S   I   A

Omsk

Trans-Siberian
Railway

Lake Baikal

Irkutsk

Karymskaya

Amur line

MANCHURIA

Chinese Eastern
Railway

Harbin

MONGOLIA

Altay Mountains

Vladivostok

Peking

CHINA

Tokyo

J A P A N

INDIA

# THE ALLIES AND THE RUSSIAN COLLAPSE

## 1917–1918

RUSSIA AND THE ALLIES 1917–1920
VOLUME ONE

# The Allies
# and the Russian Collapse
## March 1917–March 1918

## MICHAEL KETTLE

University of Minnesota Press . Minneapolis

**Library of Congress Cataloging in Publication Data**

Kettle, Michael
The Allies and the Russian collapse, March 1917–March 1918
  (Russian and the Allies, 1917–1920; v. 1)
  Bibliography: p.
  Includes index
  1. Russian—History—Revolution, 1917–1921
  2. Russian—Foreign relations.   3. Russia—Foreign relations—
  1917–1945.  I. Title.  II. Series
DK265.9.E2K43 1980       947.084′1      80–275
ISBN 0–8166–0981–0

*For my daughter*

JULIET CHRISTINA KETTLE

Take but degree away, untune that string,
And, hark, what discord follows! each thing meets
In mere oppugnancy: the bounded waters
Should lift their bosoms higher than the shores,
And make a sop of all this solid globe:
Strength should be lord of imbecility,
And the rude son should strike his father dead:
Force should be right; or, rather, right and wrong –
Between whose endless jar justice resides –
Should lose their names, and so should justice too.
Then every thing includes itself in power,
Power into will, will into appetite;
And appetite, an universal wolf,
So doubly seconded with will and power,
Must make perforce an universal prey,
And last eat up himself.

*Troilus and Cressida, Act 1, Scene 3, lines 108–24*

# Contents

# List of Illustrations

# Author's Note

THIS work has taken fifteen years to date; the first and second volumes are now ready for the press, the third is completed, and the fourth and fifth volumes, taking the story down to Denikin's forced evacuation of Novorossisk in early spring 1920, when the British washed their hands of the White Russian cause, are in final draft. Inevitably, in a work of such duration, an author incurs deep debts of gratitude.

First, I would like to express my profound appreciation of the help given me, over a period of several years, by Professor George F. Kennan, former American Ambassador in Moscow, now of the Institute for Advanced Study at Princeton University. I am also very appreciative of my appointment as Associate Member of the Russian Research Centre at Harvard University.

Secondly, I owe much to the advice and support given me by A. J. P. Taylor, who has kindly allowed me in this first volume to make use of a small number of documents from the Lloyd George Papers in the Beaverbrook Library.

Various persons have read portions of the text for me, and to them I express my thanks. Alan Houghton Brodrick and Phillip Knightley have read the text right through, and to them I am especially grateful for their comments.

Next, I wish to express my thanks to the Arts Council for various grants. In a more general sense, I would like to thank the Deputy Librarian, Mr Douglas Matthews, and his staff at the London Library for their unfailing helpfulness, cheerfulness and general kindness over a number of years. I also express my gratitude to the Librarian at the London School of Economics for occasional use of the LSE Library, which holds various books on this period, which are not to be found in the British Museum.

A work of this length has inevitably had to be typed several times. I would express my gratitude to three girls for their work: Sylvia

Northcote and Sally Kemsley, of London, and Marlene Guttman, of Los Angeles.

Next, I must record my thanks to Mr Jonathan Locker-Lampson for permission to use the papers and photographs of his father Commander Oliver Locker-Lampson; to Mrs Oona Neilson for a letter from Colonel J. F. Neilson; to various members of the Jaroszynski family in emigration for information about and photographs of Karol Jaroszynski; to Mr Noel Leech for information about and for the only photograph in existence of his brother Hugh Leech; to Mr A. H. Ruston for a photograph of the Cossack Wild Division, taken from the back of his armoured car; to the Imperial War Museum for a photograph of Major-General Poole and Brigadier Finlayson; to Mrs H. D. Fellowes for a photograph of her father, Colonel Terence Keyes; and to Mrs Vera Russell for the photographs and certain papers of her father, Vladimir Poliakov, and his friend Teddy Lessing. The *Times* archivist also kindly granted me access to Poliakov's file.

Lastly, I must thank my agent Bruce Hunter for his assiduous work on my behalf, and my editor and publisher Piers Burnett.

For the sake of clarity I have used the modern western calendar throughout (although the Russians did not officially adopt it until 14 January 1918). Thus what the Russians still call the February and October Revolutions of 1917 are here referred to as the March and November Revolutions.

Finally, I should add that as the main sources for my book are the War Cabinet, Foreign Office, War Office and Admiralty Papers, the relatively few general books quoted are merely used to amplify these primary sources; hence no bibliography is considered necessary.

MICHAEL KETTLE.

January 1979.

# I

## The Origins of Revolution

WHEN the Great War began in August 1914, Russia, on Germany's eastern front, valiantly sustained her Allies on the western front from the battle of the Marne onwards – and often at the cost of terrible casualties. But by March 1917, with the war some two and a half years old, her British and French Allies were aware that Russia, their antediluvian comrade in arms, was sick, politically, socially and militarily. But they had no cause to fear a sudden collapse. Their men on the spot were so inured to the waywardness and turmoil of Russian affairs that even when the revolution came, they reported it with remarkable sang-froid.

One of the foreigners present in Petrograd during the early days of March, when strikes, factory closures and riots presaged the blow to come, was Commander Oliver Locker-Lampson MP. Sunday, March 11, he stated, 'dawned upon the most serious situation. It was bitterly cold, stomachs were empty, brains excited. Huge crowds collected in various squares and the infantry, which were turned upon them, merely marched unoffendingly through a cheering mob. It was the same with the Cossacks, who had a tremendous ovation.' The mounted police therefore charged, and the Pavlovsky Regiment 'fired once into the people . . .'

Locker-Lampson then crossed the Nevski Prospekt and walked to the Neva quay, where 'astounding scenes met me', he records. Beyond the Neva came the 'sound of cheering, shots and the crisp crepitation of the maxims'.* The prison fortress of Peter and Paul had been stormed and a great plume of smoke was rising from another prison. 'Knots of people gathered feverishly with excitement; boys went by with swords with red flags on the points. Civilians armed to the teeth rushed about firing rifles, and car loads of yelling soldiers thundered down the Quay, drunk with revolution.' But nobody was molested, and the whole thing

* Machine guns.

[13]

resembled a 'sort of extravagant political election'. He then walked back across the square opposite the Winter Palace, which had earlier been empty, and now found it 'full of massing soldiers, orderly, without arms, but with their bands playing. I asked an officer if they were government troops or revolutionaries, and . . . he told me they were loyal troops, and that there was no revolution at all.' But as Locker-Lampson drove back down the Morskaya to the Astoria Hotel, he ran into a brisk engagement between loyalists and revolutionaries, who commandeered his car.

'That night Revolution was King,' he records; and as he opened the double windows of his room in the Astoria and looked out, 'a murmur as of multitudes cheering arose as in one huge roar from the city, and through it came the incessant rattle of shots and the sputtering of maxims. The sky in the east was quite bright and many buildings seemed on fire.'[1]

What followed next day was more reminiscent of the French revolution. As a rumour had spread that a police agent had taken refuge in the Astoria, Locker-Lampson awoke to find the revolutionaries in possession of the square facing the hotel; '. . . as I looked out of the window I suddenly realised that nearly all the soldiers in the huge Square had become stationary and were looking up. Then quite near me, as from the hotel, sounded the *plug, plug, plug*, of a maxim, and in an instant the Square was in a chaos . . . We could not imagine what had happened, and never dreamed that a maxim was actually firing from the roof over mine.'*

As the revolutionaries returned the fire, shots tore into the hotel rooms facing the square – and two maids ran into Locker-Lampson's bedroom screaming that their mistress, a Russian princess, had been hit and was dying. Two armoured cars, which the revolutionaries had commandeered, then began bombarding the doors of the hotel, through which an infuriated mob now poured, killing everyone in the hall, which was sacked, and drinking all the wine in the cellars. With great presence of mind, Locker-Lampson laid the wounded princess out in the passage, and surrounded her with blood-stained pillows; he and other Allied officers then stood, unarmed and in silence behind her, as the drunken mob came on up the stairs 'in yelling parties', firing their rifles up the lift-shaft and through the staircase windows. The dramatic scene which awaited them had its effect. The revolutionaries, abashed, soon departed. Locker-Lampson, with the blood-stained princess in

---

* Professor Katkov (the great authority on Russian events of 1917) states that the story that the Minister of the Interior (Protopopov) had stationed police with maxim guns on rooftops is false. But who then was firing the maxim that Locker-Lampson heard? This seems never to have been determined.

his arms, then descended to find all the public rooms, the lobby and the dining-room entirely wrecked, even the band, 'and a huge violin-cello lay amid awful disorder in the broken lift'. But on the walls, he noticed, the portraits of the Tsar were 'intact and undishonoured'. Having taken the princess to hospital, he walked back to the Astoria to find the 'men with the maxim' had been marched off, and sentries posted everywhere, 'smoking what I recognised as my cigars . . .'[1]

These events in Petrograd precipitated the downfall of the huge, centuries-old, Russian Empire. But what was the real cause of this downfall?

The seeds of the Russian Revolution of March 1917 perhaps lie in the previous revolution of Russian society carried out by Peter the Great (1689–1725), who had radically transformed the ancient Tsardom of Muscovy into the Empire of All-Russias; and, with the construction of his new capital, St Petersburg, had decisively directed his empire towards Western Europe. But for nearly 200 years thereafter, the unswerving desire of every successive Tsar had been to maintain what he interpreted as Peter's true legacy – complete control over the huge, and ever-growing, multi-racial, multi-lingual and multi-religious Russian Empire, by means of an oriental autocracy. This inherent schism led to two centuries of unresolved debate between 'Westernisers' and 'Slavophiles'.

By the mid-nineteenth century, Russia had acquired many non-Russian lands and peoples: Poland, Esthonia, Latvia, Lithuania and Finland; Armenia and other areas in the Caucasus; parts of Kazakhstan – even Alaska (shortly to be sold to the United States) – and was expanding into the Danube principalities in support of the Balkan Slavs. Though the Russian steamroller moved slowly, it moved inexorably. But were these new non-Russian populations to be 'russified', according to Tsarist autocratic tradition, or were they to be allowed local autonomy, in the western manner? Here the succeeding Tsars had chopped and changed in their policy. Under Peter's immediate heirs, Anna (1730–40) and Elizabeth (1741–62), German favourites had been relied on, while Catherine the Great (1762–96) was herself German. German nobles had thus been settled in the Baltic states of Latvia and Esthonia, the first conquests, to keep the local peasants down. Elsewhere, it was decided that linguistic and religious differences could remain, and the new peoples should be raised to the standard of the Russian serf, which was in itself low. But as the native élite could not be relied on, Russian officials had eventually to be sent in, thus ruling out local autonomy.

[15]

Catherine particularly alienated the Russian peasant; and in 1773, there was a serious revolt in east Russia led by the Cossack Pugachev. The Cossacks were free peasants who were settled on Russia's frontiers. In return for considerable grants of land, they undertook special military obligations, not only to defend the frontiers, but to help maintain order in the Russian interior. They were divided into separate districts, or *voiskos*; Don, Kuban, Terek, Astrakhan, Ural, Orenberg (and later four more in Siberia). They were traditional military democracies; and each *voisko* elected its own leader, or *ataman*. But under Catherine, they lost their autonomy and some of their privileges and began to sink to the level of the peasants.

The influx of western culture and Pugachev's revolt awoke even the St Petersburg aristocracy to the need for an improvement in the conditions of the serfs. In 1790, a nobleman, just back from Germany, wrote in scathing terms of the dehumanisation of the serf and the corruption of his noble landlord – and got himself banished by Catherine to Siberia.

Catherine also alienated the Russian Jews, who were then living in western Russia and catholic Poland (still at the time independent), and were detested by both Poles and Russians. Catherine marked out an area in south-west Russia, recently annexed from Poland, and forced all Jews to live in this 'Pale'.

There was further territorial expansion in the reign of Nicholas I (1825–55), who began a reign of open repression at home, after an outbreak of revolutionary agitation on the death of the previous Tsar, Alexander I (1801–25). New ideas were banned; university students were encouraged to spy on their professors and on each other. All writers were suspect. The poet Pushkin was in trouble with the authorities for years. The writer who first openly discussed the controversy between 'Westernisers' and 'Slavophiles' was declared mad by the Tsar, confined to his house, and placed under medical supervision (the methods of the KGB are nothing new). But the great territorial expansion was not now accompanied by 'russification'; the new subjects merely had to obey. When Sweden ceded Finland to Russia, the Tsar merely became Grand Duke of Finland, and it was hoped that the Finns would prove loyal. But in 1831, when there was a dispute over Lithuania, Russia went to war with her long-standing enemy catholic Poland. Russia won, and Poland was duly 'russified'. The Jewish 'Pale' now comprised all Russian Poland, Lithuania, part of western Russia, and most of the Ukraine.

Russia was relatively unaffected by the revolutionary outbreak of 1848, but Russia's defeat in the Crimean War (1853–6) made clear that she was no longer a first-rate military power, as in 1815, and that she was indeed very backward. Alexander II (1855–81) put in hand reforms, but they were inadequate and allowed revolutionaries to surface. They murdered the Tsar in 1881.

Alexander III (1881–94) at once reaffirmed the principle of autocracy without change, and reintroduced oppressive policies, and complete 'russification'. It was no longer sufficient for the Tsar's subjects to obey him loyally; they now had to become Russians. Imposition of Orthodox Christianity went hand in hand with 'russification', and did untold harm, especially to those most economically and culturally advanced, and who had been most loyal to the empire. In north Russia both the Baltic Germans and the Latvians and Esthonians suffered; while attempts to 'russify' Finland united all Finns in opposition to the Tsar. In south Russia, the Armenian Christians, traditionally Russophile, were outraged; so, naturally, were the Muslims. The worst sufferers were the Jews, enclosed in the 'Pale'. Already severely restricted in education and economic life, they now became the official scapegoats to divert popular discontent from the regime. The Tsarist police began the practice of 'pogroms' (officially sponsored riots), that led to the destruction of Jewish shops, and physical violence on Jews. Alexander III, in fact, began a process that was to end in the gas-chambers of Auschwitz and Dachau.

In the countryside, the *zemstvos* (provincial assemblies) were hampered, and were soon in growing conflict with the authorities. Nothing was done to modernise agriculture, and the existence of large estates became more and more resented. The authorities, however, were certain that the – mainly inefficient – peasant commune, or *mir*, was a bulwark of traditional Russian values, the embodiment of loyalty to the Tsar; and by the imposition of strict controls, sought to maintain it as such. The continuing demand for some sort of national consultative assembly went totally unheeded.

Industrial expansion was, however, official government policy, and foreign investors were actively encouraged. The French and Belgians invested mainly in metallurgy in south Russia, the British in petroleum, and the Germans in electricity and in banking. In 1891, it was decided to open up Siberia by the construction of a trans-Siberian railway; and work was begun simultaneously at Chelyabinsk, in the Urals, and at Vladivostok, in the far east.

That year also saw the resurgence of illegal political activity against the regime, when *zemstvo* officials were forbidden to undertake relief work after a crop failure had caused widespread famine. This activity received impetus from the accession of Nicholas II (1894–1917), the weak and irresolute son of Alexander III, and the last of the Tsars.

By the 1890s, Russian foreign policy was engaged in countering the

Triple Alliance of Germany, Austria-Hungary and Italy, and in Russian expansion in the Balkans and in the Far East – which brought her into collision with Japan. Europe, and European relationships, were by now becoming brittle; and the only safety lay in alliance. The threat from the Triple Alliance was offset in 1891 by an alliance with republican France. In the Balkans, Russia had been humiliated. In 1877, she went to war with Turkey, as Grand Protector of the small Slav states, and almost took Constantinople; but at the Congress of Berlin in 1878, England and Austria-Hungary saw to it that Russia should not control the Balkans – or the Straits into the Black Sea. Eventually, Russia and Austria-Hungary agreed on spheres of influence in the Balkans, a temporary expedient.

But it was Russian designs in the Far East that led to her complete military humiliation. After Japan and China had gone to war over Korea in 1894 – a war that Japan had easily won – Russia (together with France and Germany) demanded that Japan should return to China the Liaotung peninsula, which is in the Yellow Sea, west of Korea. This Japan agreed to do. Russia then concluded an alliance with China, which allowed Russia (whose trans-Siberian railway was now nearing completion) to construct a railway (known as the Chinese Eastern railway) across northern Manchuria to link western Siberia more easily with Vladivostok. Russia then acquired the Liaotung peninsula itself from China and built an ice-free naval base on its tip at Port Arthur. Next, she obtained China's agreement to the construction of a railway across south Manchuria, linking Port Arthur with the Chinese Eastern railway at the junction of Harbin. Japan watched these moves with growing anger. In 1904 (as the trans-Siberian railway was completed), Japan launched a sudden attack on Russian warships at Port Arthur. The Russo-Japanese war ended in the total destruction of the Russian fleet.

Russia's humiliating defeat abroad acted as an immediate detonator of social unrest at home, of which the revolutionaries took full advantage. They had a long history, going back to the Decembrists, a group of early martyrs in the post-Napoleonic period, who had seen something of European liberalism, and reacted strongly against Alexander I's military autocracy. In the general reaction against foreignness after the Napoleonic wars, they huddled themselves in secret societies and masonic lodges. When there was some uncertainty over the succession on Alexander's death in December 1825, they decided to strike. They were arrested, executed or banished. Their direct descendants were young students (*narodniki*), who were active in the 1870s, in the reign of Alexander II. The reforms he had put in hand after Russia's defeat in the Crimean War (1853–6) had made clear how backward she was.

They included the abolition of serfdom, in 1861, but the peasants remained embittered, as the terms whereby they could purchase land were unfavourable; they were still less than full citizens. In 1864, the *zemstvos* were created, but the nobles had a large number of both votes and seats. There was also a demand for a national consultative assembly, but this the Tsar turned down; and he retained the power of banishing politically undesirable persons in disregard of the courts. The insufficiency of his reforms and the slackening of repressive control allowed small revolutionary groups to appear. In 1861, leaflets demanded a full constituent assembly. Armed rebellion in Poland in 1863, which was put down with extreme severity, strengthened the forces of repression once more. So did an attempt on the Tsar's life three years later. In 1873-4, the *narodniki* went direct to the peasants, whom they thought the main potential for revolutionary action. But the peasants could not understand them and the police arrested the students. A new party, 'Land and Freedom', could not decide what to do. Some favoured assassination of prominent officials and reliance on the workers in the new industrial cities; others opposed violence and urged continued reliance on the peasants. The party split; and the terrorist wing, 'People's Will', succeeded in assassinating the Tsar in 1881. The leaders were caught and hanged.

In the early 1890s, the revolutionaries were mainly, if not wholly, drawn from the 'intelligentsia', or what would now be called 'the intellectuals'. Every intelligent Jewish youth, denied education and advancement, was a natural recruit. Many others were children of Orthodox priests, since the imposition of Orthodoxy often went hand in hand with the hated 'russification'. Action had to be clandestine. Many of the revolutionaries were as autocratic as their opponents, being mystically, even religiously, convinced that they alone knew what was best for the dark mass of the Russian people.

In the late 1890s, revolutionary socialism was divided into two main groups; in each was a section that wished for a mass movement, and a section that favoured rigidly controlled conspiracy. The Social-Revolutionaries (founded in 1901 from the 'People's Will' groups) wished to construct a socialist order based on the peasant commune (*mir*), which they saw – unlike the Tsarist regime – as a natural unit of a future socialist republic. Their terrorist wing, the 'Fighting Organisation', believed in assassination of top Tsarist officials to advance their cause. The Social Democrats (founded in 1898 from illegal working-class groups) were Marxist, and wished to construct a socialist order based on the working class in the cities, the proletariat. Lenin had split the party at an emigré meeting in London in 1903. His group were known as the 'Bolsheviks' (majority), and stood for rigid discipline and

[19]

a tightly controlled party organisation. The 'Mensheviks' (minority), also Marxist, aimed for a mass labour movement, as in Western European countries.

On January 22, 1905, a large crowd of workers marched to the Winter Palace square in St Petersburg. Troops opened fire, killing several hundred. Violent disorders followed, especially in areas inhabited by non-Russians; in Poland, Latvia, the Ukraine and Georgia. There were also pogroms, and right-wing gangs ('Black Hundreds') attacked the demonstrators. In October 1905, there was a national railway strike, and a *Soviet* (Council) of Workers' Deputies was formed at St Petersburg. The Tsar, under severe pressure, issued a manifesto promising to convene a national assembly.

In April 1906, the election produced a *Duma* (parliament) with a pronounced left-wing majority. Though the Social Democrats and Social-Revolutionaries mainly abstained, the Conservative elements obtained very few seats. The largest party were the Constitutional-Democrats (Cadets), but deputies representing the non-Russian peoples, like the Ukrainians and Muslims, also won a considerable number of seats. The Russian Empire had, for the first time, spoken. The Duma demanded redistribution of the estates, a political amnesty, equal rights for Jews and others, and autonomy for Poland. Co-operation between the Duma and the Tsar proved impossible. As the Duma could not overthrow the Tsar's ministers, the Tsar dissolved the Duma in July. For eight months Stolypin, the new Prime Minister, ruled by decree, ruthlessly suppressing peasant riots and executing hundreds by special courts martial.

Early in 1907, with revolution suppressed and discipline in the army and police restored, elections were held for a second Duma which resulted in a majority even further to the left. 'Co-operation' again proved impossible, the Duma was again dissolved that summer – and the electoral law was summarily changed in favour of the upper classes and Russian citizens, and to the detriment of the peasants and non-Russians. The third and fourth Dumas were thus more conservative, but at least there was a Duma, with political parties, open meetings, political debate, a fairly free press, and trade unions. But there was still much that was untouched. Stolypin, an able man, proceeded to apply 'russification' with vigour, and began to improve Russian agriculture. In 1911 Stolypin was assassinated and the weak Tsar was left only with mediocre officials and advisers.

But this was a period of great industrial and agricultural expansion, indeed a Russian economic boom. At the turn of the century, most of Russia's wealth was in native and unworked raw materials on such a vast scale that her existing industries and railways were quite unable to cope with it. She needed technical machinery, manufactured goods, and capital from Western Europe. This she easily obtained. But with no middle class between the illiterate masses and the effete Russian Court and aristocracy, she had to pay a very high price – foreign investment-capital quickly established control over important sectors of the Russian economy.[2]

Nevertheless, between 1900 and 1905, the gross output of Russian industry had increased by 45%; and despite the war with Japan and the accompanying depression, which lasted until 1909, went on increasing at a very rapid rate. The boom (to which even Communist writers pay tribute) perhaps reached its peak in 1910 to 1912, and was achieved by concentration of industry, in which Russia outstripped the United States. She became one of the foremost countries of the world; the increase in her industrial capital stock at this period being three times as great as the United States. By 1913, her gross industrial output was 219% higher than in 1900.

But this super-concentration of Russian industry had two important consequences. First, it herded together a mass of semi-illiterate workers in the industrial cities, where the revolutionary leaders could more easily organise them. Secondly, in the absence of a managerial middle class, it vastly increased the power of foreign investment-capital, and gave foreigners an important grip over Russian industry. The oil industry in the Caucasus was controlled by the British. The copper and platinum exploitation in the Urals and the Caucasus was the monopoly of British and American syndicates – indeed the Russo-Asiatic Corporation, controlled by British capital, and run by Mr Leslie Urquhart from London, actually owned the two largest Russian copper and iron corporations in the Urals and western Siberia. (The Azov-Don Bank, which had acted for the Russian interests in this deal, had made one million roubles clear profit on this deal; and even this amount was transferred to a London bank.) All the Russian tramways in the main towns were run by Belgian concerns. Some 70% of the Russian electrical companies were owned by German firms, trading under Russian names.

Of greatest political importance were the French investments in Russia. The loss of the coal and iron mines in Alsace-Lorraine in the war of 1871 had gravely affected the French economy. Under the Franco-Russian Military Convention of 1894, French loans in gold were guaranteed in return for Russian military support in any war for the recovery of Alsace-Lorraine. French gold, in the form of the savings of the French peasants, was soon flowing into Russia; and Russian liabilities on the Paris Stock Exchange rose rapidly. French (and Belgian) capital soon controlled all the iron mines, the coal mines and smelting furnaces in the Donetz basin and on the Don. By 1902, no less than 10 milliard francs, out of a total of 18 milliard francs invested abroad by the French, was invested in Russia.

In 1913, an inspired article in a French newspaper announced that France had already lent Russia 17 milliard francs, and would lend 2½ milliard more in annual payments of half a milliard, provided the money was partly spent in improving the strategic railways in Russian Poland (which in any future war were in the front line, and were notoriously weak compared to the German railways over the border), and partly in improving mobilisation. (The Russian military machine was notoriously cumbersome, and it was feared it would take some while to set in motion, and such delay might be crucial.) But such a disclosure in a newspaper publicly demonstrated the real motive behind these massive French investments; this gold was in preparation for war.

Finally, as all these huge sums of money – from England, France, Belgium, America and Germany – had to be routed through the Russian banks (which were huge financial conglomerates in their own right, and thus very different from European banks), they too were losing their independence and coming under the sway of foreign powers; and the actual influence acquired by Germany through German investment in Russian banking could mostly be discounted.

The economic boom was accompanied by a minor boom in agriculture, through the opening up of Siberia, and the reforms put through by Stolypin. On his insistence, the Peasant Land Bank bought up land from the private owner, and resold them to certain peasants (the *kulaks*), who broke away from the communes, and whom the Co-operative Associations and the *zemstva* supplied with agricultural implements. This naturally saddled them with more debt; and it was a reform that appealed only to the more enterprising. By 1914, only 15% of the peasants had become *kulaks*. Other peasants migrated, or resettled in Siberia, which now began an American-type economic and cultural development. Between 1905 and 1914, the Siberian population doubled, the area of cultivated land trebled and so did agricultural output; while agricultural export – mainly in the shape of grain, flax and butter – rose tenfold. The general welfare of the whole people rose too; so did their deposits in the savings banks, many linked to the Co-operative Movement, which was very popular and powerful all over Russia – and differed markedly from the British 'Co-ops'.

But on many of the great estates in Russia proper, the peasant remained a neo-serf, with his back-breaking toil, his humiliation. Where the landowner would not sell his land, and the peasant refused to take on more debt, it was realised by both sides that only an upheaval from below, which gave the initiative to the peasants, would cure the age-old evils of the Russian countryside.

After the crises surrounding the establishment of the Duma, Russian foreign policy became increasingly absorbed in Balkan affairs, while differences were composed with enemies, actual and potential. Russia co-operated with Japan; settled differences with England (over Persia, and territories adjacent to India) by the Anglo-Russian agreement of 1907; and reaffirmed the alliance with France. As England was now also in alliance with France, the Triple Alliance of Germany, Austria-Hungary and Italy was faced by Russia, France and England. Europe was dividing into hostile camps. In the Balkans, Russia, the Grand Protector of the Slavs, was organising blocs and petty alliances against Austria-Hungary. This was the setting for the murder of the Austrian Archduke Franz Ferdinand in June 1914 in Serbia, which enjoyed Russian protection. In just over a month, the whole of Europe was at war.

In the West, the Germans planned a lightning strike (under the Schlieffen plan) to knock France out of the war, while on their Eastern Front they remained on the defensive. The danger was that this would allow Russia time to concentrate her forces and set in motion her huge military steamroller from her base in Russian Poland. This, strategically, was a tongue of territory projecting from Russia proper and flanked to the north by east Prussia, to the west by the German province of Silesia, and to the south by the Austrian province of Galicia, with the Carpathian Mountains beyond guarding the approaches to the plain of Hungary. Since the German border provinces had a far better railway network than Russian Poland, it made good strategic sense to lure the Russians forward to meet a German counter-stroke.

As the French, anxious to relieve German pressure on the Western Front, urged the Russians to deliver a simultaneous attack against Germany – for which they were unprepared – the Russians played into German hands. In mid-August 1914, when the French and British armies in France fell back to the Marne before the German invasion, two Russian armies invaded east Prussia, but were decisively beaten at Tannenberg and at the Masurian Lakes (north-east of Warsaw), and expelled from east Prussia with the loss of 250,000 men – and much war material, which they could not afford. The Russian invasion of east Prussia had, however, helped to make possible a French recovery on the Marne by causing the rapid despatch of two German corps from the Western Front.

On the Galician front, two Austrian armies had invaded Russian

[23]

Poland, but were driven back through Lemberg (north of the Carpathians), and in late September had to fall back to Cracow (well to the west). Germany now came to Austria's aid. From south-west Poland, an advance was made on Warsaw, but the Russians, now approaching their full mobilised strength, regrouped, drove the enemy back, and tried to invade Silesia. By December, they in turn were driven back to Warsaw and in the south, fell back from Cracow, having exhausted their munitions which Russia was too badly organised to replenish.

Germany now reversed her policy and decided to remain on the defensive in France, while she tried to knock Russia out of the war. Russia was chronically short of supplies of all kinds and in November 1914, when Turkey entered the war on Germany's side, was completely shut off from direct contact with her Allies owing to the closure of the Black Sea. In January 1915, the British Cabinet responded to a Russian request for a British attempt to force the Dardanelles Straits into the Black Sea (it being secretly agreed that after the war Russia should retain both the Straits and Constantinople, which had long been Russia's dream).

Early in 1915, the Russian Command aimed to secure both its flanks before trying to break into Silesia again. In Poland, the Russians were preparing to strike northwards into east Prussia, but were forestalled early in February by a German attack towards the frontier of Russia proper, which enveloped an entire Russian force east of the Masurian Lakes. On the southern flank, from January to April (when the British attack on the Dardanelles opened), Russian forces strove for control in the Carpathian Mountains, but the Austrians, again with German support, parried them and Russian losses were very heavy.

In order to relieve the pressure on the Austrians, the German Command now decided on a big attack between the upper Vistula and the Carpathians in central Poland, to rupture the Russian centre. Early in May, a powerful German thrust rolled the whole Russian front up along the Carpathians and by mid-May, the Germans had reached the San river. With reinforcements from the Western Front, the Germans then again attacked, with the Austrians, and in late June retook Lemberg, thus successfully cutting the Russian front into two separate sectors.

But the Russians made good their huge losses – 400,000 had been captured – and the German Command, still anxious about the Austrians, decided to continue the attack. This time they aimed to strike north, between the Bug and Vistula rivers, where the main Russian force lay, while another German force from east Prussia struck south-east, across the Narew river (north of Warsaw) towards the Bug, so as to envelop the Russian armies in the Warsaw salient. By mid-

August, when Bulgaria entered the war on the German side, though the bulk of the Russian armies had just escaped encirclement, the Russians had lost all Poland and 750,000 prisoners.

Early in September, the Germans struck again in the northern sector. Two German armies attacked in enveloping movements, one east towards Dvinsk, the other south-east towards Vilna; and German cavalry, advancing between the two armies, overlapped Vilna and approached the main Moscow–Warsaw railway at Minsk. The Russian forces again just managed to escape the German net, but by late September, as the British attack on the Dardanelles faltered, the Russian line ran from Riga in the Baltic to Czernowitz on the Roumanian frontier. Russia had been badly lamed, though not destroyed, and in mid-December the British finally evacuated the Dardanelles. This meant that the hard-pressed Russian armies could expect no Allied supplies through the Black Sea.

The Germans now made a determined effort to force Russia out of the war by subversive means. A revolution was to be stimulated in Russia to overthrow the Tsar, then peace terms were to be offered to the revolutionary leaders. At the outset of the war, there had been a great upsurge of loyalty to the Tsar, who had banished virtually all revolutionary leaders from Russia. Now, the wheel had turned. Defeat at the front, and incompetence at home was making the Tsar more and more unpopular. To a growing number of Russians, revolution seemed the only way out. The Russian most closely concerned with the stimulation of this revolution was not Lenin or Trotsky (still condemned to impoverished and relatively futile inactivity in exile), but a Russian Jew called Doctor Alexander Helphand, alias 'Parvus', who was a member of the German Social Democrat Party.

The Germans knew that a successful revolution needed organisation, and organisation meant cash, and plenty of cash. Helphand seemed to qualify. In the 1890s, he was the leading political theorist and analyst in Germany. His books on the Russian famine, and on European free trade (in which, in 1900, he foresaw the European Common Market of the 1960s), and on many other politico-social problems, showed him to be not only an outstanding political thinker but a man who could see how to put his ideas into practice. From 1900 to 1905, his flat in Munich was the meeting place for all the leading Russian exiles – he was the only man who stood astride both the Russian and German socialist movements. Lenin admired him, and under his influence started the underground paper *Iskra* in Munich, eight numbers of which were printed in Helphand's flat.[3]

After Lenin split the Russian Social Democrat Party in 1903, Helphand met the young Trotsky for the first time. Both stood aside

[25]

from the party dispute. Trotsky was strongly influenced by Helphand's contention that the coming revolution in Russia would start with a general strike. After this had occurred, in October 1905, it was these two, not the other socialist leaders, who were the leading figures in the Petrograd Soviet. But Trotsky was the natural, dominant personality, while Helphand was the natural stage-manager behind the scenes.

After the Petrograd Soviet's collapse, and what he saw as his relative failure as a political leader, Helphand returned to Germany and devoted himself to literature and journalism. He believed in a workers' democracy. Socialism to him meant the gradual transformation of an industrial society, not the dictatorship of the proletariat; he clearly saw the dangers in an all-powerful socialist state, and did not therefore hold with the idea of a revolutionary élite. He gradually came to detest Lenin's struggle for power. Generally he was, as his writings indicated, a man far ahead of his time; and as such, he became more and more mistrusted by both German and Russian socialist parties.

It was in a mood of depression that he left Germany in 1910 for Constantinople. During the Balkan wars, he was in business supplying goods to the Turkish army, dealing in corn, and probably also in munitions, and modernising the Turkish railway system. By 1914, when war broke out, he was a rich man. Power, he had learnt, could be reached through money; and money made through political power.

As he now saw that a direct alliance between Germany and the Russian revolutionaries could overthrow the Tsarist regime, he came out in support of a German victory, and against any German revolution during the war. In February 1915, he arrived at the Foreign Ministry in Berlin, via the German Embassy in Constantinople, with a plan for the total subversion of the Tsarist Empire. This entailed German support for Lenin and his revolutionary colleagues (whom he still disliked, but respected) in preparations for a general strike which would lead to revolution; for infiltration of Russia by propaganda; and for a press campaign against Tsarism. As the aims of both the German government and Lenin's revolutionaries completely coincided, the German diplomats approved Helphand's plan – but solely as a means of influencing the Tsar to conclude a separate peace; they were not in the least interested in social changes in Russia. From now on, Helphand became the leading adviser to the German government on revolutionary affairs in Russia. His task was to unite the European socialists against Tsarist Russia and to enable the Russian revolutionaries to engineer the collapse of Russia. Late in March 1915, he received one million marks from the Foreign Ministry as a first instalment of the expenses which the plan involved.

From early in 1915 until late in 1917, this delicate operation was

[26]

handled by Diego von Bergen, a senior Wilhelmstrasse official (who was to become German Ambassador to the Vatican under Hitler), who was in constant contact with Helphand. 'The policy bore the mark of the highest security rating; its outline becomes clear from the documents . . . [but] its implementation, carried out by many agents, is obscure to a degree,' explains Doctor Z. A. B. Zeman, editor of the main official German documents on this tricky subject.[4] 'Often the search in the archives of the Foreign Ministry is unrewarding: the words "the matter was settled by word of mouth" appear too often. As few records as possible were made . . .'

The relationship between von Bergen and Helphand was shot through with mistrust. Both German diplomats and Russian revolutionaries were dealing with their potential executioners. The Germans saw the operation as an essential part of a short-term and limited policy to knock Russia out of the war, after which the revolutionaries might well become expendable. The revolutionaries saw it as a means of starting a world-wide revolution, not only in Russia, but above all in Germany. The Germans, however, were generally more willing to grant favours than the revolutionaries were to accept them. 'There is no evidence among the documents of the Foreign Ministry,' adds Zeman, 'that Lenin, a circumspect man, was in direct contact with any of the official German agencies. How much he knew about the activities of the men around him is difficult to tell . . .' (But from the time that Lenin arrived, penniless and without documents, in Switzerland in September 1914, the Germans had had their eye on him. On his arrival, a Swiss Social Democrat in Berne called Karl Moor, who was working for the Austrian and German General Staffs as an informer on socialists living in Switzerland, heped him in his dealings with the local authorities and police – and probably with small loans of cash. Even as late as 1916, the Germans were being kept informed of Lenin's activities and views by Moor, a 'shrewd and cautious man', writes Professor Katkov, whose contacts with the Germans were 'very carefully camouflaged'.)[5]

The German Social Democrats had no idea what Helphand was now up to, and thought he was simply a Russian agent. 'A very splendid case indeed: an ultra-radical revolutionary; a Russian informer, a scoundrel, a confidence trickster (Gorky affair!*), and now a Turkish

---

* In 1902, Helphand had founded a publishing firm to propagate the works of Russian writers abroad. He presented Maxim Gorky to the European public and his play *The Lower Depths*, was a great success in Germany. It was agreed that a quarter of the proceeds should go to Gorky and the rest to the Russian Social Democratic Party. But Helphand kept much more than the 20% commission he had claimed; neither Gorky nor the Party, in fact, ever received a penny – Helphand kept the lot. This financial unscrupulousness was never forgotten.

agent and speculator,' wrote a German comrade. The radical left called him a '*souteneur* of imperialism'. His old friend Trotsky, now running a defeatist emigré paper in Paris, broke with him and called him a 'political Falstaff' – after receiving a substantial subsidy from him.

Little did Helphand care. He was now in his element. The first Marxist millionaire, he clearly saw himself as the stage-manager of the Russian revolution; with his high-level contacts and unlimited financial resources, the factious little cliques of Russian conspirators could be converted, under his influence, into a really effective revolutionary instrument to bring Tsarism crashing down. Any political aims, he believed, could be realised with enough money – which the socialist leaders could resist no more than any other group of people.

In mid-May 1915, Helphand arrived in Switzerland to see Lenin; if he could come to terms with him, all the other Russian factions would follow him. Lenin wanted an immediate revolution. He also wanted money. Helphand could provide both. But there was now a glaring contrast between the two men. Lenin lived a Spartan life, of extreme poverty, moving from one wretched boarding-house to another. Helphand, on arrival in Zurich, moved into the most expensive hotel, and ostentatiously lived it up with his 'retinue of rather well-endowed blondes', as his biographers put it, smoking cigars and drinking champagne. This high life, though, was already beginning to tell on Helphand. 'His massive, gigantic figure was more puffed out than ever,' write Zeman and Scharlau. 'The broad, bull-like face with its high forehead, tiny nose, and carefully trimmed beard, had developed a flabby double-chin, behind which his neck completely disappeared. The small lively eyes were deeply embedded in fat. His short legs were barely strong enough to support his body, and when he was standing up or walking, he seemed to use his arms to maintain himself on an even keel.' The penniless Russian comrades regarded this extraordinary figure with a mixture of horror and furious fascination. This was not the man they remembered from the 1905 revolution. But Karl Radek (the Polish socialist, and friend of Lenin) paved the way for him.

Late in May, Helphand appeared at a small café, where the Russian exiles usually lunched, and asked to see Lenin and the two went off for a private talk. Helphand, according to his own account, expounded his views in fairly arrogant terms. Lenin told him, according to his account, that Helphand was simply a German socialist turned chauvinist, and he would have nothing to do with him. Whatever was really said, they did not reach agreement; Lenin obviously feared that Helphand, with his undoubted ability and vast financial backing, might well take over the Bolshevik movement.

Having failed to unite the revolutionaries, as requested by the

German Foreign Ministry, Helphand therefore recruited some of the Russian exiles in Switzerland, and set off for Copenhagen to start his own import-export business. Whatever he may have said to Helphand, Lenin kept in close but unofficial touch with him; for the most notable of Helphand's recruits was a Polish socialist called Jacob Furstenberg, one of Lenin's close friends, who undoubtedly joined Helphand with Lenin's approval.

In Copenhagen, Helphand and Furstenberg took advantage of the lax wartime trading regulations in Russia. Armed with German licences and money, they bought up not only German, but Allied goods (including anything from heavy machinery to silk stockings, from chemicals to contraceptives) for export to Russia. In return, they exported, via Copenhagen, Russian copper, rubber, corn and tin to aid the German war effort. Some of the goods went into Russia officially, others were smuggled over the frontier, where the Petrograd firm of Fabian Klingsland took them in hand, their agent, Eugenia Sumenson, keeping in close touch with Furstenberg (her cousin), and depositing the considerable profits with the Siberian Bank in Petrograd. Other business agents of Helphand's continually combed Russia and Scandinavia, and thus maintained contact with and financed underground cells and strike committees. By these means German funds were infiltrated into Russia to build up an organisation, aptly described as 'the only company in the Russian revolutionary business'. A fair proportion of the profits, however (Russian exports to Germany were especially profitable), came back to Copenhagen, and found their way into Helphand's pocket. He prospered greatly, and soon had a large house in Copenhagen, lavishly furnished and guarded by thoroughbred mastiffs; in the garage was a huge Adler limousine. Helphand was now well ahead of Lenin, who, still penniless in Switzerland, could do practically nothing.

Soon the Allies launched a virulent press campaign against Helphand, which made the Russian emigrés think he was simply a German agent. The German Foreign Ministry therefore agreed that the German Minister in Copenhagen should henceforth keep in touch with him. In their first talk early in August 1915, Helphand argued strongly for his revolutionary policy in Russia and against a separate peace with the Tsar. He intended to found a paper to unite the European socialists against the Tsarist regime. German military policy, he urged, should be co-ordinated with his plans, and must above all prevent Russia obtaining control over the Straits, which would bring the Tsar tremendous prestige at home. The German army should thus strike in southern Russia and give Turkey a respite. (The British campaign to force the Dardanelles was then in full swing.) The German army should also seize and secure the Donetz basin, which would cut across Russia's main artery. 'There can be no question that he [Helphand] is an extraordinarily important man,' reported the German Minister to Berlin, 'whose unusual powers I feel we *must* employ – whether we personally agree with his convictions or not.'

When Helphand arrived in Berlin in mid-August, he found that German peace feelers had been rejected in St Petersburg. His task now, in fact, was to stir up the European socialists against the Tsarist regime (publication of his paper was readily agreed to), and to prepare a general strike in Russia, which was to spark off the revolution. Helphand fixed January 22, 1916, the anniversary of 'Bloody Sunday' in 1905, as the date for launching the strike.

In September 1915, when his paper *Die Glocke* (*The Bell*) first appeared, he made some absurd claims. The German General Staff, he stated, was the proletariat's protector in the struggle against Tsarism, and the way to socialist victory led through German defiance of the Tsarist threat. As for his links with the German government, he claimed to be forging 'a spiritual link between the armed German and the revolutionary Russian proletariat'. Helphand, not unnaturally, failed to start an international propaganda campaign against Tsarism. Karl Kautsky, the leading German socialist opponent of the war, called him an 'imperial Falstaff'. Lenin now let fly at him, but made no mention of their meeting in May, did not call him a German agent, and left open the possibility of co-operation, should the need arise. Furstenberg had no doubt kept Lenin informed of what he and Helphand were up to in Russia.

Lenin had now come to the attention of the Germans from another source. In September 1915, an Esthonian emigré in Switzerland called Alexander Keskula, who was mainly interested in Esthonian independence, contacted the German Minister in Berne, and informed him of Lenin's attitude to the war. Keskula was contemptuous of Russian revolutionaries as a group, except for Lenin, whom he had met only once, but considered outstanding. On September 30, 1915, the German Minister in Berne reported on Lenin's programme for a separate peace with Germany. The Foreign Ministry in Berlin took this report very seriously, and through the German Legation in Berne, Keskula put small sums of money, the source carefully camouflaged, at Lenin's disposal.[5]

Late in 1915, Keskula went to Stockholm to organise contacts with the revolutionaries in Russia, his main interest still being Esthonian independence. He did not think much of the Russian revolutionaries' organising abilities and tried to organise them himself, but unlike Helphand, he had no independent means. On arriving in Stockholm, however, he contacted the local Bolshevik committee, and printed leaflets and pamphlets for clandestine distribution in Russia. He also arranged for a Danish Social Democrat to pay two visits to Russia, both on his own and Helphand's behalf, to contact Bolshevik organisations in Petrograd and Moscow.

On November 20, Helphand told the German Minister in Copenhagen that one of his agents was just back with news from St Petersburg: the Russian army's morale was low, the situation in the interior was getting worse, and starvation was expected in St Petersburg and Moscow that winter; but the Russian army would not rebel until after the war. With the Russian workers, however, it was different. 'Certainly 100,000 men' could be brought out on strike in St Petersburg at twenty-four-hours' notice. But the strike committees and other organisations needed to be better co-ordinated, and also needed to be linked with the army. In making this report (which should have made clear to the Germans that it was highly unlikely that a revolution would follow such a strike), Helphand ignored the Bolshevik groups in Russia. They were so weakened by the war and by their lack of finance that they could have given no effective support, even if Lenin had consented to their use; and he had not. He too was still paralysed by lack of money. 'No money. There is no money here. That is the main trouble,' he wrote to a friend in mid-December. (This indeed makes clear that the subsidies from the German Legation in Berne, paid to Lenin by Keskula and Karl Moor, must have been very small – and irregular.)

From what we now know of the collapse of Russian morale, and the unwillingness to continue the war, Helphand's reports at this stage were only marginally exaggerated. The crucial point was – would the Russian army join the revolution? Helphand said 'no, not yet' – and in this he was right. Something of the steady drop in morale at home is reflected in this table (whose figures must be taken as approximate):

|                              | 1914  | 1915  | 1916  | 1917                        |
|------------------------------|-------|-------|-------|-----------------------------|
| Increases in industrial profits | 16·5% | 39·7% | 53·1% | 72·5% (1st six months only) |
| Rise in retail price-index   | —     | 23%   | 79%   | 124%                        |
| Rise in wages                | —     | 10%   | 15%   | 50%                         |

These huge paper profits were largely obtained by cornering raw materials, and reducing output, so as to sell at high monopoly prices, thus causing rampant inflation of some 55% by 1916, and an ever more embittered proletariat, whose wage increases were so very limited. These industrial profits were then sent safely abroad in the form of credit to the English and French banks, whose increasing involvement in the rapidly deteriorating Russian economy was rapidly becoming the subject of a major conflict in its own right between England (the major financial power of the Entente) and Germany. Already in 1915, confidential Board of Trade reports were exhorting the British government to use the war finally to capture the Russian market from the Germans.

To return to Helphand. On November 30, he again saw the German Minister at Copenhagen, and warned him against a German deal with the Tsarist regime – Helphand's abiding fear – which, he claimed, no longer wielded the necessary authority. Germany would lose the political results of her military achievements. If there was no peace made with the Tsar (and the German government had in fact abandoned all such attempts), peace would become the revolutionary movement's main policy. The moment, he thought, was now ripe. The revolutionary organisations were now stronger than before 1905. (This was *not* what he had said ten days previously.) A German seizure of Riga and Dvinsk would destroy Russia's last hopes of victory, and precipitate events in St Petersburg and Moscow. Helphand then proposed that the Russian market should be flooded with forged currency. The rouble was already in a weak state and this would push it still lower and undermine the Russians' confidence in their own currency; if it was discovered that there were two notes with the same serial number in circulation, there would be a panic which would further harm Russia's already tarnished credit abroad. Finally, he urged a well-organised propaganda campaign within the Russian army (which seems to indicate that he supposed that it could still maintain moderate discipline).

Helphand was summoned back to Berlin. Between December 16 and 20, he discussed his plans both with the Foreign Ministry, who approved them, and with the Treasury, who strongly disapproved of the introduction of forged currency into Russia (a measure later adopted by the Bolsheviks themselves, whose printing presses were to pour out roubles, all with the same serial number). But Helphand came away from Berlin with the promise of a further one million roubles for defeatist propaganda within the Russian army.

On his return to Copenhagen, however, Helphand warned the German Minister that it was by no means certain that the January strike would be a success; he would need another 20 million roubles (a huge sum) to complete the organisation of the revolution, which was to follow the strike. The German government should put the measures he had suggested into immediate operation, but should also prepare for another winter campaign. Helphand, however, was only given one million roubles, and this he took with him to Stockholm early in January.

The strike, which began later that month, started vigorously enough. On the 11th, some 10,000 workers came out at the naval base of Nicolaiev, near Odessa. On the 22nd, 45,000 came out in St Petersburg and were able to stay out for some considerable time, Helphand having seen to it that the strike committees had ample funds. Helphand was convinced, so his biographers claim, that all this was his own achievement; but one cannot be sure. Certainly no revolution followed the strike. He had relied too much on flair, hard cash, and hasty improvisation. There was no cohesive organisation at this time such as might have ensured the success of a mass movement. Again, his paid agents in Russia may have misled him; and he had not had the 20 million roubles from the Germans for which he had asked at the last moment. Was it likely that they would have handed over so large a sum at such short notice? Was this Helphand covering himself against the failure that he now foresaw?

On returning to Copenhagen, he told the German Minister that his confidential agents in St Petersburg had opposed his directive to launch the strike even on January 22; the leaders had therefore postponed it, but the organisation was still ready for action. This, it is felt, was partly true; but it was doubtful, as Helphand himself now admitted, whether they could really bring 100,000 men into the streets at twenty-four-hours' notice.

Somewhere among all this may be detected the precise state of the revolutionary organisation in St Petersburg, and of Russian morale generally, at this time. It was Helphand who had told the Germans that he could turn a mass strike into a revolution. In January 1916, he failed. Exactly a year later, a general strike did turn into a revolution. There can be no question that Helphand's ground work largely contributed to success in early 1917.

The failure of the revolution in 1916 thoroughly depressed the Foreign Ministry in Berlin. Von Jagow, the Foreign Secretary, who had never liked the plan and thoroughly mistrusted Helphand, believed that a large part of the revolutionary funds, supplied from German sources, had come to rest in Helphand's pocket. This was partly true. The Foreign Ministry banished Helphand, and cut back on its revolutionary activities.

Helphand was undismayed. The revolution, he knew, was inevitable and events would rehabilitate him. He had to wait, and find another supporter. Meanwhile, he kept up his subversive activities in Russia from his Copenhagen base, probably now backed, his biographers feel, by the German General Staff (whose archives were destroyed during the Second World War). But by now, he was a financial giant in his own right. His firm either continued to finance revolutionary activities in Russia, or, more probably, to accumulate capital in Russia to ensure that there would be ample funds there when the revolution did break out. Not a great deal more seems known about his political activities during the rest of 1916. Throughout that spring and summer, however, it is known that Keskula's organisation supplied the Petrograd Bolsheviks with revolutionary literature.

In 1914, the centre of gravity had been on the Western Front. In 1915, it had shifted to the Eastern Front. In 1916, it shifted back to the Western Front, when the German Command decided on a battle of attrition at Verdun to break the French army, and a simultaneous submarine campaign to cripple England.

Again, as in 1914, Russia came to the rescue. In the spring of 1916, Germany had 46 divisions on the Eastern Front and Austria had 40, while Russia had 130 divisions but was short of supplies and equipment. Allied munitions and supplies of all sorts were now being poured into Vladivostok in the far east, and into the north Russian ports to enable Russia to struggle on. With them came Commander Oliver Locker-Lampson MP, who witnessed the outbreak of the revolution in March 1917, in command of a British armoured car squadron, sent out to keep the British flag flying after the failure of the Dardanelles operation.

In March 1916, however, Russian troops attacked – to relieve Verdun – at Lake Narocz, east of Vilna, a very costly move. The main Russian offensive was to begin in July, in conjunction with a British offensive on the Somme. But early in June, General Brusilov, the Russian commander on the south-west front, attacked suddenly and prematurely (this time in response to an Italian appeal) against the Austrians north of Lemberg and in the Bukovina. The Austrians quickly collapsed, and Brusilov took 200,000 prisoners. His successful offensive lasted for three months – and led Roumania to enter the war on the Allied side.

Roumania had 23 divisions, but only six weeks' supply of ammunition. Late in August, Roumanian troops moved slowly north-west through the Carpathian Mountains to co-operate with Brusilov in the Bukovina. But early in September, the enemy countered vigorously and advanced into the Dobrudja, by the mouth of the Danube. Early in October, they attacked the Roumanians' centre and in mid-November finally broke through the Transylvanian mountain passes. Late in November, they crossed the Danube near Bucharest, which fell on

December 6. The rest of the Roumanian troops retreated into the north-east corner of Roumania, between the Carpathians and the Russian border. The Germans and Austrians had thus gained the bulk of Roumania, with all its oil and wheat – in just three months of fighting.

By now, Brusilov's offensive had ended. Although it had compelled the withdrawal of German troops from France, and thus caused the abandonment of the Verdun attack, it had cost the Russians one million lives, and virtually ruined Russia as a military power. Consequently, the Germans could now strike through Roumania into southern Russia and the Ukraine, where they could obtain untold quantities of raw materials and supplies, which they now desperately needed for their very survival, and thus break the Allied naval blockade of Germany.

This was the significance of the Roumanian collapse at the end of Brusilov's offensive – which had finally broken the Russian army. If Helphand's assessment was right, Russia indeed seemed ripe for revolution. From now on, she was a passive object in the Great War. On the home front, inflation was raging worse than ever, and Russia's state debt was steadily mounting. In 1916, it was already 30 milliard roubles, the interest on which was more than half the country's revenue for that year – and it was rising rapidly. Revolution apart, Russia was heading for bankruptcy.

# 2

# *Kornilov and the British*

IN 1917, the British Embassy in St Petersburg was a massive building, 'more like a barracks than a residence', thought the Ambassador's daughter. Blood-red in colour, it stood at the corner of the Troitsky bridge, opposite the fortress of Peter and Paul, and gave on to the Neva embankment and the Champ de Mars. It had been built by Giacomo Quarenghi, whom Catherine the Great, bored with her French architects, had summoned from Italy in 1780, and who had impressed a Palladian magnificence on the architecture of St Petersburg. But Catherine overworked Quarenghi; and the palace which he built for her lover Sergei Soltikov had little to recommend it except its size. For nearly a century, the great house except for a small wing where the Princess Soltikov lived, had been leased to His Majesty's government by the Soltikov family.

Inside, a scarlet and white staircase led up to a suite of four saloons which opened out into a large white ballroom and an oval dining-room. Only when the windows were open did that strange Russian smell of leather and fish oil penetrate this airless and private world; with it came the scent of blood. This was the recollection of the young Harold Nicolson of a visit to his father, British Ambassador to Russia from 1906 to 1910. Diplomatic circles in Russia were entirely isolated from the lives of the people. Like the Imperial Court, they did not even speak the same language – indeed, no British ambassador since at least 1906 had been able to speak Russian; Sir Arthur Nicolson spoke to the Russians in Spanish, his successor, Sir George Buchanan in French, the language of the court.

In appearance, Buchanan was the schoolgirl's ideal of a British diplomat – and as such pilloried by Somerset Maugham in his short story, 'His Excellency'. He was well supported by his wife and daughter and a large staff, headed by his Counsellor, Francis Lindley, a Wyke-hamist, whose calm manner and kindly smile nothing ever disturbed, and by his Military Attaché, Major-General Alfred Knox (formerly ADC to Lord Curzon, when Viceroy in India), an upright, plain-speaking man, much respected by the Russian army, but now rather feared by Russian officers for his open criticism of Russian inefficiency and incompetence.[1]

At Moscow, the British Consul-General was a young, round-faced Scot called Robert Bruce Lockhart, who was fluent in Russian, and mixed widely in political circles, and was thus of great use to his Ambassador. An intelligent, energetic and clever young man, Buchanan thought him his most able subordinate.

At Russian GHQ at Mogilev ('Stavka'), the British military representative was Major-General Sir Charles St Leger Barter, who had commanded a division in France up to September 1916, and hence had little knowledge of the Russians – and none of politics, which were coming to play an increasing role in every Russian's life; and at the age of sixty-one, Barter was unlikely to acquire any such knowledge, since not far beneath his precise, military manner, there lay an over-excitable temperament.

Literally swanning around between Petrograd, Moscow and the 'Stavka,' was Commander Oliver Locker-Lampson, with his British armoured car squadron, who took orders from no one in Russia. He wore a Lieut-Colonel's crown and pip on his shoulder, and a Naval Commander's rings on his sleeve, since his unit formed part of the Royal Naval Air Service. He reported to and took occasional orders from the First Lord of the Admiralty, but his prime allegiance seems to have been to King George V, with whom he was in frequent correspondence.

This varied support should have lightened the burden of Buchanan. But inside the Ambassador's long study, with its white bookcases and dark red walls, a frail man, with a tired, sad face, could be seen behind the large Sheraton writing table. For by January 1917, Buchanan was an exhausted man. He had to bear the full burden of the War Cabinet's mounting disapproval of and exasperation with Russia and the Russian army.[1]

The Prime Minister in the new Coalition government was Lloyd George, who had ousted Asquith in December 1916. He was in fact the only Liberal in the Cabinet; but, as the *Manchester Guardian* commented, was 'a sort of coalition in himself'. He was a Welshman and a highly complex character. 'One could say fifty things of LG that might appear contradictory, and all would be true,' writes the assistant Cabinet secretary. There was his courage in great crises (and his capacity to sleep soundly during them). There was his physical cowardice; he was 'all of a tremble' during an air raid over London, and took to his bed.

There was his extraordinary vitality. But at other times, Hankey (the Cabinet secretary) found him 'restless and neurotic, unstable and rather infirm in purpose, neuralgic and irritable' (September 1917). In January 1918, Hankey found him impossible to work with, or for. 'He is petulant, irritable, perpetually demanding impossible information which he doesn't need, abusing and quarrelling with the soldiers, suspicious, sly, and dog-tired but refusing to rest.' But his Cabinet secretary was devoted to him. He could indeed inspire a small, devoted circle of brilliant young men, like Philip Kerr (later Lord Lothian, Ambassador to the United States) and Hankey; but he also relied on other very dubious cronies, like William Sutherland, whom Hankey found an 'odious fellow . . . some sort of political parasite of L G's'. Then there was Maundy Gregory, the honours tout, who finally had to flee the country to escape a murder charge – and whom Lloyd George later openly visited in Paris.

There was his imagination and flair, his compulsive wenching, his magnanimity, his capacity for drawing out young people to make them feel they were the only ones who mattered – in fact, to elicit information. The young Duff Cooper, a perceptive young man, records in 1918 that Lloyd George created the impression of a great man, 'and he does it without seeming theatrical and without seeming sincere'. He radiated magnetism. Twenty years later, a young journalist met L G, then aged seventy-five, at his home at Churt in Surrey. 'An electric current went through the air as he entered the room,' he writes. Hankey, and many others, saw him as the only man to win the war, but in June 1917 recorded sourly: 'With him "nothing succeeds like success" and honesty and good faith don't matter.' Other supporters knew this too. 'Of course, he would not pick your pocket if he knew there was nothing in it,' remarked F. E. Smith, later Lord Birkenhead and Lord Chancellor.

Above all, there was Lloyd George's tremendous oratory. His relative lack of education give some passages a slightly stilted feeling, but they come across, even today, and in cold print, with terrific passion. He was stimulated by anxiety and trouble, which disturbed and 'upheaved' his whole nature, wrote Frances Stevenson (who became his second wife) of a speech given in January 1917. He 'had worked himself up into a perfect fever . . . As the time drew near for the delivery of the speech, he was quite pitiful, & almost ill with fright . . . But he delivered it magnificently, & was splendidly received. It was a great speech.' A month later, when Hankey met him in a corridor of the House after another great speech, he found him 'literally trembling in every limb' with excitement.[2]

But men of power, men of influence, saw in these contradictory elements a statesman who now alone could lead England to victory.

Nearly all the other Cabinet ministers were Tories. Andrew Bonar Law, the Conservative Party leader, was Chancellor of the Exchequer and leader of the House of Commons. A Scottish-Canadian iron-merchant from Glasgow, he had become Tory leader as a compromise candidate on Balfour's resignation in 1911. He was a manic depressive and teetotaler whose only relaxation was contract bridge. Asquith thought he 'had not the brains of a Glasgow baillie'. Invariably he relied on a more energetic personality than himself and if one was not available, he would wait 'for a course which was inevitable', as Lloyd George remarked. Bonar Law openly regarded the new Prime Minister as a dictator, but 'meant to give him his chance', as he said, calling him 'George' (which he knew infuriated Lloyd George) when he wanted to annoy. But though admittedly ignorant of military affairs, he could be extremely effective in the House of Commons, which Lloyd George was glad to leave in his care. Debating with Bonar Law, it was said, 'was like having handfuls of fine, stinging gravel thrown in one's face. There was never a big stone one could fling back.' He could keep most of the Tory dogs in check, and in general was a good second to Lloyd George during the war.[3]

The Lord President of the Council and leader of the House of Lords was Lord Curzon, who had become Viceroy of India before he was forty. He had a profound knowledge of the Middle and Far East and was a prodigious worker – masterly in exposition, though somewhat weak in making decisions. He wore a brace and girdle to protect a weak back and leg and this added a rigidity to an appearance already over-bearing and pompous. 'Curzon is an intolerable person to do business with – pompous, dictatorial and outrageously conceited,' records Hankey. 'Really he is an intolerable person . . . Yet an able, strong man with it all . . .' The constant pain he suffered from his back only increased his great capacity for work. With a bottle of champagne beside him, he sometimes sat up at night over his papers until 3.30 a.m., minuting them in an appalling handwriting. His harassed staff were quite unable to read his instructions, but were too frightened to approach him because in the mornings he was very bad-tempered, 'but better as the day advances', according to Baldwin. 'He has plenty of brains, but is feeble in a crisis,' remarks Lloyd George, who had to have him in the Cabinet to please the Tories, but 'loathed the Curzon set, and all they stood for – loathed their mannerisms, their ideals, their customs, their mode of life'. Curzon himself was extraordinarily energetic, but mercilessly ill-treated and ill-used his staff and secretaries, to whom he could occasionally be charming, but was too often a vindictive tyrant. While he busied himself winding the clocks or choosing picture frames, at the same time drafting foreign despatches and haranguing his maids, government officials were made to keep his domestic accounts, pay his servants, type his books – even pack up cushions and draperies in tissue paper and boxes.[4] The verdict on Curzon must be that of Robert Horne: 'He does not understand the ordinary man, and most men are ordinary.'

Lord Milner, who had been born at Hesse-Darmstadt in Germany, was a rigid bureaucrat by inclination and an imperialist by experience. He had been educated in Germany too, before going up to Balliol, then became a journalist and later a civil servant. He had made his name as British High Commissioner in South Africa from 1897 to 1902, when the Boer War ended. Though a strong critic of the Liberal Government in the House of Lords, he joined Lloyd George's Coalition government in December 1916 and was the Prime Minister's right-hand man for over two years. Many people in England, particularly young people, suspected him of extreme reactionary views. 'Tell me that Lord Milner is not set on my doing my duty after the war according to his lights,' wrote a young officer from the trenches to the assistant Cabinet secretary, who was a friend. This reputation was not undeserved.[5] Milner's close friends confided that he was 'a real democrat in theory – but inhuman when he comes to deal with men'.

Arthur Henderson, a former Trade Unionist from Newcastle, was Labour Party leader in the House of Commons – and pro-war. A tall, thick-set man, with fair skin and fair hair, he appeared a typical, stolid Englishman, but his massive strength of mind and warm heart had led him to be universally known as 'Uncle Arthur'. He was not overawed by his Tory colleagues. In April 1917, Frances Stevenson records sitting in her room in Downing Street, 'when suddenly I heard someone shouting & banging their fist on the Cabinet Room table. This went on for a long time & there was no doubt it was someone in a great rage.'[6] It was not the Tory Ministers threatening to resign in a body, but Henderson putting his case on Electoral Reform, which the Tory ministers did not like. (Henderson was later to be Home Secretary in 1924, and Foreign Secretary from 1929 to 1931.)

The Secretaries of State were all Tories. At the War Office was Lord Derby, a public figurehead with an enormous, but quite undeserved reputation. Hankey found him 'pitiful', 'feather-brained', a 'flabby jelly . . . on the point of resigning for the 28th time or thereabouts', while the assistant Cabinet secretary thought him 'a public danger'. This enabled Lloyd George, who had been Secretary of State for War under Asquith, to maintain practical control of the War Office himself for over a year. The Chief of the Imperial General Staff (CIGS) was General Sir William Robertson, a careful and competent officer, who had risen from the ranks, but whose lack of imagination and obstructiveness had somehow – in the general wartime atmosphere of the 'untouchability' of the generals – created a legend of resolution.[7] (The French called him '*Le Général Non-Non*'.) Given to long silences, Robertson countered any argument he did not like in Cabinet with the phrase 'I've 'eard different' – which too often got him his way.

At the Admiralty, the First Lord was Sir Edward Carson, the great advocate and Ulster leader. He had played a considerable part in the negotiations which had led to the replacement of Asquith by Lloyd George; but even in November 1916, he had told Lloyd George that he was 'too tired & is sick of the whole thing'. Lloyd George sent him to the Admiralty, where he was not a success in coping with the twin problems of convoys and submarines.[8] Hankey's comments on Carson are severe: a 'veritable "dismal Jimmy" ' (September 1915); 'positively pitiful, and worse than Bonar Law' (December 1916); and in January 1917, a 'fearful pessimist – but he always was'.

At the Foreign Office, the Secretary of State was A. J. Balfour, the former Prime Minister, and former Tory party leader. He stood head and shoulders above his Tory colleagues and made little effort to conceal his realisation of this; together with his unhurried, casual manner, this had infuriated the Tories and in 1911 had lost him the party leadership. As Foreign Secretary, his attraction to philosophy enabled him to see both sides of a case with 'almost crippling' clarity. 'Balfour followed with a very typical speech 20 minutes long, nicely balancing the arguments,' records Hankey of an Allied conference in Paris. 'Clemenceau replied: "Very well – are you for or against?" ' But his dilettante manner concealed a brilliant mind and a highly professional approach to politics.[9]

The Under Secretary of State, and Minister of Blockade, was Lord Robert Cecil, a very tall man, with a marked stoop and an air of great intellectual penetration and moral force. He was a deeply religious man and was shocked by the horrors of war. In September 1916 he had submitted proposals for the avoidance of future wars, which formed a basis for the Covenant of the League of Nations. Like all the Cecil family, members of which have been influential in public affairs since the days of Queen Elizabeth I, Lord Robert's reforming zeal could not conceal his ambition for power. On joining the Coalition government in December 1916, the 'tortuous mentality' of the Cecils, as Lloyd George termed it, did not prevent him enforcing the Allied blockade of Germany with 'unwavering efficiency'. For Cecil, reared in the isolation of his ancestral home, Hatfield House, the Bolshevik was a foreign anti-Christ, outside the pale of decent order and – rather gradual – political progress; he deserved no mercy. Not all were taken in by the dichotomy in Cecil's character. 'He is spiteful & malicious & will do D.

[41]

[Lloyd George] no good,' recorded Frances Stevenson, on hearing that he was to join the Coalition government. In 1921, by which time he was a fervent supporter of the League of Nations (of which he was later President), a Tory colleague remarked: 'He is the worst type – the sentimentalist with some of the wisdom of the serpent.'[10]

The heavy predominance of Conservative ministers in the Coalition government did the Prime Minister a good deal of harm. As late as December 1917, a report reached Downing Street that in South Wales there was 'widespread distrust of the Cabinet, owing to the presence in it of Milner, Curzon and Carson'. A month later, a further report stated that the Labour rank and file 'have no faith in Milner, Curzon, Carson, as likely to work for a democratic peace'.[11]

The real reason for the War Cabinet's concern over Russia was whether she would now stay in the war. The state of the Russian army and of affairs on the home front was known to the Cabinet; so was her near bankruptcy. But although massive British loans, and great quantities of military material and supplies were now being shipped into Russia, they seemed to do little good; very few of the supplies ever seemed to reach the front.

In late January, as a hastily-constructed railway line from Petrograd up to the ice-free port of Murmansk neared completion (thus hopefully enabling Allied supplies to reach the Russian front more quickly), it was decided to send an Allied mission out to Russia to encourage the Tsar to fight on. The British delegation was led by Lord Milner and General Sir Henry Wilson.

Sir Henry Wilson, an Ulsterman, was both the ugliest and cleverest man in the British army; which quality he had often to conceal, as he was a highly ambitious military politician, and the phrase 'too clever by half' had ruined many other talented men. Before the war, he had been one of the first senior British officers to see that conflict was inevitable, and as early as 1911, he had advocated conscription. As commandant of the Staff College in 1909, he had visited his opposite number in France, a Brigadier Foch, and the two became fast friends. Wilson had travelled, often on a bicycle, all over the terrain that a German invader might be expected to occupy. As Director of Military Operations (DMO) he put new vigour into Anglo-French military conversations and military plans, and carefully prepared for the landing of a British expeditionary force in France. In the autumn of 1915, he and General Sir William Robertson were the two most likely candidates for the post of Chief of the Imperial General Staff (CIGS). But Asquith never forgave Wilson, that 'poisonous tho' clever ruffian', he called him, for actively fomenting the Curragh mutiny early in 1914 from inside the

War Office. Robertson therefore got the job. During the war, Wilson, a born intriguer, supported Robertson, as that dour officer blundered on, with the casualty lists ever mounting. Later, Wilson became liaison officer with the French, and then British Military Representative on the Supreme War Council at Versailles.[12] His cleverness, and close relations with French officers, were still a liability. When someone lightly remarked that his job at Versailles required 'more suppleness than was perhaps usual in men of the British race', he nearly came to blows in the corridors of the Travellers Club.

Milner and Wilson brought out Brigadier-General F. C. Poole to take over the vital task of handling British supplies sent to the Russian army, which were now largely being wasted. But both Milner and Wilson proceeded warily, for Milner knew that the Russians were 'very sensitive' about British interference. At first, things went quite well. At a reception, the Tsar had 'quite a twinkle in his eye', and the Tsarina 'nearly laughed' at one of Wilson's jokes. (Edward VII is the only Englishman known to have wholly succeeded in this difficult task.) But in spite of optimistic Russian promises, the truth could not be concealed – there was now open talk of revolution. Milner, convinced that the autocracy 'alone holds Russia together', and must therefore be upheld, pressed strongly for Poole's appointment.[13] The Tsar agreed, and Poole set to work.

Unfortunately, he was not the best choice Wilson could have made. During some twenty-five years' service with the Gunners, mainly in Africa, he had risen to the rank of Major, whereupon he had retired. He had returned to the colours in 1914, and in 1916 had been attached to Wilson's staff, when the latter was in command of the 4th Army Corps in France. The two men were alike in certain ways: both had considerable charm and apparently got on well together, but behind Wilson's gangling and garrulous manner there lay one of the sharpest brains in the British army; behind Poole's, little except a cheerful and bustling optimism, and a taste for Russian gypsy girls. But Poole had some powerful connections at home. His father-in-law was Sir Charles Hanson, a Liberal MP and at this time Lord Mayor of London. Poole chose Brigadier R. G. Finlayson, also a Gunner, as his Chief of Staff. ('Copper' Finlayson was to become C.-in-C. Western Command in England early in the Second World War.)

On the British delegation's return to London, the 'Milner Committee' was set up to co-ordinate and support Poole's work in Petrograd, and Milner appointed as his secretary and general manager Colonel H. F. Byrne, a wily political animal well versed in Cabinet committee in-fighting.

Soon after the Allied mission left for England in late February, Buchanan came to the conclusion that Russia, with her 'happy knack of muddling through', would be able to carry on the war, and he left Petrograd for a holiday in Finland. But it was a risky time to leave. There was now no bread and little fuel in the city. 'The Putilov works stopped yesterday,' noted General Knox, the Military Attaché, on March 8. 'The Tula works have stopped . . .' So had others. Striking factory workers began to crowd the streets. On Saturday the 10th, though the British Embassy heard that the factories were restarting work, martial law was proclaimed; but 'the Nevski [Prospekt] was quiet when I crossed it at 3.30 p.m.', Knox records.[14] Half an hour later, however, the 'gendarmes were charging the people', and that evening there was more serious rioting. But when walking back from a dinner party at midnight, Knox found the streets deserted, except for Cossack patrols, and a 'few lonely policemen'.

Locker-Lampson has vividly described the tumultuous events of Sunday, March 11. But it was the defection of the Petrograd garrison that was crucial to the success of the revolution. Locker-Lampson, in fact, in his account of the events of that Sunday, was wrong in inferring that only the Pavlovsky Regiment fired that day at the strikers and demonstrators. Troops of the Pavlovsky and Volynsky regiments, among others, also took part in the firing. But when the Pavlovsky fired (as Professor Katkov points out in his *Russia 1917*), the demonstrators induced some of their comrades in barracks to mutiny. That evening, however, their colonel quelled the revolt, but as he was leaving the barracks, he was killed. Next morning, the 12th, after the colonel of the Volynsky had been killed in his barracks, the Volynsky rushed out and induced the Preobrajensky and other regiments of the garrison to mutiny. The details of these murders, which are crucial to the mutiny of the Petrograd garrison, still remain obscure.[15] (Katkov, indeed, makes clear that there is still a great deal which remains unknown about the March revolution.)

While Locker-Lampson was conducting his soap-opera with the Russian Princess and the revolutionaries at the Astoria Hotel on March 12, General Knox was with the General Staff on the Liteini Prospekt, when news came that the entire garrison had mutinied, and were coming down the street. 'We went to the window and waited,' he records. 'Craning our necks, we first saw two soldiers – a sort of advanced guard . . . Then came a great disorderly mass of soldiery, stretching right across the wide street . . . led by a diminutive but immensely dignified student . . . They looked up at the windows, which were now crowded with officers and clerks, but showed no sign of hostility . . . What struck me most was the uncanny silence of it all . . .'

When they finally broke in to the General Staff building, the Russian officers left hastily by a back door, and as Knox looked down over the banisters, he saw the men of the Preobrajensky Regiment taking the officers' swords. On his return to the British Embassy, he telephoned the news to Buchanan, who had now come racing back from Finland, and that morning had gone to the Foreign Ministry, and Knox heard him repeat it in French to the Foreign Minister and the French Ambassador.[16]

The Duma quickly nominated a provisional government, mainly of Constitutional-Democrats (or Cadets), who were, as their name implies, on the right wing of the revolutionary parties, with the colourless Prince Lvov as Prime Minister, and Milyukov, the Cadet leader, as Foreign Minister, to govern Russia until a constituent assembly could be called.

On March 13 Knox and two other British officers set off to the Duma at Buchanan's request; they were given a lift on a sledge 'crowded with peasants in holiday dress'. An old soldier, who smelt strongly of vodka, breathed into Knox's ear as they drove along, clinging to one another, that the 'Emperor was a good man', but was surrounded by traitors, who would now be removed, 'and all would be well'. On arriving at the Duma, they found the whole street crowded with lorries filled with 'joy-riding soldiers'. Rodzianko, the President of the Duma, and a 'pale-faced lawyer', a deputy called Alexander Kerensky, urged the men to keep order, but they had little success. The Russian army had gone over to the Revolution.[16]

On the 15th, the Tsar abdicated. Knox asked Rodzianko whether Russia would fight on. 'My dear Knox, you must be easy,' replied Rodzianko. 'Everything is going on all right. Russia is a big country, and can wage a war and manage a revolution at the same time.' But the Duma had only just moved in time. For the factory workers, soldiers and peasants had begun to form their own councils or soviets, headed by the Petrograd soviet (as in 1905).[16] This was under the control of the Social-Revolutionaries (or SR). As Russia was primarily an agricultural country, the SR were still the main revolutionary party. The Duma maintained a link with the Petrograd soviet by the appointment of the SR deputy, Alexander Kerensky, as Minister of Justice.

'There never was a more bloodless and orderly Revolution,' concluded Locker-Lampson in his report to the Admiralty. 'It may be that the Russian lacks imagination, but this tremendous change has been wrought without excess, without insult to women, without any cruelty. The crowds are not nearly as noisy as those in an English election . . . It has been the Revolution of a noble, generous-hearted people. The first days they took down the Tsar's portraits . . . but already in the hospitals the wounded want their Monarch's picture back and all the

moujiks are saying: "We want a Republic, but we want our Tsar".'
But, he added, 'to what extent German money was to blame for this
[Revolution] no one knows'.

In fact, hunger and anger with the corrupt Tsarist regime had precipitated events, and brought the crowds out into the streets. But much
of the organisation that initially kept the ensuing revolution going (and
especially the provision of the finance that kept the organisation going),
were undoubtedly due to the efforts of Helphand and his German
backers over the previous two years. History, especially in this century,
has repeatedly shown that intolerable conditions alone will generally
*not* start a revolution. Organisation is vital to canalise the upsurge of
feeling – and organisation means money, and a great deal of money.
Without such organisation, the State can often force its subjects to
accept what seem the most intolerable conditions.

By early April, the revolution was seemingly over. America entered
the war, which strengthened the provisional government's resolve to
fight on, so Milyukov assured the Allies; a Russian offensive would
shortly be launched, and Russia would stand by the Allied secret
treaties, which gave her Constantinople and the Straits, and parcelled
out the Turkish Empire in the Middle East among all the victorious
Allies. Russia's Allies were reassured.

But British observers badly under-estimated the importance of the
Petrograd soviet as an alternative power. It continued 'to act as if it
were the Government', wrote Buchanan, and was already trying to
force the Russian Ministers to approach the Allies about a general
peace. However, Kerensky (the Minister of Justice, and link man with
the Petrograd soviet) told Buchanan that the Petrograd soviet 'would
die a natural death, that the present agitation in the army would
pass . . .' But though Milyukov tried to placate both the Allies and the
Petrograd soviet, Buchanan warned Lord Milner that the military
outlook was 'most discouraging'. Russia was 'not ripe' for a democratic
government, and neither a republican nor a federal system would
prevent Russia disintegrating.[17]

Other more astute observers of the Russian scene held different views.
On April 1, Helphand went to see the German Minister in Copenhagen
to press for continued support of the Bolsheviks. Germany, he argued,
must now abstain from further military action against Russia, or it
would create a patriotic mood for the defence of liberties already
achieved. The Russian revolution must now be left alone to allow the
logical development of the clash of class interests, which would reduce
Russia to complete anarchy in two to three months. Germany could
then launch a powerful attack to conquer and hold southern Russia,

after which there must be ruthless political exploitation of the victory to break up the centralised Russian Empire. If there was no German attack, Russia would again grow into an aggressive military power, all the more bent on revenge on Germany. To prepare the ground for the attack, the 'extreme revolutionary movement will have to be supported, in order to intensify anarchy', Helphand urged.[18] But if all this was thought undesirable, Germany must conclude an early peace, without bitterness. This required a stable situation; there would then be no need to intensify anarchy. Helphand clearly preferred the first option – which entailed full German support for Lenin and the Bolshevik party. His was a brilliant assessment.

In March, in fact, with the approval of the German General Staff, Helphand had curtly informed Lenin, via Furstenberg, that it had already been arranged for him and Zinoviev to return to Russia at once; similar arrangements were being made about the other exiles. Lenin turned this down flat. He obviously could not accept German help to return on his own. Helphand knew of Lenin's refusal when he saw the German Minister in Copenhagen, who strongly supported Helphand's proposals in his report to the Foreign Secretary in Berlin; and the German Minister in Berne was instructed to offer all the Russian exiles free transit through Germany, via Stockholm, back to Russia, while Helphand would discuss the technical details with Foreign Office officials.[18] On April 13, Helphand was in Stockholm, as representative of the German Socialists, to meet Lenin on his arrival. Lenin flatly refused to see him. Helphand therefore asked Furstenberg to discover what plans Lenin had to achieve peace. Lenin replied, according to Helphand, that 'he was not concerned with diplomacy; his task was social-revolutionary agitation'. Helphand sent back an angry warning to Lenin that 'he may go on agitating; but if he is not interested in statesmanship, then he will become a tool in my hands'. Helphand then went to see Radek, and arranged to provide massive financial support for the Bolshevik movement in its struggle for power in Russia. Helphand, who clearly saw himself as the real leader of the revolutionary movement, who would take over the Bolshevik movement at the critical moment, then returned to Berlin, where he had an audience with Zimmerman, the Foreign Secretary, to whom he stressed the importance of backing the Bolsheviks, and of not launching a new German offensive.

The Bolsheviks, however, though avidly accepting Helphand's money, saw him mainly as a gambler, who had finally decided to go banco on Bolshevism. The Bolshevik Foreign Mission in Stockholm (run by the three Polish Jews, Furstenberg, Radek, and one Vorovski), whom Helphand haunted all through the early summer, were in touch with other minor German agents, and probably with the German Legation in Stockholm itself, in their vital task of channelling money into the Bolshevik movement in Russia in mid-1917.

Something of the activity of these other German agents is now known. Just after Lenin returned to Russia, the German Minister in Berne instructed his Military Attaché, Walter Nasse, to discover how money could best be passed to Lenin and the other Russian emigrés who had returned with him. Nasse reported that Karl Moor (who had been keeping an eye on Lenin for the German General Staff ever since September 1914) had asked the Bolsheviks and Mensheviks, who still remained in Switzerland; they said finance would indeed be acceptable, provided it came as a gift from an 'unobjectionable source'.

For some reason which is still unclear, this matter was now handled by the German General Staff and Treasury, and kept secret from the Foreign Ministry (perhaps their previous contacts with Helphand had become too well known). Some time in May, a certain Doctor Gustav Mayer, a biographer of Engels, approached the Foreign Ministry in Berlin and offered to go to Stockholm, where socialists from many countries were assembling for a conference. His offer was accepted, and he was asked to report on what was happening. Now Dr Mayer happened to be very friendly with Nasse – who happened to be a close relative of the Secretary of the Treasury, Count Roedern. Just before leaving for Stockholm, Mayer was approached by a Treasury official (who also happened to be a relative of Count Roedern) and asked to make contact in Stockholm with someone he already knew, and help him; this matter, it was explained to Mayer, was of 'extreme political importance', and must be kept secret even from the Foreign Ministry. On arrival in Stockholm, Mayer found that this person was none other than Nasse, for whom he was required to act as a post-box. Now Mayer makes clear that he was in close touch with both Furstenberg and Radek; and that Karl Moor was also in Stockholm at this time. The clear deduction is that Nasse was passing on German Treasury funds, via Dr Mayer, to Karl Moor, who was in turn handing them over to the Bolshevik Foreign Mission as a gift from an 'unobjectionable source'; indeed, later that year, when the Bolsheviks were openly charged with taking German money, their central committee noted that Karl Moor had offered money – which came from a 'large inheritance', which he had 'unexpectedly' received.[19]

These were some of the ways (there may well have been others which still remain undetected) in which between 30 and 50 million gold marks (some £1 million to £1·7 million) of German money were channelled into the Bolshevik movement in Russia in mid-1917.

Back in Petrograd, Lenin installed himself in a deserted palace; he was regarded by the British Embassy as a fairly harmless lunatic, and 'as we drove to the islands in the afternoon', records Buchanan, 'we sometimes saw him or one of his followers addressing a crowd from the balcony'. But from now on, the Bolshevik party, calling incessantly for an immediate peace, began to attract serious attention, and Bolshevik agitators made the most of large demonstrations which occurred when in mid-May the clash finally came between the provisional government and the Petrograd soviet. The Cadets made a counter-demonstration. Buchanan spoke to the crowd from his Embassy balcony. General Kornilov, the Petrograd commander, tried to bring out the Cossacks. But it was the Petrograd soviet that finally calmed the crowd. Milyukov, Gouchkov, the War Minister, and Kornilov thereupon resigned. Members of the Petrograd soviet were invited to join the provisional government, which now consisted of ten Cadets and six socialists, and Kerensky became War Minister. The balance of power was shifting. 'We have got to face the fact that Socialism is now dominant', Buchanan warned the Foreign Office.[20]

In London, the War Cabinet feared that this meant that Buchanan was no longer popular with the new Russian regime. They therefore sent one of their number, Arthur Henderson, out to Petrograd to replace Buchanan, if he saw fit. Henderson arrived in Petrograd on June 2. He quickly saw that things were very different in Russia – that Buchanan was popular, and knew more about the Russian situation than he ever would. On June 14, he therefore wrote to Lloyd George urging that Buchanan be retained as Ambassador.[21]

The Petrograd soviet welcomed all Allied socialists. On April 22, various neutral socialists had issued an invitation for an international socialist conference to be held at Stockholm. On May 8, the Petrograd soviet, uneasy at being by-passed, had issued an invitation for all socialists to come and confer in Petrograd before going on to Stockholm. In late May, as neutral and German socialists arrived in Stockholm, and patriotic socialists turned up in Petrograd (but had little success in urging the Russians to continue the war), the American, French and Italian governments all refused permission for their socialists to go to Stockholm; only the British government havered.[21] On June 2, the Petrograd soviet issued a further invitation to all socialists to come and confer in Petrograd before going on to the Stockholm Conference; but the conference was then postponed.

In the face of all this socialist activity, the Russian right-wing now began to retaliate. While the Russian officers grouped together, the leading Russian financier, Putilov, founded the 'Union for the Economic Revival of Russia', of which Gouchkov became chairman after his resignation, and which various Russian bank directors and others joined, ostensibly to raise funds to support moderate candidates in the coming elections for the constituent assembly; and together with General Kornilov (now Commander of the 8th Army on the south-west front), they formed the 'Republican Centre'. Money changed hands, and gradually a plot began to crystallise, of which British officers could hardly fail to become aware. Their views, as soldiers – which they openly expressed – were very different from the diplomats and and politicians. 'Have Knox, who is causing trouble, recalled from front,' Kerensky wired back to Petrograd impetuously.[22] For as Kerensky began to campaign for the Russian offensive on the southern front, he knew that the Russian soldiers had to be very carefully handled, or they would not fight.

The sole British observer and participant at the front was thus Commander Locker-Lampson, whose squadron had been sent to give support. In late June (the Russian offensive was still delayed), he received a letter of encouragement from Buckingham Palace.

Dear Commander Locker-Lampson,

The King desires me to thank you for your letter of the 4th June. His Majesty was greatly interested in all you told him of the doings of the Squadron of British Naval Armoured Cars under your Command.

You certainly rendered the most useful service in Roumania last year and up to the time of the Revolution, and His Majesty looks forward to your having a chance of proving to the present Russian Government your value in the coming advance, which the King trusts will not be long delayed.

What you say about the political situation also interested His Majesty . . .

Yours very truly,
Stamfordham.[23]

The Russian offensive finally began early in July. 'One of the Corps Commanders prayed silently during the fateful minutes preceding the appointed time,' reported Locker-Lampson. 'When, punctually at 9 a.m., the troops swarmed over and the attacking waves rolled onward, this General devoutly crossed himself.' The Russian troops drove the rather demoralised Austrians back quite rapidly.

The Germans then launched a combined political and military offensive, designed to force the provisional government to make peace. For some time, it had been known that the remaining Cadet ministers, who were keen to continue the war, were about to resign; and the Germans were impatient with Lenin's lack of success in seizing power. The Germans thus stirred up disaffection through agents in the Baltic fleet at Kronstadt, and in certain Russian regiments, notably a machine-gun regiment; and the coming outbreak, alleged to be due to mass indignation at the recent Russian offensive, was made known in advance to the Russian troops at the front in subversive leaflets. As soon as the Cadet ministers resigned on July 15, disorganised rioting broke out, started by the machine-gunners and the Baltic sailors, who had poured into Petrograd. The surprised Bolshevik leaders, deeply concerned at this revolutionary adventurism, had no choice but to grant hasty approval to this sudden outbreak and try and control it.[24]

The provisional government just managed to seize the initiative. On July 18, the Russian Ministry of Justice (originally tipped off by Allied sources) began to publish a series of documents, which they had seized, to prove that Lenin and the Bolshevik party had received German money, and were thus guilty of high treason. This turned the tide. Some of the regiments, who had remained neutral, decided to support the provisional government, and the Baltic sailors began to drift back to Kronstadt. The deserted palace, which the Bolsheviks used as a headquarters, was seized; so were the offices of *Pravda*. Trotsky and other leaders were (temporarily) arrested, and Lenin fled to Finland. The uprising known as the 'July days' thus ended with the complete discredit of the Bolshevik party, with whom the provisional government was now determined to settle accounts.

The Germans resorted to military pressure. On July 20, they launched a vigorous counter-offensive on the Russian front. During the preliminary artillery barrage, the Russian soldiers in the trenches 'would kneel down, place their hands together, and pray, overcome with fear', Locker-Lampson informed the Admiralty. But when the enemy advanced, 'as one man the Russians flung away their rifles, abandoned their Maxims, and ran screaming out over the fields. In their desperation they would only stop to sit down and tear off their high boots so as to run the faster. In vain their officers caught at the men's legs in a useless effort to stop them, and then turned back quite alone to fire ineffectual pistol shots against the Austrians, until they themselves were killed.'[25]

The old Russian army, in fact, was routed. Locker-Lampson's armoured cars did all they could to cover the retreat. But as soon as they set up a new base, they again had to pull back. The pandemonium was awful. Once, when encamped beside the open road, 'quite suddenly, not only the skyline of the road, but the whole horizon of the plain became black, black and crawling with cars, carts, horses, and creatures flying for their lives,' Locker-Lampson reported. 'It is impossible to reproduce the feeling of despair which overwhelmed me.'

But their liaison officer, a Baron Girard, dashed out, armed only with a revolver and a walking stick, overturned the leading cart, and began 'striking the deserters in the cart repeatedly over the head with his stick. A huge lorry behind crammed high with at least thirty armed soldiers was brought abruptly to a stop.' Girard attacked the driver, then the soldiers; other Russian officers joined in. 'These new-fledged freedmen were slaves still,' Locker-Lampson reported, 'obedient to any strong man who forced his will upon them. Really it was as if the old regime had not disappeared. The soldiers stood up as of yore, stiffly at attention, while the officers beat them in the face, tore their beards and kicked them for cowards. Others fell on their knees making the sign of the cross and prayed for mercy.' Soon the whole mob was streaming back in the opposite direction.

But it was all to no avail. The enemy now left the road, and 'clearly through my telescope I could see grey coats advancing through the corn', adds Locker-Lampson. The rout went on; and the Russian soldiers were soon streaming back over the frontier. General Kornilov, the local Russian commander, however, was highly impressed with the help which British officers had given their Russian officer-colleagues in trying to stem the retreat, and wrote Locker-Lampson a heart-felt letter of thanks, and sent him twenty-four St George's Crosses.

It was at this moment that Locker-Lampson received a rather delayed and inopportune message from the First Lord of the Admiralty. 'Please inform officers and men under your command how glad I am to learn that the Squadron . . . has taken part in the recent successes stop I congratulate all concerned . . .'[25]

Locker-Lampson, however, appears to have seen quite quickly that, in certain circumstances, these two messages, together with the King's letter, could be profitably combined; he kept them by him.

By now, the great garrison towns in south Russia were in uproar and confusion, the Russian soldiers began to pour home, and as order began to break down, Kerensky, now Prime Minister, began to lose control, and the provisional government was too weak to settle accounts with the now thoroughly discredited Bolsheviks.

In documents seized and published by the Russian Ministry of Justice, it was in fact Helphand (Parvus) who appeared as the central figure in the Bolshevik movement, organising everything in the background. 'Parvus is not an agent provocateur,' the Cadet paper had stated. 'He is more than that: he is an agent of Wilhelm II.' As the Bolsheviks could not reveal the true facts, they neither received Helphand into the fold, nor denounced him as a German agent, but simply replied with flat denials and considerable abuse. Early in August, however, Help-hand published 'My reply to Kerensky & Co', from the sanctuary of Switzerland, in which he firmly stated that he had always supported the Russian revolutionary movement. 'You lunatics, why do you worry whether I have given money to Lenin?' he added, somewhat dangerously.

But the Bolsheviks remained in real trouble, even though the provisional government was too weak to settle matters with them, and some of the financial channels between Stockholm and Petrograd undoubtedly broke down, including, Professor Katkov thinks, the Nasse–Moor link, for Dr Mayer, Nasse's go-between, left Stockholm early in August. Karl Moor, however, stayed on, and was soon looking for other ways of resuming transfers of money to the Bolsheviks; for now that they were practically an underground party again, they were more than ever in need of German money. But if German money was crucial, so now was Bolshevik discretion. In August, Lenin wrote from Helsinki warning the Central Committee to maintain extreme caution and to avoid all contact with Karl Moor.[26]

In London, where there was now real concern about the Russian ability to fight on, there had now been two additions to the War Cabinet.

General Jan Smuts, a non-party outsider, had joined the Cabinet on June 22. Having fought the British as a general in the Boer War, he afterwards became Colonial Secretary under Botha. He took part in the 1914–15 campaign in German South-West Africa and commanded the Allied troops that penetrated into German East Africa in 1916, capturing Dar-es-Salaam in September. In March 1917, he came to an Imperial Conference in London, where he made a strong impression. 'I hear on all sides that Smuts is one of the great men of the Empire, much the biggest of the Premiers now in London,' records the assistant Cabinet secretary; and Hankey found him a 'delightful and attractive creature'. Smuts, an intellectual, who had allegedly read Kant's *Critique of Pure Reason* when bivouacked at night during the Boer War, and who 'still had in his eyes the look of the man who has been in a tight corner, who is ever on the watch for a potential enemy', also made a strong impression on Lloyd George, who asked him to join the War Cabinet. 'There was a deep understanding between the two men,' records Frances Stevenson. Neither ever gave himself away, 'though both had an uncanny capacity for knowing what the third man might think or do'. Smuts, who rarely spoke in Cabinet, soon came to the view, largely under the influence of the Dutch Ambassador, that the war would end in a draw; and Lloyd George used him more as an adviser – in particular on secret negotiations to try and take Austria out of the war.[27]

Then in mid-July, Lloyd George finally had to remove the depressed Carson from the Admiralty (but in order not to offend the Tories, had to 'boot up' Carson to the Cabinet, 'without his realising that he is really "degommé",' as Hankey reported).[28]

The First Lord was now Sir Eric Geddes, a railway expert: 'Transport is my religion,' he liked to say. Lloyd George had sent him to France in 1916 to improve the transport arrangements behind the lines. In this he had been highly successful, and as a result was made Inspector-General of Transport in all theatres of war. Described as 'painfully shy' and a 'loveable sort of giant', who could give forceful renderings of Harry Lauder's songs in the manner of a music-hall favourite, success soon made him 'most aggressive and pushful'. Faced with terrible shipping losses due to the German submarine campaign early in 1917, Lloyd George appointed him as Controller of Shipbuilding at the Admiralty, and in July as First Lord – with instructions to make changes at the Admiralty. For Admiral Jellicoe, the First Sea Lord, had reported that England could not survive the submarine campaign beyond December 1917; the Prime Minister was certain that England could survive, and that Jellicoe was tired out.[29]

But the submarine menace had forced the Prime Minister to agree to a major attack in Flanders to try to capture the submarine bases. He was certain that it would result in losses out of all proportion to any likely gains, but finally he acquiesced. On July 22, a terrific artillery bombardment had opened on the Flanders front, entirely destroying the intricate drainage system and turning the whole area through which the British troops were to advance into a swamp. On July 31, in torrential rain which lasted for days on end, the troops advanced – and immediately and literally floundered in the morass. The attack had clearly failed – but orders were issued that it should continue.

On July 31, the War Cabinet discussed what action to take if the military disasters on the Eastern Front and the internal dissensions in Russia should lead to a Russian collapse. Though it was generally felt that this would not happen immediately, and that a recovery was still possible, it was realised that a complete Russian débâcle would allow some of the 80 German and 40 Austrian divisions on the Eastern Front to be transferred to France, and 'that this would convert our present superiority of force into an inferiority; and that we should no longer be in a position to take the offensive'. In fact, on a purely arithmetical basis, the elimination of Russia would make the achievement of the Allied war aims, ie, complete victory, 'very problematical . . .'

On August 2, the CIGS wired to General Barter at Russian GHQ that restoration of discipline in the Russian army was essential, and that 'appeals from Russia for co-operation should be preceded by measures for putting her own house in order'. The War Cabinet would discuss with the Allies whether to exert pressure on the Russian government.[30]

Russia now had a new Commander-in-Chief. On July 29, Kerensky had presided at an important military conference at Mogilev, attended by all the front-line commanders, save for Kornilov, who was detained by the military situation on his own south-western front. Most of the generals at the conference attacked the revolutionary innovations in the army. By contrast, Kornilov sent a message, suggesting that commissars and committees indeed had their functions in the armies, but should be placed under definite limitations. To Kerensky, this sounded like a necessary liberal and progressive outlook for a potential C.in-C. Could Kornilov by these means restore discipline in the Russian army? Then in his mid-forties, Kornilov was of humble Cossack origin, a small, sinewy man, intensely brave and patriotic, with light olive skin, prominent cheek-bones, and piercing, slanting eyes. But in the present Russian turmoil, the position required considerable political judgement; and Kornilov, like most Cossacks, had no knowledge of politics. For him, Bolsheviks and socialists of all types were the enemies of the Russia he knew and served.[31]

But he had a valuable political friend and guarantor in the person of Boris Savinkov, former leader of the SR terrorist 'Fighting Organisation', well-known novelist, and at present commissar of the south-western front (who may well have drafted Kornilov's message to the conference), whom Kerensky had now decided to appoint as acting War Minister, while remaining in nominal charge himself. For Savinkov, a stronger and more resolute character than Kerensky, for whom 'socialism' merely meant a fairly liberal republicanism, was a fervent believer in the restoration of order and discipline in the army, and was convinced that General Kornilov, if supplied with proper political guidance, could achieve this.

So Savinkov at the War Ministry, and his deputy attached to Russian GHQ as Chief Commissar, did their best to inspire more military firmness in Kerensky, and more political discretion in Kornilov to enable the Premier and his new C.-in-C. to work together. Though their characters were strongly contrasted, their main objectives were not so very different. Kerensky, like Kornilov, wished to see a Russian army where the soldiers would obey orders, not debate them; while Kornilov, of humble origin himself, had no desire to restore the monarchy.[31]

On August 3, the War Cabinet were told that General Barter had found General Kornilov's 8th Army to be in a better state of discipline than any other army, and he thus had great hopes that Kornilov's appointment as Russian C.-in-C. would lead to the regeneration of the Russian army. The War Cabinet were also informed that Locker-Lampson's 'fleet' of armoured cars had survived the Russian retreat.[32]

Once the armoured cars were back on Russian soil (where some of the Russian soldiers began to turn and fight), Locker-Lampson was asked to train Kornilov's crack Cossack Wild Division in the use of his Lewis guns. He imagined they were to stop deserters, for these Cossacks, he found, 'consisted of dark-skinned cavaliers who loathed the revolution and hated deserters and who dreamt only of shedding blood. They had a great sense . . . of loyalty to their leaders, but felt under no obligation to any one else,' he reported.[33] In fact, the Wild Division was the personal bodyguard to Kornilov, who had been approached by the big financiers to lead a movement to seize Petrograd, and take over the provisional government. Locker-Lampson paid a visit to Russian GHQ at Mogilev, where his suspicions were confirmed that a military coup was in the air. Kornilov, much impressed by the British armoured car squadron, strongly urged him, for the good of the Russian army and a successful outcome of the war, to act with him when he moved. Locker-Lampson returned to his advance base at Proskurov by the frontier and began to move his stores, part of them to his main base at Kursk and part 'to a new base which', he informed the Admiralty, 'I decided to start, not at Kiev itself (which may fall), but beyond it and over the river [Dnieper] at Brovari.' Now this base had been carefully chosen; it was nothing more than a tiny hamlet, but was strategically placed along the road on which the armoured car squadron would have to move, either to join Kornilov at Mogilev, or to return to their main base at Kursk. But the Admiralty were told nothing of this reasoning.

On August 7, the War Cabinet considered telegrams from Buchanan and Knox, both sent from Petrograd on the 4th. Buchanan was being urged by Barter to impress on Kerensky the need for immediate restoration of disciplinary powers to Russian commanders and for the Russian government to put the grave military situation before any political objective in the present crisis. Both telegrams emphasised to the War Cabinet that the time had come for some Allied warning to the Russian government that unless effective steps were taken, Russia faced inevitable disaster. A separate message from France, however, might be of 'particular value', since France had originally declared war to support Russia, when she could – it was claimed – have escaped war. The War Cabinet also considered a later wire from Knox, dated August 6, stating that the Russians were complaining of the cold attitude, shown by the British, to whose opinion more weight was attached than to that of any other ally, and adding that 'it might be of real assistance in this crisis if we gave a hint that, while we were ready to make any sacrifice to help a Russia which had a strong government, our duty to ourselves and our other Allies might make us question the advisability of helping a government that delayed to take the necessary steps to restore discipline'. The War Cabinet decided to refer the matter to an approaching Allied conference, which should be urged to send a joint note of 'exhortation', and to request France to send a second special message.[34]

Kornilov's first act, after his appointment as C.-in-C., was to despatch a telegram to the provisional government, declaring that he could accept the post, and 'bring the people to victory and to a just and honourable peace', only on the following conditions:

1. Responsibility before his own conscience, and before the whole people.
2. Complete non-interference in his operational orders, and thus in the appointment of the higher staff commands.
3. Extension of the measures which had recently been adopted at the front (presumably the re-introduction of the death penalty) to all places in the rear, where army reinforcements were stationed.
4. Acceptance of the proposals (presumably the limitation of the powers of commissars and committees) which he had sent by telegraph to the conference at Mogilev on July 29.

The provisional government, however, did not take these demands very seriously, attributing the first point, which in fact implied the establishment of an independent dictatorship, to Kornilov's unfamiliarity with political niceties. He at length accepted Savinkov's deputy's interpretation of his first point, who suggested that 'responsibility before the whole people' implied responsibility before their representatives, *ie*, the provisional government. The other points were noted rather than accepted.[35]

General Barter did not report these matters correctly. On August 9, the War Cabinet were informed of General Barter's most recent wire, giving General Kornilov's conditions for accepting his appointment as Russian C.-in-C., 'namely, that he should be responsible to legal Government only and not to any Committee; that the application of disciplinary measures and death penalty should be extended to all troops in the [Russian] Empire; that sanction should be given to inflict death penalty on commanders who do not repress lack of discipline with sufficient energy. These conditions,' stated Barter, 'had been accepted by the Government.' Barter also stated that there was some improvement in Russian morale. 'Some troops in retreat had come to a halt, and some had even resumed the offensive.' (This is confirmed by Locker-Lampson's report.) But the CIGS then informed the War Cabinet that some 10,000 Russian troops fighting on the Western Front had mutinied. They had been surrounded by French troops; some had surrendered, 'and part were being starved into submission'. Russian troops on all fronts had had enough.[35]

On August 12, the CIGS sent this private telegram (no. 39420) to General Barter.

Following for General Kornilov:

I thank you for your telegram of 10th instant, and desire to express my sympathy with you in your responsible and heavy task of re-establishing discipline. I have no doubt that after you have succeeded in this that the Russian troops will again assert their superiority over the enemy. Very bad weather on the Western front has latterly impeded operations, but it is now improving and I hope for further good results shortly. Many reports show that the morale of the enemy's infantry is much inferior to what it was a year ago, and that there is a shortage of food and of material of various kinds.[36]

Next day, the War Cabinet were informed that all the Russian troops, who had mutinied in France, had now been disarmed, save for one brigade, which was still holding out. 'The French authorities were finding great difficulty in knowing what to do with these men,' stated the CIGS.[37]

On August 15, the War Cabinet had an exhaustive discussion on Russia. By now, Arthur Henderson had left the Cabinet. He had returned from Petrograd in late July convinced that the only way to keep Russia in the war was to send British delegates to the Stockholm conference. But the American, French and Italian governments had all refused permission for their socialists to go to Stockholm, and the War Cabinet naturally disliked Henderson's proposal. He also incurred the Cabinet's displeasure by insisting on going to France with Ramsay Macdonald to negotiate details of the conference, Macdonald being widely unpopular because of his pacifism. On August 10, Henderson persuaded a special Labour Party conference in London to pass a resolution in favour of sending British delegates to Stockholm. That evening, he was harshly condemned by his War Cabinet colleagues, and was virtually dismissed by Lloyd George next day. The Stockholm conference was then again postponed, and the whole proposal eventually fizzled out. Henderson's place in the Cabinet was taken by George Barnes, a former docker, who had been Minister of Pensions in 1916–17; a man with a 'calm, rather slow, but completely unprejudiced mind', writes Frances Stevenson.[38]

The immediate issue before the War Cabinet on August 15 was whether or not to despatch more guns to Russia. General Poole (who was making a brief visit from Petrograd) stressed that 80% of the Russian people were anxious for immediate peace, and that only a small minority backed Kerensky in his support of the Allies, 'and that this minority depended to a very large degree upon the help and assistance of every kind which the Allies, particularly Great Britain and France, could now render them . . .' The Russian government, in fact, considered the continued shipment of guns to Russia as the 'all-important symbol' of continued Allied support. We had sent no guns since last March; some should be sent at once, before the port of Archangel closed, even though they could not be used in the front line this year, for the moral effect of sending some, as promised, 'would be as good as the continued refusal to send guns would be bad, if not disastrous'.[39]

But Poole was not supported by his colleagues at the War Office. The CIGS opposed the despatch of any more guns to Russia; most of those already sent had never been used, and 'it was vital that no more diversions should be made from the decisive Western Front'. The Master-General of Ordnance agreed; Field-Marshal Haig 'wanted every gun he could get for immediate use . . .' Lord Derby also supported the CIGS; political considerations must here give way to military. The one military consideration was where the guns would best be used, 'and he urged the War Cabinet not to send any guns whatsoever to Russia'.

But Lord Milner (who, since his visit to Russia in January, had been watching the Russian situation for the War Cabinet) disagreed. He had 'recent and definite evidence' that Russian feelings on this question were becoming embittered, 'and that we must now either send more guns, or justify to M. Kerensky the breaking of our promise to send guns. It was impossible to temporise any longer, and we must let the people who are keeping Russia in the war know definitely what we are going to do, one way or the other. The position in Russia was very serious, and, quite apart from the political point of view, in his [Milner's] judgement we should lose the war from the military point of view if we did not keep Russia in the war.' Two batteries should be sent at once; and Kerensky informed that more would follow in due course.

Balfour said that the position was 'quite clear; we must act on the psychology of M. Kerensky and his colleagues in the Russian government'. It would be 'well worth sending at least 20 heavy guns, however great our need in France might be, to keep Russia in the war. We had to balance the possible military loss of a small number of guns against the possibility of large numbers of German and Austrian divisions being withdrawn from the Russian front to oppose us in the West, and, as far as he [Balfour] was concerned, he had no doubt that the War Cabinet would be well advised to send the guns.' This settled the matter. It was even suggested that the despatch of eight guns to Russia 'seemed like a mockery', and Kerensky should be informed that we would eventually send all the 150 guns we had promised, as soon as weather conditions in France made further operations impossible. The

War Cabinet, having paid lip service to the War Office's view, thereupon decided 'that the risk of discouraging Russia by a neglect to continue the supply of guns was too great to be ignored'. The War Office was to despatch two batteries to Russia at once, and Balfour was to explain the whole position to Buchanan, who was to inform Kerensky.[39]

On August 17, the War Cabinet had to consider another telegram from General Barter, sent from Russian GHQ on the 12th, stating that he had just returned from Petrograd, where he had found the political situation worse than expected. He and Buchanan agreed that it was of the utmost importance that the Russian government should clearly understand that the British government 'cordially approves' of Kornilov's measures to restore discipline. 'I suggested to the Ambassador that he should congratulate Kerensky on his support of Kornilov, whether he be genuine or not, if only to indicate what view is taken by the British Government.' Buchanan would speak to Kerensky in this sense, and also 'delicately hint' that the British might refuse to send more guns, unless assured that they would be put to good use. 'In my opinion it is of the greatest importance that Kornilov should feel that he has support from outside, in order that he may not weaken in his intention, as, otherwise, I think he very possibly may. If he goes, I see no hope of any improvement of efficiency for a considerable time,' stated Barter. 'Tomorrow I am seeing Kornilov to try to keep him up to the mark.'[40]

It is probable that this War Cabinet also considered a further telegram from Barter to the CIGS received on the 16th. (All Barter's wires of this period were printed as Cabinet papers, unless otherwise stated.) This stated that on the evening of the 13th, Barther had had a 'confidential interview' with Kornilov, who had shown him a document, for immediate presentation to the Russian government, which contained 'definite conditions' for the restoration of discipline, and the general reorganisation of Russia. These conditions included the restoration of proper authority – and proper pay and pensions – to the officers, who must be saluted by their men; military discipline, including the death penalty, to be applied on the railways; military control of all food supplies; and authority to deal with disorders 'in the whole interior' by military force. 'These conditions are in addition to those regarding disciplinary measures at the front which have already been demanded,' stated Barter. 'I presented your telegram 39420 (dated August 12) to General Kornilov, and I assured him that you entirely approved of the disciplinary measures already reported to you.' Kornilov was determined to make a firm stand, but was not confident that the Russian government would support his conditions. 'He expressed the opinion that Kerensky was an opportunist and that he could not be relied on.' Barter then asked Kornilov directly whether 'severe' Allied pressure should be applied to the Russian government, if they hesitated to adopt his conditions. Kornilov replied 'emphatically' that this would then be the only step that could save the situation.

'It was then arranged between us that this premonitory message should be sent to you by me,' Barter informed the CIGS. 'He [Kornilov] promised that he would give me the earliest possible information regarding the course of events in order that I might transmit it to you. He thought that it might probably be in about three days; but in that case the question of time would be of great urgency.' Barter told Kornilov that he was the only man to put these demands through. But Barter warned the CIGS that, after conferring with Buchanan, he felt that the provisional government might not be strong enough, 'even if willing', to impose these demands on the Petrograd soviet, which was now so strongly represented in the present Ministry; even the SR leader was included, whose mere presence was an 'ominous presage in connection with Kornilov's ultimatum'. (This was the first mention of this word.) As time was now short, Barter strongly urged that Buchanan be given authority to apply pressure on the provisional government 'immediately and collectively at the psychological moment . . .'[41] Barter, it was clear, was now getting deeper and deeper into Kornilov's pocket; he was indeed most peculiarly ill-suited for the post of (independent) British military representative at Russian GHQ at this crucial stage in Russian affairs.

On August 16, General Kornilov arrived in Petrograd with a paper outlining the measures which he regarded as necessary for the restoration of the fighting capacity both at the front and in the rear. Savinkov and his deputy looked over the paper, found it politically unacceptable, and suggested that Kornilov leave it with them for modification. This he agreed to do. But in the course of his interview with Kerensky, he showed the latter the unaltered paper, which the Premier later said contained a number of proposals, 'the vast majority of which were quite acceptable', but they were expressed in such a form, and supported by such arguments that their publication 'would have led to unfavourable results'. Chamberlin goes on:

'Kerensky seized this opportunity of sounding out Kornilov's political sentiments. Hinting vaguely at the possibility of a military dictatorship, he warned the General in the following terms. "Suppose I should withdraw, what will happen? You will hang in the air; the railroads will stop; the telegraph will cease to function." To Kerensky's questioning as to whether, in Kornilov's opinion, he should remain at the head of the state, the C.in-C. gave the somewhat reserved reply that, although

Kerensky's influence had declined, nevertheless, as the recognised leader of the democratic party, he should remain at the head of the Government.'[42]

Another incident during this visit to Petrograd apparently made a strong impression on Kornilov, and very possibly encouraged him to listen to his more adventurous friends. While he was reporting on the military situation to the Cabinet, Kerensky and Savinkov warned him to be discreet in discussing where an offensive might be launched. Some of the ministers, they explained (apparently there was a special insinuation against the SR leader and Minister of Agriculture, Chernov, who was already a marked man at Mogilev), were in close touch with the executive committee of the Petrograd soviet, among the members of which were German agents. This convinced Kornilov, who never understood that there was any distinction between the Bolsheviks and the more moderate socialist parties, which at that time constituted the majority in almost all the soviets, that not only the Bolsheviks, but also other parties in the Petrograd soviet were traitors and German agents and that they exercised an unwarrantable degree of influence upon the provisional government.

The War Cabinet were told nothing of all this. 'General Kornilov left suddenly yesterday evening for Petrograd,' wired Barter to the CIGS on the 16th.[42] 'It is rumoured in well-informed quarters that the Government is cavilling at his conditions . . .' (But this telegram was never printed for the Cabinet.)

The same day (the 16th), Commander Locker-Lampson, who had already made preparations to back Kornilov if necessary, without informing the Admiralty, but – one must surely presume – with Barter's blessing, or at least his knowledge, sent a further report to the Admiralty. He said nothing of any plot; but after a brief reference to the 'shocking state of Russian politics', ended by warmly praising Kornilov. 'He is now the outstanding figure in this country and lacks nothing to succeed except perhaps knowledge of western life and sympathy with democratic ideals. As a Tartar, a Cossack and a soldier he inclines to solve all problems with the sword and believes with Cromwell that "Stone dead hath no fellow". His strength lies in his age (he is only 47), his solid Cossack backing, his force of character and the legend of his name.' In the present state of the Russian army, Locker-Lampson warned, the Germans might march straight through to Odessa. 'Moreover, may not this be just what Monarchists like Kornilov want?' he asked. 'In a sense, the worst [sic] of the present disaster, the more his hands will be strengthened . . . It is difficult as yet to saddle the soldiers' committees and spy socialists with the blame and to make Russia as a whole sick of their interference. It requires the loss of some *Russian* territory and perhaps a winter of famine to make the prayer for a dictator and for order universal and profound . . .'[43]

The Admiralty were left to deduce what they wished from this. Nor were his officers and men given any real inkling of what was afoot. Locker-Lampson merely posted up, both at Proskurov and Kursk (his advanced and main bases), King George V's letter (of late June), the First Lord's message, and Kornilov's letter of thanks to the British squadron (both received after the failure of the July offensive); and to the latter he added a rather fulsome preface in praise of the new Russian C.-in-C.[44]

On August 17, as General Knox prudently left Petrograd for London (he drove at midnight to have a talk with Kornilov, 'but did not learn much', he records), the War Cabinet considered Barter's messages, but 'felt it would be unwise to put pressure on the Russian Government to adopt General Kornilov's full programme, because it might be said that the British Government were urging the Russian Government to shoot soldiers. Such advice, it was pointed out, by an Allied Government, would, in similar circumstances, be strongly resented by a British Government.' Balfour particularly stressed how delicate the matter was, with its bearings on Russian psychology, 'of which our Ambassador was the best judge'. It was suggested that 'some careful message' supporting the restoration of discipline might be sent to Buchanan, to be used at his discretion after consultation with the Allied ambassadors. Balfour undertook to draft such a message for submission to the Prime Minister for his approval. It was already clear that the War Cabinet would be able to do very little in the fast developing crisis in Russia. What, though, would British envoys and officers do on their own?[45]

Kornilov's visit to Petrograd, which was straightway attended by rumours about his differences with the provisional government, and about his drastic programme for the restoration of discipline, stirred up passions on all sides. The left wing launched a press campaign against him, conservative and military organisations rallied round him. On the 19th, with ever-growing rumours of plots on all sides, the Council of the Union of Cossack troops made a ringing declaration of support for Kornilov, which was a direct challenge to the provisional government. The Knights of St George (holders of the highest Russian military decoration) and other organisations quickly followed suit. In Moscow, a group of conservative politicians, led by Rodzianko, sent Kornilov this telegram: 'In this threatening hour of heavy trial, all thinking Russia looks to you with hope and faith.' This, of course, was open to various different interpretations; but to Kornilov, intensely susceptible to flattery, it was all too much – and he made his first move. On either the 19th or 20th, he instructed his Chief of Staff, General Lukomsky (a competent officer, who had also been Chief of Staff to Brusilov) to concentrate the Wild Division and another Cossack corps in the neighbourhood of towns within convenient railroad striking distance of Petrograd and Moscow. Lukomsky suggested to Kornilov that such a move could hardly strengthen the northern front at Riga, then threatened by the Germans, but was quite convenient for an eventual blow at Petrograd or Moscow. He asked Kornilov to tell him frankly what his intentions were. This Kornilov promised to do.[46]

In London, the CIGS was dealing with a request from General Kornilov for yet another British attack in France to relieve pressure on the Russian front. He wired to Barter on August 20. 'Explain to Kornilov that we have been fighting hard on the Ypres front since 31st July. Continuous rain, which makes Flanders mud impassable, has much hampered our operations. Weather is now improving, and we shall continue our operations with all possible vigour.' Since the attack opened, the Allied forces had inflicted 'very heavy losses' on the enemy, forced him to relieve 22 divisions, and taken over 10,000 prisoners and 30 guns, stated the CIGS (in wire no. 39852).[47]

The Bolsheviks, meanwhile (who were meant to be organising a new rising in mid-September), were still exceedingly uneasy about the revelations, following the disastrous July riots in Petrograd, of their connections via Helphand with their German patrons. On August 10 (two days after Helphand had issued 'My reply to Kerensky & Co' from the safety of Switzerland), the German Minister in Copenhagen, Helphand's chief patron, warned the Foreign Ministry in Berlin that the Cadet paper had stated on July 20 that two German staff officers had told a Russian lieutenant 'that Lenin was a German agent. It also said that Jacob Furstenberg and Dr Helphand (Parvus) were German agents acting as intermediaries between the Bolsheviks and the Imperial Government.' The paper had further stated, according to a Copenhagen report, that the German Social Democrat leader, Haase, had told a Russian journalist 'that Helphand was an intermediary between the Imperial Government and the Russian Bolsheviks, and that he had transferred money to the latter'.[48] It was essential to issue a categorical denial; and the Bolsheviks wanted wide publicity given to Helphand's answer to Kerensky. On the 16th, the German Minister therefore asked the Foreign Ministry in Berlin to publicise it through the 'Wolf Bureau', the official German news agency.

The Foreign Ministry refused; they would only publicise it in Switzerland and Sweden (the two main neutral havens for Russian exiles); they added, however, 'The suspicion that Lenin is a German agent has been energetically countered in Switzerland and Sweden at our instigation. Thus the impact of the reports on this subject supposedly made by German officers has also been destroyed. The statement claimed to have been made by Haase has been denied.' The Foreign Ministry would go no further.[49]

By now, Kerensky had caught his political breath and was set on taking the initiative. Russia, he claims – somewhat optimistically – had made something of a recovery after the fall of the monarchy in March, despite the military débâcle of the July offensive, which had loosed several millions of armed deserters into the Russian villages. Many of the 'zemstva' and urban councils had been reorganised on the basis of universal suffrage, he goes on. In the soviets, Bolshevik influence was rapidly waning after the fiasco of the 'July days', and many soviets were indeed breaking up. In this quasi-limbo, Kerensky was acutely aware of the need to forge closer links with all sections of the people. Otherwise, his Russian government would be very vulnerable to demagogic pressure from the military and political opposition, especially if there were another breakdown at the front. Kerensky thus convened a State Conference at Moscow to 'take the pulse of the nation', and to enable him to explain his policies and his problems – and at the very least, to keep all sides talking, rather than rushing into precipitate action.[50]

On the 21st, the War Cabinet considered a wire from Barter, dated the 18th, stating that Kornilov had returned the night before from Petrograd, where he had had 'satisfactory', if short, interviews with both Kerensky and Savinkov; 'latter especially strongly supporting him,' claimed Barter. Neither Kornilov nor Kerensky thought it advisable as yet to inform the Russian government of all Kornilov's conditions, probably because Kerensky feared that the Russian ministers would at once inform the Petrograd soviet. Kornilov, stated Barter, would disclose his conditions just before the coming Moscow conference, due to open on August 25, 'when the Government would be clear of Petrograd. He [Kornilov] said also that he was already putting some of his discipline measures into operation without reference to Government.' Kornilov did not yet know if he would attend the Moscow conference; but if he did, Barter would accompany him. 'I venture to suggest,' concluded Barter tactfully, 'that it might have useful effect as showing in polite way that British Government approve of Kornilov's policy if before the [Moscow] Congress he was given a high British decoration and that British Ambassador at Petrograd were to be immediately informed for notification to Russian Government . . .' But the War Cabinet turned this down.[51] 'Your suggestion for giving decoration to Kornilov has been carefully considered by War Cabinet,' the CIGS wired to Barter later that day, 'and they have decided that for political reasons the award might do more harm than good . . .'

But the idea was evidently much favoured at Mogilev. 'This morning C.-in-C. sent for me nominally to confer on me the Order of Saint Vladimir,' wired Barter on the 20th, 'but really I believe to tell me how matters stand between Provisional Government and himself. He informed me without reserve that Government is too weak to support his programme and dare not act. He himself is determined to maintain his conditions and it was quite clear to me both from his attitude and from some veiled allusions which he made that he is out of patriotism considering expediency of adopting, if necessary, a vigorous political initiative which, should foreign diplomatic action fail, is, in his opinion, the only way to save the army and country. One sentence especially led me to this supposition. He said Cossacks were ready to a man to act by force in support of his military policy.' But Barter unfortunately made no mention of the fact – of which he must have been aware – that the Cossacks did *not* represent what remained of the Russian army.

'Kornilov has definitely decided to attend Congress at Moscow and has asked me to accompany him,' Barter went on. 'I shall take with me a secret code book and a staff officer. I shall of course be most discreet and careful in my behaviour . . .' Kornilov had also given the 'strongest possible hint' that the only peaceable way to save the Russian situation was by Allied diplomatic intervention. 'It was perfectly evident that he ardently desired this diplomatic intervention but wished to be able to declare if necessary that he had not solicited it.' Barter then gave a dark hint that he would not add his private opinion in this present cypher of what Kornilov was 'prepared to do should this diplomatic alternative fail . . .' Even though the cypher clerks managed to garble some of this sentence, the meaning was very clear. Barter emphatically urged that if Allied diplomatic pressure was being contemplated, 'it should be applied without a day's delay'. It should certainly be applied before the Moscow conference of August 25. Barter again urged that each Allied government should wire to the Russian government, via the Allied ambassadors, conferring a high decoration on Kornilov. 'This would constitute courteous yet clear evidence that they approved of military policy adopted by Kornilov.'[52] Barter concluded by asking for 'some indication' of British policy on these points for transmission to Kornilov. Matters were obviously, and rapidly, reaching a crisis at Mogilev.

On the 21st, Barter transmitted the resolution by the Cossack council, 'to which greatest importance is attached'. This stated that the Cossacks were 'entirely opposed' to the Petrograd soviet's condemnation of Kornilov's measures for the restoration of discipline; that Kornilov was the 'real popular leader', who the majority of the Russian people thought was the only man who could save the country, and thus could not be replaced; that if he were replaced, the Cossacks would not fight on against the Germans, but might well take action against the internal enemy. The resolution ended strongly: 'Council [of Cossacks] expresses with loud and determined voice its full and devoted subordination to its hero Chief, General Kornilov.' Though the majority of the Russian people certainly did not think of Kornilov as the only saviour of their country, such a resolution obviously foreshadowed immediate action. Barter added that the council of the Knights of Saint George had issued a similar resolution at Petrograd. 'I shall see Kornilov tomorrow and shall send you his latest views,' he concluded.[53]

Barter wired the CIGS again next day: 'This morning I saw Kornilov and communicated your telegram no. 39852 [of August 20] to him. He was very pleased and begged me to transmit his sincere appreciation.' Kornilov then showed Barter various messages of 'emphatic support' from officer and veteran organisations. 'He also informed me that he has been called by Government to Petrograd to discuss his programme, before attending Moscow Congress and he added with significant expression of face that he did not know if he could find time to go. I laughed and said that as he could not take a train full of his Turcomans with him, I should, if I were he, find that work was too pressing to allow him to leave GHQ before going to Moscow. Turcomans referred to,' explained Barter, 'are a wild cavalry regiment which he recently called to GHQ, and which is wholly devoted to him, as his mother was one of the tribe. He is safe from *coup de main*,' added Barter, 'as battalion of St George, which has also declared its fidelity to Kornilov, is permanently quartered here.' But Kornilov was still very anxious to know whether Allied diplomatic pressure would be applied on the Russian government. 'He is a genuine patriot and would rather attain his object by peaceable means,' stressed Barter again. 'In any case, it is very doubtful if the time is yet ripe for playing a very high stake at a different game.' Barter had had to tell Kornilov that he had had no information from London. But there was good reason to believe that the Russian government now intended to abolish the post of C.-in-C., and appoint a War Council, to sit at Petrograd, directly under Kerensky's control. 'This measure, if it is really contemplated, as I believe, may bring matters to an early and violent crisis.'[54]

For all these varied reasons, Kornilov's second visit to Petrograd on August 23 was even more difficult and strained than his first. Some of his friends strongly advised him not to leave Mogilev, as Kerensky might arrest him. Only constant reminders by Savinkov and his deputy that they had defended him against his enemies in Petrograd induced

Kornilov to make a second visit at all. And when he did set out, he took with him a Turcoman bodyguard with two machine-guns, whom he proceeded to station – with their two machine-guns – just outside Kerensky's office when he went to pay his official call on the Prime Minister in the Winter Palace.

This was the somewhat bizarre background to a discussion of Kornilov's military programme. It had been revised and toned down by Savinkov's deputy – who also added proposals for the militarisation of the railroads, and of the war industries. Kornilov handed this paper to Kerensky, who asked for time for further consideration of these new proposals – at the same time blaming Savinkov for signing such a document without his consent. At the end of the interview, Kornilov told Kerensky that he had heard rumours that he was about to be removed from his post, and bluntly advised the Premier not to adopt this course.[55]

The paper was further discussed with Kornilov by Kerensky and some of the Russian ministers. Finally Kornilov's original paper was preferred to the amplified and edited version by Savinkov's deputy. But Kornilov received only the vaguest assurances about the precise time of carrying out his recommendations. The Cabinet merely agreed: 'To recognise in principle the possibility of applying various measures, including the death penalty in the rear, but to carry them out only after the discussion in legislative order of each concrete measure, according to the circumstances of time and place.'

Kornilov returned to Mogilev thoroughly disgusted with Kerensky's weak temporising, and now told Lukomsky the real purpose of the cavalry concentration.

'It's time to hang the German supporters and spies, with Lenin at their head,' he burst out. The Petrograd soviet must be finally and definitely dispersed. 'You are right,' he went on. 'I am shifting the cavalry corps mainly so as to bring it up to Petrograd by the end of August, and, if a demonstration of the Bolsheviks takes place, to deal with these traitors as they deserve.' The operation would be commanded by General Krimov, who was not to hesitate, if need be, 'to hang every member of the Petrograd soviet'.

But Kornilov was more uncertain about the political side of his projected move. He did not intend to come out against the provisional government, he told Lukomsky, and hoped to reach an agreement with Kerensky and Savinkov, although he was prepared to strike at the Bolsheviks on his own account, if he did not come to terms with them. 'I want nothing for myself,' Kornilov concluded. 'I only want to save Russia, and I will obey unconditionally a cleansed and strengthened provisional Government.'[55]

When Locker-Lampson then returned to Mogilev, he found that Kornilov had issued secret orders to his Russian generals. In mid-September, there would be another Bolshevik rising in Petrograd, to coincide with a German attack on Riga. This time they must nip it in the bud. Groups of reliable young Russian officers (more than 3,000 in all) were to be sent to Mogilev, ostensibly to study 'British mortar and machine-gun techniques' under Brigadier Finlayson – but in fact to go straight on to Petrograd, while the Cossack divisions were to be despatched to points just north of Mogilev as agreed, whence they could easily move to Riga, Petrograd or Moscow.[56]

Though Kornilov's final decision was not known in London, it was clear that General Barter needed firm instructions. On the 23rd, the CIGS replied to his wire of the 20th that the War Cabinet had authorised Buchanan to inform the Russian government, after consulting the French Ambassador, that the British government 'cordially approve of General Kornilov's measures to restore discipline'. But, the CIGS explained, Buchanan had replied that, after due consultation with the French Ambassador, he thought the present moment inopportune for the presentation of such a note, 'but thinks authority to do so may on some later occasion be useful. You should keep in as close touch with Buchanan as possible on all questions of a political or semi-political nature,' he warned Barter.[57] Hindsight shows that the failure by the British and French ambassadors to deliver such a note to Kerensky at this time was a disastrous error.

On August 24, the CIGS brought Barter's 'two important telegrams' of August 20 (to which he had just replied) and 21st, before the War Cabinet. But after due consideration, it was decided that it was 'inadvisable at present' to exert any diplomatic pressure beyond that agreed on August 17 – which Buchanan had just rejected. The CIGS therefore sent a strong warning to Barter on August 25: 'Your recent telegrams seem to indicate that Kornilov may shortly be deeply involved in politics. You should not fail to remember that your mission is purely military.'[58]

# 3

## The Kornilov Adventure

KERENSKY saw the Moscow conference not as a legislative but as a consultative assembly, a rallying point of national unity, whereby he could take the 'pulse of the nation' and gain support for what he saw as moderate policies in the face of rising military adventurism. He thus saw to it that the conference was attended by as wide a spectrum of Russian national opinion as possible, with himself as the central arbiter. He took great care to balance the right against the left. There were seats for members of the four Dumas; for the Co-operative Societies; for the Trade Unions; for commercial and industrial organisations, and the banks; for the Municipalities; for the Executive Committee of the United Soviet of Workers', Soldiers' and Peasants' deputies; for the Army and Navy; and for the Soviets of Workers' and Soldiers' and Peasants' Deputies.

'Today I attended the opening of the Moscow conference,' reported General Barter to the CIGS on August 25. 'Kerensky made a speech of hysterical and snarling character,' he stated excitedly, and wrongly. 'He [Kerensky] threatened Bolsheviks directly and Military Chief by allusion' (both of whom were absent; the Bolsheviks, like the monarchists, refused to attend; Kornilov had not yet arrived). French and other diplomatic envoys were present, 'but no British official except myself', stated Barter. Kerensky reluctantly admitted the necessity for the death penalty, but insisted that the soldiers' committees should be on the courts martial. His speech was mainly devoted to the defence of the Russian government and the safety of the revolution; not to the defence and safety of Russia. It thus made an unfavourable impression, as it contained no definite pronouncement of policy. The Russian government had thus lost the chance of prolonging its own existence by a 'frank endorsement' of Kornilov's programme. 'My private opinion,' stated Barter, 'is that a climax is rapidly [? approach]ing and that the present Government will soon be replaced by a Bolshevik ministry which in its turn will be immediately knocked out by a military counter revolution'. (This prognosis, a reflection of the thinking at Mogilev, was shared by other Allied envoys, but was based on a fallacy. The Bolsheviks, at that moment, were far too weak to form a government; though that very day, on the opening of the Moscow conference, they had succeeded in their attempt to bring the Moscow workers out on strike.) The military party, Barter went on, was fast gaining in power; and Savinkov had now resigned to support Kornilov. On the 23rd (the day of Kornilov's bizarre second meeting with Kerensky), Rodzianko, President of the Duma, had held a meeting attended by Alexeiev, the former Russian Chief of Staff, other military chiefs, and leading Cadets; which, Alexeiev told Barter, had been 'most successful as regards unanimity of opinion and firm determination'. But what exactly this entailed, Barter did not say. 'Kornilov sagaciously postponed his arrival until tomorrow,' Barter added.[1]

On the 27th, Rex Leeper, of the Political Intelligence Department of the Foreign Office, in his weekly report on Russia, outlined the internal political background to the Moscow conference for the War Cabinet. The main questions were political, he wrote, and their acuteness was due to class rivalry. The military questions concerning General Kornilov were secondary, he claimed, though if the bourgeois parties failed to get what they wanted, they might appeal to the discontented army leaders to attempt a *coup d'état*. It was impossible to prophesy what would happen during the next few days – though Leeper failed to point out that Kornilov was a power in his own right. 'Kerensky, in his opening speech, has made the attitude of the [Russian] Government unmistakable. His speech means that, if the bourgeois parties attempt a *coup d'état*, the Government, backed by the Socialists, will fight for it.' But Leeper totally failed to point out that this would also entail the reinstatement and rearming of the Bolsheviks. It was to be hoped, he went on, that the differences between Kerensky and Kornilov would not be aggravated by Kerensky's political rivals, for Kerensky undoubtedly desired to see the restoration of the fighting powers of the army just as much as Kornilov did, 'and in the main the two are in agreement'.[2] Kerensky's slowness was due to political reasons, and his desire to prevent any drastic measures which might provoke bloodshed within the country on a large scale. 'Kerensky has now shown his hand; the next week will show what sort of reply his political opponents and and the army leaders intend to make.'

On the 27th, Barter wired again from Moscow. 'Today I had cordial reception from Kerensky.' Barter assured him of continued 'energetic' British action in France to relieve pressure on the Russian front, and of the CIGS's 'best wishes for the success of vigorous measures for restoration of discipline'. In reply, Kerensky sent his 'cordial appreciation' to the CIGS, and assured him that his Russian government would never consent to a separate peace, nor to terms that would dishonour Russia or her Allies; but he 'complained that the Military party is urging the adoption of measures which, if applied precipitately, would only lead to mutiny and to disorder and general acts of violence'. Kerensky produced telegrams showing that some commanders were already abusing their new powers by cruel use of the lash, and added that the abolition of soldiers' committees and commissars now would inevitably lead to disaster. 'I agreed with this latter opinion,' stated Barter.[3]

In reply to Barter, who had asked Kerensky if the troops would remain in the trenches that winter, Kerensky said he was confident that they would. Barter hinted that time was short; if the officers' authority was not restored by then, the men would probably refuse. Kerensky merely replied that he was confident that discipline would be sufficiently restored in the next three months 'to avert this calamity'. On general policy, Kerensky remarked 'somewhat slyly' that the dissatisfaction of both right and left was the best proof that his middle course was sound. 'My general impression,' wired Barter, 'was that Kerensky was honest in his views, but that he is too absorbed with the maintenance of the revolution, and that he puts this consideration before the safety of Russia.' Many of Kerensky's bitterest opponents also thought him honest, 'but all agree that he is expecting too much merely from words, from his own personal influence amongst troops', and that the internal anarchy and low morale at the front demanded the 'immediate and stern application of force. They are undoubtedly right in this view,' Barter added erroneously. A smack of firm government was not indeed called for, but very delicate nurturing of a war-weary people. Barter was also of course equating 'Russia' and the 'safety of Russia' with continued Russian participation in the war, and with continued Russian offensives, which were now obviously impossible.[3]

Barter had also had a long talk with Alexeiev, who was an unselfish patriot of moderate and sound views. Though he did not think matters disquieting at present, the application of 'immediate and drastic measures' was vital. 'Alexeiev is very apprehensive of German advance on Odessa and Nicolaiev, the possession of which would paralyse Black Sea Fleet. He thinks the fall of Riga very probable, but regrettable rather for its moral than strategical reasons. He does not think Germans would advance in any case beyond Riga before next spring,' Barter reported.

'I shall see Kornilov tomorrow. Conference did not assemble today.

I understand Kerensky is endeavouring to muzzle all opponents, but the members of the Duma are fighting hard for the right of speech, as Vice-President informed me today with much bitterness. Am keeping on friendly terms with all parties alike.'[3]

That evening, Kornilov finally arrived in Moscow to an 'enthusiastic reception from large crowd at station', reported Barter on the 28th. There were flowers, banners, guards of honour – but no member of the government to meet him. Later that evening, there was a bitter exchange between Kerensky and Kornilov about the speech which the general was to make the next day. Kerensky, extremely anxious to keep the Moscow conference on an even keel, insisted that Kornilov should restrict himself to military and strategic questions, while Kornilov retorted that he would speak as he wished. Actually, the speech, drafted by Savinkov's deputy, was not designed to provoke a breach with the provisional government. While it hinted broadly at the necessity for applying drastic measures in the rear as well as at the front, it did not directly attack the government, and Kornilov even declared that he was – still – not an opponent of the army committees, merely demanding that they should not interfere in operational matters.

In opening the second session of the Moscow conference on the 28th, Kerensky allowed opposition speeches, and appealed for all speakers to be given a fair hearing. Kornilov delivered a 'moderate but earnest' speech, describing the condition of the army and the situation at the front. He underlined the need for the restoration of authority to the officers and the limitation of the soldiers' committees to administration; for increased output of munitions, which had fallen by 60%; and for urgent measures to improve the supply position, now seriously disorganised, to meet the army's needs during the winter. 'In conclusion, he faced Kerensky and signified that he had no doubt that these measures would be taken. Kerensky made no sign of protestation,' stated Barter. 'Both on entering and on conclusion of his speech, Kornilov met with great ovation.' A block of soldiers' delegates in the centre of the theatre had remained sullenly silent, 'but practically all the civilians in the audience loudly applauded him'. Kerensky's reception had been more noisy, 'but not so solid or universal'. The sullen attitude of the soldiers' delegates had been very conspicuous. They had remained quiet when any reference was made to the honour of the Russian army, or the need to drive out the Germans, and only applauded when their chief speaker advocated an early peace. 'The assembly generally was evidently painfully affected by this attitude,' remarked Barter.[4]

The words and arguments that Kerensky feared that Kornilov would utter were finally voiced by General Kaledin, Ataman (elected leader) of the Don Cossacks. To a predictable chorus of cheers from the Right, and jeers and hisses from the Left, Kaledin boasted that the Cossacks had never been serfs, and therefore took the new liberties in their stride. They had no deserters either. He called for the abolition of all soviets and committees both in the army, and in the rear. The Cossacks had always done their duty at the front, 'and were ready to do it in the interior against traitors', reported Barter. 'He made severe and effective attack against Government's inaction.' Rodzianko and the Cadet leaders urged the government to take immediate action, but indicated that they would continue to support it, 'even in form of dictatorship in order to secure immediate and strong measures and freedom from party politics'. Several influential speakers violently attacked the sr leader Chernov, Minister of Agriculture, as an enemy of Russia; others who incited their hearers to class warfare received enthusiastic applause from the soldiers' delegates.

'Kornilov left this afternoon; he told me before departing that a crisis was inevitable unless Government took immediate steps demanded by the moderates. He seems determined,' Barter added. Kornilov had told him confidentially that he was to be appointed honorary C.-in-C. of the Cossacks at a meeting of Cossack leaders in some twelve days' time in the Caucasus. This might have great significance, as a conflict between the Cossacks and the disorganised rabble in the interior was 'extremely probable', and the Cossacks would easily win. 'Kornilov thanks you for your assurance of continued action on Western front,' concluded Barter to the cigs.[4] What Barter did not report, and very possibly did not know, was that, just before leaving Moscow, Kornilov summoned Putilov and various other leading financiers of the 'Union for the Economic Revival of Russia' to his coach, where they met General Krimov, who was to command the Petrograd operation, and whom Kornilov had secretly brought with him in his train. The financiers were told what was going to happen, and that Krimov needed finance for his operations. They told Kornilov that funds were already available, and could be paid through the 'Republican Centre'. The meeting broke up.

The same day, the British mission in Roumania also wired the cigs that Locker-Lampson had arrived with some transport lorries. 'Regarding their employment, I am in correspondence with General Barter . . .' (The War Cabinet were not informed of this latter wire.)[5]

On the 29th, Barter sent his final wire from Moscow. 'Early this morning, [Moscow] Conference closed. Impressive speech by Alexeiev marked the last session.' The good effect of the speeches of both Alexeiev and Kornilov was shown by the 'expressed determination' of all speakers the day before to conclude the war honourably.

'In a fine speech Kerensky opened the road to conciliation and united effort. His presidency of this Conference has been impartial and distinguished, and on a level with the best parliamentary traditions. He did not once allow any speaker, whether a friend or opponent, to attribute to another party unworthy motives.' This had undoubtedly corrected the unfavourable impression of his first speech, 'and his position [has] been strengthened', stated Barter. 'I think if the Government immediately start reorganising thoroughly, regardless of opposition of the extreme left, it will occupy very strong position. My own opinion of Kerensky as a statesman has risen considerably. He certainly is a leader of great personal magnetism and quick resource.' (Whether 'personal magnetism' was meant to be an euphemism for hysteria is not known, but Barter never mentioned that Kerensky's closing speech was a mixture of banalities and rising hysteria. Kerensky indeed worked himself up into such a state that he had to be applauded into stopping his rambling address. Without thinking, he then wandered off the stage, and had to be recalled to bring the conference to a proper close.) But Barter added that though Rodzianko and the Cadets had shown they were ready to compromise with the government to get things re-organised, 'an attempt at counter-revolution will, I believe, shortly be made by military party and the Government are preparing for it'. Barter had had an interview with Alexeiev just after his speech. 'He said that time was not yet ripe for action by force. I believe he himself is against any commotion at present moment if the Government will only act, but I believe Kornilov on the other hand considers that in any case such action is indispensable.' The military party was thus divided.[6]

On returning to Mogilev on the 30th, Barter sent a further wire, which he had evidently not wished to despatch from Moscow. While there, he informed the CIGS, he had been visited by a 'very influential' member of the Cadet party, who had asked for a loan of £250,000 from the British government for expenses for the Cossacks 'in the event of his party taking forcible military action'. A verbal guarantee would be sufficient. Barter had replied that this was out of the question, 'as my Government would never favour an intrigue against friendly government . . .' This ended Barter's somewhat jumbled account of the Moscow conference.[7]

The British Embassy in Petrograd saw things rather differently. Each of the opposing parties, into which the Moscow conference had been divided, claimed to have won the day, 'and I can find no two people whose opinion agrees as to the result of the Conference', the Assistant Military Attaché, Lieut-Colonel James Blair, wired to the Director of Military Intelligence (DMI) at the War Office on September 1: 'The only point on which everyone is agreed is that Kerensky came out of it very badly . . .' Rodzianko, whom Blair had interviewed on his return from

Moscow that day, said that the difference between the two contending parties, into which Russia was now divided, 'cannot be settled, and the position which the Left adopts is leading the country to civil war'. The Moscow conference had also shown that the Left was unfit to rule Russia, 'but that the Right parties have not sufficient power to take matters into their own hands. He [Rodzianko] says there cannot and will not be a counter-revolution as no party is sufficiently strong or well enough organised to do so . . .'[8]

But to other members of the British community, Rodzianko had been telling different tales. 'Rodzianko and others have been talking far too much about a counter-revolution,' notes Buchanan on September 3, 'and have been saying that a military *coup d'état* is the only thing that can save Russia . . . In a telegram which General Barter sent me on his return to headquarters from Moscow, he spoke as if some sort of *coup d'état* might be attempted at any moment. I have told him that anything of the kind would be fatal at present, and would inevitably lead to civil war and entail irreparable disaster.'[8]

In London, Rex Leeper gave the War Cabinet that day an entirely different picture of the Moscow conference. 'Kornilov's speech produced an enormous impression, and can only do good. From first to last, it was that of a soldier and no one can doubt his sincerity. By his conduct at Moscow, he has undoubtedly increased the chances of an agreement between himself and the Provisional Government.' On the whole, the conference had strengthened the government, claimed Leeper, and the extreme right wing had been isolated. 'What will still further increase the prestige of the Government is an immediate agreement with Kornilov. If Kerensky seizes the present moment for strong action, he may gain very strong support.' In other words, Kornilov was virtually a moderate. This seriously misled the War Cabinet.[9]

In fact, as soon as the Moscow conference closed, Kerensky veered towards the right wing. There had just been a series of explosions in munitions factories, indicating that the lack of discipline was giving a free rein to German agents – and Riga was about to be surrendered to the Germans. Kerensky decided that he must move to the right to hold on. On August 30, he told Savinkov, now reinstated at the War Ministry, that he was now prepared to accept Kornilov's paper of August 23. This not only called for the reintroduction of the death penalty, but for complete militarisation behind the lines, including the railroads and the war industries. Savinkov promptly passed this news on to Mogilev, where Kerensky was by now thoroughly distrusted and despised, and his latest move was simply taken as a sign of weakness; and preparations for the plot continued.[10]

[76]

Meanwhile, the Germans had attacked Riga, as predicted. On August 20, the DMO had informed the War Cabinet that this German advance was 'not appreciable and had no strategic significance'. The only serious matter was the further evidence provided of the continued lack of Russian morale. 'The official news from Riga front bad as expected,' wired Barter from Mogilev on September 2. Kornilov, however, had shown him a telegram from the Russian government, 'in reply to fresh demands he made for drastic measures'. The telegram stated that in a few days' time, measures would be published, based on Kornilov's programme, which would be adopted. 'Kornilov is very pleased with this announcement, but Chief of Staff is not enthusiastic.' Barter felt it would allow matters to be delayed and the programme to be reduced, as the Bolsheviks were violently opposed and were pressing the government to abolish the death penalty even at the front.[10] Discipline was getting worse every day.

As soon as Riga fell, Kornilov wired to Kerensky demanding that all troops in the Petrograd district should be placed under his direct command. Kerensky refused; up to now, the Petrograd district had been commanded by a general responsible to the provisional government, and Kerensky insisted that Petrograd and its outlying areas should remain subordinate to him.

The military plot had now been carefully worked out. On September 3, Kornilov's quartermaster-general had hand-grenades issued to the Cossack troops who were to envelop and seize Petrograd from the north and south. A date for the operation was now fixed. 'As soon as news is received about the beginning of disorders in Petrograd, and not later than the morning of September 14th.' For it was believed that the tighter measures for the restoration of discipline, which the provisional government would soon announce, would provoke some protest demonstration by the Bolsheviks, and probably by the Petrograd soviet as well. Furthermore, September 9 was exactly six months from the outbreak of the March revolution. Kornilov's supporters felt that some sort of Bolshevik outbreak was sure to occur on this day, which would be sufficient excuse for really decisive measures of repression. Inside Petrograd, it was believed at Mogilev, some 2,000 armed men could be counted on, who would, if need be, provoke or even simulate Bolshevik outbreaks, in case no disorder did occur, and would then be ready 'to seize armoured vehicles, to arrest the Provisional Government, to arrest and execute the more prominent and influential members of the Petrograd Soviet, etc.'

'Great indifference displayed generally regarding loss of Riga,' wired Barter from Mogilev on the 4th, 'partly because it was expected.' Another reason was that the Bolsheviks hoped it would help secure an early peace, while the military party thought it would increase the chance of an early success for their plot, and hence in taking over the state.

But the indifference had vanished that evening when Barter wired again. 'Riga retirement still continues . . . Russians flying in all directions . . . Panic reported at Petrograd. Kerensky arrives here tomorrow to confer with Kornilov. The political change, which I have already foretold, and which in my opinion may be the only way to save Russia as an active ally, may be expected at any moment.'[11]

In fact, it was Savinkov who arrived at Mogilev on September 5, with a set of requests for Kornilov, which almost placed Kerensky in the position of plotting against himself. These were Kerensky's requests:

1. To get rid of certain officers, and Kornilov's political department, since they were involved in a plot.
2. To give Kornilov command of Petrograd district, but not of Petrograd itself.
3. To ask Kornilov for a cavalry corps to enforce martial law in Petrograd, and to defend the provisional government against any attacks, especially from the Bolsheviks.

For Kerensky was convinced, on the basis of some foreign intelligence reports (probably British) that there was danger of another 'July days' episode, in conjunction with a German landing in Finland. He was also probably anticipating the Petrograd soviet's opposition to his adoption of Kornilov's military programme. But he could not have realised that he was thereby putting himself into the hands of conspirators who, if their conspiracy succeeded, would sweep him aside. For his part, Kornilov was delighted that his conspiracy now, at the last minute, had legal sanction; and he readily agreed with Kerensky's specific requests also, such as not appointing General Krimov, who was thought to be a monarchist, and not sending the Wild Division, whose officers were thought to be politically unreliable. (In fact, though he agreed, Kornilov made no changes whatever, and both Krimov and the Wild Division were sent on the operation.) Kornilov and his entourage were encouraged by Savinkov's very strong language about the need for smashing the Bolsheviks – and the Petrograd soviet as well, if it sided with them. General Lukomsky, the ablest officer at Mogilev, distrusted the government's intentions; but Kornilov, after his talk with Savinkov, was satisfied that the strongest members of the government were now with him, and that Kerensky himself could be swept aside, or easily managed now. That evening, Kornilov told Barter that it would be a crime to disguise the 'extreme seriousness' of the situation. 'He [Kornilov] was not even sure of saving Petrograd. He has been, however, given command [of] Petrograd.'[12] (Kornilov was probably seeing to it that Barter was kept worked up. There was, in fact, no chance of the Russians losing Petrograd. But Barter was now starting to succumb to the political pressure against which the CIGS had warned him on August 25.)

Hectic plotting and planning was now going on at Mogilev between Russian generals, bankers and colonels and Kornilov had got himself into the hands of some very dubious hangers-on, in particular Zavoiko and Aladin V. Zavoiko, who simply called himself Kornilov's orderly, and refused all military rank, was an elderly financier of no great ability, whom Kornilov liked to say he had taken on because of his impressive literary style; in fact, Zavoiko was a nephew of the great financier Putilov. Alexis Aladin was rather a different fish. He had been a member of the first Duma, but as a man of the extreme left, he had been forced to go abroad and had spent many years in England, where he had become a man of the extreme right. He had recently returned to Russia in the uniform of a British lieutenant; this, together with his violent speech and exaggerated stories of support for Kornilov in England, gave Kornilov to believe that he had found a politician of real ability. Aladin had no ability. (For decades, Kerensky accused Aladin of bringing out a letter for Kornilov from Lord Milner, approving his plans for the establishment of a military dictatorship in Russia. This is extremely unlikely, in view of the very cautious attitude of the War Cabinet. No such letter has been traced in Milner's papers; and in his final book of memoirs, *Russia and History's Turning Point*, Kerensky dropped the charge.)

On September 6, Barter sent a crucial wire to the CIGS (which was never circulated to the Cabinet) reporting that Kornilov had had a satisfactory interview with Savinkov. 'The Government have decreed the death penalty in the interior, which is a very important advance. Riga disaster has enabled Kornilov to move as a logical measure four divisions to the neighbourhood of Petrograd.' One would go to the north, three to the south, and the 'trustworthy' Knights of St George to the coast, west of Peterhof. 'Petrograd will then be entirely cut off from interior.' Kerensky had appointed Kornilov as C.-in-C. of the forces defending Petrograd on both sides of the Gulf of Finland, 'and he is going to Petrograd in a few days', stated Barter. 'It is clear, however, though he did not say so, that Government has been driven to seek his support. This seems to indicate that for the present, at any rate, Kornilov and the Government are in accord. From my knowledge of the man it is my opinion that once he has secured power he will do just what he thinks best to meet the emergency, with Government if possible, but without if necessary.'[13]

Barter went on: 'He told me in strictest confidence that he intended to declare a state of siege in Petrograd in four days' time, and he significantly intimated that he was going to deal with the internal enemies of the country first. I earnestly beg that this information may be kept entirely secret, especially from our Ambassador in Petrograd. I am coding this by myself for greater secrecy.' (And the War Office did keep this information to themselves.)

Kornilov fully realised the 'grave insecurity' of the present situation, but 'complained bitterly that the Government had been blind to his repeated protestations regarding imminence of danger and indispensability of stern measures. He also complained that Alexeiev had assured Government that attack at Riga was impossible, when he himself urged the contrary several times.' (This alleged statement by Alexeiev is clearly contradicted by Barter's wire of August 27.)[13] As he considered, 'against the opinion of our Ambassador', that only Kornilov now had sufficient power and influence to save Russia from complete ruin, Barter strongly urged joint Allied diplomatic action, 'without a moment's delay', in support of Kornilov 'at right moment'. One chance of exerting such pressure had been missed before the Moscow conference, owing to the failure of the Allied envoys to appreciate the 'real state' of the military situation. A last chance would shortly present itself. Kornilov had made no suggestion of such action, but he clearly attached great importance to some Allied mark of approval in the event of his success, 'and if possible to official recognition'.[13]

But Buchanan was not kept entirely in the dark. On September 5, the leading Russian financier Putilov (who had been present at the crucial meeting with Kornilov in his railway coach in Moscow, and assured him of the necessary finance for the Petrograd operation) had marched into the British Embassy, and officially informed Buchanan of a movement which would begin on the following Saturday, September 8, whereupon the provisional government would be arrested, and the Petrograd soviet dissolved. 'They hoped that I,' reported Buchanan in dismay to the Foreign Office, 'would assist them by placing the British armoured cars at their disposal, and by helping them to escape should their enterprise fail . . .' Buchanan threw his arms in the air; he would not give them away, however, but warned Kornilov to wait until the Bolsheviks moved, and then come and put them down. But Buchanan never sent any message to Locker-Lampson – whose future plans in support of Kornilov had clearly now been approved by Barter.[14]

Meanwhile, there was a pause. 'Kerensky in an Army order issued today praises the part played by officers during and since the Revolution,' reported Colonel Blair to the DMI from Petrograd on September 6. This 'tardy recognition' was evidently meant to restore the authority of the officers; distrust between officers and men, claimed Kerensky, had been brought about by the old regime, which 'obviously shows how impossible it is to trust in Kerensky or expect any good to come while he is in power', wired Blair. In the light of the Riga disaster, the Petrograd soviet had demanded the removal from Petrograd of all reactionary generals, and complete control of the Petrograd garrison. In the recent municipal elections, the SR had obtained most of the votes, second came the Bolsheviks, and third the Cadets. 'There are no signs of unity to meet the present crisis,' stated Blair; in fact, with the coming influx of refugees and German agents from Riga, and the absence of any police control, 'it is easily seen that trouble may break out in Petrograd at any time . . .' People generally felt, he went on next day, that matters could not improve until things were brought to a head by food riots in October, or by a Bolshevik rising, which might come sooner. 'All parties appear to be waiting at present for something to happen . . .'[15]

On September 7, the War Cabinet asked General Knox, just back from Petrograd, to report on the Russian situation. Knox warned that there were three 'powerful forces' tending to drive the Russians to make a separate peace. First, the great mass of the soldiers did not want to fight on. Secondly, the workmen were making such 'huge economic demands' on their employers, that the factories were closing, and there would soon probably be a general lock-out. Thirdly, the railways were in complete chaos, which meant that no grain could be brought up from the Caucasus or western Siberia, and the northern cities would be faced with starvation.

In reply to questions about the likelihood of a *coup d'état* headed by Kornilov, Knox said 'that he did not know what preparations were being made'. (How far this is true, one cannot know. Knox certainly did not know of the details.)[16] When he left Russia on August 18, Knox went on, Kornilov and Savinkov were in agreement. Kornilov was a strong character, an honest patriot, 'and the best man in sight'. (Knox was later to use the same expression about Admiral Kolchak, who was also to prove a disaster to the British cause.) Kornilov had the support of 150,000 Cossacks, Knox claimed, who had no faith in Kerensky, and he had 'heard rumours that Kerensky's party had accepted money from Germany'. (German money had indeed been syphoned into Russia via SR agents.) Kerensky was letting matters drift towards anarchy, as he was afraid of shedding blood. 'A force of 10,000 loyalists would be enough to subdue Petrograd – the main source of disorder – for the Russians were cowards.' (This appears to be the first mention of the highly dangerous argument, to be vigorously propagated in 1918, that a small compact Allied force, preferably British, could go through

Russia like a knife through butter and accomplish virtually anything.)
If Kerensky were to suggest a separate peace, Knox warned, 'he would
certainly have the great majority of the country with him'. Knox
strongly urged the War Cabinet that joint Allied pressure should be
exerted on the Russian government, and he recommended that 'in
view of Russia's desperate situation and the peril of putting back
democracy [sic], General Kornilov should be fully supported in the
measures which he wished to take to restore discipline at the front, on
the railways, and in Petrograd.'

The War Cabinet gave 'careful and prolonged' consideration to
Knox's suggestions, and discussed three proposals:

1. The despatch of a joint Allied note to the Russian government.
2. The despatch of a British note to Washington, asking President
   Wilson to urge the Russian government to support General Kornilov's programme – a draft note to President Wilson to be submitted
   to the Prime Minister (who was absent) forthwith.
3. The prior despatch of the proposed note to Buchanan, asking if it
   was advisable to present it to the Russian government.

At the War Cabinet's request, Lord Robert Cecil submitted a draft
note to President Wilson. The Cabinet recognised that the despatch of
such a note in the terms contemplated was a 'matter of grave importance and might be strongly resented by Kerensky and the Government. Interference might be construed as helping Kornilov to a *coup
d'état*. On the other hand, the serious menace of the situation had to be
faced and some risk taken.' Knox stressed that a joint Allied note would
carry much greater weight in Russia than an American note. Cecil
retorted that it was 'unlikely that the President of a Republican Government would be willing to suggest to the Russian Government what
would, in effect, be the establishment of a Military Dictatorship'. In
any case, American would probably prefer to send a separate note. The
War Cabinet then adjourned their discussions. No subsequent action
was taken and thus the last chance for British mediation between
Kerensky and Kornilov was lost.[16]

Whenever there is a plot afoot in Russia, there is an overwhelming
desire in the Russian soul to meddle in it, to spring it before its time,
in fact to act as agent provocateur. The man who now stepped forward
was a well-meaning minor politician: a certain V. N. Lvov (not to be
confused with Prince Lvov, the first Premier of the provisional government), who had been Procurator of the Holy Synod in one of the
provisional governments.[17]

After some talks with Kornilov's unreliable entourage, Lvov had come to see Kerensky, to acquaint him with the facts, late on September 4. Kerensky told him to make further soundings.

Late on the 6th (just after Savinkov had left Mogilev), Lvov arrived to see Kornilov, and said he had Kerensky's authority to discover Kornilov's demands. This request, coming so soon after Savinkov's visit, convinced Kornilov that Kerensky was now ready to capitulate, and that the conspiracy was no longer necessary.

Early on the 7th, Lvov saw Kornilov again, who put forward these demands:

1. Declaration of martial law in Petrograd, and the handing over of all civil and military authority to the C.-in-C., whoever he might be.
2. Invitation to Kerensky and Savinkov to come to Mogilev; Kerensky might become Minister of Justice, and Savinkov the Minister of War.

But Zavoiko then privately told Lvov that it was intended not only to remove Kerensky from power, but assassinate him.

Late on the 8th (while Buchanan, warned by Putilov that the coup was to be launched that day, kept well out of the way on the British residents' golf course), Lvov had his second talk with Kerensky, who was amazed at these demands, which he asked Lvov to put in writing, which he did; and warned Kerensky that it would be dangerous for him to go to Mogilev.[17]

Kerensky, bearing in mind that Kornilov had only recently promised to Savinkov to co-operate, got in touch by telegraph with Kornilov, who told him that the information given to Lvov was correct, and asked him urgently to come to Mogilev. Kerensky said – falsely – that he would leave for Mogilev the next day.

Kerensky then had Lvov arrested. At 4 a.m. on the 9th, Kerensky called a cabinet session, after rejecting Savinkov's advice for direct negotiations with Kornilov. The astonished ministers gave Kerensky full powers. Kerensky then sent this message to Kornilov:

'I order you immediately to turn over your office to General Lukomsky, who is to take over temporarily the duties of Commander-in-Chief, until the arrival of the new Commander-in-Chief.

'You are instructed immediately to come to Petrograd.'[17]

Kornilov, after his talk with Kerensky on the 8th, was confident that his plan would meet no opposition. He was thus completely surprised, next morning, to receive Kerensky's curt wire of dismissal. Lukomsky refused Kerensky's order to take over from his chief, and so informed the other Russian generals.

On the 9th, a war of words took place between Kerensky and

Kornilov, in which the role of Lvov was variously interpreted. Kornilov instructed the cavalry units to proceed to Petrograd, according to plan, and issued a flowery declaration, written by Zavoiko. Kerensky proclaimed martial law in Petrograd, ordered all troop movements towards Petrograd to be stopped, and 20,000 troops of the Petrograd garrison were despatched to defend the city from Kornilov. 'These troops are chiefly composed of the reformed regiments that joined in the Bolshevik rising in July,' wired Colonel Blair from Petrograd on September 9. 'Although there are continued rumours of another Bolshevik rising, the Chief of the Staff of [Petrograd] district does not think that it will come off . . .'[18]

There would indeed be no Bolshevik rising. The Kornilov adventure brought the Petrograd soviet to life in a truly electrifying way. The humiliation and disgrace of the 'July days' was speedily forgotten; and on the evening of the 9th, the Mensheviks proposed formal co-operation with the Bolsheviks, and the formation of a 'Committee for Struggle with Counter-revolution'. A delegation called on Kerensky the next day, offering full co-operation, and demanding the complete suppression of the Kornilov movement. The Bolsheviks then made all possible use of legal means in winning the masses away from the moderate socialists, and induced the 'Committee for Struggle with Counter-revolution' to form an armed workers' militia, which was nothing other than the old Bolshevik Red Guard, which had been driven underground after the 'July days'. Within a few days, 25,000 recruits had been enlisted and the Bolsheviks, through their supply of rifles and machine-guns, had effective control of them.[18]

At Mogilev there was great confusion. 'Kornilov has been relieved of his command this morning,' wired General Barter at 8.56 p.m. that evening (the 9th). At 10.50 p.m., he wired again that he and his French and Italian colleagues had been summoned that afternoon by the Russian Chief of Staff, 'who asked us to keep his name secret' (it was in fact General Lukhomsky), who handed them a note for transmission to their governments – and ambassadors in Petrograd. This stated that in the last few months, the Petrograd soviet had become an 'insurmountable obstacle' to the reorganisation of the Russian army, whose disorganised state would force Russia to leave the war in two or three months' time, and cause grave disorder inside Russia. Kornilov had 'continually and insistently' informed the Russian government that the only solution was the formation of a really strong government. Kerensky and Savinkov, after negotiations which they themselves had begun, had recently accepted Kornilov's programme and had agreed to visit Mogilev that day (the 9th) to arrange matters; but after a telephone conversation with Kornilov, they had then deferred their arrival until the 10th. On the strength of this, Kornilov had invited Rodzianko and other political leaders to come to Mogilev for a 'combined' conference, to set up a 'strong national Government'.[19]

But that morning (the 9th), Kornilov had been instructed to come to Petrograd urgently, after handing over command to his Chief of Staff, General Lukhomsky. But Lukhomsky had replied that in view of Kerensky's previous consent, and the gravity of the situation, orders had already been issued which could not be countermanded. 'He [Lukhomsky] could not, in consequence, even for a brief period, assume the responsibility of replacing Kornilov.' The Russian High Command would not be responsible for the catastrophes which might befall Russia, should the provisional government now decline to form a strong government of national defence with Kornilov, who had 'given the Government his positive assurance that he is inspired by no personal ambition.' This ended the Russian Chief of Staff's note.[19]

Barter urged upon the CIGS that it was 'most highly desired' by the Russian High Command that the Allied governments should immediately bring the strongest possible diplomatic pressure to bear on the Russian government to accept Kornilov's terms, 'if only in the interests of the Allies themselves, as the continuation of the war by Russia would otherwise be impossible. It is expected here that Savinkov, the virtual Minister of War, who, as reported, visited Kornilov on September 5th, will endeavour to deny the arrangements then arrived at, on behalf of his Government.' Barter had been assured by the Russian High Command that 'Kerensky proposed that Kornilov should form a Government, and that he himself would form part of it, or not, as thought best. Kornilov replied that in his opinion Kerensky's presence would strengthen the Government, in which were to be included Rodzianko and other representative men of worth and patriotism. He [the Russian High Command spokesman] also informs me that Kornilov has decided not to go to Petrograd. Both Kerensky and Kornilov are afraid to place himself in the other's power,' Barter explained. 'There are now 4 divisions of Cossacks within 30 miles of Petrograd, and on these divisions the course of events largely depends.'

Once again Barter emphasised the need for immediate Allied diplomatic pressure on the provisional government, 'which is showing itself hopelessly weak and vacillating. So long as the extreme left remains powerful, the situation cannot possibly improve. The only means of suppressing this party is military power, preferably with a Government which will include Kerensky,' he stated. 'Kerensky clearly is intensely nervous and undecided. The vigorous insistence of the Allies should be sufficient to weigh down the scale in favour of the only course which can yet save the country, but the sands are running out. I am persuaded absolutely that Kornilov is the only horse to back to win, with Kerensky for a place in his Government . . .' The Russian High Command, he added, did not wish to be quoted as the source of this information.[19]

In a postscript to this despatch, Barter added: 'I have just been informed on the best authority that Kornilov has refused to give up his post . . . Kerensky maintains that the envoys [ie, Lvov] did not represent his propositions correctly.' (This at all events was glaringly true.) 'I am communicating this message to the Ambassador,' Barter concluded.[19]

This despatch was probably not before the War Cabinet when they met on the 10th. Bonar Law (Chancellor of the Exchequer) informed the Cabinet, that, as a result of their discussions on the 7th, the Prime Minister (who was not present) had despatched a draft of the proposed note to Buchanan, asking him if it should be presented to the Russian government.

It was now further suggested that as an impression prevailed in Paris (according to the British Ambassador's wire from Paris of the 9th) that the Japanese government would be willing to send troops to assist the Allies, 'it might be desirable to urge that any available Japanese troops should be used in Russia as a nucleus that could serve to stiffen the resistance of those Russian troops who were prepared to stand firm.'[20] The War Cabinet were indeed clutching at straws, since all Russians loathed all Japanese. Nevertheless, the War Cabinet instructed the CIGS to ask Kornilov, via Barter, whether he wanted the support of Japanese troops.

On September 11, Barter sent another report to the CIGS. 'Kornilov persists in his refusal to resign.' All the Russian military commanders had protested at his removal, including the general appointed to take over as C.-in-C., who had refused to do so point-blank. Three battalions of the Wild Division had arrived at Mogilev. 'St George's battalion, which is here, is said to favour the Government. The streets are being patrolled by Turcoman Cossacks.' He went on hopefully: 'The Cossack divisions are closing in on Petrograd. All communication between the front and Petrograd has been stopped by Kornilov . . . Opinion is prevalent here that Kornilov is gaining [upper] hand.'

Barter had wired this report to Buchanan, and had urged him to press the Russian government, 'if it is acting in good faith', to publish 'correct' statements about the Allies' sympathy with Russia, and their successful efforts to relieve German pressure on the Russian front. At present, the Bolshevik press was 'spreading pernicious reports about the Allies without hindrance, stating that our armies are everywhere being routed by the Germans, and accusing the Allies of disloyalty to Russia. These statements, which are being readily believed by civilians and soldiers, are doing much mischief,' wired Barter to the CIGS. 'I am afraid that Ambassador does not realise,' he added, 'that the continuance of state of affairs hitherto existing must inevitably be disastrous to Allied cause and that the situation can only be saved by vigorous measures.' Barter was not against Kerensky, whom he believed to be honest, and thought he should be included in any new Russian government. 'He is not at present however playing quite a straight game as regards Kornilov and it can hardly be doubted that some of Kerensky's Ministers are pro-German. There is every reason to believe that a few days after the Riga defeat, he was ready to come to any arrangement with Kornilov. The Government recovered from its panic when the Germans suspended their advance for two or three days and now refuses to acknowledge the combination arranged with Kornilov by Kerensky's envoys . . . Several senior officers were present at this interview and Kornilov told me next day that it was satisfactory . . .'[21]

Later on the 11th, Barter wired again. 'Kornilov is confined to his room with slight chill which probably is more assumed than real.' Lukhomsky, his Chief of Staff, had just told Barter that if Alexeiev was called upon by the provisional government to form a new government, 'Kornilov will have obtained all he wanted and is quite ready to stand aside. Alexeiev and Kornilov are working together in complete accord,' he stated. 'Trustworthy telegram from Petrograd states that Petrograd troops are moving out to meet Cossack divisions, but that they are only an undisciplined mob. All the railways are still obediently under Kornilov's order.'[22]

This was quite untrue. The whole Russian army, save for the officers and a few Cossacks, was bitterly hostile to Kornilov. So were the railway workers, the Red Guard and a host of agitators under the command of the 'Committee for Struggle with Counter-revolution'.

In fact, the Kornilov adventure – not that the War Cabinet or their chief informant, General Barter, knew it – was already over, and Kornilov's unofficial British support had failed dismally. Late on the evening of the 8th, Locker-Lampson had arrived at Proskurov, and had told one of his officers that they were leaving at once for Mogilev to join Kornilov. The two of them would go on ahead in his private Rolls-Royce car, and the armoured car squadron would follow later. If they were stopped, he explained, they would simply say they were on their way to their new base at Brovari, near Kiev; there was no need to mention Kornilov – which was indeed the first that any of his officers had heard about the coming coup. They set off in haste early next morning (the 9th). But before the great sage-green limousine had gone 60 miles, a tyre burst. Much to the driver's embarrassment, and Locker-Lampson's fury, it was discovered that there was no spare, and they had to bump along the chaussée to join the counter-revoultion with one flat wheel.* That afternoon, as the Rolls drew up in Berdichev, Locker-Lampson saw General Anton Denikin, commander of the Western Front, seized by revolutionaries as he drove by in a droshkie – and then seized back again by a squadron of 'whooping and roaring' Cossacks. The two British officers drove hurriedly on.

The coup was hanging fire. On the 10th, as Russian officers were arrested, and Bolshevik agitators and saboteurs sallied forth to win over the advancing troops, Kornilov had an urgent message sent to Proskurov: 'Immediately instruct the Commander of the British Armoured Car Division to despatch all fighting machines . . . to Brovari.' The British squadron set off.

In Petrograd, everything went wrong. The Russian officers realised that the Bolsheviks had decided to postpone their rising – if indeed they ever had any intention of launching one. As the Wild Division had been primed to suppress disorders, the officers had to try to provoke some.

While the provisional government remained paralysed, Kerensky took action. Though Buchanan and the Allied ambassadors urged him to come to terms with Kornilov, he had a statement published on the 11th that 'General Kornilov cannot count on Allied support'.[23] (The provisional government had, in fact, been intercepting Buchanan's wires to the Foreign Office. And from those exchanged – and intercepted – between August 10 and September 21. Buchanan seems to have taken no part in the Kornilov affair, and indeed to have opposed it. The whole tenor of his advice was that Kornilov was an excellent fellow, but that British support for his movement would only worsen the general situation and probably defeat the main British objective, which was to keep Russia in the war. But he took no action, it seems, to try to stop Locker-Lampson.)[24]

Kerensky's statement helped to turn the scale. The attempt to stage street rioting was a dismal failure, the Wild Division refused to move; and that morning (the 11th), on the dusty road between Zhitomir and Brovari, revolutionary troops signalled to Locker-Lampson's Rolls Royce to stop. It was not difficult to recognise it, as Locker-Lampson had been careful, for purposes of propaganda, not to repair or repaint the scars of battle inflicted on the Caucasus front. He was in fact expected. The revolutionaries were quite polite. They had reason to believe, they said, that he was going to join Kornilov, who had just been arrested for starting a counter-revolution. (This was a little premature.) Locker-Lampson replied that they were merely on their

* I am grateful to the British officer, who drove with Locker-Lampson, for details of this episode, which is supported by documentary evidence in his possession.

way to their base across the River Dnieper; and after some palaver, they sped off to Brovari, which they reached later that afternoon. The British squadron was also stopped, and gave more or less the same excuse, then hurried on to Brovari as well, whence the reunited convoy, thankful to get off so lightly, set off with all speed to their main base at Kursk, where they discovered that Locker-Lampson's 'poster' had apparently given them away. For during the uproar in Kursk they captured a Bolshevik courier who had in his pockets the copies of King George V's letter, the First Lord's message, and Kornilov's letter of thanks to the British squadron, which Locker-Lampson had stuck up for his men to see.[25]

By the afternoon of the 11th, the counter-revolution was all over. The Commander of Kornilov's own Wild Division shot himself, Locker-Lampson had to hastily re-assemble his armoured cars – some were still en route – prior to their immediate embarkation for England; and Brigadier Finlayson, who was to have organised a course on 'British mortar and machine-gun techniques' for young Russian officers at Mogilev, as a blind, did not escape detection.[26]

Mercifully for Locker-Lampson and Finlayson, this was unknown to the War Cabinet when they again considered the Russian situation on September 12. The DMI admitted that it was doubtful what was happening in Petrograd, where there were some 100,000 troops, 'of whom about 20,000 had been sent into the surrounding districts on defensive lines against any advance by General Kornilov'. These were reformed regiments, and their fighting value 'was not of a high order'. All the Russian generals were apparently against Kerensky, he added. Lord Robert Cecil said that the last telegram from Buchanan was dated September 10; it was thus 'doubtful if we were in possession of the facts of the matter in all its aspects'.

In the discussion that followed, the view was expressed that General Kornilov 'represented all that was sound and hopeful' for an improvement in the Russian situation, 'and that he should not be condemned on telegrams received from Russian sources, as the case as now presented was one-sided, prejudiced, and possibly untrue'. (So, alas, were Barter's reports.) 'It was really a duel between M. Kerensky and General Kornilov, and it was possible that the latter had jeopardised the success of his movement by premature action, after failing to obtain the support, which he deemed essential to the welfare of Russia, of M. Kerensky.' But, the Cabinet minutes emphasise strongly, 'to talk of General Kornilov as a "traitor to his country" was monstrous, and it should not be forgotten that in the past we have been in general sympathy with his endeavours to aid the cause not only of Russia but of the Allies'.[27] Difficult though it was for the British government to interfere, without appearing to take sides with General Kornilov, it was felt 'impossible, in the interests of the Allies and of democracy generally, to make no effort to improve the situation, though it was realised that any steps in that direction would have to be taken through M. Kerensky, as he was the representative of the existing Government'. It was suggested that he be informed that the British government 'viewed with the greatest alarm the probabilities of civil war', and urged him 'to come to terms with General Kornilov', both in Russian and Allied interests. But it was pointed out, with reference to the meeting of the War Cabinet of the 7th (as a result of which the Prime Minister had wired to Buchanan, asking if a joint Allied note should be presented to the Russian government), that Buchanan already knew that the War Cabinet wished to support Kornilov's previous programme.

The War Cabinet decided that the Foreign Office should – again – instruct Buchanan to make an appeal to Kerensky, as he saw fit; and that the French government should be urged to give similar instructions to the French Ambassador in Petrograd.[27]

The DMI stated that the CIGS wished the War Cabinet to know that he had refused to ask Kornilov if he wanted the active support of Japanese troops. The Cabinet acquiesced in this decision.

Kerensky, who had 'won', then assumed almost 'supreme power'. He formed a Council of Five, had Kornilov and the other Russian generals arrested, and proclaimed Russia a republic. But all the Russian officers and the non-socialist parties were utterly humiliated.

Lenin wrote from Finland (where he had been in hiding) that after Kornilov's revolt, which was an 'almost incredible turn of events', and 'completely unexpected', they must now overthrow Kerensky himself; and though Kerensky sent out an urgent order that the 'arbitrary formation of detachments under the pretext of a struggle against the counter-revolutionary uprising be stopped immediately', it was already too late. By September 13, the Petrograd soviet had fallen into the hands of the Bolsheviks, who now had an armed force, the 'Red Guard', and began in their turn to demand the suppression of the provisional government, and 'Dictatorship of the Proletariat'.[28]

Late on the 13th, Barter wired the CIGS that he had had a long conversation that morning with Kornilov, who was now ruminating on his failure. 'He believed Cossack divisions were ready to march against the Bolsheviks, but were not willing to act against Government.' In any case, they were too far away to strike at the opportune moment. 'He states at celebrated conference [? with] Savinkov here, Kerensky's envoy [ie, Savinkov] asked him urgently to send as much cavalry as possible preferably of the line to Petrograd to act against Bolsheviks who were expected to rise against Government on or about 10th instant.' Kornilov then read to Barter the 'full record of negotiations between Alexeiev, speaking for Government, and himself . . . he [Kornilov] only wanted country's good and if Alexeiev had Government's guarantee that necessary measures would be taken, he would stand aside[29] . . . Kornilov is evidently very anxious that the Western Powers should know [he] has throughout only been inspired by patriotism. It may be assumed that further complications with Kornilov are at an end.' Indeed they were not.

On the 14th, Barter wired again. 'This morning Kornilov sent for me. He is submitting unconditionally and has notified Alexeiev, who is at Vitebsk, that he will give his command to him this afternoon . . . He is also from patriotic motives using all his influence with the Cossacks to induce them to remain at the front, as they are saying at present that with Kornilov gone, all is over and they may as well go home.' Now indeed were the evil results of Kornilov's fiasco being realised. Kornilov, Barter went on, had submitted so that 'bloodshed and civil war might be avoided'. Barter added, 'Kornilov is confiding to me private papers which he positively assures me are connected with his defence and which for a safe custody he wishes lodged at our Embassy. I leave for Petrograd today to see Ambassador . . .' Thus the proofs of the British involvement with Kornilov disappeared into the British Embassy at Petrograd. They have not been located. But if they contained only copies of the messages from the CIGS, which are printed in this chapter, they would be sufficient to suggest that the British were indeed compromised with the rebellious Russian general.[30]

That day, when the War Cabinet again considered the Russian situation, they once again had to debate matters which were in fact over and done with. It was a short and depressing discussion. Many of Barter's wires had not yet arrived. The DMI stated that from Barter's wire of the 11th, 'it appeared that General Alexeiev and General Kornilov were working together in complete accord'. But Colonel Blair's wire of the 12th from Petrograd stressed that the delay in Kornilov's advance on the city had enabled the 'Petrograd garrison to organise itself and for the Kronstadt garrison to arrive at Petrograd'. Blair also reported that Putilov's works were on fire, and that it was 'not unlikely that other Russian munition factories would meet the same fate'. But the DMI had discouraged Blair's suggestion that England 'should organise a secret service in Russia to counter that of the Germans and help to put down sabotage'. Lord Robert Cecil added that he had heard that it would be difficult for Russia to face the prospect of a separate peace until they could cope with the serious problem of demobilisation, which also entailed the restoration of discipline.[31]

The War Cabinet's policy of official non-intervention and scrupulous adherence to the diplomatic rules during the Kornilov adventure had not proved a success. For by confining their action to appeals to the Russian government, which the British Ambassador had sedulously refused to present to Kerensky, the War Cabinet had created a kind of void into which Barter and Locker-Lampson, without any authority, had immediately plunged – with disastrous consequences. The British, and in particular the unfortunate Buchanan (who was thought to have approved these unauthorised activities), were now hopelessly compromised by their supposed part in the Kornilov affair. It appeared that they had not only backed the rebel general, but had sent their armoured cars, whose commander (according to Locker-Lampson's 'poster', seized at Kursk) had the active support of the Tsar's cousin, that arch imperialist, the British King. The Bolsheviks raged at the British in their newspapers, and threatened reprisals.

On September 15, Brigadier Finlayson (whose role at Mogilev had also been exposed) wrote a line to Colonel Byrne (whose brief visit from London, no doubt in connection with the Kornilov affair, had gone undetected), regretting that Byrne had not come to see them the previous evening 'for a buck & a parting "dram" before leaving this benighted country'. (Byrne had evidently left in a considerable hurry.) 'It was a wise decision in view of the rumours, but, as it turns out, you'd have been all right, for "not a shot was heard; not a funeral note, etc etc, as the drams to our tummies we hurried," & we had quite a cheery evening. I understand, however, that we are to be killed tonight instead. Do you know that the Consulate was so "windy" last night that they sent most of the British from the Viborg side of the river over here last night & many people in the [Astoria] hotel were flooded with refugees, to whom we have parted with a priceless tin of oatcakes & a loaf of nearly-white bread . . .'[32]

On September 15, General Barter arrived at Petrograd and duly deposited Kornilov's private papers at the British Embassy; but he told Buchanan nothing, it seems, of what had really been happening at Mogilev. That day, Colonel Blair wrote a full report on Kornilov's *coup d'état* for the DMI. 'Although it is officially announced that the Kornilov "venture" has been "liquidated", it is extremely difficult to ascertain the real preliminaries which led up to this disastrous episode,' he wrote from the British Embassy. Two views were current:

1. The Russian government's view, 'which the Government has taken such pains to spread throughout Petrograd and the country', that

Kornilov 'really intended to declare himself absolute dictator and had long prepared for doing so'.

2. Kornilov's view, which he has 'definitely stated to be the case', that he was 'asked by Kerensky to make himself dictator and after making definite preparations to do so, was thrown over by Kerensky and then decided to carry on in spite'.

Blair commented: 'It is obvious that prodigious lying has been going on in some quarter, at present unknown,' and two points should be borne in mind. First, Kerensky's attitude to Kornilov, after he became C.-in-C., and especially during the Moscow conference. 'Kerensky feared and so hated Kornilov. This was no secret.' Secondly, the characters of the two men. 'Kerensky, weak, vacillating, very ambitious, and continually struggling with his ideals, which he knows to be impracticable but is too weak to definitely renounce. No mention is made of the rumours now so frequently circulated as to Kerensky's honesty. Kornilov, on the other hand, strong, fearless, admittedly straightforward and a true patriot, though no politician.[33]

'Kornilov's attempt has failed, failed as it was obvious to anyone that it must fail, because it hadn't the Army behind it. Looking back on it, it seems incredible that Kornilov should have attempted it unless his version of the affair is correct, and there seems no reason to doubt it, while there is every reason to doubt the Provisional Government's version, which was daily dished up for the Petrograd public, while the crisis lasted and which was undoubtedly inspired by the Soviet.'

A senior Russian general had commented that 'Kornilov, being a determined and hasty man, might easily undertake a venture without proper preparation, but that if Lukhomsky [his Chief of Staff], a cautious and very methodical organiser, was associated with it, it must be based on some solid foundations'.

Of these two views of the events leading up to the attempted coup, wrote Blair acidly, 'if it was a plot long prepared, it must surely have been known to the British Military Mission in the Stavka. If it was known to the British Mission there, it seems strange that no communication was sent on the subject to the British Embassy in Petrograd.' But whatever prospects of success the plot may seem to have had from Mogilev, it was obvious to anyone in Petrograd that it must fail, since the support of the Russian army could only be obtained (via the various committees) through the Petrograd soviet, 'unless it was known that the Government would throw in its lot with Kornilov and denounce the Soviet. And even then,' wrote Blair, 'it is doubtful whether the plot could have succeeded, as the [Petrograd] Soviet would probably have immediately thrown in its lot with the Bolsheviks and the extreme left parties . . . Hence it seems extremely unlikely that the plot was one long prepared beforehand.' Thus, the second view, that Kornilov received some proposal from Kerensky, 'is the more probable'.[33]

Blair went on: 'One of the arguments used against Kornilov by the Government in their absolutely unjustifiable propaganda in the press during the crisis was that they had given in to him on all his demands for the introduction of disciplinary measures. That this was so seems to be yet another proof that Kornilov would not have attempted a *coup d'état* to make himself sole dictator.' But whatever the real truth of Kornilov's ill-fated attempt, 'there is absolutely no doubt of the results. The consequences both for Russia and for the Allies are fatal.' The Russian officers' authority was at an even lower ebb than just after the revolution. 'Officers have again become suspects, and from all quarters are coming in reports of the murder of officers . . .' The soldiers' committees, on the other hand, had now regained their former authority, 'with its fatal consequences. In a word, it may be said that the introduction of discipline into the Army which was so tardily undertaken has now had a setback from which it is not likely to recover during the war . . .

'The Government has been in the hands of the [Petrograd] Soviet, and has now been thrown even more into their hands,' concluded Colonel Blair to the DMI. 'As the Soviet is against the introduction of all the military disciplinary reforms demanded by Kornilov, it may now be assumed that no measures will be taken by the Government to increase the efficiency of the Army. The outlook is extremely bad, and the Soviet is in its turn drifting more and more into the direction of the Bolsheviks. The Bolsheviks, supported by German money, are organising as they have not organised before. An outbreak at no very distant date is almost a certainty, and the triumph of the Bolsheviks will be the first step towards a separate peace.'[33]

Hindsight, however, shows that both Kerensky's and Kornilov's views of the origin of the *coup d'état* were accurate. Kornilov had for some time prepared to make himself dictator, and Kerensky at one point asked him to do so, but then drew back; whereupon Kornilov went ahead. But for the British Embassy, the complicating factor was General Barter, who had known all along what was to happen, and had not only deliberately withheld the information from the British Ambassador, but had begged the War Office to see that it was not provided from London either.

On the morning of the 16th, Barter called on Kerensky, who was not pleased to see him. To try and elicit some information, Barter claimed that he must know how the political situation was affecting the Russian military position; the 'violent' British offensive in France, aimed at relieving German pressure on Russia, and British supplies to Russia might have to be stopped. (It is not clear whether Barter had any authority to make such a threat.) Kerensky replied shortly that the strategic position had 'somewhat improved'. Barter asked if the troops could be properly supplied at the front before winter. 'He [Kerensky] did not seem disposed to give much information on this subject.' But in answer to a direct question, 'Kerensky replied that he was confident Army was behind him and would obey his orders as Commander-in-Chief.' Barter then asked directly if the Petrograd soviet in fact wanted peace at any price. Kerensky replied angrily that many Russian people thought England and France wanted to make peace with Germany, 'and to leave Russia in the lurch'. Barter protested emphatically; if the Allies 'could count on Russia as surely as they could count on us, we should be well satisfied'. Kerensky claimed hotly that German peace propaganda was now aimed at England and France rather than Russia, and that Germany intended to offer them favourable terms at the expense of Russia. Barter then openly pleaded for Kornilov; he and Buchanan agreed that if Kornilov were put to death, 'it might lead to rising of Cossacks and perhaps to civil war'. Kerensky said there was no danger of this; Kaledin, the Don Cossack Ataman (who had come out so strongly for Kornilov at the Moscow conference, but when called on for support by Kornilov had been threatened with arrest by the Voronezh soviet, and had to make his way back to the safety of Don territory by a roundabout route) had wired to Kerensky dissociating himself from the Kornilov affair. If the Russian government were weak over this, 'it would be impossible to restore discipline', he added for Barter's discomfort, 'as soldiers were being shot at the front at the present moment for insubordination. He could not make any difference between Generals and soldiers after he had reluctantly assented to death penalty.' Barter hastily dropped the subject, and instead asked flatly if the Petrograd soviet were likely to create 'immediate disorders' in Petrograd. 'He laughingly replied "Today was the day on which disorders were supposed to occur" and remarked that everything was perfectly quiet.' This ended the interview. Kerensky had clearly had enough of the British envoys in Russia.[34]

In London, the further deterioration in the Russian situation was now evident. On September 17, the CIGS informed the War Cabinet that General Knox had wired from Petrograd that German agents had destroyed large quantities of ammunition at Kazan. On the 18th, they were told that Knox had reported that the Russian Foreign Minister had asked what steps were being taken to protect the British Embassy, 'having regard to the fact that war had been declared by the new

[Russian] Government on the [Petrograd] Soviet and that trouble was expected in the immediate future'. It was considered undesirable to have a Russian guard outside the Embassy; but since the 11th, stated Knox, there had been a guard of British airmen and gunners, who had been withdrawn from Tsarskoe Selo when Kornilov began his march on Petrograd. (Trouble was indeed expected; but not on account of any aggression by Kerensky.)[35]

On the 19th, however, Rex Leeper, in his weekly report on Russia, headed 'After the Kornilov Rising', showed that the rise of the Petrograd soviet and the decline of both the military party and the right wing, was still not properly appreciated in London. 'In the interests both of Russia and the Allies,' he informed the War Cabinet, 'it seems essential not only that there should be a Coalition Government strongly backed by the Cadets, but that those Socialists who may join it should free themselves from the influence of the Soviet.' All this, of course, suggested that Kerensky, or any other Prime Minister, was still backed by a coherent state apparatus; that such an apparatus still existed in Russia; and that the Petrograd soviet, now under Bolshevik control, was still in some way responsive to the provisional government. 'Thus Kerensky's Government ought to be able to move to the right, and act just as strongly against the Soviet as against Kornilov.' In fact, 'the whole Kornilov episode may prove to have done good.' But Kerensky now had no force with which to move against the Petrograd soviet. Yet Leeper saw the only difficulty in whether or not Kerensky would show the necessary power of decision. Once again, he was seriously misleading the War Cabinet on the Russian situation.[36]

'But the first thing that must be done is the suppression of the Maximalists. Alexinski, Burtsev and others are busy unearthing further proofs of the guilt of Lenin, Zinoviev and many of their followers. Any further evidence against them that can be collected in England or France would be useful. Action against them would have to be taken quickly by the Russian Government, as until they are suppressed they will grow in numbers . . .

'If the Russian Government does not take the initiative in putting down the Maximalists,' concluded Leeper, 'the probability is that there will be another rising in Petrograd . . .'[36]

But again the idea that Kerensky could now take open action against the 'Maximalists' (ie, the Bolsheviks) was sheer lunacy. Whether any further 'evidence' against Lenin and the Bolsheviks was unearthed in England is unclear. But the 'proofs of guilt' collected by the Russian journalists Alexinski and Burtsev (first published in the Russian press after the failure of the Bolshevik riots in the 'July days') were later incorporated into the notorious forged documents which came to the surface in Petrograd early in February 1918 and which alleged that Lenin and Trotsky *themselves* were simply German agents.

Leeper's erroneous views were corrected, however, on the 20th, when Buchanan wired from Petrograd straight to the DMI that he had just had a visit from Rodzianko, President of the Duma, who had told him that the Russian army would desert on the first approach of cold weather, that there would be a further Bolshevik rising as soon as the composition of the new Russian government was announced, and that, thanks to the weakness shown after their July rising, the Bolsheviks were now probably too powerful to be put down. Buchanan emphasised that conditions could not improve so long as the Russian government adopted a weak attitude towards the Bolshevik movement, whose whole strength 'lies in the amount of German money with which it is financed. The only way of combating the movement is to spend sufficient money, and take the most decisive measures against spies and German agents.' In this respect, the Russian government was doing practically nothing. 'One excuse is that they have not sufficient money. If the Allies wish the present chaotic conditions of Russia to improve, I am convinced they must take steps to help Russia to deal with the German spy and agent menace. In the coming struggle, the main issue is whether the Bolsheviks are to form a Government or not. On all sides I am convinced that if the Bolsheviks win, they will immediately set to work for a separate peace . . .' (What happened when British officers and agents began to spend what Buchanan called 'sufficient money' will be seen in the next chapter.)

But reports from Russian GHQ at Mogilev were contradictory. On September 24, the CIGS informed the War Cabinet that Barter had wired that the Allied military envoys had jointly paid their respects to Kerensky (the official C.-in-C.), 'who had promised to endeavour to restore the discipline of officers in the Russian army, and had given an undertaking that representatives of the soviet would not be allowed to interfere at the front'. This was sheer moonshine. But on the 27th, the CIGS reported that Barter admitted that it was felt 'in some quarters' that the Bolsheviks might get into power, 'in which case there was a possibility of a separate peace'.[38]

The Germans, in fact, had good cause for satisfaction. On the 29th, Baron Richard von Kühlmann, the new Foreign Minister, summarised their Russian policy in a lengthy telegram to the German High Command: 'The military operations on the Eastern Front, which were prepared on a large scale and have been carried out with great success, were seconded by intensive undermining activities inside Russia on the part of the Foreign Ministry. Our first interest, in these activities, was to further nationalist and separatist endeavours as far as possible and

D

to give strong support to the revolutionary elements. We have now been engaged in these activities for some time, and in complete agreement with the Political Section of the General Staff in Berlin. Our work together has shown tangible results. The Bolshevik movement could never have attained the scale or the influence which it has today without our continual support. There is every indication that the movement will continue to grow . . . According to the most recent reports received here, the situation in Russia is that the country, whose economic life has been shattered, and which is only just being held together by English agents, could be expected to collapse as a result of any further, fairly powerful shock . . .'[39] (In fact, the Bolsheviks at this moment were extremely chary of accepting any further German money. On October 7 the Bolshevik central committee carefully recorded in their minutes that they would not accept money from the German agent Karl Moor – though Professor Katkov feels that they may well have done so *sub rosa*.)

In Petrograd, the Bolsheviks continued to hammer away at the British connection. In particular, they still raged in their newspapers at the British support for Kornilov and still threatened direct action. On October 2 (as the War Cabinet in fact refused an official Russian request for British anti-aircraft guns to protect Petrograd), Kerensky, at Buchanan's urgent request, had a categorical denial published in the Russian press that British armoured cars had taken any part in Kornilov's revolt.[40]

On October 8, after much wrangling, Kerensky formed a coalition government of sorts to rule Russia until the Constituent Assembly met. Trotsky, the new president of the Petrograd soviet, at once denounced it as a 'government of civil war', and refused to support it. 'The Bolsheviks, who form a compact minority, have alone a definite programme,' Buchanan warned the Foreign Office. If the provisional government could not put them down by force, the 'only alternative will be a Bolshevik Government.'

By now, October 1917, Russia was bankrupt as well. The total Russian state debt amounted to 70 milliard roubles, of which 15·7 milliard were internal long-term loans, 25 foreign long-term loans (15·5 owing to France, 7·5 to England, and 3·23 to other countries), and 28·3 in paper money and short-term loans. The interest and sinking fund on all this was 4·5 milliard roubles, which was more than the whole state revenue in 1916. Of this, over 2 milliard were directly payable to foreign banks and governments. Soon, the whole Russian debt would have to be taken over as a mortgage to foreign banks in guarantee for further financial assistance in carrying on the war. Indeed, the process of handing over native industries to foreign banks was already far advanced by the autumn of 1917. As the final economic crash approached,

British and French banks (particularly the British in Petrograd and Moscow) became more and more the trustees for their Russian clients, whose deposits and shares they held; and Russian industrialists, mine-owners and financiers were only too anxious to hide behind Allied banks.

On October 9, Buchanan and the French and Italian ambassadors came, on instructions, to see Kerensky. Under great emotional stress, Buchanan, as spokesman, began to read out, in a 'quavering, nervous voice', a very strong note, which stated that the Allies could not allow 'anarchy' to continue in Russia, that Kerensky must now apply the energetic measures, which had been so long delayed, otherwise the Allies could not undertake to give 'necessary material and financial support to Russia'.[41]

The Russian bourgeoisie had to watch out now, or else British banks would no longer provide the necessary asylum for paper war-profits, or take over the shares of Russian industrial syndicates at other than knock-down prices, or guarantee further loans.

Since it was only Kornilov's 'lunatic action' that had created such disorder, Kerensky was 'really incensed', returned the Allied note, delivered a few crisp words, and with a wave of his hand, strode out of the room – and went straight to the American Embassy to thank the American Ambassador, Francis, for not having participated in this démarche. Buchanan also was incensed; Kerensky had no business to treat Allied ambassadors 'so cavalierly', he complained to the Russian Foreign Minister, Tereschenko. Events in Petrograd were becoming a little unreal.[41]

On October 11, the War Cabinet called in several very senior British officers to advise them on the general military position, as some very important decisions now had to be taken. 'The fourth military campaign of the war was drawing to a close without promising prospects of decisive results, and there were elements of great difficulty in the situation,' stated the Prime Minister, Lloyd George. One of the factors which caused the 'most anxiety' to the War Cabinet was the 'military collapse of Russia, which introduced a new situation. Since the beginning of the Revolution, the [British] Government had always hoped for a recovery,' state the Cabinet minutes, 'but up to now their hopes had been dis-appointed. Telegrams arrived from time to time suggesting that a solid [Russian] Government had now been formed, and that the troops would be better, but there was no real improvement, and the Russian Army had failed completely. The recent incident in which General Kornilov had been concerned had only made matters worse.' It was thus prob-able that in 1918 Russia could virtually be ruled out of the war. Next day, the CIGS informed the War Cabinet that 59 third line Russian divisions were to be disbanded; this would reduce the total number of Russian divisions from 229 to 170. But even this figure proved to be a gross exaggeration.[42]

'Nothing very exciting here,' wrote General Poole in Petrograd to Colonel Byrne in London on October 15, 'a sort of political truce at present, but on the whole I think the Bolsheviks are top dog, so directly the Govt. try to do anything they will kybosh them . . . I am taking up the question of the smuggling from Finland to Sweden to Germany which is reaching a serious stage,' he stated. 'Will you see that *The Times* which is addressed to me daily at your office comes along always in the bag,' he reminded Byrne.[43]

Then a new idea was put forward to resuscitate the Russian army. On October 23, the War Cabinet considered a paper by the Russian expert, Professor (later Sir) Bernard Pares on the movement in Russia for the formation of a volunteer army, to meet the need for a 'more conscious discipline in the Army, as produced by the Revolution', so as to counter the present disruption of discipline, 'and the consequent disasters'. Professor Pares, in a paper written in Petrograd on August 16, before Kornilov's coup, stated that the originators of the movement were officers and men in the Russian army and navy, who were 'all convinced adherents of the Revolution, principally from the Socialist parties . . .' The movement, he wrote, 'declares clearly for war till complete victory in absolute union with the Allies, the strictest discipline, allegiance only to the provisional government, obedience only to the Military Chiefs, no regimental committees, except for household purposes, exclusion of all who break this oath, also for the rights of smaller peoples.'[44] On these lines, various units had sprung up, like the League of Knights of St George (which had played a prominent part in Kornilov's revolt), which were all grouped together in the 'semi-official' All-Russian Central Volunteer Committee, under the then Russian C.-in-C., General Kornilov. (This paper was written, it must be re-emphasised, on August 16, before Kornilov's revolt.) 'The attitude of this Committee towards England was of the most cordial character,' Lord Derby, the Secretary of State for War, told the War Cabinet, 'and Professor Pares had been asked to act on it as connecting it with England. Professor Pares submitted that we had every political and military reason for giving the strongest moral and, where possible, material support to this movement.' Pares urged that permission be given for Colonel Blair in Petrograd, and for carefully selected British military instructors to help the committee to organise the movement. But the War Cabinet (already clutching at straws as over the proposal for the use of Japanese troops in Russia) approved Lord Derby's action in informing Professor Pares that it would be 'quite impossible' for us to make such a suggestion to the Russian government, 'but that if asked for such assistance officially, we would do our best to give it'. The Colonial Secretary, Walter Long, however, urged that the proposal should be wired to Buchanan, who should be told that if he could bring the matter informally before the Russian government, and secure their support, 'we would most gladly give our assistance in every way possible.' The War Cabinet was thus divided. It was agreed that Balfour should discuss the matter with the Russian envoys who were shortly coming to this country, en route for an Allied conference.[44]

(The War Cabinet would undoubtedly have shown more interest at this early stage if they had known that the guiding spirit, if not the actual leader, of the movement for a volunteer army was none other than General Alexeiev, Chief of Staff both to the Tsar, and now to Kerensky – and Russia's most distinguished soldier. A quiet, modest and retiring man, of delicate health, with an intellectual and scholarly approach to the science of war, he was quite unlike the average Russian general. Though no slavish courtier, he had been completely trusted by the Tsar when appointed Chief of Staff in mid-1915, and was constantly in the Tsar's company and at his table; but Alexeiev was an effective Russian C.-in-C. He was popular with all Russian officers, who respected his military knowledge and knew that he had risen to the highest rank solely on his merits. His reputation as a strategist was respected by the Allies. He was thus a very different general to Kornilov; and after the failure of Kornilov's adventure, Alexeiev set about approaching the Russian officers, who were now in a high state of demoralisation, about the formation of a new type of Russian army, based not on the principle of military adventure, but on the moral values, essentially liberal, of the March revolution. As many Russian officers were now of humble origin, and some had even welcomed the revolution, this was an effective approach, and officer groups were soon assembled, ready to move off to southern Russia, where Alexeiev intended to build up his volunteer army, far from the big cities of the north.)[44]

After the political lull which had followed Kornilov's revolt, things were now hotting up again in the Russian capital, and there was never any chance to discuss this idea. On October 20, Lenin had returned in disguise from Finland to Petrograd. On the 23rd, the Bolshevik central committee decided to launch an armed uprising, and Trotsky created a 'Military Revolutionary Committee' to organise a 'Red Guard' of 20,000 armed factory workers. This soon became known. On the 25th, Kerensky told Buchanan that the Bolsheviks 'would probably rise in the course of the next few weeks . . .' Major Percy Banting (Poole's new Chief of Staff, who had taken over from Finlayson, who was ill) confirmed this in a letter to Colonel Byrne in late October. 'We are all due to have our throats cut on Friday of this week [probably November 2] – so says the Bolshevik. It is to be a real good rising this time, but as it is published everywhere I am sure nothing will happen . . .'[45]

On October 31, Somerset Maugham, who was acting for the Secret Intelligence Service, saw Kerensky who urged the Allies to make an immediate offer of peace, without annexations or indemnities, to Germany; only if the Germans refused would Russian troops fight on – and then only to defend Russian territory. Kerensky also again complained of the lack of regular Allied aid – and demanded the recall of the *Times* correspondent in Petrograd, and of Buchanan – in that order. (He had been sent out, Maugham writes, as a 'private agent' to contact parties hostile to the provisional government and to 'devise a scheme' to prevent the Bolsheviks seizing power, and thus keep Russia in the war. Some task! Maugham's secret report (now in the Lloyd George papers) is of some interest, not only in view of his extremely unflattering portrayal of Buchanan in the short story 'His Excellency', but also because of his Ashenden stories. The report is written in a sort of baby talk. Perhaps Maugham wished to give an impression of how Kerensky actually spoke. It certainly reads very oddly. It was of no use, however, as it only reached the Prime Minister via Sir William Wiseman in Washington, on November 18.)[46]

On November 1, the Director of Military Operations informed the War Cabinet of two further telegrams from General Barter at Mogilev, which gave a 'more encouraging' account of the state of the Russian army; some 400,000 'good' troops would be ready by January 1918, and the volunteer movement, of which Professor Pares had given the first news, was 'more promising'. Balfour stated, however, that he had just had a telegram from Lord Reading (then British Ambassador in Washington), who stated that the Russian situation was reported to be worse than ever before, 'and that peace would probably be made within two months, unless Japanese and American divisions were sent to pull the nation together'. The Russian Ambassador in Washington was already 'talking peace'.[47]

The War Cabinet were then told that in a telegram from Tokyo, dated October 20, it was stated that the Japanese Foreign Minister had categorically informed the Russian Ambassador 'that the question of the despatch of [Japanese] troops to Europe had been decided once and for all, and that the [Japanese] Government would not change its mind'. The War Cabinet, clutching at more straws, then considered the other alternative, the use of American troops in Russia. It was pointed out that there would be too many American troops to be brought across the Atlantic; some could therefore be sent across the Pacific – which would result in a 'net gain' to the Allied forces in Russia. The War Cabinet decided that Balfour should inform Reading tactfully that 'while it was not for this country to indicate to the United States what they should do in the matter of strengthening the moral of the Russian Army, at the same time, if the United States Government saw their way to send a force to Russia, His Majesty's Government felt that the effect would be very good'. Lord Reading should also be informed of General Barter's telegram, and told that this confirmed information already received from other quarters about the 'good prospect' of the volunteer movement in Russia. Thus, the War Cabinet were pressing the United States government to send American troops to Russia even before the Bolshevik revolution.[47]

In Petrograd, the die was now cast. 'The Bolshevik trial of strength is expected for Wednesday, November 7th,' noted Knox on the 1st. 'The political situation is not improving,' wrote Poole in a letter to Colonel Byrne on the 3rd. 'There was a great demonstration planned by the Bolsheviks for yesterday to dam [sic] the Government, but it has not come off so far. Both sides are afraid of each other – Kerensky is well defended in the Winter Palace with the troops he can depend on, and machine-guns; Lenin and Trotsky are equally safe across the river . . . The worst feature of all is the growth of anti-Ally and pro-German feeling – particularly at Moscow . . . Sir G.B. [ie, Buchanan] is going home next week. A little rest will do him good, and he will be able to bring the F.O. ideas up to date.'[48]

Another of Poole's officers, Captain Frank Pinder, was more explicit about the situation when he also wrote to Colonel Byrne on November 3. 'The Bolsheviks were expected out yesterday again, but nothing happened. At the Winter Palace there were several armoured cars in the square, surrounded by soldiers, in case of emergency. The Government and the Bolsheviks are, however, equally afraid of each other, and so both hesitate to begin the fight. The population are of course very pessimistic, and rumours and scares consequently abound. My impression is that the muddle is worse than at the time of your departure [on September 14], and there appears little chance of the Government doing anything. Razgromi (burglaries with violence) are exceedingly numerous in Petrograd, and the latest departure is for gangs of hooligans to hold up women and girls and deprive them of their footwear and purses. In the country, there is a far worse state of things, and estates and houses are burned and pillaged to an alarming extent. Unfortunately the "Intelligentsia" is too down in the mouth to do what would happen in any other country, ie, to organise and at least defend themselves against burglary and breaches of the peace. Their constant wail is "Why do not the Allies send the Japanese into Russia to put things right?" This cry you may have heard previously, but it is now the one refrain.' Their Russian liaison officer had just heard, 'on what he claimed to be unimpeachable authority, that two officers belonging to his regiment had been boiled alive,' concluded Pinder wearily. 'The sale of boots, rifles and precious stones and jewels is still proceeding apace on the Fontanka . . .'[49]

Major Banting also added a note for Colonel Byrne that day, but in lighter tone. 'There is very little to report . . . we have not had our throats cut as per schedule. We have a small but very select supper party on tonight at a doubtful place. I will give details in my next letter. There are rumours of beautiful maidens dancing round the supper tables, etc.'[49]

On November 5, the War Cabinet were told that General Knox had reported that there was now great difficulty in feeding the Russian army. 'Supplies at Petrograd are very short, and there was said to be only one day's reserve of forage.'[50]

Everyone in Petrograd was now more or less resigned to the impending Bolshevik coup. Bank directors, in anticipation, withdrew very large sums in cash from the State Bank, on which they depended for their supply of rouble notes. But even if the provisional government were overthrown, the Bolsheviks 'would not be able to hold out for long', Buchanan reported on the 5th, 'and would sooner or later provoke a counter-revolution'. News came through that a Cossack conference had been convened early in October in the Caucasus, under General Kaledin, the Don Cossack *Ataman*, and had formed a 'South-Eastern Union', and was going to set up a Russian federal republic.

The provisional government called out the only reliable troops it could find in Petrograd – some young officer cadets and a battalion of women, whom Knox watched marching past the British Embassy 'with a lump in the throat', he admits. On the evening of the 6th, after the Cossacks in Petrograd decided not to support Kerensky, who had called them counter-revolutionaries and Kornilov a 'traitor', the Bolsheviks seized the railway stations, the bridges and the State Bank. Only the Winter Palace held out.[51]

Next morning, however, as Kerensky set out for the front to find more loyal troops, Knox was surprised to find 'perfect order' prevailing. That afternoon, while Buchanan walked down to the Winter Palace square, and watched events from a distance, Knox called on the unfortunate Petrograd commander, who 'thanked me quite touchingly for having come to see him'. On his way, Knox met a friend, a Russian officer who had been at the Cossack conference in the Caucasus and was now in Petrograd on 'purely private affairs. He was in high spirits,' Knox records; and as they walked across the Winter Palace square, he told Knox that the Cossacks would hold back grain, coal and oil from the north. Knox also found the General Staff 'quite unperturbed'; the quarrel between the provisional government and the Petrograd soviet, it was explained, 'did not concern the General Staff . . .'[52]

On the evening of November 7, Major Banting wrote a further note to Colonel Byrne. 'The Bridges over the river are closed tonight & there are many indications of trouble brewing, but no one seems to know quite what [it] is all about. The Bolsheviks are supposed to be going to fight, the only thing we can't quite find out is "with whom they are going to fight", as the Govt seems to have no following at all amongst the so-called soldiers here – all merry & bright @ 104 (Moika).'[53]

Later that evening, while the trams in fact ran as usual over the Troitsky bridge, Buchanan and his wife watched from the windows of the British Embassy as the Bolsheviks opened up a haphazard fusillade against the Winter Palace; and early next morning, it fell to the Red Guards.

So the Bolshevik revolution became a fact. 'Quite probably an ultimate victory of Bolshevism was predetermined by the entire political, economic and social condition of Russia in 1917,' writes Chamberlin. 'But Kornilov's futile, clumsy thrust for power facilitated and expedited this victory.' In fact, there was nothing 'inevitable' about Lenin's revolution in November 1917 at all. He was handed his 'revolution' on a plate by a myopic general and an hysterical premier. History in this century has recorded many instances when a revolution looked 'inevitable', but has not taken place. Something, the right thing, has to trigger it off. Lenin, as he himself admits, never dreamed that the Kornilov–Kerensky combination would virtually hand Russia over to him.[54]

# 4

## The Bolsheviks in Power

ON November 8, the day after the fall of the Winter Palace, the second congress of Soviets, then in session at Smolny, approved the formation of the new Bolshevik government (officially known as the Council of People's Commissars). Lenin became President, and Trotsky the Commissar for Foreign Affairs. It was at once decided to make an immediate peace, to distribute land to the peasants, and for the workers to take over the factories.

The initial local British reaction to the Bolshevik coup, and to the disjointed events that followed, can best be seen in some extracts from a series of letters from General Poole and his officers in Petrograd to Colonel Byrne in London.[1]

'On Nov. 6th, the Bolsheviks began to act and completely cornered the Govt,' wrote General Poole. 'By daylight on the 7th, they had complete control of the Town except for the Ministers themselves who held out in the Winter Palace, guarded by the Women's battn, and a detachment of boys!!'

By now, went on Captain Frank Pinder, the Baltic fleet had sent up the large cruiser *Aurora*, two small cruisers, two torpedo boats, a gunboat and two transports to support the Bolsheviks. 'On the night of 7th instant, the Maximalists [*ie*, the Bolsheviks] opened fire on the Winter Palace from 3″ field guns ranged in the Square. The affair started at 10 to 9 p.m., & at 10.10 the *Aurora* opened with her big guns, probably firing blank, just to make a noise.' (Major Percy Banting expands on this: 'They brought up a field gun under the arch leading into the Winter Palace Square from the Hotel de France & there was some small naval gun firing from a boat which arrived from Kronstadt. There was also a considerable amount of rifle & m/c gun fire.')

Pinder goes on: 'The Palace was held by the Women's Battalion & some cadets. The place was carried at 1 a.m., the cadets slaughtered

& the women submitted to the usual treatment. Kerensky escaped ["in a motor lent him by the Americans, on the morning of the 7th," states Poole], the remaining Ministers were taken & subsequently released. The Palace has been pillaged & the booty taken to Kronstadt. Most of the wall-pictures were bayonetted, & upholstery slashed.'[1]

Poole continues: 'There was absolute order & quiet in the Town & the B[olshevik]'s issued very stringent orders against looting.' (That morning [the 8th], General Knox walked down to the General Staff offices, where their 'unconcerned aloofness' astounded him. Loyal troops were coming from the front, he was told. One Russian politician told him that he gave the Bolsheviks 'about two days'. The non-Bolshevik socialists, he heard, were forming a committee of public safety.)

'The B's began to form their Govt, but they were not supported by any other section of the Socialistic party, so they were soon up against it,' writes Poole. 'Meanwhile Kerensky had got to Gatchina, where he began to raise the opposition, with the Cossacks as a foundation. Gradually his influence began to tell. He occupied Gatchina yesterday [the 10th] – after a "bloody battle"! (Ewart [another of Poole's officers] walked over the battlefield during the fight and didn't know it was going on!!!) The Bolsheviks were driven out of Tsarskoe Selo and fell back on Petrograd, & K's troops followed. Last night K's advanced troops were a mile or two outside Pet. and today the great battle is taking place. I hear a few shots now as I write. The attitude of the officers here is extreme terror – most of them are disguised in plain clothes & unshaven! I suppose the latter is a sop to the Bolshevik prejudices. The soldiers & sailors don't much want to fight either way. They want to sit on the fence & join the winner. The "Red Guard", *ie*, armed workmen, put up a little show but they are not experts with the rifle so won't stay long.

'I suppose Kerensky will be on top by nightfall. I don't fancy he'll stay long . . . All sorts of rumours of plots & counterplots are on foot, but nothing definite.'[1]

Major Banting continued with his own account: 'Apparently he [Kerensky] marched on Tsarskoe Selo on Friday [the 9th] & took it the same evening & was expected in Petrograd on the Saturday. However, he did not turn up & in the meantime the Bolshevik sailors from Kronstadt had arrived. On the Sunday [the 11th] Kerensky had apparently arranged to definitely march into Petrograd & consequently his supporters in Petrograd took action here.

'The Astoria was seized & the Bolshevik guard turned out & the Telephone Exchange was held by the Cadets & various armoured cars manned by the Cadets were rushing about the place.' (During the firing, Knox met a Russian officer friend walking arm-in-arm with a lady in the next street. 'I expressed my astonishment that he took no interest in the fighting, and he said that it had nothing to do with him!' records Knox.)[1]

'The whole show was messed up owing to the fact that, as might easily have been anticipated, there was trouble with Kerensky's soldiers & Kerensky himself started sending & receiving delegates. This played straight into the hands of the Bolsheviks, who had been in a real funk on Saturday night [the 10th] & would have run like rabbits if K. had come on – as it was, they got the upper hand on Sunday afternoon & smashed up two of the Cadet schools, killing about 80 Cadets, retook the Telephone Exchange & Astoria, etc. There were also minor scraps & shooting all over the place.

'The net result of the whole show on Monday [the 12th] was that the "Bolsheviks" were in full power & the town was perfectly quiet except for a few murders of cadets & officers. The Russian officers in the Astoria were mostly chucked out or locked up in their rooms. Except for the excitement, the Allied officers in the Astoria had no trouble, the restaurant, etc. there was of course out of action.' (Pinder added: 'The better-class population is in a state of complete panic & all doors are shut & guarded by occupants of the various apartments in turn, as arranged by the house committee. At night, the streets are practically deserted.')

'The Bolsheviks are by no means in a position to "carry on" here,' Banting went on, 'as the various Govt Depts are closed due to the staffs refusing to have anything to do with them. Although Bolsheviks guard the State Bank, the latter refuse to pay out anything. A possible solution is the formation of a Socialistic Govt which will amalgamate all the various socialistic parties. Kerensky is apparently a wash out – not being wanted by either side. From all sources of information it wd appear that we shall probably have the Bolsheviks on top for 2 or 3 weeks. The key note of the whole situation is *Food*. If they cannot keep up the supplies of food in Petrograd, they will soon be chucked out.

'The news from Moscow is very scrappy. Most of the reports say that the Bolsheviks have been beaten down there.

'There is no news from the front, but the Germans are not thought of at all here. The Bolshevik programme when they came into power was:

1. Immediate armistice on *all* fronts for three months to settle peace terms.
2. Division of all land without compensation amongst the peasants.
3. All Industrial concerns to be under the management of the Workmen.

Looks quite good on paper for the "Bolshevik" soldier, peasant & workman. Lenin himself said in one of his speeches that it would take some time to arrange the peace.

'There is one aspect of the situation which may be beneficial to the Allies. By fraternization with the Germans, the poison of the Bolshevik programme may spread into Germany, and anyhow the programme must be very distasteful to the German authorities & for this reason they could not very well treat for peace terms with a party holding such views.[1]

'From the above you will see that there is generally a pretty kettle of fish here & it is impossible to say what may happen next.'

Poole added in his own hand a postscript to Banting's letter:
'My ideas are

1. There is little or no fight in either side and whatever happens, they will be no further use in the war, either for offensive or defensive purposes. We can practically rule them out of all court.
2. The Bolsheviks are now in complete control of the City. There is a strong feeling against them on the part of the more educated classes – and the result will be a sort of coalition Govt – which may or may not last – probably the latter.
3. In a few days I will advise definitely as to the desirability of sending any more supplies.
4. Damn all these chicken-hearted peoples who have no guts to stick out a war!!!'

But some British officers were now lapsing into amused but apathetic despair. 'I can't see how room can be found for the English much longer in this mad house,' wrote Colonel John Neilson on the 19th. 'I think Petersburg and the Nevski Strasse will miss us but as few of us can speak German we would be rather out of place! Perhaps we will be interned!! Can you picture it? The Ambassador with a straggling beard leaning against the barbed wire luring insects from their fastnesses in his *shuba*. He will wear his eye-glass still and still look the Diplomat. Lady G. [Buchanan] with unpowdered nose and straw in her hair. Poole will be cheerful – Knox blasphemous . . .

'Nice friendly Allies we have chosen, haven't we? No Englishman is allowed to leave the country. Are we being kept to drag the conquerors' chariots? Make sport for the soldiery? General von Sauerkrout in his carriage being dragged down the Nevski by Sir George and Knox while Lady G. and Meriel [her daughter] wave palm branches over his head! I wonder what job I will get?'[2]

Knox and Buchanan took a more sober, but equally pessimistic view. 'I agree with Trotsky that the only opposition the Bolsheviks had to fear was from Kornilov's and Kaledin's party,' records Knox, 'and that is now past.' Buchanan agreed. 'At the present moment force alone counts,' he wrote in his diary on the 19th, and as the bourgeois parties had failed to organise themselves, the situation was 'now hopeless'. This was quite correct.[3]

The German reaction to the Bolshevik coup was more complicated. The Germans, of course, wanted to make an immediate peace with the Bolsheviks, their former clandestine protégés, and now their official Russian adversaries; but to enable the Bolsheviks to agree, the Germans had to continue to give them discreet financial support to keep them in power. The first warning of the dangers inherent in this dual policy came from the German Legation in Stockholm, the main German listening post for events in Petrograd, and now also the main point of contact between the Germans and the Bolsheviks, since it was the only place outside Russia where there was already a Bolshevik foreign mission. 'I urgently recommend that all public announcements of amicable agreement with Russia be avoided in the German and Austrian press,' wired the German Minister in Stockholm to the Foreign Ministry in Berlin on November 8 (the day after the Bolshevik coup). 'Amicable agreement with imperial states cannot possibly be accepted as a watchword by the Bolsheviks. They can only justify peace with Germany by citing the will of the people and Russia's desperate position.' The Bolsheviks, he was assured, could only explain 'friendly words' from Germany as proof of German weakness in face of the British. 'It would be advisable for the [German] press to exercise moderation, especially as the extent of the Bolsheviks' victory is not yet certain, since they control the Telegraph Agency.' A copy of this wire was sent to the German High Command.[4]

On November 9, the Petrograd Telegraph Agency broadcast conditions, approved by the Bolshevik government, for a peace offer. The German High Command refused to have it published. Kühlmann, the Foreign Secretary, agreed. 'The view that the utmost moderation should be exercised is shared here,' he assured the German High Command the same day. 'The press has been instructed accordingly.' Reports from Stockholm warned that it would also be inadvisable for any German peace offers to be made at the front; and if the Russians made any general peace offers, these should merely be accepted, and no more. 'According to further reports from Stockholm, the Bolsheviks there have said that the new government could only remain in power if it achieved a cease-fire in the immediate future,' Kühlmann added.

But Count Czernin, the Austro-Hungarian Foreign Minister, rushed ahead. On the 10th, having commented favourably on the Bolshevik peace offer in his foreign news bulletin, he wired to Berlin strongly urging Kühlmann to do likewise. Kühlmann wired back that all his reports agreed that the struggle between Lenin and Kerensky was not yet over, and the Bolshevik regime was therefore by no means stable. Hence by a premature acceptance of the unofficial Bolshevik peace offer, which had only been reported by the Telegraph Agency, 'we should only be taking the risk of appearing weak'. Czernin, desperate for peace with Russia, wrote at length the same day to the German Chancellor. The latest Russian revolution had come sooner than imagined, he wrote. But there were numerous signs that Bolshevik power would be more than temporary; Lenin had to achieve a democratic peace, and the Central Powers must therefore reconsider their war aims. Whether Lenin could maintain his power *'for any considerable time'* was a question nobody could answer. 'For this very reason, however, it would seem essential to exploit this moment, and to offer them all the help that they would need . . . If the Leninists were to succeed even in bringing about the promised armistice, then, it seems to me, we should have won almost a complete victory on the Russian sector, for . . . the Russian Army, in its present state, would surely pour back into the hinterland in order to be on the spot when the estates are distributed.' Lenin first seemed to want to renew his attempt to achieve a general peace. If the Allies refused, as was certain, he would then have to conclude a separate peace with the Central Powers. 'However, he will only wish to do this, or be able to, if we accept the formula, peace "without annexations or reparations",' Czernin emphasised. He urged Kühlmann to give a press interview to explain this. In view of their recent great military successes [*ie*, on the Italian front], there was 'no reason to fear that a statement in these terms could be interpreted as a sign of our weakness,' he wrote. Indeed by such a step, 'we should take every gust of wind out of the sails of our Socialist parties, with whom Lenin is already trying to open relations . . .' The present moment should not be lost. There was also the economic factor, 'for, after a break with the Western Powers, Russia will be forced to rely economically on the Central Powers, who will then have the opportunity of penetrating and reorganising Russian economic life . . .' The Chancellor passed Czernin's letter on to Kühlmann for his observations.[4]

On November 12 (when the Bolshevik peace conditions appeared in the German press), Kurt Riezler, a counsellor at the German Legation in Stockholm and an expert in subversion in Russia, submitted to the German Chancellor an explanatory report on the new Russian situation. Both Lenin and Trotsky had great strength of personality, he said, 'and both are practical revolutionaries in the grand manner'. He stressed Trotsky's 'burning hatred' of the British, as a result of his temporary imprisonment in Nova Scotia on his way back to Russia from New York. 'Even if the power of the Bolsheviks in Russia only lasts a few weeks, the country will almost certainly have to face terror such as even France under Marat hardly experienced . . .' The Bolsheviks would completely eliminate the existing administration, and give all power to the soviets. 'If they are successful in this, even for only a few weeks and even if no cease-fire agreement should be reached, the country will cease to figure in . . . the World War, and it would take the old regime, which would presumably be restored in this case, years to restore order among the chaos.' Riezler, the Russian expert, foresaw a short life for the Bolsheviks.

Kühlmann sent the Chancellor his observations on Count Czernin's letter on the 13th. As he had already told Czernin himself, a premature answer to the unofficial Bolshevik peace offer would only give an impression of German weakness. 'I am still not prepared to drop this objection,' stated Kühlmann. He had just received an unconfirmed report from Stockholm that Kerensky, Kornilov and Kaledin had occupied Petrograd, and that Lenin and his followers were entrenched in the Smolny quarter. 'Informed Russian circles here [ie, Stockholm] believe that the Bolshevik rising has, for the moment, been liquidated,' the report stated, 'and that any future government in Russia has no choice but to follow a determined peace policy.'

'According to [other] reports from our Legation in Stockholm,' Kühlmann went on, 'the Entente Powers are reckoning with the collapse of the Bolshevik Government within two to three weeks.' It would thus be better to await the further course of events in Petrograd. 'A nervous and hasty policy in this matter would only spoil things.' Though Kühlmann's reports from both Petrograd and Stockholm were inaccurate, he proved himself a good, cautious diplomat.[4]

Helphand (who had been banished after the revelations in July of his financial connections with the Bolsheviks), now reappeared on the scene. On November 14, as he was being received by Count Czernin in Vienna, he had a wire from Radek, head of the Bolshevik mission in Stockholm, urging him to return to Sweden at once; the Bolsheviks needed immediate German and Austrian socialist support. Helphand called at the Foreign Ministry in Berlin and urged that there should be a swift response to the Bolshevik peace offer, which would cause the Russian army to disintegrate, consolidate the Bolsheviks in power, and enable them to win over the constituent assembly, which was soon to meet. The Russian market and penetration of Russian industry, he added, were more important than the seizure of more Russian territory. (Helphand, in fact, was largely repeating Czernin's arguments to Kühlmann.)[5]

Now that the Bolsheviks were actually in power, Helphand thought that the German socialists would be more useful than the German diplomats. But the socialists turned down the Bolshevik request for demonstrations and strikes in Germany; they would not at present attack the German government, only agitate for a negotiated peace. It was therefore decided that Helphand should go at once to Stockholm to discuss with the Bolshevik mission a draft German socialist resolution expressing sympathy with the Bolshevik victory, which would be read out at mass meetings in Germany. Helphand reached Stockholm on November 17, and Radek at once approved the German resolution. But Helphand had other business to discuss as well. He offered his services to the Bolshevik government and asked Radek to obtain Lenin's permission for him to return to Russia. As he knew that his wartime policy was suspect in Bolshevik circles, he would defend himself before a workers' court, whose verdict he would accept. Helphand, with all his high-level contacts, vast financial resources and general ability, would have been a great asset to the struggling Bolshevik party at this difficult moment; but he knew too much about the financial dealings between the Germans and the Bolsheviks – indeed, he had been the main intermediary, and had been exposed as such in July. What might he say before a workers' court? Radek set off in haste to ask Lenin.[5]

Helphand then went to the German Legation in Stockholm to have the approved resolution despatched to Berlin. There he met Kurt Riezler, who strongly disapproved of its being sent. The resolution, however, was despatched in time for the meetings in Germany, which were to take place on November 18; but the Foreign Ministry thought it too explosive, and sat on it until after the meetings had taken place. As a result, the German socialists attacked Helphand in the Reichstag, the German diplomats strongly criticised him in Stockholm – and the German General Staff placed him under close surveillance. But for Helphand, the great moment had arrived; it was now or never. On the 18th, as he waited impatiently for Lenin's answer, the Austrian Ambassador in Stockholm explained in a wire to Vienna what Helphand was really up to. He had entirely different aims to those of the German Foreign Ministry, and 'wants to crown his endeavour by bringing about, so to speak, a peace of brotherliness, under his own auspices . . . Helphand is working, if I may say so, one third for the Central Powers, one third for Social Democracy, and one third for Russia . . .'[5]

But all this time, while discussions continued between Berlin and Vienna on whether or not to respond to the Bolshevik peace offer, and while Helphand wove his own, highly personal web, the Germans were continuing to give the Bolsheviks discreet financial support in order to keep them in power. On November 8, the day after the

Bolshevik coup, Riezler wired cryptically from Stockholm to Diego von Bergen, the senior Foreign Ministry official responsible for relations with the Russian revolutionaries, 'Please forward two millions of the War Loan for agreed purposes.' (This was perhaps about £60,000.) As a result of this, Bergen had immediate discussion with the Treasury. On the 9th, Kühlmann wrote privately to the Secretary of the Treasury requesting the allocation of 15 million marks (about £500,000) to the Foreign Ministry, as a result of Bergen's discussions, for 'political propaganda' in Russia, and reserving the right to ask for more in the near future. Bergen wired equally cryptically to the German Minister in Berne: 'In view of the events in Russia, Baier's journey to the North is desirable.' Baier was the code-name for Karl Moor, who was now resting in Switzerland, after having spent the summer and autumn channelling German funds into the Bolshevik mission in Stockholm. On November 10, the Treasury having agreed to the allocation of 15 million marks, Bergen replied to Riezler in Stockholm: 'Half of desired sum will be taken on Sunday [the 11th] . . . Remainder on Tuesday. Further sums available if necessary . . .'[6]

But the Bolsheviks were not the only Russian revolutionary group receiving discreet German financial support. Since August 1916, the Germans had been supporting an SR politician, who was close to the SR leader, Chernov – but whom the provisional government had reportedly imprisoned on a charge of high treason, since they had proof of his connection with the Central Powers. This, it seems, had cut the Germans off from the SR (but explains the strong feelings of Kornilov and others towards Chernov). On November 10, the German Legation in Copenhagen wired that one Löwenstein, a friend of the imprisoned SR politican, urgently needed 20,000 marks to finance the despatch of two confidential agents to Petrograd to maintain contact with the SR party. 'It appears essential to speed up the matter, as longer inactivity may arouse suspicion,' the legation stated. An appreciation of the Russian situation by Löwenstein was also sent, which closely resembled that of Count Czernin, and asked for guidance for his confidential agents. '20,000 marks for Blau [Löwenstein's cover name] approved,' replied the Foreign Ministry on the 11th. 'He can send a message to Russia that the Imperial Government still stands on the basis of the Reichstag resolution.* If necessary, this can be stressed publicly when the opportunity arises.' (Professor Katkov remarks that this channel of communication, via Blau, was 'rather ineffectual'.)[6]

---

* On July 6, 1917, the German Catholic Deputy, Matthias Erzberger, had proposed in the Reichstag that Germany should renounce territorial annexations in order to facilitate a negotiated peace. On July 19, the Reichstag had passed a rather watered-down peace resolution along these lines.

On November 15, the German Minister in Berne replied to Bergen. 'Baier asked that Nasse [the German Military Attaché at Berne, then in Berlin, and the great German spymaster for delivering German funds to the Bolsheviks] should be told of the following telegram from Stockholm: "Please fulfil your promise immediately. We have committed ourselves on this basis, because great demands are being made on us. Vorovski." Baier let me know that this message may make his journey to the North more urgent.' (The 'basis' referred to by Vorovski – of the Bolshevik mission in Stockholm – for which Karl Moor had evidently promised further support, was probably the conclusion of peace between Russia and Germany.)[6]

Thus, the German Foreign Ministry was unofficially channelling in funds to the Bolsheviks to keep them in power, and to the SR, at least to maintain contact with them, while officially still considering whether or not to take up the Bolshevik peace offer. In this, they were being seriously hampered by two persons. For while Helphand was agitating for an international socialist conference, the German deputy, Matthias Erzberger (whose proposal had resulted in the Reichstag peace resolution of mid-July) was negotiating for Reichstag deputies, not socialists, to take part in the peace talks. Both were negotiating with Vorovski, the only remaining member of the Bolshevik foreign mission left in Stockholm, who supported Helphand. This much alarmed the Foreign Ministry in Berlin. Helphand thought that the German and Russian socialists would reach agreement much more easily than the diplomats; both the socialist conference and the peace talks should take place in Copenhagen, he urged, and the former could bring pressure on the latter for a really democratic peace, and thus counter-balance the strong German military position. Erzberger was carrying on his negotiations, with considerable *naïveté*, through confidential agents, who were talking too much to Vorovski and crediting him with too much authority. They too were alarmed by Helphand's proposals. Even the Bolsheviks, Erzberger was informed from Stockholm on November 22, objected to the German socialists entrusting such a delicate mission to Helphand, since it would give their opponents a powerful weapon; while the anti-Bolsheviks were saying that 'hardly are the Bolsheviks at the helm before Parvus pays them their allowance'. Riezler, at the German Legation, did his best to discredit both Helphand and Erzberger in the eyes of the Bolsheviks; only direct talks with the German government, he assured them, would achieve results. With Kühlmann's approval, he informed the Bolshevik government that as soon as peace was concluded the German government would grant it a substantial loan.[7]

But Riezler still did not think the Bolsheviks would last long. 'For the moment, we are dealing with what is simply the forceful dictatorship of a handful of determined revolutionaries, whose domination is held in complete contempt by the rest of Russia, and is only tolerated because these men promise immediate peace and, as is generally known, will bring it,' Riezler reported to the German Chancellor on the 26th. 'By any reasonable judgement, the supremacy of these people will shake the whole Russian state to its roots and, in all probability, in not more than a few months, when the *raison d'être* of the new government has ceased to exist, and the war against other nations has finally been brought to an end, it will then be swept away by a flood of violent hostility throughout the rest of Russia.' Riezler strongly criticised Erzberger for trying to open negotiations between the German majority parties and the Bolsheviks. 'It would probably be a grave political error even to seem to bind the future of Russo-German relations to the fortunes of the men now in power in Russia. The duration of their government will bring no more than a cease-fire and possibly a formal peace,' Riezler pointed out.[7]

The German Minister in Stockholm strongly supported Riezler. In a report to the German Chancellor the same day, he warned that Erzberger had let the Bolsheviks know, 'some considerable time ago, that the German people wanted peace and that an agreement with him, Erzberger – as the representative of the majority parties – would bind the Imperial Government. ['An end should be finally put to this,' minuted Kühlmann in the margin.] This has undoubtedly created the double misconception in the minds of the Bolsheviks – who are very naïve in political matters – that there is a great hunger for peace in Germany, and that there is a split between the representatives of the people and the government, of which the latter can be ignored.' All this made Riezler's task more difficult. But on the 27th, it was agreed that there should be an armistice on the Russian front, and that German and Bolshevik delegates should meet at Brest-Litovsk, the German headquarters on the Eastern Front, early in December to discuss peace terms.[7]

Meanwhile, the Foreign Ministry were continuing their financial support of the Bolsheviks to keep them in power. On November 22, Bergen had agreed that Karl Moor should set out from Berne with German funds for the Bolsheviks. But on the 26th, the German Minister in Berne reported that Moor had had to postpone his departure by a week on medical advice. Nasse, the Military Attaché and spymaster, was also remaining in Berne for the time being. 'In the meantime, the requested financial aid is being despatched through safe channels.' Bergen wired back to warn that he had information that the new Petrograd government was in great financial difficulties. 'It is therefore very desirable that they be sent more money.'

Thus, as the peace talks at Brest-Litovsk were about to open, the Bolsheviks were still receiving discreet German financial support and had been promised it more openly, in the form of a substantial German loan, on their conclusion.[7]

The War Cabinet in London had not yet considered the consequences of the latest revolution in Russia – just another setback in an already hopeless situation, and coming on top of appalling news from both the French and Italian fronts. After the widespread mutinies in the French army in the spring of 1917, the British army had launched a major offensive in Flanders in late July to drive the Germans from their submarine bases in the Belgian ports and relieve German pressure on the French army while it was reorganised by General Pétain. But heavy autumn rains, coupled with the heavy bombardment by the British guns, which had destroyed the dykes and drainage system, had turned Flanders into a swamp; and all through that autumn, as the attack ground on, the casualty lists mounted. By late October, when British troops had nearly reached the village of Passchendaele, the casualties had attained horrific proportions; and the attack had failed. A few days later came news that the Italian army had been decisively defeated at Caporetto.

On October 30, General Sir Henry Wilson (who had gone out to Russia in January to encourage the Tsar to fight on) made this entry in his diary, comparing the meagre results of British efforts in France, with the major German achievements on other fronts.

1. We take Bullecourt, they take Roumania;
2. We take Messines, they take Russia;
3. We don't take Passchendaele, they take Italy.[8]

It was horribly true. It really seemed that the Allies might not now win the war.

Even by November 16, there was still no firm news in London of what was really happening in Petrograd. All wireless communication between Archangel and Petrograd and Moscow, had broken down for three days, the War Cabinet were told. The latest news to reach the British Admiral at Archangel was dated November 12, and simply stated that there was anarchy in Petrograd, owing to a general strike, and severe fighting in Moscow. Balfour said he had had no telegrams from Russia later than the 11th, but he had received one that morning from Teheran, which stated that Odessa and the Black Sea fleet were reported on the 14th to be in Bolshevik hands, that civil war was raging in Kiev, and that there was general disorder in southern Russia as the estates were being seized. The revolution, in fact, was not confined to Petrograd and Moscow. The latest telegram from General Knox at Petrograd was dated the 10th, and merely stated that Kerensky was trying to collect three Cossack divisions. It was not much for the Cabinet to go on.[9]

On the 21st (the day after the Bolsheviks had instructed the Russian C.-in-C. to open peace talks with the Germans), Balfour drew the War Cabinet's attention to a 'very important' telegram, sent by the King of Roumania on the 17th, stating that if the Allies would continue to support him, despite the Russian collapse, he would try to force a passage with some Roumanian troops in north-east Roumania (which the Germans had not occupied), through southern Russia to join up with the Cossacks, and then, if possible, with British forces in Mesopotamia. But if Allied support could not be continued, the King might have to come to terms with Germany and Austria.

Balfour stressed to the War Cabinet that it was of the 'greatest importance' that we should in no way approve Roumania making a separate peace with Germany. The only practical way out of the difficulty was to contact the Don Cossack *Ataman* Kaledin, through Roumania, in order to obtain Cossack support for the Roumanians.

Sir Edward Carson supported this proposal. He and the DMI had had an 'important' meeting the day before with the Polish representative in London, Count Horodysky, as a result of which Carson believed the formation of a nucleus of Poles, Cossacks and Roumanian troops was a 'practical proposition', if we could 'get at' General Kaledin through Roumania. 'It was quite clear that the British were most unpopular in Russia at the present moment,' stated Carson, 'and that it was questionable policy for Great Britain to approach General Kaledin, who was still only the leader of a faction, officially or direct.' We must not appear to take sides in the internal dispute now raging in Russia.

The War Cabinet directed the CIGS to select 'an individual' to be sent, either from England or from Roumania, to get in touch with General Kaledin.

It was thus decided to contact an anti-Bolshevik general in south Russia, but solely in order to support the Roumanians; and largely on the advice of a Polish count, whom the War Cabinet recognised as, to say the least, fairly unreliable. Hankey, the Cabinet secretary, thought him 'a self- seeker and possible spy', but the Foreign Office, he records, thought well of him; and it was on his advice that the War Cabinet decided on November 21 to send an agent to Kaledin.[10]

On the 22nd, the War Cabinet continued the previous day's discussion, and debated how far it was possible for the Allies to take 'any effective action' in Russia against the Bolsheviks, who had now issued a wireless message to the world announcing that they were determined on an immediate armistice. The Allied governments, it was pointed out, had not so far recognised Lenin and his colleagues as a Russian government, and could not recognise them as an Allied government, if they officially put forward peace proposals to the enemy. The difficulty was that any overt official step taken against the Bolsheviks might only strengthen their determination to make peace, and thus 'inflame' anti-Allied feeling in Russia, 'and so defeat the very object we were aiming at'. Nor was it known if we would be justified, at this moment, in backing either Kaledin, 'or any other leader of the party of law and order'. Steps might, however, be taken to build up in Russia 'some sort of unofficial organisation' to counter the German organisation. Meanwhile, the best 'immediate' step might be to let the Roumanians get into touch with General Kaledin, on purely military grounds, assuming, of course, that he was strong enough to help them.[11]

Balfour approved. The previous afternoon, he stated, he and the Prime Minister had discussed the matter with Colonel House, President Wilson's special envoy, and drafted and despatched a telegram to Roumania (which had been later shown to the French Ambassador in London), stating that there could be no separate Roumanian peace with Germany, and suggesting that the Roumanians should get in touch with Kaledin. A Roumanian appeal to Kaledin, as the Cabinet suggested, on purely military grounds, 'as the Commander of the nearest effective Russian Army', would not be an intervention in Russian internal affairs as a direct Allied appeal to Kaledin would, while it might succeed in discovering what Kaledin's 'real strength and intentions were'.

The War Cabinet felt this would be preferable to sending envoys like General Ballard (the British Military Attaché in Roumania) or a civilian to General Kaledin. Anyone, moreover, who tried at this moment to get to southern Russia from England would encounter 'very serious' difficulties. The War Cabinet directed the CIGS to wire to Ballard, 'putting frankly before him the whole difficulty', and asking him to consult General Berthelot, head of the French mission in Roumania, to advise on the 'best procedure' for approaching General Kaledin, 'or otherwise securing Russian help for Roumania'. Balfour was also asked to discuss the matter fully with the French Ambassador. Thus the decision of the previous day was reversed.[11]

The War Cabinet were right to be cautious about Kaledin. In fact, when General Alexeiev, the former Russian Chief of Staff, had arrived at the Don Cossack capital of Novocherkask on November 15 to found a volunteer army, he had received a very lukewarm reception from

Kaledin, who told him that a counter-revolutionary movement would cause trouble on the Don; his younger Cossacks, like most other Russian troops, had no wish to fight on. (It is difficult to know exactly how many troops Kaledin commanded at that moment. The question is largely academic – whether it was several Don Cossack divisions, or a Cossack corps – because military disorganisation and moral disintegration had by now cut such a swathe through even the Cossacks, that Kaledin, who had been so outspoken at the Moscow conference in support of Kornilov, could not now count on more than a few thousand – and then only to defend the boundaries of the Don country.)

General Alexeiev went on further south to the Kuban Cossack capital of Ekaterinodar, then returned to the Don, where Kaledin finally allowed him to form his volunteer army, provided it was understood that it was Alexeiev's private organisation, and that he considered himself simply a guest of the Don Cossacks, who could give him no support. Alexeiev's idea was that such a volunteer army force would form the backbone of a movement to fight on with the Allies, and 'restore' Russia – but it was all very vague, and there was no idea of restoring the monarchy.[12]

In Petrograd, as in other Russian areas under Bolshevik control, the Russian economy, such as it was, had now come to a standstill. For as soon as the Bolsheviks occupied the State Bank, and the workers seized control of the factories, the Russian banks refused them any further money – but paid one month's salary to all civil servants, bank clerks and any other workers who agreed to strike. Russia was primarily an agricultural country, and the main Russian merchant and joint stock banks controlled – *inter alia* – the entire Russian grain trade, and thus had effective control over the Russian economy. But as Russia had drifted towards total bankruptcy, this control (as already detailed) had gradually been passing into Allied hands. It was already clear to British observers in Petrograd that whether the Bolsheviks remained in power for a few weeks or rather longer, control over the Russian economy, through the Russian banks, was going to be vital, so that there could be no chance of the Germans obtaining large-scale grain supplies that would enable them to break the Allied blockade.[13]

In Petrograd, the Cadet press had appealed to all civil servants and factory and railway workers to continue to refuse to obey the new régime. But as the rouble notes held by the Russian banks were already running out and the State Bank would advance no more, people began to return to work and the factories to reopen. On November 23, as the Bolshevik paper *Izvestia* began to publish the Allied secret treaties, the

Russian banker, Prince Shakhovskoy (formerly Russian Minister of Trade and Industry from 1915 until the March revolution, and a director of the Russian Commercial and Industrial Bank) came to the British Embassy and told Buchanan that Kaledin, Alexeiev and Savinkov were at Novocherkask, and Rodzianko, the President of the Duma, and Kornilov, the former Russian C.-in-C., were on their way. (This was incorrect. Kornilov was still interned near Mogilev; Rodzianko was nowhere near the Don; and Savinkov did not arrive till late in December.) They were going to form a council, Shakhovskoy told the Ambassador, with Kaledin as military dictator and Alexeiev as C.-in-C.; and after gathering sufficient forces, would march on Petrograd and put the Bolsheviks down. But they required financial support. As there were no banknotes in southern Russia and it was impossible to send rouble notes across Bolshevik-held territory, Shakhovskoy outlined a scheme for the formation of a Cossack bank, whose capital would be guaranteed by the grain and mineral wealth of south Russia, and to which the Allies could give immediate financial support by the purchase of shares. Here was a chance for further British control over the Russian economy, for a Russian bank completely under British control.

But Buchanan, who had already recorded on the 19th that it was too late for any counter-revolutionary movement, clearly thought little of Shakhovskoy's scheme. The British government, he replied, could not intervene in Russian affairs, and he asked his visitor not to say he had been received at the British Embassy; but he could tell the Cossack leaders that the Allies would welcome any strong and legal Russian government that would keep Russia in the war.[14]

Meanwhile, General Barter had protested strongly, in the name of all the Allied military missions at Russian GHQ at Mogilev, at the very suggestion of peace talks with the Germans; any such action, the Russian C.-in-C. was warned, would entail the 'gravest consequences', which was taken to imply Allied support for an attack on Russia by Japan, a country loathed by all Russians. Trotsky replied that this 'flagrant interference' by the Allies would simply start a civil war. Buchanan sympathised with him; Barter's 'ill-advised' protest had done the Allies much harm. Knox went further. In a wire to the War Office on the 25th, he pointed out that as neither the Bolshevik, nor any other Russian government could fight on, if the Russian army refused to do so, it was 'useless as well as cruel' to reproach the Russian officers. The Allies should release Russia from the treaty of 1914, and allow her to make a separate peace.[14]

On November 26, the CIGS read out to the War Cabinet an earlier wire from Knox, sent on the 22nd, stating that it was quite clear that, 'whatever happened politically in Russia', the bulk of the Russian army refused to continue the war, while the Russian troops at the front were 'insisting upon an armistice'. The CIGS next read out Barter's protest at peace talks with the Germans, which the War Cabinet approved. But the CIGS then read a wire from General Ballard, in Roumania, stating that the Ukrainians were now anxious to make peace 'at the earliest possible moment'. The War Cabinet simply confirmed that they could not approve a separate Roumanian peace with the Germans, and agreed that the Roumanians should as soon as possible contact those Russian leaders who were still prepared to fight on.[15]

But on the 27th, as the German High Command agreed to an armistice on the Russian front, Buchanan decided that Knox was right. The only thing to do was *faire bonne mine à mauvais jeu*. The situation was now 'so desperate', he wired the Foreign Office, that the only safe course was to let Russia make peace if she wished. 'Every day that we keep Russia in the war against her will does but embitter her people against us.'

That day, General Poole was writing in much the same vein to Colonel Byrne. 'The elections [for the Constituent Assembly] are now going on,' he wrote. 'In Petrograd it will be a close thing between the Bolsheviks and Cadets. I don't know yet how the country will go. In any case, it's fairly certain that, if a non-Bolshevik party is elected, they will be promptly deposed by the Bolsheviks, who have all the real power in the country in that they have the rifles. Any socialistic party elected would have practically the same Peace ideas as the Bolsheviks. So whatever happens you may – in my judgement – count Russia out of the war.' He confirmed his recent advice that no more British supplies should be sent out.[16]

Poole then made a strong attack on Buchanan, an attack that was not undeserved. 'I'm distressed beyond measure at the present situation. I always preached & now I'm convinced that it might have been avoided by strong & resolute handling. A weak policy, feebly interpreted by a not very strong but charming gentleman, is not and never will be the right policy for our dealings with this country. We made the great mistake of not clearing out the whole of our old regime at the time of the revolution. We accentuated the mistake by allowing our suspicions that all was not well to be lulled by Tereschenko [Kerensky's Foreign Minister], who told Henderson that he was delighted with "things as they were". Of course he was! However it's no use crying over spilt milk. What we must do now is to try to save something out of the wreck by propaganda to try to increase British popularity & to get a place in the sun for our trade out here after the war.'[16]

But news of Prince Shakhovskoy's visit to the British Embassy to seek support for a Cossack bank had leaked out, and Trotsky was now thoroughly suspicious of Buchanan. A French officer told Knox on the 28th that Trotsky had told him that he knew Buchanan was in 'constant touch' with Kaledin; and Trotsky sent Buchanan a fierce note stating that the detention in England of two Bolsheviks called Chicherin and Petrov could not be tolerated while British subjects in Russia carried on 'active propaganda' in favour of counter-revolution.[16]

On the 28th, the DMO informed the War Cabinet that Barter wished to know what action to take if Lieutenant Krilenko (whom the Bolsheviks had sent to replace General Dukhonin as Russian C.-in-C.) arranged an armistice with the enemy. It was pointed out that if Barter and the rest of the British mission at Russian GHQ were to join Buchanan in Petrograd, he would be going further away from General Kaledin, whom it was desired to encourage. If Barter proceeded to Roumania, he might be out of Russia at a moment when a sudden change might render his presence there desirable. But if he joined Kaledin, it would amount to recognition of his party 'as the existing Government of the country'. The War Cabinet found it difficult to decide what to do about this important matter. The DMO urged joint Allied action, so the War Cabinet referred the matter to an Allied conference, then meeting in Paris, as they did not feel they had sufficient information to enable them to come to a decision.[17]

On November 29, a political bombshell burst in London. Lord Lansdowne published a letter in the *Daily Telegraph* urging an immediate compromise peace with Germany. His letter could not be ignored by the Tory ministers in Lloyd George's coalition government, since he was a respected Conservative elder statesman, and had been both Foreign Secretary and Viceroy of India; he had also had two sons killed in the war.

That morning, the War Cabinet considered three telegrams from Petrograd, and three from Jassy in Roumania, dated the 26th and 27th. Lord Robert Cecil stated that, apart from the 'large issues of policy' raised in these telegrams, there were also two minor questions. The first was Trotsky's demand for the release of Chicherin and Petrov, who were interned in England, and the virtual threat of reprisals against British subjects in Russia should these two agitators not be released. To release them at Trotsky's bidding would greatly add to his prestige, argued Cecil, 'and would be tantamount to a recognition of his Government'. The second question was Buchanan's complaint that Barter had put the Ambassador in a 'very embarrassing' position by his threat of 'serious consequences', which accompanied his protest at possible peace talks with the Germans. The DMO, however, defended Barter. The War Cabinet decided that:

[123]

a. No notice should be taken of Trotsky's request to release Chicherin and Petrov.
b. The War Office should enquire into the complaint against Barter, and a 'suitable' telegram should be sent to Buchanan.[18]

The War Cabinet then considered the general Russian situation, as set forth in the Petrograd and Jassy telegrams. On the 27th, it was stated, Trotsky had issued a note saying that the Bolsheviks were trying to bring about a general, not separate, armistice, but might be driven to a separate armistice if the Allies would not negotiate. If the Allied governments would not recognise the Bolsheviks, they would appeal to the peoples as against their governments. Since Trotsky's proposal for a general armistice only reached the British Embassy nineteen hours after the Russian C.-in-C. opened negotiations with the enemy, Buchanan urged an immediate reply to this 'insolent communication', stating that the Allies would continue the war until they had obtained a permanent peace. Buchanan further urged that, as the situation was now 'desperate', it was advisable to release Russia from her 1914 agreement, so that she could act as she chose, 'and decide to purchase peace on Germany's terms, or fight on with the Allies'. Bolshevik policy was to divide Russia and England, and so pave the way for what would virtually be a German protectorate over Russia. If Buchanan's proposal were adopted, it would be impossible for the Bolsheviks to reproach the Allies 'with driving Russian soldiers to slaughter for their Imperialist aims'. But in a telegram from Jassy, the British Military Attaché in Roumania proposed that if Kaledin were 'well-disposed' to the Allies, an Anglo-French mission should be sent to guarantee him financial support up to £10 million, with full powers to act 'without waiting instructions from England'.

Lord Robert Cecil said it was vital for the Cabinet to arrive at a decision 'at the earliest possible moment' on the questions raised in these telegrams. 'Kaledin was in command of the resources of Russia,' he stated, 'and if he and his Cossacks could be united against the Germans, supplies would thereby be prevented from reaching the enemy. There was no evidence to show that the Bolsheviks had anything like general support throughout Russia. There was reason for thinking that the peasants were against the Bolsheviks. Kaledin had with him Alexeiev, and possibly Savinkov and Rodzianko. The one man with an organised force was Kaledin, and, as Chief of the Cossacks, he had great prestige'. Cecil urged that General Ballard be sent to Kaledin, and, if he was 'genuinely' in favour of the Allies, Ballard should take whatever steps he deemed wise, and be authorised to incur expenditure up to £10 million.[18]

Some members of the War Cabinet, however, were impressed with the objections to entering into active co-operation with Kaledin without further information, which was being obtained, but had not yet arrived. Little was definitely known of Kaledin's personality, 'and there were signs that the Cossacks were not prepared to fight'. On Ballard's own admission, the scheme could not be regarded as hopeful, and its only result might be to drive the Russian government into the arms of Germany. If we waited for a short time, we should learn what terms were being offered by Germany, 'and these might open the eyes of the Russian people to what a German peace really meant'. There were two alternative courses: to follow Buchanan's advice; or to wait a little in the hope that the situation would subsequently become clearer. In any case, the subject should be referred to the Allied conference now meeting in Paris.

When the Cabinet's attention was called to the position of the Roumanian army, some members again thought there was less objection to securing Kaledin's support for the Roumanian army than for an 'open expedition' against the Bolsheviks. 'Against the policy of drift,' state the Cabinet minutes, 'it was urged that for the past eight months we had sedulously refrained from intervening in the policy of the Russian Government, and we were now confronted with the fact that the Russians were negotiating with the German Government.' It had also to be remembered that Kaledin did not know what the British view of the Russian situation was.

The War Cabinet decided that Cecil should wire to Paris, referring these telegrams to the Prime Minister, Balfour and Milner, and should add that the War Cabinet in London were divided on what immediate steps should be taken.[18]

This was a wise decision. There is fair reason to believe that General Ballard, when urging massive support for Kaledin, in fact knew absolutely nothing about him, and was acting under the pressure of the powerful French mission in Roumania (which more or less had the remnants of the Roumanian army under its control). For though the French were anxious to re-create the Eastern Front, they were also very anxious to protect their enormous investments in the Donetz and the Ukraine; and as the Ukrainians had stated that they intended to make peace 'at the earliest possible moment', it was Kaledin or no one. But Cecil was simply indulging in wild conjecture when informing the War Cabinet that Kaledin was 'the one man with an organised force'. He knew even less about Kaledin than General Ballard.

Sir Edward Carson drew the War Cabinet's attention to various Russian wireless messages, mainly Bolshevik propaganda, whose publication he had temporarily stopped. The Press Bureau's director claimed that the whole question of Russian press messages was so difficult that the only solution was for him to pass, stop, or censor them at his discretion; in this case, there should be some public announcement. The alternative was to pass everything from a press correspondent abroad. Carson explained that 'some of the messages were appeals to the people as against their Governments, and were in many respects of a violent character'. Balfour and Milner, who had been consulted before they left for Paris, were against publication.[18]

Cecil urged the removal of censorship from Foreign Office matters, save for telegrams passing through England to a foreign country, as had been done in late 1915. It was better to throw the onus on to the press, 'and let them risk prosecution under the Defence of the Realm Act'. He was in favour of publishing these propaganda messages, for, if withheld, they would only leak out later, and the British government would be blamed for suppressing them. On the other hand, it was urged that these were simply propaganda messages from an unrecognised government. Some newspapers were complaining that they were only allowed to see mutilated copies of their telegrams. The War Cabinet decided that these messages should not be published for the present, but that the Press Bureau could show them to the newspapers concerned at their discretion. Thus, Bolshevik propaganda was officially denied entry to Britain.[18]

On November 30, the War Cabinet were informed that Cecil had wired to Petrograd about Chicherin and Petrov, and the CIGS to Barter as instructed. It was pointed out, however, that if the British government were to give way to Trotsky's demands, 'it would not by any means ensure that the British residents would be allowed to leave Russia in return, and that to give way to these demands, which were in reality due to a German plan to force Russia to do something irrevocable, would form but a precedent for further demands of the same nature'. Cecil undertook to obtain the latest details of the Russian situation by December 3, by which time the Allied conference in Paris would have ended.

Carson then raised another matter. *The Times* that morning had carried a report of a speech by the German Chancellor, who had referred to a wireless telegram sent by Trotsky from Tsarskoe Selo. The Press Bureau's director had stopped many such telegrams, said Carson; one, addressed to Reuter's, 'contained the full text of the manifesto to all the belligerents, signed by Trotsky and Lenin', and the director again wished to know what to do. The War Cabinet confirmed that the telegram should not be published.

At Carson's suggestion, it was then agreed that the manufacture of all munitions and warlike stores for Russia, whether in England, or on

British credit in America, should be suspended. They should be converted for the use of the Allied governments. General Poole's advice was thus accepted. But the despatch to Russia of clothing, boots and other non-warlike equipment should be continued, it was agreed, to demonstrate the 'friendly feeling' in England towards the Russian people.[19]

On major policy, the War Cabinet had to await the results of the Allied conference in Paris.

# 5

## *Kaledin and the British*

In Paris, the British, French and Italian premiers and foreign ministers that day (November 30) began discussing the Russian situation with Colonel House, President Wilson's special representative, at the Quai d'Orsay, unaware that peace talks between Russia and the enemy were so imminent. Lloyd George first brought up Buchanan's proposal that the Allies should release Russia from her 1914 agreement, and let her make a separate peace if she wished.

Pichon, the French Foreign Minister, said that Maklakov, the Russian Ambassador in Paris (who was a former Russian Minister of the Interior, and a prominent Cadet politician) did not agree with Buchanan's proposal. Maklakov thought the German Chancellor's recent speech 'very astute', for it appeared to offer the peace that Russia wanted, 'although, in reality, it would result in what was practically a German protectorate'. But this German trap could be avoided, thought Maklakov, by an Allied declaration offering to discuss war aims, not with the Bolsheviks, 'but with a reasonably constituted Russian government'. Pichon agreed that this might be a possibility; for like some German diplomats, he foresaw a short life for the Bolsheviks. Since the Austrian Foreign Minister had agreed to take up the Bolshevik armistice offer as a basis for peace negotiations, the 'English proposal' was dangerous, and would assist the Bolsheviks, Pichon declared. So far as the Allies knew, many Russian people, like the Cossacks, the Ukrainians, and the moderate socialists, had never supported the Bolshevik proposals. 'To make the [British] declaration would be to desert "our friends", and perhaps to throw them into the hands of the Bolsheviks.'

Balfour and Baron Sonnino, the Italian Foreign Minister, both agreed. Lloyd George retorted that this was not the British government's proposal, it was Buchanan's; but before it was rejected, he said (being suspicious of Pichon's interpretation of Maklakov's views), he would like to hear the views of Maklakov himself.

Clemenceau, the French Premier, retorted that it was simply a matter of common sense. If Russia made a separate peace, she would betray her Allies. They should keep the moral advantage of being betrayed. 'If Maklakov and all the celestial powers asked him to give Russia back her word, he would refuse.'[1]

Sonnino agreed. If we gave Russia back her word, what would be the effect on Roumania, on Serbia, and indeed on Italy? This, with the Caporetto disaster all too fresh in everyone's mind, strongly affected the Allied conference.

Balfour tried to reconcile the two points of view, but Sonnino insisted that once anyone started to talk peace, the French and Italian peoples would not take up arms again. Sonnino himself would do nothing. He would wait to see what action 'our friends' in Russia took.

Colonel House urged the conference to make some answer to the German Chancellor's speech in order to hearten everyone, including the smaller powers.

When Maklakov arrived, Lloyd George explained Buchanan's proposal by saying that as the Bolsheviks claimed that the Allies were forcing Russian soldiers to fight on to realise Allied war aims, it would assist the moderate party in Russia if an Allied declaration stated that, if Russia wished to be free, we should not hold her to the 1914 agreement. In fact, if we did not demand 'the execution of our Shylock bond', it would harm the Bolsheviks, and strengthen 'our friends'. (This interpretation of his proposal would have shocked Buchanan.) Maklakov said he thought Buchanan really meant that the Allies could discuss their war aims with a loyal Russian government, if one were formed. This was what he would advise the Allies to do. As Lloyd George now realised that Maklakov was indeed opposed to Buchanan's proposal, he said he would drop it.

Maklakov, he understood, supported an Allied declaration to discuss war aims. Maklakov said he only meant some intimation through some channel, not necessarily the Allied conference. 'The Bolshevik party were continually asserting that the Allies were insisting on their fighting to obtain their own war aims. Against this, the moderate party had no argument to put up.' Some such intimation would give a 'platform' to the moderate party. (By moderates, Maklakov seems to have meant the SR.) When Colonel House suggested an adjournment to consider this proposal, Lloyd George asked Maklakov to draft a declaration on 'how we could assist the moderates in Russia'. But as Buchanan had made abundantly clear, it was already too late to support the moderates. The conference then adjourned.

When it was resumed on December 1, various drafts were produced. Balfour criticised them all, since they said, in effect, that the Allies would be willing to discuss their war aims with a 'decent' Russian government, 'which we had not really intended to do'. They gave the impression that the Allies were being 'frightened' into a discussion of war aims. House agreed; and only those states who had signed the London pact of September 1914 should sign such a declaration. This meant that the American government could not do so. But it was felt that it would be better to send no declaration at all, rather than one in which America declined to participate. Sonnino wished to wait until after the elections for the Constituent Assembly. 'At present, we had no idea how events would develop.' Balfour now agreed that it would be impossible to send a joint declaration. Each Allied government should send their own.

Lloyd George interrupted at this point to say that he had just heard from London that the Russians had asked the Germans for three days in order to communicate with their Allies before they gave their answer about an armistice. This was broadly correct, though the message was much delayed, and gave the Allied ministers the impression that they had ample time to consider the matter. In fact, peace talks were only hours away. Lloyd George warned the conference that this Russian note would either have to be answered, or ignored. America could hardly refuse to answer if the other Allies did, he added. He said he had also just heard that four Russian armies had already accepted an armistice, and that the others would follow suit. 'It was fairly clear, therefore, that Trotsky and Lenin did, in fact, speak in the name of the Russian armies, and probably of the Russian peoples, and that some answer would have to be given to them.' Lloyd George now saw that the moderates counted for nothing, and that Buchanan had been right all along.

But after considerable discussion, which made it increasingly clear that it was impossible to reach agreement, Lloyd George said that the more he considered the matter, the more alarmed he became at the very idea of trying to make any joint declaration. 'Even in Great Britain, it was more difficult to make any announcement of our consent to discuss war aims after Lord Lansdowne's letter,' he pointed out. If any document were published in Paris, it would be regarded as support for Lansdowne's view. This made any form of declaration much more difficult. He feared 'a rot would set in' over waging war. Each Ambassador in Petrograd should simply make it clear that we were ready to discuss war aims. There really was some case for this. Consider Russia's war aims. They had wanted control of Constantinople, the Bosphorus, the Dardanelles. 'What was the use of talking of that now?' At present, Russian war aims stood in the way of a separate peace with Turkey. He favoured Balfour's proposal. There was general agreement with this

view. But this was a futile decision. The only way the Bolshevik government could achieve stability was by means of a diplomatic success at
Brest-Litovsk, *ie*, by making peace with the enemy – the one thing the
Allies wished to avoid. Balfour concluded the discussion by warning
that the Bolshevik government might very soon obtain the support not
only of the Bolshevik army, but also of the Constituent Assembly. 'If
so, we might have to enter into relations with it as a de facto
Government.'[1]

They then discussed the question of Japanese co-operation. In view of
the growing shortage of Allied manpower, this was a tricky subject.
Up to now, recalled Pichon, Japan, though an Ally, had co-operated
very little. The Russian collapse, however, had greatly changed things.
It was now in Japan's interests to co-operate much more. If Germany
won the war, Japanese penetration in the Far East would end. Lloyd
George pointed out that Japanese willingness to co-operate was a 'very
big assumption'. Japanese troops could not be sent to Russia, because
Russia would not have them; they could go only to Mesopotamia, but
then there was the shipping shortage. Was it not more important to
ship American rather than Japanese troops?

Pichon suggested asking for general Japanese help. They had been
'greatly enriched' by the war, he said, 'and had obtained colossal
advantages'. Colonel House recalled that American attempts to obtain
even a small amount of Japanese help had been entirely unsuccessful.
But Lloyd George stressed that they had given the Russians hundreds
of thousands of rifles, many guns, and great quantities of war material.

When the Japanese ambassadors in London and Paris then joined the
conference, Pichon explained the present serious military situation,
due to Russia's collapse. 'It was proper and fit that Japan should
examine what further assistance she could give,' he said. The ambassadors stressed that Japan had sent warships to the Mediterranean, and
munitions to France and Russia. But it was impossible to send troops,
since the Japanese army was not organised for such a contingency,
Japan did not have the tonnage, and the Japanese people were against
it. Pichon retorted that the Japanese government 'should do something'.
But it was a despairing request. Little was to be hoped for from Japan.

The Allied conference then considered the question of financial aid
to Russia. At present, France was paying 125 million francs a month to
Russia, mainly for military purposes, said Pichon. America had stopped
all financial support. These Allied arrangements should be concerted.
Lloyd George said it was only necessary to stop the supply of goods.
Pichon agreed. So it was decided that no further supplies should be
sent to Russia, but at Balfour's suggestion, it was agreed that the
machinery for restarting the despatch of supplies should be retained,

'in case a more stable form of [Russian] government should be introduced'. This was in line with the War Cabinet's recent decision.

A proposal by General Niessel, head of the French military mission in Russia, for large financial credits for propaganda in Russia was next considered. General Foch, it was stated, wanted it handled on an Allied basis. Pichon suggested referring the matter to the military attachés in Petrograd. Lloyd George asked whether they were the right people, but Pichon's proposal was accepted. Money, in fact, was still to be spent in Russia. Instead of direct financial aid and supplies, it was now to go on pro-Allied propaganda to try and retain the goodwill of Russian hearts and minds.

Various proposals by General Berthelot, head of the powerful French military mission in Roumania, next came up for discussion. (Roumania, it will be recalled, had finally entered the war on the Allied side in mid-1916, encouraged by the success of Brusilov's offensive. Roumania had then been rapidly conquered by the Germans, who had occupied the capital of Bucharest in December 1916. The remnant of the Roumanian army, supported by a powerful French military mission, had retired to the mountainous north-eastern corner of the country, and were now based on the provincial town of Jassy, near the Russian border, where the Germans let them be. In their predicament, the Roumanians were naturally much influenced by events in Russia. They had finally entered the war on the high tide of the – last – Russian successful offensive, and were now likely to come out of the war if the Russians did.)

Berthelot's first proposal dealt with the reconstruction and reorganisation of the Russian railways, on which Roumanian supplies were dependent, and which were in very poor shape. His second proposal was for the setting up of an Allied commission in Odessa to purchase supplies for Roumania. Despite doubts expressed by Balfour, this was accepted in principle. His third and most important proposal concerned the reorganisation of various armies in southern Russia under Berthelot's command, namely all 'fighting forces' in Roumania (which included some Russian troops), and the formation of what the minutes call a 'Tzek-Slavic' army. (This referred to two divisions of Czechoslav troops, formed from Czechs living in pre-war Russia, and Czech prisoners and deserters from the Austrian army, who had been attached as a separate unit to the old Russian army, and who had kept their cohesion in the general breakdown of discipline.)

Balfour said he fully recognised Berthelot's great services in reorganising the Roumanian army. 'But if we made him Commander-in-Chief of large Russian forces, how should we stand towards a properly constituted Russian government, if one came into being?' How, in fact, could the Allies 'put Russian troops under a foreign General?' To this there was no answer. (This was the first mention of the Czech troops.)

Lloyd George next read out the telegram from General Ballard, in which he proposed that an Anglo-French mission should be sent to General Kaledin to guarantee him financial support of up to £10 million, and consider his plans in detail, with special regard for the state of the local railways, and the supply position. After some discussion, General Ballard's suggestion was approved.

Next, Sonnino stated that the King of Roumania had asked if the Allies would guarantee that Roumania should retain her pre-war territory, and that, in the event of a Roumanian collapse, the Roumanian royal house would remain in power. Balfour said the King's request should be accepted. Roumania, he pointed out, 'had little chance of success unless General Kaledin came to her help'. It was agreed to give the guarantee the King requested, to encourage Roumania to fight on.

Then finally came the subject of Poland, who had asked for an Allied declaration in favour of Polish autonomy. This subject had become more acute owing to Bolshevik publication of the Allied secret treaties, which allowed Russia 'to organise her western front as she wished', *ie*, to do whatever she liked with Poland. In view of recent Allied military reverses, both Balfour and Lloyd George thought such a declaration undesirable. Since some Polish territory was claimed by Austria, Lloyd George thought the present moment 'most unpropitious', when we had 'almost broken' with Russia, 'and had some hopes from Austria'. And if the Allies undertook new responsibilities on behalf of the Poles, he warned, they would have to do the same for the Jugoslavs and the Czechoslavs, who were also under Austrian control. The question was hastily dropped. Lloyd George said that he must leave Paris before the final meeting on Monday, December 3; and this ended the discussion.[1]

On December 2, with Lloyd George back in London, Balfour, after consulting Colonel House, wired to Buchanan in Petrograd that the Allies would reconsider their war aims with Russia, as soon as there was a stable Russian government, acceptable to the Russian people. Balfour then wired the Foreign Office that as the British officer sent from Roumania to the Don had not yet reported, no British military mission should yet be sent to Kaledin, as the Bolsheviks would consider such an 'ostentatious act' as clearly hostile, and might retaliate against the British Embassy in Petrograd.[1]

As more requests for support for the Don Cossacks reached the British Embassy on November 29, Knox reported from Petrograd that he had just heard that the Cossack Union in south Russia was very weak (which was correct), as the Cossacks were so divided. But if they could unite, and finance was available, they might assist Georgia and Armenia against the Turks, and occupy the Donetz basin, thus denying Russian minerals and oil and Siberian grain to the Germans; a Captain Noel should be sent from Tiflis, said Knox, to Novocherkask, the Don Cossack capital. This was as far as the British Embassy would go in supporting the Cossacks and they agreed to do so only for limited anti-German, not large-scale anti-Bolshevik, measures.

Pokrovsky, the last Tsarist Foreign Minister, and Chairman of the Siberian Bank, who was acting for Rodzianko, Alexeiev and Kaledin, then came to the British Embassy, probably on the 30th, to ask for financial support for the Cossack Union. Buchanan apparently would not see Pokrovsky as he well knew of Trotsky's suspicions; and merely agreed to the despatch of Captain Noel. It was at this point decided – apparently by Rodzianko – to ask the Polish financier, Jaroszynski, to act as banker for the Cossack Union.[2]

Karol Josephovitch Jaroszynski, then aged forty, came from an old Polish family that had strong connections with the Vatican and large estates near Vinnitsa in the Ukraine. Through various judicious speculations, initially in the sugar industry, he had managed to acquire enough capital to buy control of the Commercial and Industrial Bank, and by mortgaging various properties he was able to buy out the majority shareholders. He prospered rapidly, and with the bank's money he bought into another bank, and so on, since he had seen that the big Russian banks, which were financial conglomerates, were very undervalued.

There were two types of Russian bank:

1   *Merchant Banks*

*The Russian Bank for Foreign Trade* controlled the entire grain trade on the Volga and owned the two largest Russian sugar companies and the largest Russian insurance company. (This bank was formerly closely connected with the Deutsche Bank.)

*The International Bank* controlled the entire south Russian grain trade, most of the jute trade and coal production, and owned a large number of coal mines and the three biggest Russian metallurgic works. (This bank was formerly closely connected with the Disconto Geselschaft and the Dresdner Bank.)

*The Azov-Don Bank* had big property holdings in the Rostov area, and controlled the largest platinum works in the Urals. (This bank had originally been entirely financed by the Mendelssohn Bank, of Berlin.)

[134]

*The Volga-Kama Bank* had extensive interests in the upper Volga region.

*The Russo-Asiatic Bank* had vast concessions in the Urals and Altai district, and controlled the Chinese Eastern Railway. (The chairman was the Russian financier A. I. Putilov, and it had close connections with the French Société Générale.)[3]

### 2  *Joint Stock Banks*

*The Siberian Bank* controlled the entire grain trade in Siberia, and the gold and platinum trade.

*The Commercial and Industrial Bank.*

The Grand Duke Alexander Michailovitch, in a book called *Once a Grand Duke* (London, 1932), pp. 276–81 (which probably reflects current Court and Stock exchange gossip), states that on the outbreak of war, the big three bankers of St Petersburg were Putilov, Batolin and Jaroszynski, known as 'The Three Horsemen of the Apocalypse'. They really controlled the Russian economy, their wealth being largely based on the extreme leniency of the Russian banking laws, since a bank could be controlled by the purchase of not more than 15% of the capital; and the banks controlled nearly everything else in Russia.

A British officer who called on Jaroszynski in Paris during the peace conference, describes him as a tall and portly man, with very shiny finger nails; that slightly finicky manner that fat men often have; very boastful, and with the rather dandified air of an Austrian Pole. The British Consul in Odessa, however, who knew him well, said that his financial position was often 'very straitened owing to the lack of ready cash', but he was not a speculator; his genius was 'essentially a creative one'.

By now (December 1917), Jaroszynski was beginning to see himself as the Cecil Rhodes of Russia and, in fact, of all eastern Europe. He had been providing the imperial family with 25,000 roubles a month since their arrest, and had dreams of a Polish-Ukrainian federation. Amidst the turmoil of the revolution, in fact, he was fast expanding his already vast interests through the Commercial and Industrial Bank, part of whose capital he had prudently transferred (like many other Russian financiers) to his London agents, the London City and Midland Bank (later the Midland Bank). He already controlled navigation on the Dnieper and the Volga, and had bought large holdings in the Russian Bank for Foreign Trade and the International Bank (which together controlled the Volga and the south Russian grain trade). But these 'pyramiding' operations had almost bankrupted the Commercial and Industrial Bank, which was now being heavily supported by the Russian and English Bank in Petrograd.[3]

While the British Ambassador and his Military Attaché were awaiting a response to their joint advice that Russia should be allowed to leave the war, other more devious British operators now appeared in Petrograd, with all their murky contacts in the Russian financial world, bent on keeping Russia in the war. The spooks and half-spooks now emerged from the embassy woodwork.

Jaroszynski already had contact with one such character at the British Embassy in the person of H. A. F. Leech, a young Englishman who called himself – as did many – a 'commission agent', and ran a firm in Petrograd with a friend, W. E. G. Firebrace, called Leech and Firebrace. Leech also ran the British Propaganda Bureau, known as the 'Cosmos Agency', and had a room in the British Embassy. One of his main tasks was the distribution of large sums of money, originating from the London City and Midland Bank and transferred to him through the Commercial and Industrial Bank, to newspapers in Petrograd and Moscow for publishing anti-Bolshevik articles. Hugh Ansdell Farran Leech,* then aged thirty, was the son of a banker, who had formerly worked closely with Sir Edward Holden, who in 1918 was chairman of the London City and Midland Bank. Leech studied accountancy at Manchester University and afterwards engineering at Hamburg. In about 1912, he went to Russia. There he married a girl from Rostov, and first worked in the Galician oilfields. A seemingly erratic and reckless character, with an enormous capacity for vodka, he had then plunged into pre-war Tsarist high finance and made a good deal of money. These aspects of his career were public knowledge. Known to only a very few was the fact that he had long been a British secret agent. The Secret Intelligence Service, being passionately interested in developments in the Russian oil industry, invariably recruited young Englishmen in the Russian oil business, who had an engineering background.

What the London City and Midland Bank paid Leech for his work in the Cosmos Agency is not known, but it was evidently a good deal. He had also had an advance of more than £70,000 from the London bankers Higgs & Co., which he should later have repaid, apparently, from another source. In 1920, Higgs and Co. sued him for the recovery of £20,000 which he still owed them, but no British government department would cover him.

Leech knew Jaroszynski well through their Russian banking connections. It so happened that when Jaroszynski was asked to act as banker for the Cossack Union, he was engaged in a crucial financial operation of his own. Desperately short of ready cash, he had just told

* This information about Jaroszynski and Leech, which is well backed by documentary evidence, comes from family sources.

his agent, Isidore Kon, who had been managing director of the Commercial and Industrial Bank up to 1914, to find him 150 million roubles, promising him 2% commission if he were successful (Jaroszynski needed the money to enable him to secure *final* control of both the Russian Bank for Foreign Trade and the International Bank.) Kon went to see Benenson (manager of the Russian and English Bank in Petrograd, and father of Manya Harari, the distinguished translator of *Doctor Zhivago*, and founder of the Harvill Press), and offered him 75,000 shares in each of the two banks at 1,000 roubles a share in return for a loan of 150 million roubles. But Benenson would only lend him 50 million roubles (of which some 12 to 14 million roubles had been advanced by early December).

It was now decided that Jaroszynski must be contacted by General Poole's mission, at whose personnel it is necessary to look rather closely. Colonel Terence Keyes (a brother of Admiral Keyes, of Zeebrugge) had been an Indian Army intelligence officer, and had also seen service as a political agent in the Persian Gulf. He attended to political matters for Poole. A Treasury official, Major Macalpine, saw to the finances. He is described as tight-lipped, and of somewhat dull vision, 'and consequently a tool in the hands of clever people'. (One gathers the word 'clever' here means rather more than sharp, and refers to the Russian banking community.)[3]

After the Bolshevik revolution, and above all after their decision to open peace talks with the enemy, the main task of Poole's mission changed abruptly. It was no longer to help the Russian army to make the best use of British supplies, but to prevent the Germans seizing them, or possibly obtaining them from the Bolsheviks. There were two ways of doing this. Friendly station masters and railways workers could sometimes be induced to dispatch goods from the Petrograd area to east Russia free of charge, though it was obvious even now that Allied armed force or Bolshevik good will would be needed to protect the immense stocks of Allied stores at Archangel, and at Vladivostok in the Far East. Secondly, the mission could buy up, through the Russian co-operative societies (which had branches all over Russia, and which the Bolsheviks had not touched), all other stocks of potential use to the Germans (*eg*, sunflower seeds, oil, glycerine, textiles, flax, hemp, metals and grain), either for export, or for distribution within Russia.

A. E. Lessing, who had long been established in the Russian metal and grain trades, which had brought him into close contact with the co-operative societies and various Russian businessmen, was of particular use to General Poole at this time. But to the other members of the mission, especially to Colonel Keyes, he was a man of mystery.

Keyes, who actually ran the mission for General Poole, was puzzled by Lessing's erratic movements. 'During the whole time Lessing has been floating about in the background in both Petrograd and London,' he later noted. But unknown to Keyes, Lessing was a link of sorts between Lloyd George and the Russian bankers, since he had close connections with both William Sutherland, the Prime Minister's press secretary, and with Vladimir Poliakov, a rich Russian banker and railway engineer.[3]

Poliakov and Lessing were both close friends and probably secret colleagues. The grandson of Lazar Poliakov, the great Russian railroad king, who had built many of the first Russian railways, Poliakov had been an engineer officer during the war. But it was as a director of the Siberian Bank that he had been taken on in October 1917 by the British Embassy as financial adviser. As such, he played a considerable role in secret banking operations between London and Petrograd; and when he had to flee Russia in late 1918, he arrived in England penniless. He began a new career as a journalist. In 1920, he joined the *Daily Telegraph*. But it was his outspoken articles in the *Fortnightly Review*, under the pen-name of 'Augur', that caused people to take notice. In 1924 he became Diplomatic Correspondent for *The Times*, a post he held for twelve years. Poliakov was fiercely anti-Hitler, but a warm supporter of Mussolini, whom he somewhat resembled. Extremely argumentative in conversation, he became a well-known Fleet Street figure, often to be seen preceded by two large white poodles, or two red salukis. His provocative exterior hid a very warm heart, however, and he often helped young journalists. At this time, he carefully concealed what he had been doing on behalf of the British in Russia in 1917 and 1918. So did *The Times*. In his obituary, it was simply stated that he had served as a Russian engineer officer, 'but in the confused period which culminated in the collapse of Russian resistance, found himself isolated. Determined, if possible, to keep Russia in the war, he made contact with the British diplomatic representatives in Russia. After Lenin's triumph, Poliakov escaped to the United Kingdom.' This omitted a good deal. He finally left *The Times* in 1936, in protest over the editor Geoffrey Dawson's appeasement policy. He died in 1956. In Poliakov's file in *The Times* archives, there is an internal office memo to the effect that, while working for that newspaper, he was 'chiefly' engaged in journalism. He was thus probably engaged in secret work as well.

The Lessings were a rich German-Jewish family (direct descendants of Lessing, the philosopher), who were in the brewing and grain trade in both St Petersburg and London. But they were now very English, and like certain other families with business interests in Russia, now only went to St Petersburg for a few months each year. Teddy Lessing (cousin of the novelist Doris Lessing) was an Edwardian dandy – a 'masher' in the parlance of the day – but had much charm and many friends. Some saw him simply as an agreeable ass, but to others he seemed more like a character out of one of Sapper's 'Bulldog Drummond' novels – only an ass on the outside. He spoke German, French and Russian, and though lacking in initiative, had a native sharpness and excellent contacts in the world of banking and high finance, and – through his uncle the MP Edward Strauss – with some Liberal politicians. From the age of about twenty-two until nearly the end of his life he was an SIS agent. In 1917, then aged twenty-seven, Teddy Lessing was a captain in the Grenadier Guards, attached to General Poole's mission – and keeping an eye on the family business.

'Lessing has turned up and we are using him for metals,' wrote Colonel Byrne to General Poole on October 27. 'He sends off mysterious wires about conferences and negotiations at Downing Street. What is it all about and cannot I help? He dearly loves mystery . . .' On November 7, the day of the Bolshevik coup, Byrne was writing again: 'Lessing is more mysterious than ever . . .'[4]

On November 9, Poole replied to Byrne's letter of the 27th. '*Lessing*. There is no need of mystery, especially with you! When he was coming home on leave I discussed & explained to him my views as to the absolute necessity of much stronger action to be taken on the part of the Allies. You know the views I have always held as to the absolute futility of our present "milk & water" policy . . . Well I told him, as he knows & is in political circles, to impress my ideas on all & sundry – particularly L.G. if he could get hold of him.

'Recent events out here have convinced me that my policy is the right one. If only we had had a strong man who would handle the situation resolutely, I think we should have stiffened the [Provisional] Govt. into action & avoided the present calamity.

'You well know how I value your help, and you said you would back me all the way when we discussed the matter here at the time of the Henderson meeting, but you also said that in your view the policy was not the right one. For this reason I never urged you to be a "whole hogger" & press it at home. If you *do* by any chance agree with me, discuss the matter with Lessing & if you can, press it along. Even now, although things look desperate, I think something might be done.'[4]

Colonel Keyes knew nothing of all this when he received instructions to make contact with Jaroszynski. First, he guardedly approached Leech (whom he had apparently not met before), and told him that 'besides certain anti-Bolshevik activities, he was a member of a Commission for getting control of [Russian] businesses and counteracting

German influence in Russia'. He would therefore like to contact Jaroszynski. Leech explained that Jaroszynski had just obtained a partial loan for this very purpose (this was hardly true!) from Benenson, who was strongly suspected of being pro-German and the Germans were already making strong efforts to capture certain banks. Keyes replied that the British government would find *all* the money that Jaroszynski wanted. At this, Leech went to see Jaroszynski, who at once told his agent, Kon, to cancel the 50 million rouble loan from Benenson, but said that Kon could keep his 2% commission (*ie*, 1 million roubles).

Keyes and Leech were soon in consultation with Jaroszynski, who said that if the British government would lend him 200 million roubles, he could obtain complete control of the Russian Bank for Foreign Trade, the International Bank, the Commercial and Industrial Bank, the Volga-Kama Bank, and the Siberian Bank; and with their resources, he could then set up a Cossack bank, which could issue bank notes in south Russia. Keyes much favoured this scheme and put it to Buchanan, who, somewhat reluctantly, said that he would approve if Pokrovsky (the late Foreign Minister) and Krivoshein (the late Minister of Agriculture), both of whom Buchanan trusted, approved; he would not become involved. Pokrovsky and Krivoshein, however, both approved this scheme which Keyes passed on to London (early in December), without mentioning Jaronszynski, but simply referring to 'a financier', since the Bolsheviks now had him under surveillance.[5]

Unfortunately, these plans remained far from secret. On December 3 (the day after Kornilov, Denikin and the other Russian generals, whom Kerensky had imprisoned near Mogilev, escaped and set out for the Don, on learning that the former Russian C.-in-C. Dukhonin had just been murdered at Russian GHQ by his own troops), Trotsky angrily told Woodhouse, the British Consul, that no British subjects would be allowed to leave Russia until Chicherin and Petrov were released from prison in England; and if the British government refused to release them, he would arrest 'certain British subjects whom he knew to be counter-revolutionaries'. This, as Buchanan knew full well, meant Leech and his propaganda bureau. Then that night, the French Military Attaché called at the British Embassy to warn Buchanan that Trotsky had told a French officer that he had a 'special grudge' against him, as he now knew that Buchanan had been financing Kaledin as well. He was therefore thinking of arresting both Buchanan and Knox.[6]

In London, on the morning of Monday, December 3, Hankey produced a paper for the War Cabinet summarising the decisions taken in Paris on the Russian question, as the War Cabinet now had some very important decisions of their own to take, since it was now known that peace talks between the Russians and the Germans had actually begun the day before at Brest-Litovsk. First, it had been decided that the Allies should each inform their own ambassadors in Petrograd that they were prepared to discuss war aims with a decent Russian government; and that each ambassador should make this known in the way he thought best. Balfour had taken the necessary action. Next, an Anglo-French mission was to be sent to Kaledin to guarantee him credits up to £10 million, and an Allied commission was to be set up at Odessa to procure supplies for Roumania. Balfour again had taken the necessary action. Then there was the question of a great extension of propaganda in Russia, 'involving the expenditure of very large sums of money'. It was agreed that the military attachés in Petrograd should prepare a scheme. Hankey himself had arranged for the necessary action to be taken before leaving Paris. 'He [Balfour] felt some doubt as to whether the military attachés were the right people to communicate with, and I think he intended to discuss the matter further,' wrote Hankey. 'This decision was rather rushed, and I doubt if half of those present realised that it had been taken,' he added. Next, there had been a proposal to make a declaration in favour of the establishment of a Polish state, but it had been dropped after a very strong appeal by Lloyd George, as it might be considered a new war aim, just at a time when the realisation of our existing war aims was becoming extremely difficult. Finally, it was decided that the Japanese ambassadors should ask their government to consider further co-operation. 'The impression I formed from their attitude,' remarked Hankey, 'was that not much is likely to come of this.'

On leaving Paris, Hankey had reminded Balfour that certain questions were still outstanding, namely what the Allied military missions at Russian GHQ were to do while the armistice was being negotiated – a question which Balfour undertook to raise. But, added Hankey, 'I do not think that Mr Balfour is likely to take any action on this in Paris, as he evidently did not consider the occasion very favourable.'[7]

On December 3 (the day after peace talks had opened at Brest-Litovsk), Bonar Law informed the War Cabinet (now all, except Balfour, back in London) that the Russian Embassy in London had told him that the Russian army in the Caucasus was remaining loyal to the old Russian provisional government, and that the Georgians, Armenians and Tartars were raising a 'national' army to fight on against Germany. The local Russian commander in the Caucasus wanted a loan of 300 million roubles, of which 70 million were needed forthwith. The British Minister at Teheran, in telegrams of November 30, had supported this proposal, and also urged financial support for the Persian Cossack division, which was now cut off. This was a wildly optimistic proposal; the Russian Caucasus army was rapidly disbanding, while the secular hatred of Tartar for Armenian made any such co-operation unthinkable. But the War Cabinet decided that 'Any reasonable demands for money from the Russian Caucasus Army and the Persian Cossack Division should be met by the Treasury,' and that the British Minister at Teheran, and the Russian Embassy in London, should be so informed.[8]

The War Cabinet next proceeded to discuss the need for making a 'tremendous effort' to maintain south Russia on the Allied side, and the steps that would have to be taken. Both the Cossacks and Ukrainians would also need financial support, 'and the War Cabinet decided that such assistance should be forthcoming . . .' Cecil was instructed to wire to the British Minister and Military Attaché at Jassy in Roumania in this sense, and to inform Buchanan of the action taken, and to advise him, with reference to his wire of November 28 (urging that Russia be allowed to make a separate peace), that British policy was to support 'any responsible body' in Russia that would 'actively' oppose the Bolshevik movement, and to give money freely to those bodies that would help the Allied cause; and that the detailed arrangements for the organisation of Ukrainian, Cossack, Armenian and Polish banks were left to Buchanan's discretion. That night, the CIGS wired to Ballard instructing him to finance Kaledin 'up to any figure necessary', and to go himself, if possible with his French colleague, to Novocherkask; while Lord Robert Cecil, informing Buchanan of the War Cabinet's decision, explained that every effort had to be made to prevent Russia making a separate peace – and in fact told him to proceed with the proposal for setting up a Cossack bank, as put forward by Colonel Keyes. 'These decisions,' Hankey reminded the War Cabinet nearly three months later, in a summary of their Russian policy since the Kornilov adventure, 'inaugurated the policy of secret support to partisans in the political strife in Russia'. These were, in fact, momentous decisions, since there was still no news of Kaledin's strength and intentions; and they went far beyond those just taken in Paris. They were undoubtedly occasioned by the Bolsheviks actually opening peace talks with the enemy. But they took no account of what British relations were to be with the Bolsheviks.[8]

On the 4th, the War Cabinet discussed another telegram from Buchanan stating that failure to release Chicherin and Petrov would probably entail reprisals against British subjects in Russia (like Leech) who were conducting propaganda 'in sympathy with the counter-revolutionary movement'. The *Daily News* stated that Chicherin had been appointed Russian Ambassador to Great Britain, and if he were not released, this might be made a pretext for the arrest of Buchanan, 'and for picking a quarrel with the British Government'. The War Cabinet realised that they were in a dilemma. If threats by Lenin and Trotsky were heeded and negotiations were begun, 'it would be tantamount to the recognition of the Bolshevik Government by the British Government'. But if nothing were done, there was 'real danger' that Buchanan and British subjects in Russia would be interned, 'and possibly starved'. An alternative was simply to deport both men without saying anything, but this might be taken by Trotsky as a submission to threats, 'and would lead to renewed and more offensive demands'. Another alternative was to inform Trotsky that the two Russians would be deported if he would undertake not to oppress any of the British in Russia. Or he could be informed that Chicherin and Petrov had been arrested for carrying on propaganda work against the British government, and the Russian government's right to intern British subjects working against it in the same way in Russia was recognised. The War Cabinet did not like this, and decided that the best course for the present was to take no action.[9] They, in fact, shied away from granting *de facto* recognition to two Russian governments – one in south Russia, the other in Moscow.

Both Buchanan and Knox were appalled at the War Cabinet's decision to back the Don Cossacks and others. Buchanan replied sharply on the 5th that it was 'useless' to found exaggerated hopes on promises made by Don Cossack emissaries, whose 'constant visits' and indiscretion would end by seriously compromising the British Embassy. It was not realised how very precarious their position was, he warned. If Trotsky could prove either his or Knox's complicity in a counter-revolutionary plot, he would certainly arrest one or other of them. Any such dealings should be handled from Roumania. Knox was even more scathing. It was 'fantastically unlikely' that the Don Cossacks and others would fight on; and to ask the British Embassy to intrigue with them while in the Bolshevik government's power, was 'merely to get our throats cut to no purpose'. These wires seem to have had their due, though temporary effect in London; and there was no immediate reply to Colonel Keyes about the 200 million rouble loan to Jaroszynski.[10]

But meanwhile, he had a chance to obtain complete control of the Russian Bank for Foreign Trade (which controlled the grain trade on the Volga), if he could find 6 million roubles in sterling at once, as all the directors, including Davidov the chairman (a former head of the Foreign Department of the Russian Ministry of Finance), feared for their imminent arrest by the Bolsheviks and wished to leave Russia at once. Leech, acting as intermediary, put this proposition to Colonel Keyes in the form of an advertisement (probably to try and catch his attention in a moment of stress), and scrawled this across a single piece of paper:[11]

> *'Does the right to place*
> *Two Directors*
> *on the board of*
> *The Russian Bank for Foreign Trade*
> *interest H.M.G.?'*

These men, Leech explained, must be bought out by the British Embassy, who must therefore guarantee the money, or else it would be found elsewhere (*ie*, possibly from German sources, he hinted). But at this critical moment, Leech retired to bed with tonsilitis. His partner Firebrace, therefore, went to the British Embassy to see Lindley, the counsellor, who was terribly overworked and replied that he could not guarantee sterling which he did not hold. So Firebrace went to see Benenson, of the Russian and English Bank, whom he knew Lindley disliked, and made a temporary arrangement with him to lend the money. He then went back to the British Embassy and told Lindley, who was furious. 'I will not be under obligation to that squirt Benenson,' he said angrily; and promised that the British Embassy would guarantee the 6 million roubles in sterling. Lindley, without knowing it, had just taken a very important step. From now on, the matter of financing Jaroszynski's attempts to set up a Cossack bank became inextricably entwined with British efforts to use Jaroszynski as an agent to obtain control of all the major Russian banks for the British government.[11]

In more letters home, General Poole and Major Banting gave a good picture of the Russian scene at this time, but appear not to have known what Keyes and Leech were planning with Jaroszynski.

'These Bolshevik boys are rushing ahead to try & get peace @ any price, but they do act, which is more than can be said of any other crowd out here,' wrote Banting to Colonel Byrne in London on about the 4th. 'Troitsky [*sic*] is twisting the British Lion's tail a bit over here & is out to do everything to annoy the British (German propaganda) – it would appear that we are ably assisting him by keeping two interned Russian Jews in England rather than sending them back here & by refusal to recognise the Bolshevik power. I can understand the policy of non-recognition of the Bolshevik Govt,' he wrote, 'but I cannot understand why we want to keep Russian Jews, when some other fool wants them. However, high diplomacy is a wonderful art. It is rather amusing that in spite of the refusal [of British recognition], Troitsky has to be asked for permits for the Embassy cars, tickets to travel in Russia, etc. Personally, we have rec'd nothing but courtesy from the Bolshies . . . Troitsky's latest is to stop all British (women & children included) from leaving Russia. Things are all quiet here except for a small bust up @ the Winter Palace last night, when a number of troops broke into the cellars & many of them got very tight & the usual promiscuous firing took place all round the neighbourhood. We heard afterwards that some of the wine was being sold, but we missed that chance.

'The Bolshies have merely a "destructive" policy with no idea of a "constructive" one, but they have absolute power all round. Stavka talked a lot about fighting to the end, but yesterday they surrendered to the Red Guard.[12]

'Everything is @ a stand-still here now. The Govt. Depts are in a chaos. Lenin & Troitsky are just running the show and all the various districts of Russia – Finland, Ukraine, Poland – also Caucasus, Siberia, etc., etc. – are forming independent Govts, none of which know how to start a show or how to carry on. It is really an amusing show – if there were not the serious side, and all sorts of reports keep pouring in . . . The petrol shortage is getting very difficult . . . and nothing is coming up from the South. We have some good rogues with not too high morals on the job of getting it . . . We have just received the [English] papers giving an account of the Bolshevik regime here. It would appear that the "man-in-the-street" [in England] will get a very poor idea about what a Govt. of this sort means.'

He went on: 'I was in Moscow @ the beginning of this week to have a look round. Works are all half paralysed, they can't get money for wages & labour comes & goes as it likes. The R.F.C. Show under Maund would have been a great success if conditions were normal over here. The amount of stores found @ the Sklad [a junction on the Petrograd–Moscow line] is really amazing. About 50,000 pds [1,000 tons] of aluminium & a huge quantity of steel, etc. Aeroplanes complete in cases which have been lying in the open for two years.

'I stayed @ Cazalet's flat in Moscow – had quite a good time. On the last evening C. collected a party of the fairest & best . . . The Turkestanoff Princess sent her love to you. Prices are almost worse in Moscow than here . . .'

Banting added a note about the American railway mission and Allied stores in the Far East. 'The American control of the Trans-Siberian Railway has been a complete farce as regards relief of the block @ Vladivostok. It is the old story – good advice, without personnel to see that action is taken, is valueless over here. No one has seen or heard anything of the Stevens* mission, which is supposed to be somewhere on the line, for six weeks or more . . .'

* Stevens, an American railway expert, who was in charge of Russian railway reorganisation with the former Russian Provisional government's approval, was then either en route for or at Vladivostok to welcome a large party of American railway engineers.

Banting went on to show that some minds in Russia were already turning to the question of the economic opportunities now on offer, but these were not the diplomats, but people like Banting and Poole, who were most frustrated by the military collapse, and less aware of the political dangers. 'Have any steps been taken to consider the question of "after-the-war" commercial trade with Russia?' Banting asked Byrne. 'The great advantage that Germany has over the British is the rate-of-exchange. Owing to the low rates of exchange in Germany & Russia, they will be able to trade together more easily ... If there is any organisation considering this question in England, could you send some information out as to the lines on which they are working, as we could probably assist at this end ... Nothing more can be done here [by British businessmen] till the Treasury Dept here re-opens, as it has done nothing now for about three weeks ... The industrial business of Russia is becoming a very serious one,' he warned, 'thousands of workmen are now out of employment & production is dropping fast.[12]

'We are absolutely dry as regards whisky, but otherwise all merry & bright,' he added cheerfully.

General Poole was also writing to Colonel Byrne on the 4th: 'A mail may go out tonight so I send you a few words on the political situation –

1. Disabuse your mind and that of all others in London as to the idea of any "war party" existing. A few stalwarts talk big about wishing to go on with the war, but it's all talk & no chance of action. The people are tired & will never fight again.
2. Dukhonin was the mouthpiece of the war party outlined in (1). He talked big & wouldn't recognise Krilenko. When the Bolsheviks attacked the Stavka, the GHQ party surrendered forthwith. Dukhonin was lynched. *Moral.* It's no earthly use to shake a stick at determined men unless you are prepared to use it on their heads.
3. Our present policy appears to be exactly as outlined in (2). We won't recognise the Bol. Govt. We threaten that if they make peace it will have terrible results for them. The result is that the Bolsheviks now dislike us & humiliate our Govt, by pin-pricking British subjects out here. If we want to help the Hun we are being successful. It all fits in with the Hun-anti-British propaganda. If it goes on it will tend more & more to drive Russia into German arms. If it is driven to extremes it may even make Russia eventually an active enemy instead of a passive one.
4. I should prefer to see a policy of realising the truth – that Russia is out of the war. Then follow it up by trying to save as much as possible from the wreck by keeping a "place in the sun" for us & our

trade out here after the war. We should realise that the ship has been run on the rocks & is breaking up. Now is not the time to "strafe" the skipper, but to try to salve all we can.

'These are my views for what they are worth . . . Don't let anyone sail for our mission until the situation is cleared one way or another.'[12]

These letters from Poole's mission crossed with a letter from Colonel Byrne. 'Many thanks for all your letters,' he wrote to Poole on December 5. He confirmed that no more British supplies would be sent to Russia. 'What about yourselves, and is there any policy you would like pushed?' he asked. 'There are many things I would like to put in this letter, but I am afraid . . . it may get into Trotsky's hands. Meanwhile I will continue to do all I can about promotions . . . The W.O. are impossible and appear to delight in obstructing everything we do,' he added in a sudden outburst of inter-departmental venom.[12]

# 6

## *The Ukraine and the Don – Spheres of Interest*

As the various elements in the British Embassy were locked in dissension about whether or not to give massive financial support to the anti-Bolsheviks far away in the Don country, the German government were discussing what their long-term relations with Russia were to be on the conclusion of peace. The Foreign Ministry was not in accord with the German High Command. On November 29, however, Kühlmann received a wire from the Imperial Court stating that if there were to be peace talks with Russia, Kühlmann should still try, 'in spite of everything', to reach some alliance with the Russians. 'He [the Kaiser] said that, as after the Russo-Japanese war, this might be easier than we now thought.' The German High Command had already agreed to help to put the Russian railways in order. 'In the more distant future, the Emperor also hopes to set up a close commercial relationship with the Russians.'[1]

Underneath this wire, Kühlmann minuted to Bergen (the Foreign Ministry expert on the Bolshevik movement), 'Please draft a reply which would not be binding.'

But on December 1, while Bergen was working on the draft, the German newspaper *Neue Freie Presse* printed an interview with Field-Marshal Ludendorff in which he expressed a different opinion. 'I do not regard the Bolshevik announcement as an offer of peace,' he was quoted as saying. 'We can conclude an armistice with Russia only when we are certain that it will be observed.' The Russian revolution was the 'natural and inevitable result of our conduct of the war . . . It is the outcome of our victory.' This considerably hampered the efforts of the Foreign Ministry.

On December 3, the day after the peace talks opened at Brest-Litovsk, Kühlmann despatched a reply to the Imperial Court, based on

Bergen's draft. 'The disruption of the Entente and the subsequent creation of political combinations agreeable to us constitute the most important war aim of our diplomacy,' stated the Foreign Secretary. 'Russia appeared to be the weakest link in the enemy chain. The task therefore was gradually to loosen it, and, when possible, to remove it. This was the purpose of the subversive activity we caused to be carried out in Russia behind the front – in the first place promotion of separatist tendencies and support of the Bolsheviks. It was not until the Bolsheviks had received from us a steady flow of funds through various channels and under different labels that they were in a position to be able to build up their main organ, *Pravda*, to conduct energetic propaganda and appreciably to extend the originally narrow basis of their party.

'The Bolsheviks have now come to power; how long they will retain power cannot yet be foreseen. They need peace in order to strengthen their own position; on the other hand it is entirely in our interest that we should exploit the period while they are in power, which may be a short one, in order to attain firstly an armistice and then, if possible, peace. (The words: "There can be no question of further support of the Bolsheviks", apparently here in Bergen's draft, were omitted by Kühlmann.)

'The conclusion of a separate peace would mean the achievement of the desired war aim, namely a breach between Russia and her Allies . . . Once cast out and cast off by her former Allies, abandoned financially, Russia will be forced to seek our support.'

German help for Russia could be provided in various ways: first, a German-Russian commission, under German control, to restore the Russian railways; then a 'substantial' German loan to keep the Russian state machine going, which could be advanced 'on the security of grain, raw materials, etc., etc., to be provided by Russia'. Such aid, to be increased 'as and when necessary', would bring about a 'growing rapprochement' between the two countries.

'Austria-Hungary will regard the rapprochement with distrust and not without apprehension. I would interpret the excessive eagerness of Count Czernin to come to terms with the Russians as a desire to forestall us and to prevent Germany and Russia arriving at an intimate relationship inconvenient to the Danube monarchy. There is no need for us to compete for Russia's good will,' Kühlmann stated. 'We are strong enough to wait with equanimity; we are in a far better position than Austria-Hungary to offer Russia what she needs for the reconstruction of her state. I view future developments in the East with confidence, but I think it expedient for the time being to maintain a certain reserve in our attitude to the Austro-Hungarian Government . . .'[1]

A reply came on the 4th stating that the Kaiser approved this. But it was now clear that though the Russian specialists at the Foreign Ministry, and at the German Legation in Stockholm, who had fostered the clandestine Bolshevik revolutionary movement during the early war years, often against the sentiment of previous Foreign Secretaries, were now for withdrawing support from the Bolshevik government, since they felt it could not last, the present Foreign Secretary held that it could and must remain in power – and must therefore continue to receive German financial support.

It remained to counter the ill effects of Ludendorff's recent press interview. The opportunity came in a wire from Berne of December 5, stating that Karl Moor was now sufficiently well to travel to Stockholm in a few days time. Was his journey still desirable? The 'much-publicised' interview in the *Neue Freie Presse* had had an 'unusually powerful' effect everywhere, remarked the German Minister in Berne. But it was believed that Moor, with the strong influence which he had with the Bolsheviks, could actively counter the 'hostile exploitation' of this interview, 'which was, of course, immediately unleashed with all the means available'.[1]

'Journey desirable,' replied Bergen by return.

In discussions on December 6 and 7, however, the German High Command and the Foreign Ministry agreed on the preliminary conditions for peace talks proper with the Bolsheviks. These were:

1. German annexation of Latvia and Lithuania, 'in order to feed the [German] nation'. Polish independence, in association with Germany. Russian evacuation of Esthonia and Finland; of East Galicia and Moldavia (east of Poland and Roumania respectively); and of Armenia, in the Caucasus.
2. No German interference in Russian affairs. No war reparations. General exchange of prisoners. Self-determination in the territories lost by Russia (but apparently conditional on their not being occupied by the British).
3. German help and financial support for the reorganisation of the Russian railways and the Russian economy. 'Close' German economic and commercial relations with Russia. 'Delivery of [Russian] cereals, oil, etc., to Germany at favourable prices.'
4. A German guarantee not to attack Russia, in case of Japanese intervention.
5. A German alliance with Russia 'at a later date'.[2]

Kühlmann was satisfied. 'Preliminary peace could be concluded in a very short time,' he minuted to Foreign Ministry officials on the 9th.

'If Trotsky or Lenin came in person, I myself would appear for the negotiations, and this would offer a guarantee of a speedy conclusion...'

There remained one troublesome matter to settle. The same day, Kühlmann warned the German Minister in Stockholm that if the neutral countries did not recognise Bolshevik diplomatic envoys, the Bolshevik government might break off relations with their envoys in Petrograd, 'and since, moreover, we lay particular value on the continuation of the activities of the Swedish Minister in Petersburg, I request that you discuss the matter confidentially with the Swedish government, and recommend them to recognise the Bolshevik representatives as soon as possible'.[2]

This was soon settled. The Swedes obliged by recognising Vorovski, the Bolshevik envoy in Stockholm. But now Helphand, fearful of being squeezed out by both Germans and Bolsheviks, was creating difficulties by strongly influencing Vorovski (and hence, it was feared, Trotsky) in favour of holding the coming peace talks at Stockholm, not Brest-Litovsk. The Foreign Ministry in Berlin were alarmed. 'Please ask him [Helphand] urgently to help to promote the peace negotiations, which begin in a few days, by influencing his friends,' wired the Under Secretary of State to the German Minister in Copenhagen on the 17th. 'The Bolsheviks are fighting, according to reliable reports, against growing internal difficulties,' he explained, 'and therefore have every interest in strengthening their position by an early peace.'[3]

But Helphand had no friends in Petrograd. Lenin had now decided to get rid of him once and for all. The same day (the 17th), Radek had returned to Stockholm and had told Helphand that Lenin would not allow him to return to Russia; 'the cause of the revolution', Lenin had said, 'should not be touched by dirty hands'. Thus Lenin thought he had rid himself, and the Bolshevik party, of the taint of German money.

For Helphand, this was the end of his great gamble. But he quickly recovered himself. Assured of Lenin's hostility, he went to see Counsellor Riezler to make his peace with the German Foreign Ministry. Having founded a new Russian newspaper, which was to be distributed free in Russia, he planned to attack the Bolshevik leaders for their mistakes and their dictatorial attitude; his main target was to be the middle ranks of the Bolshevik party. Riezler welcomed Helphand back. On December 24, as Helphand left Stockholm for Berlin, Riezler wrote privately to Bergen, the German specialist on the Bolshevik movement: 'At this moment, when his [Helphand's] interests and ours are running parallel again, he is once more very important, and I would strongly recommend you to ask him, in confidence ... for his advice in Berlin ... He really is a very considerable man and he has excellent ideas. It may well be that we shall soon feel that it would be an advantage to base our position in Russia on wider circles than those around Lenin, and in that event he will be essential to us.' Riezler, in fact, the Russian expert in Stockholm, once again made clear that he did not feel that the Bolsheviks would last.[3]

In Petrograd, despite a violent appeal by Lenin to the Indian Moslems to revolt against British rule, relations between the British Embassy and the Bolsheviks now slightly improved. Buchanan, who felt that they would be the ruling power 'for some time to come', decided to be conciliatory when he heard of the Bolshevik government's disapproval of Trotsky's recent threats to imprison him. If British subjects could leave Russia, he informed Trotsky on the 6th, he would advise the British government to release Chicherin and Petrov. Trotsky took the hint. In answer to Buchanan, he said that in his recent note he had only wished to emphasise that Englishmen in Russia must suffer the same treatment as Russians in England, and to warn Buchanan that he 'knew as a fact' that he, Buchanan, was in touch with Kaledin's agents; Buchanan had been ill-advised and ill-informed ever since the Russian revolution, 'especially by Kerensky,' warned Trotsky. ('I gather that he was referring to the fact that I had under-estimated the strength of the Bolshevik movement – and in this he was right,' admitted Buchanan. 'Kerensky, Tereschenko, the late Foreign Minister, and some of the other Ministers had all misled me on this point, and had repeatedly assured me that the [provisional] government would be able to suppress them,' he wrote in his diary. Trotsky may well, in fact, have had various sources for his knowledge of the British Embassy's contacts, not only the undoubted indiscretion of the Don Cossack emissaries. It is for consideration whether the Bolsheviks were not successfully tapping all wires sent from the British Embassy. The provisional government had certainly been doing so.)[4]

At a press conference at the British Embassy on December 8, Buchanan answered the various Bolshevik charges. After the Allied agreement to discuss war aims with a stable Russian government was read out, and a defence made of British policy in India, Buchanan made a speech in defence of Leech's Propaganda Bureau and repudiated the charge of 'being in league with counter-revolutionaries'. There was 'not the slightest foundation' for such an accusation, he stated; while Russia was fighting, it had also conducted war propaganda, 'but it no longer does so'. He then gave this assurance: 'I wish the Russian people to know that neither I myself nor any agency under my control have any wish to interfere in the internal affairs of their country.' This was a false assurance. Whatever they may have wished, they were indeed interfering – on orders from London.[4]

But the situation on the Don, which they were meant to be supporting, was lamentable. When the escaped Russian generals, except for Kornilov, reached Novocherkask early in December, Kaledin insisted that all of them, except Alexeiev, must leave at once for the Kuban or the Caucasus; his Don Cossacks were tired, and local Bolsheviks and mutinous Black Sea sailors in Rostov were threatening action. The British envoy sent from Roumania was equally pessimistic. 'Cossacks absolutely useless and disorganised,' he wired on the 7th.* Just before the newly-arrived Russian generals moved on to the Kuban on the 9th, Alexeiev told them that he had decided to form a volunteer army; and though he had very few supplies for his few recruits, and refused to issue a general appeal for more, groups which he had set up in Petrograd and Moscow, he claimed, would help Russian officers come down to the Don. It did not look very promising.

But when the Bolsheviks in Petrograd heard of the arrival of the Russian generals on the Don, they arrested the Cadet leaders in Petrograd and ordered an attack on both Kiev and Rostov. On December 10, local Bolsheviks and Black Sea sailors seized Rostov. As his Don Cossacks refused to move against them, Kaledin had to appeal to Alexeiev, whose small volunteer army retook Rostov; whereupon it was agreed that his troops might remain on the Don. Thus the Russian civil war began.[5]

Two days later, another British military envoy, Major J. K. L. Fitzwilliams (sent by the British Military Attaché at Jassy on November 27 to investigate matters at Novocherkask) reported, on his return to Kiev, in concise and depressing terms on Kaledin. This he did in question and answer form.

1. *Question:* Is Kaledin their leader?
   *Answer:* Yes. In accordance with the custom of the Don Cossacks, he was elected *Ataman* in July 1917 for a period of three years. By the formation of the 'South-Eastern' Alliance, however, he became Chief of all the tribes on both sides of the Caucasus . . . also of the Orenburg and Ural Cossacks' territory to the east of the Volga. This alliance is for *interior defence only* . . . I had four interviews with him in three days and he gave me the impression of being very tired, very afraid of the Bolsheviks, and very uncertain of his power over his troops.
2. *Question:* What are his plans?
   *Answer:* To reorganise and bring into order the territories mentioned above. At present vendettas exist between many Caucasian

---

* But this wire was not transmitted from Jassy until December 9th.

tribes . . . All Kaledin's ideas for the present and near future are based on *internal* reconstruction and he has publicly stated that he will have nothing to do with affairs outside his own territories.

3. *Question:* Does he favour a firm continuation of the war?

*Answer:* No. He has expressed his *personal* opinion that the Cossacks will not recognise the Bolsheviks and will not agree to a separate peace, but privately he told me that he cannot see how to avoid acknowledging the B[olshevik]s in the future. The fact has to be recognised that the Cossack units lately acting on the front, etc. are deeply imbued with B[olshevik] ideas and are not to be relied upon . . . The old men are trustworthy, but the younger ones are quite unreliable. Kaledin knows this and is terrified by the threats of a possible B[olshevik] attack on the Don. In case of such an attack it is probable that the men would fight in defence of their homes, but any idea of sending troops into Russia to undertake offensive operations is not to be thought of.

4. In the above [Fitzwilliams continued], I have confined myself to answering the questions given to me. There are, however, so many outside factors bearing on the situation that the following remarks may be of use in clearing up the very complicated position of the Caucasus today. The Caucasus is crowded with refugees of all parties.

Firstly: the Cossacks have given refuge to them all, but Kaledin refuses to associate himself with any of them for fear of embroiling himself with the B[olshevik]s.[6]

Secondly: the railway junction at Tsaritsin is wholly and that at Rostov is partially held by the B[olshevik]s. This hampers him badly, and he is not strong enough to seize and hold them.

Thirdly: the various parties led by Alexeiev, Rodzianko, Kral (Czech) etc., etc., are all plotting to gain their own ends and all jealous of one another. They are all penniless and all have large staffs, but small followings. Of them all, and they gave me every facility for studying them in the hope of possible financial assistance, I consider the Czech organisation the best and the most likely to lead to the possible formation of a strong government. Reasons as follows: The Czechs know that they sink or swim with Russia; therefore they are more likely to take an unbiased view of the situation and not to be prejudiced by the claims of any one party. They are also the possessors of two well-equipped and well-disciplined divisions, which is more than any other party can claim to. Lastly; their organisation is the best and their leaders are cleverer and more hardworking than the Russians.

5. If the Allies are prepared to risk the money, I think that in six

months time a force of half a million good troops could be collected and armed. The cost will be great, but the results would be invaluable.[6]

This was a remarkably accurate report on conditions on the Don. Its detailed assessment of the Czech force in Russia supplemented one that had been supplied by General Berthelot, but which had been rejected by the Allied conference in Paris on December 1. This Czech force, it will be recalled, was composed of Czech prisoners and deserters from the Austro-Hungarian army, and Czech citizens who had been living in Russia since before the war. This compact, disciplined and democratic force had been attached to the Russian army and was now set on getting home to found a democratic Czecho-Slovak state. The Czechs felt a deep sense of gratitude to Russia, heightened by the achievements of the Russian revolution, principally the overthrow of Tsarism, and they had no wish to see Russia succumb to another dictatorship. But their main desire now was to go home.

Fitzwilliams's report took some time to reach London. It was sent to General Poole, who wrote a strong letter, probably under its influence, to Colonel Byrne in London, in which he heartily condemned British policy towards Russia. 'Our present policy,' wrote Poole on December 19, 'seems to me to be not only disastrous to us from a national point of view, but also humiliating in the extreme. We will not recognise Trotsky officially, but not a day passes without the Ambassador being obliged to send someone round from the Embassy to ask a favour from him. If only we could make up our minds to recognise that this is the *de facto* government, and treat with it as long as it is in power, it would help us enormously. For example – we want to stop the exit of goods from Archangel, or we want to re-buy all goods which are there. Now, as we cannot recognise this government, we are practically powerless, as everybody is too afraid of them to work for us without a government order. If only we could go round to Trotsky, we could square it all in ten minutes.

'The result of our policy is to help the Germans in every way, as these people spread themselves on anti-British propaganda. We should look forward to the probable position next year. Russia will be neutral, and unless we come into the picture Germany will have a free hand to exploit to the full Russia's resources. Even with the disorganisation of railways and labour troubles the result for Germany should be that she gets enough out of Russia to render our blockade innocuous.

'Our counter should be that we come into the Russian market as competitors of Germany and buy against her every time. If we play our cards carefully now we can do this with Russian goodwill which will be a great asset. As things go at present, I think we shall be up against open hostility and that the Hun will be welcomed as the saviour of Russia.

'The French have hypnotised us. They make themselves believe that things are what they would like them to be. They will not look cold facts in the face. My firm opinion is, and it gets firmer every day, that it is pure folly to count on any more fighting on the part of the Ukraine or Cossacks, or what our people at home now call "the S.E. Federation of Russia". If we count on this, we are leaning on a broken reed, I fear.'

In a postscript Poole added: 'I wish I were an artist and I would send you a picture of what I foresee in future, *viz* – the German Ambassador sitting at table with Lenin on his right and Trotsky on his left, getting all the plums of Russia. At the back door is a clerk from our Embassy, who has to scavenge for scraps, which is all we shall get.'[6]

He attached the report from Fitzwilliams, 'which bears out my views'. But as Poole did not send this letter until December 29, Fitzwilliams's report cannot have reached London until about January 18.

On the 20th, Kornilov, the former Russian C.-in-C., arrived at Novocherkask. The other Russian generals, whom Kaledin had earlier insisted should go on to the Kuban, returned to meet him. Kornilov insisted that there should be only one man (himself) in command on the Don, while Alexeiev wished to manage the financial and political side. There was considerable argument. Kornilov, in fact, was thinking of leaving to form a movement in Siberia, where he had been brought up, when Milyukov, the Cadet leader, arrived from Moscow and induced the three men to form a triumvirate. Kornilov became military commander; Alexeiev took responsibility for administration and finance, and Kaledin was to be in charge of the Don Cossacks. A document to this effect was signed and sent to the (mainly Cadet) 'National Centre' party in Moscow.[7]

In London, it had been agreed to support the Don Cossacks and others in south Russia, but no decision had been reached on British policy towards the Bolsheviks. This was now the crucial matter. During December, the War Cabinet received a lot of advice from their men on the spot on which of the contending parties in Russia to support. Knox was simply against supporting the Cossacks. The British agent sent from Roumania wired that they were useless and disorganised. Fitzwilliams, via Poole, gave a detailed assessment of how hopeless a proposition the Cossacks and others were, but reported favourably on the Czechs. Buchanan felt the Bolsheviks would be the ruling power for some time to come, and was thus inclining towards *de facto* recognition. Poole strongly urged *de facto* recognition, and was totally against all support of any forces in south Russia.

The advice from Russia was thus inclining all one way. But the War Cabinet's efforts to reach some coherent decision on British policy towards the Bolsheviks remained confused because of their ingrained prejudice and basic ignorance of Russia; but above all because Bolshevik power – whether temporary or semi-permanent – rested on their ability to make peace. Thus it appeared impossible to reconcile any sort of *de facto* relations with keeping Russia in the war, which was the War Cabinet's main aim. This was the conundrum the War Cabinet had to face.

On December 7, Balfour read to the War Cabinet a telegram from Petrograd stating that Lenin was 'openly inciting our Indian subjects to revolt', and that Buchanan intended to put the British case before the Russian public at a press conference – which might lead to a rupture with the Bolshevik government. It might thus be desirable to anticipate the crisis, which was evidently approaching, by withdrawing the British Embassy, and leaving British consuls to protect British interests in Russia. Balfour was authorised to wire Buchanan to consult his Allied colleagues, and then advise whether such action should be taken.

The main problem was then faced. The many questions arising out of the Russian problem, it was suggested, could be more easily settled if Allied policy was 'more clearly defined'. It was open to the Allies:

a. to recognise the Bolsheviks, 'and make the best arrangements possible with them'; or
b. to refuse to recognise them, 'and take open and energetic steps against them'.[8]

A decision should also be taken about the release of Chicherin and Petrov, the two Russian agitators interned for spreading Bolshevik propaganda among shipyard workers on the Clyde. But, it was pointed out, the British government had 'already undertaken risks' in contacting General Kaledin and the Ukraine, and offering them financial help. The inference clearly was that no risks could be taken with the Bolsheviks. The War Cabinet shied away from the problem.

On December 10, when the matter was again considered, it was suggested that the British government was not primarily concerned with the 'composition' of the Russian government, nor with the 'local aspirations' of the Bolsheviks or other Russian political parties, except in so far as they affected the war with Germany. 'This was the line we had taken during the Tsar's reign, and there was no reason to depart from it.' The dominant British purpose throughout the Russian revolution should be:

a. if possible, to keep Russia in the war until our joint war aims were realised; or
b. if this could not be secured, then to ensure that Russia was as helpful to us and as harmful to the enemy as possible.

Now the problem was being faced. If, as seemed likely, the Bolsheviks remained in power for the next few months only, 'these months were critical', it was emphasised, 'and to antagonise them needlessly would be to throw them into the arms of Germany'. This aspect of the War Cabinet's appreciation of the Bolshevik movement was thus very similar to the German Foreign Ministry view. At present, there were signs that the elections for the constituent assembly would in a few days time give the Bolsheviks not only *de facto*, but also constitutional power. Buchanan, in his wire of December 8, reported that there had lately been a remarkable change in the official Bolshevik press, 'the Allies not being attacked, for the first time for several weeks'.

But *The Times* that day, it was argued, had reported that the Germans in their peace terms were demanding:

a. German control of the Russian wheat market;
b. German goods to be imported into Russia duty free;
c. German retention of all Russian territory now occupied by German troops.[9]

This was broadly true. The CIGS, however, then read out a wire, sent on the 5th, stating that the new Bolshevik Commander-in-Chief Krilenko appeared 'most anxious' to make a favourable impression on Allied officers, and had carried out all their suggestions for safeguarding the lives of officers and their families. In a wire on the 6th, Buchanan reported an interview between Trotsky and a British officer concerning the embargo on British subjects leaving Russia, and the possible release of Chicherin and Petrov, of which Buchanan was now in favour.

This led to further dispute within the War Cabinet. The continued internment of Chicherin and Petrov, it was suggested, might endanger the lives of thousands of British subjects in Russia, while the case for their internment was 'not a very strong one'. But, it was argued, there was 'very real danger' of any traffic with the Bolsheviks, whose strength lay in their support for peace, and if they abandoned their efforts for peace, they would 'probably be overthrown'. Further, any such action was hardly consistent with British support for Kaledin in south Russia. 'Was it desirable to treat with both Trotsky and Kaledin at one and the same time?' the Cabinet minutes asked. 'Our policy towards Kaledin had been decided upon. Would it not be wise to wait and see whether the Bolshevik government was going to last?' But British support for

Kaledin was directed against the Germans, it was argued, and not against the Bolsheviks, 'and was specially intended to help the Roumanians'.

The War Cabinet decided, 'without making any change in their recent policy towards Russia', it was stressed, that Balfour should inform Buchanan that his wire of the 6th was approved, and that he should deal with Chicherin and Petrov as best he could. The main problem, after being briefly faced, was thus again shelved.

Balfour then enquired about British policy towards Roumania. So far, the Cabinet had been trying to keep the Roumanian army in 'active hostility' to the enemy, but they had been forced to join the armistice together with the Russians. They had as yet made no treaty, but they might have to do so if and when the Bolsheviks did so. The War Cabinet had to decide what guidance to offer Roumania.

The CIGS said that the Roumanian army was helpless. It could not be withdrawn any distance into Russia because of the breakdown in the railways and supplies. So far, no answer had been received about Kaledin, but the press that day had printed a Bolshevik proclamation declaring war against Kaledin and the Don Cossacks. The CIGS also quoted a letter dated November 25 from Captain Noel (the British envoy sent from Tiflis), in which the Don Cossacks 'were said to be weary of the war and unlikely to embark on a new campaign. The Don party might be useful in preventing supplies from the Caucasus falling into the hands of the Germans, if the Germans get control in western Russia,' reported Noel.

It was further shown from wires from other sources, including Teheran, that there was a 'strong tendency' for areas in southern Russia, like the Caucasus, the Terek, the Kuban, the Don, the Ukrainian Rada, and possibly the Black Sea littoral, to dissolve into independent political groups, pending the restoration of an 'universally recognised' central Russian government. This was also the case in Finland.

The War Cabinet recognised that in certain eventualities it might be the 'greatest kindness' to Roumania, 'and least embarrassing to us', to release Roumania entirely from her agreement with the Allies not to make a separate peace. Thus, the main reason for British support for Kaledin disappeared.

The War Cabinet decided that the CIGS should advise about those areas of Russia 'which showed a disposition not to accept Bolshevik rule'; and that the War Office, the Admiralty and the Ministry of Blockade should advise what conditions Buchanan should press for, 'if circumstances enabled him to do so', in any Bolshevik-German peace terms.[9]

But it seems extremely unlikely that the War Cabinet fully realised how turbulent were those areas in southern Russia from which they hoped for so much. As invariably happens during revolutions, events occurred now and then that bordered on farce. On November 14, Poole's mission sent to Colonel Byrne in London this extract from a report from southern Russia: 'There are one or two rather amusing changes which the Committees have decided should be made in the form of religious service and these are, M. le Dieu to be Citizen God, King of the Heavens to be President of the Heavenly Republic, and in the service where the expression "Peace of all the World" occurs, the addition of "without annexation and without contribution" should be made. Here at Sevastopol, a priest reading the lessons came across the expression Czar David, he was so afraid of even mentioning the word Czar, that he "tactfully" changed it to David's provisional government; it sounds more amusing in the Russian.'[10]

On the 14th, the DMI read out to the War Cabinet a wire from General Knox at Petrograd, giving a summary of the eleven German armistice conditions, which the Bolsheviks had refused, though Knox thought that 'something of the sort would eventually be accepted by the Russians'.

The War Cabinet then considered the Caucasus, and the general dissolution that was taking place there. On December 3, they had approved large-scale financial support for the Russian Caucasus army, and for a so-called 'national' army being raised by Georgia, Armenia and the Azerbaijani Tartars. But the Russian Caucasus army had now entirely disintegrated, and the other three small states were at each others' throats because of the secular hatred of Tartar for Armenian. As a result, British officers on the spot, with considerable funds to disburse, found themselves in danger of financing little local massacres and their inevitable reprisals, instead of joint action against the Germans. This had led to a local British policy of financing only the Armenians, which naturally involved alienating the Tartars. Meanwhile a body called the Transcaucasian Commissariat, consisting of Georgian, Azerbaijani, Armenian and Russian socialists, had been formed at Tiflis in Georgia. It had begun peace negotiations with Turkey early in December, and an armistice had been arranged. But this body had no real power over the various Caucasus states.

The matter had been touched on in the War Cabinet of December 10 and now a decision had to be made about British policy. The DMI reported that he had heard from Tiflis that it was proposed to form a local Caucasus Cossack federation, which would fight on against Germany, if financed and supplied. There had been a tendency 'in one quarter' (presumably the Foreign Office), to blame the War Office for

Major-General Poole and Brigadier Finlayson.

Commander Oliver Locker-Lampson.

*Above :* General Kornilov arrives in Moscow for the State conference, August, 1917.

*Opposite above :* Commander Locker-Lampson making a river crossing. The stranded car is the Rolls Royce in which, in September 1917, he set off to join Kornilov.

*Opposite below :* The Wild Division, photographed from one of Locker-Lampson's armoured cars.

Captain Teddy Lessing.

*Opposite :* Russian troops stream off a train on their way home in July 1917 – 'voting with their feet,' as Lenin put it.

Hugh Leech; this photograph, taken on Wimbledon Park Golf Course in 1922, is the only one known to exist.

*Opposite :* The Red Flag is hoisted by Russian soldiers in the aftermath of the defeats of July 1917.

*Above left:* Vladimir Poliakov.

*Below left:* Colonel Terence Keyes; this photograph was taken after he had been promoted to Brigadier-General in 1920.

*Above right:* Karol Jaroszynski and (*below right*) the hall of his palace in St. Petersburg.

Милостивый Государь

Владиміръ Лазаревичъ,

Прошу Васъ управлять и распоряжаться принадлежащимъ
мнѣ нынѣ и могущимъ принадлежать впослѣдствіи движимымъ
и недвижимымъ имуществомъ и завѣдывать всѣми моими дѣла-
ми. Уполномочиваю Васъ открывать въ Государственномъ
Банкѣ, его Конторахъ и Отдѣленіяхъ, въ Городскихъ Обще-
ственныхъ, Коммерческихъ, Взаимнаго Кредита и другого
наименованія Банкахъ и вообще кредитныхъ и другихъ учрежденіяхъ текущіе счета, а также и счеты спеціальные,
обезпеченные векселями или процентными бумагами, съ вы-
дачею отъ моего имени соло-векселей на сумму открытаго
мнѣ кредита, вносить на храненіе, а также и на управле-
ніе принадлежащія мнѣ государственныя и разныя процентныя бумаги и всякаго рода документы и имущества и
получать обратно вклады какъ внесенные Вами, такъ и
мною или другими лицами на мое имя; равно дѣлать на
мое имя вклады срочные и до востребованія изъ процен-
товъ, получать купоны и обратно вклады съ наросшими
процентами и деньги по трансфертамъ и переводамъ, а
также съ текущихъ и спеціальныхъ счётовъ; по чекамъ за
Вашею подписью и закрывать таковые счеты; покупать на
мое имя процентныя бумаги и принадлежащія мнѣ продавать
брать для меня во всѣхъ безъ исключенія банкахъ и кредитныхъ учрежденіяхъ во временное пользованіе для хра-
ненія моихъ цѣнностей безопасные ящики. Всему, что Вы
по сей довѣренности законно учините, я Вамъ вѣрю, спо-
рить и прекословить не буду. Довѣренность эта принадле-
житъ Инженеру Путей Сообщенія Владиміру Лазаревичу По-
лякову.

*P. Keyes.*

Тысяча девятьсотъ восемнадцатаго года Февраля
двадцать седьмого/четырнадцатаго дня въ Петроградѣ.
Настоящая довѣренность явлена у меня Павла Терентье-

A facsimile of the power of attorney given by Colonel Keyes to Poliakov on February 27th
1918. The document empowered Poliakov to negotiate the purchase of the Siberian Bank on
behalf of the British Government.

The details of the sale of the Siberian Bank, drawn up in Poliakov's own hand. They show how the crucial sum of 15 million roubles was to be passed through the Siberian Bank, under the guise of a down payment, and on to the Don Cossacks and the Volunteer Army.

the fact that the local British mission at Tiflis had not handed out more money. It was pointed out that the British Minister in Teheran (Sir Charles Marling), in a wire to the Cabinet on the 13th, had accepted responsibility for financial outlay incurred in those regions; that financial support for this Cossack federation was really separate from finance for the Caucasus states; and that there was 'some danger, if care were not taken, of support being given to different separate organisations which had varying, if not actually hostile, views'. The DMI recalled that the Cabinet had already agreed to advance £10 million to the Ukraine, £10 million to General Kaledin, and a lesser amount to the Armenians.

The War Cabinet again decided to support local Cossacks, and laid down that 'any sum of money, required for the purpose of maintaining alive in south-east Russia the resistance to the Central Powers, considered necessary by the War Office, in consultation with the Foreign Office, should be furnished; the money to be paid in instalments so long as the recipients continued the struggle'.[11]

On December 19, the Prime Minister reported to the War Cabinet on a talk he had had with an American called Thompson, just back from Russia, who had given a 'somewhat different impression' of affairs in Russia from what was generally believed. This was Lieutenant-Colonel William Boyce Thompson, a wealthy financier and copper magnate, who had personally financed and, since August, run the American Red Cross mission to Russia. On his arrival in Petrograd, however, he had launched out into other fields and had advanced $1 million for propaganda measures to keep Russia in the war and to counter the German menace; newspapers were started, printing plant bought, and news bureaux supported. Thompson's multifarious activities caused much concern in Washington and his efforts to raise more official money there were unsuccessful. After the Bolshevik coup, Thompson swung round and urged the Allies to support them. In late November, increasingly disturbed by the blindness of Allied policy, he left the American Red Cross mission in the hands of his assistant, Colonel Raymond Robins, and went to stir up support for the Bolsheviks in the Allied capitals.

'The gist of his remarks,' Lloyd George told the War Cabinet, 'was to the effect that the Revolution had come to stay; that the Allies had not shown themselves sufficiently sympathetic with the Revolution; and that Mm. Trotsky and Lenin were not in German pay, the latter being a fairly distinguished Professor.' Thompson thought the Allies should conduct 'active propaganda' in Russia by some 'specially selected' men, and that the Allies were not now well represented in Russia. He thought the Allies must realise that the Russian army and people 'were out of the war, and that the Allies would have to choose between Russia as a friendly or a hostile neutral'.

Colonel Thompson, an outsider, had thus again raised the crucial problem that the War Cabinet were continually unwilling to face – British policy towards the Bolsheviks. He had also raised a problem discussed at the Allied conference in Paris on December 1, and which the War Cabinet had never even considered, *eg*, a great extension of Allied propaganda in Russia. Some discussion now took place in the War Cabinet about whether the Allies should change their policy, 'the Bolsheviks being stated by Mr Thompson to be anti-German'.

Lord Robert Cecil said he believed that the German armistice conditions provided for German trade with Bolshevik Russia, 'the whole arrangement being obviously dictated by the Germans'. He thought the Germans would try to continue the armistice 'until the Russian army had melted away'.

Sir Edward Carson then read out a manifesto by Trotsky, a copy of which he (Carson) had been given by the British manager of the Vauxhall Motor Company, just back from Russia. This indicated that Trotsky was, ostensibly, hostile 'to the organisation of civilised society', rather than pro-German. On the other hand, it was argued, such an 'assumed attitude' was not inconsistent with Trotsky being a German agent.[12]

Lord Robert said that the best plan was to continue to rally and support all those elements in southern Russia that were resisting the Bolsheviks; Jewish sources claimed that the Ukrainians also were prepared to do so. To make this policy more effective, funds should be placed at the disposal of Sir Charles Marling, the British Minister in Teheran, who should be given 'a free hand to do the best he can by agents, propaganda, and any other means, to keep the people of south Russia on our side'. The Jews were very powerful in the Ukraine, 'and it might be possible to obtain their support', he added.

But it was argued that it was impossible to influence southern Russia from so far away as Teheran, and also difficult to find people who spoke Russian. If, moreover, the Bolsheviks should gain the upper hand 'and eventually achieve complete success', this evidence of British support for their opponents 'would intensify their irritation, and throw them even more into the hands of the Germans than they are now'.[12]

On December 20, the War Cabinet continued its discussions ('interminable and unprofitable discussions on Russian policy', complained Hankey, which wasted much time, and were solely due to 'Ll. G. having got [it] into his head that we ought to support the Bolsheviks'.) Carson and Milner undertook to find suitable people to conduct 'active propaganda' in Russia.

[162]

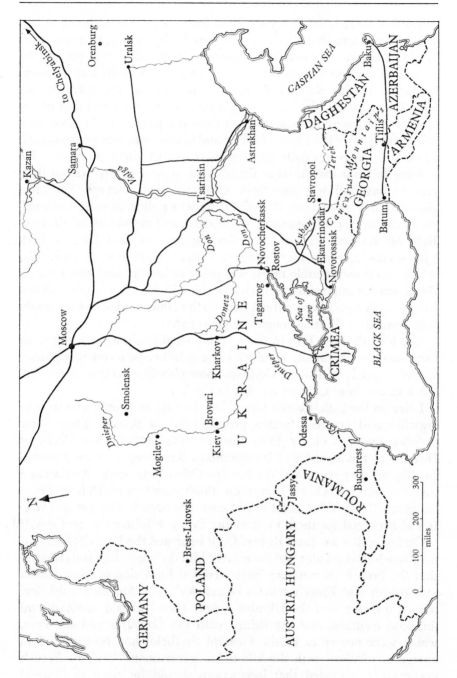

Southern Russia and the Ukraine

Lord Robert Cecil, however, now forced the War Cabinet to face the real problem that they were continually bypassing, criticised their 'vague' attitude towards developments in Russia, 'and pressed for some definite policy to be laid down'. There were really four different problems in the Russian situation – Roumania, the Ukraine, the Don Cossacks, and the Caucasus Cossacks – which formed part of one question, but were at present being treated separately. The need for a 'clear analysis' of the whole situation and of what was being done in each of the four areas was daily growing more urgent, since the information coming in from the different British local representatives varied from day to day and was sometimes mutually contradictory. The chief difficulty in carrying out the War Cabinet's policy, already 'outlined' on December 14, of financing 'those races and organisations' likely to fight on against Germany, was finding roubles, said Lord Robert. (Jaroszynski's proposal for forming a Cossack bank in southern Russia, which could issue rouble notes, was going to be of crucial importance.) But it was felt impossible to reach a decision in the absence of the Prime Minister, though it was agreed that further information, which might help towards a decision, might be collected.[13]

The idea that the Jews in the Ukraine would help to resurrect what they would undoubtedly consider to be neo-Tsarist forces was plainly absurd – but Lord Robert Cecil was now clearly emerging as the real hawk in the War Cabinet on Russian policy.

Later on the 20th, Carson assembled the various people who were to organise and conduct 'active propaganda' in Russia. These were Colonel Byrne, Colonel John Buchan (the author, then Assistant Director at the Ministry of Information), Rex Leeper, of the Political Intelligence Department at the Foreign Office (who spoke Russian and was the Foreign Office expert on Bolshevism), and Robert Bruce Lockhart, the British Consul in Moscow now back in London on leave. It was arranged for them to meet the Prime Minister the next day.[14]

On December 21, Lord Robert Cecil informed the War Cabinet that the French Ambassador had been to see him the day before and reported that the French government 'suggested a delimitation of south Russia into British and French spheres of activity'. The French should deal with Roumania and the Ukraine, where they had both military and financial facilities, and the British with the Caucasus and the Don, which were nearer to Persia. General Berthelot had been placed in charge of relations with the Ukrainian government, 'and the French government suggested that instructions should be given to General Barter not to interfere with General Berthelot'. The British, in fact, were being faced with a French *fait accompli*.

Lord Robert Cecil went on to say that he understood from newspaper reports that the Cossacks had captured Rostov, had killed 800 Red Guards, and that the Bolsheviks admitted defeat. (This, of course, was untrue. The Don Cossacks had refused to move, and the infant volunteer army had had to retake Rostov. But Cecil could not have known this.)

The conflicting policies advocated by Buchanan in Petrograd and by the Allied representatives at Jassy in Roumania 'raised an important and deep question of principle', said Cecil, continuing his argument of the day before. 'It would be impossible any longer to go on running two horses; we must decide definitely whether we are to support the Bolsheviks in their claim to be the supreme Government throughout Russia, or whether we are to recognise and assist the other *de facto* Governments in Russia. We must either support the Ukrainians, Cossacks, Georgians, and Armenians, or the Bolsheviks; we could not do both. In his opinion, the forces in South Russia had a fair fighting chance of success in the event of our supporting them. If we did not support them, the blockade of Germany would be at an end, and the terms of the armistice involved the despatch of grain and other raw materials of South Russia to Germany via the Danube. Nearly all the supplies in Russia that were of value to the enemy were in South Russia, and now in the hands of the people who were opposing the Bolshevik Government. The separatist sentiment in the Ukraine was an old story, and it appeared that the Bolshevik Government were prepared to recognise the principle of self-determination in regard to the Ukrainian people, and to recognise the Rada. The Ukrainians had been fighting with the Bolsheviks in Odessa, and here they appeared to have the support of the Jews against the Bolsheviks.

'We could hope for nothing from Trotsky,' continued Cecil, 'who was a Jew of the international type, and was solely out to smash Russia and to revenge himself, not only on the governing classes, but upon the peasants of Russia. Money was now being spent by the French and ourselves in the Ukraine, and it was a question for the Cabinet to decide whether this should continue.'

The DMI pointed out that the Roumanian army had fifteen 'good fighting' divisions, with 300 French officers attached to it, which would form a 'valuable support' to the Ukrainians, if Ukrainian supplies were available for the Roumanian army. (This was hardly borne out by what the War Cabinet had been told on the 10th, when the CIGS had admitted that it was 'helpless'.) The DMI estimated the Cossacks' strength at 250,000, and read out a telegram, received through General Berthelot, from a French officer who had seen Alexeiev on December 17, which gave a 'very hopeful account' of the Cossack situation. This was sheer rubbish.[15]

But it was argued that the information available was 'somewhat scanty and insufficient' to justify the Cabinet in coming to 'so momentous' a decision as Cecil proposed. 'There was a danger that, by backing a losing horse in South Russia, we were destroying any hope of preventing the Germans appearing in Petrograd as the friends and helpers of an all-powerful Bolshevik Government.' It was essential to take a long view, 'as that Power which assisted the future Russian Government in the reconstruction of the country would have the whole of Russia's resources at her command'. Much turned upon the south Russian peoples' military resources and military value, and it appeared that the French government had more information about their prospects than we had.

Carson stated that he and Milner had had an 'important and interesting' conference the day before with various officers and others familiar with Russia, some of whom felt that present German policy was designed to produce as much anarchy and chaos as possible in Russia, so that Russia would be compelled to make a separate peace, which would include repudiation of her Allied debts, and that German prisoners and officers now in Russia would then be used to restore the autocracy under the Germanophil Grand Duke Paul Michailovitch, the Tsar's uncle. (The first part of this statement was accurate; the second, regarding the use of German prisoners, was based more on fantasy and fears, since little was known about the prisoners.)

The War Cabinet thereupon decided that Milner, Cecil and the DMO should confer with Clemenceau in Paris on Allied policy towards Russia, and that the British Military Representative at Versailles should be asked whether the 'provisional governments' of south Russia could be relied on to 'resist a Bolshevik army under German control'.[15] Thus Lord Robert Cecil had finally forced the War Cabinet to face the main problem, but the Cabinet had again evaded a decision before consulting the French.

The Prime Minister then saw the various people recruited by Carson for propaganda work in Russia. Colonel Byrne told the Prime Minister that 'Petrograd must sooner or later fall into German hands. We should therefore keep there a nominal representation which would keep in touch with the Bolsheviks & "mess things up" for Germany. We should concentrate on the Ukraine in an unofficial manner, as it was from there: (1) Germany could get most help, & (2) we could more easily conduct propaganda both in Austria and Turkey. [Byrne] Suggested Lindley should be in nominal but Poole in active charge in Petrograd, and that Lockhart should go to Kiev.'[16]

On December 23, as peace talks proper between the Germans and Bolsheviks opened at Brest-Litovsk, Milner, Cecil and the DMO conferred with Clemenceau and General Foch in Paris. On their way over,

Milner and Cecil had drawn up a paper outlining various British proposals.

'At Petrograd, we should at once get into relations with the Bolsheviks through unofficial agents, each country as seems best to it.' It was proposed to send Buchanan on leave for reasons of health, since his long residence in Petrograd had 'indelibly' associated him, to the Bolsheviks, with the Cadet party; to them, he stood for much the same as Milyukov did. It was not, however, suggested that the Allies should follow this example, and remove their Ambassadors. 'We should represent to the Bolsheviks that we have no desire to take part in any way in the internal politics of Russia, and that any idea that we favour a counter-revolution is a profound mistake,' stated the paper firmly. 'Such a policy might be attractive to the autocratic Governments of Germany and Austria, but not to the Western democracies or America.' But it was necessary to keep in touch with the Ukraine, the Cossacks, Finland, Siberia, the Caucasus, etc., because these 'semi-autonomous' provinces contained most of the strength of Russia. 'In particular, we feel bound to befriend the Ukraine, since upon the Ukraine depends the feeding of the Roumanians to whom we are bound by every obligation of honour,' it stressed.

'As for the war, we should carefully refrain from any word or act condoning the treachery of the Russians in opening peace negotiations with our enemies. But we should continually repeat our readiness to accept the principles of self-determination, and, subject to that, of no annexation or indemnities. We should press on the Bolsheviks the importance of not being satisfied with empty phrases from the Germans . . . [for] their powers of resistance are melting away, and they will soon be, if they are not now, at the mercy of the German Kaiser, who will then snap his fingers at all their fine phrases and impose on them any terms he pleases.' The Bolsheviks should be told that it was now probably too late to save the Russian army, but the artillery material could still be preserved, 'and at the very least it should not be transferred to our enemies to be used against the Western democracies. Most important of all, the Bolsheviks should prevent, if they can, the wheat districts of Russia, such as the Ukraine, falling into the control of, or being made available for, the Central Powers.' This was another reason for supporting the Ukraine and for urging the Bolsheviks not to coerce it, but co-operate closely with it.[17]

'In southern Russia, our principal object must be, if we can, to save Roumania. Next, we must aim at preventing Russian supplies from reaching Germany. Finally, we are bound to protect if possible the remnant of the Armenians . . .' This was not only to safeguard the flanks of the Allied force in Mesopotamia in both Persia and the

Caucasus, but because an independent Armenia, together with Georgia, was the only barrier to the development of a Muslim movement from Constantinople to China (threatening India *en route*), which would provide Germany with a weapon of even greater danger to world peace than control of the Baghdad railway. 'If we could induce the southern Russian armies to resume the fight, that would be very desirable, but it is probably impossible. To secure these objects, the first thing [required] is money to reorganise the Ukraine, to pay the Cossacks and Caucasian forces, and to bribe the Persians.' The sums involved were not enormous, but there were 'great difficulties' over the exchange. Besides finance, agents and officers would be needed to advise and support the provincial governments and armies; this must be done 'as quietly as possible so as to avoid the imputation – as far as we can – that we are preparing to make war on the Bolsheviks'. It was suggested that the Ukraine should be dealt with by the French and the other south-eastern Russian provinces by the British.[17]

This paper was a curious compromise. Cecil had got rid of Buchanan, and replaced him with an 'unofficial agent', but now agreed that it was 'probably impossible' to induce the Russian armies in the south to fight on – though on the 21st, two days earlier, he was assuring the War Cabinet that the local anti-Bolshevik forces there had a 'fair fighting chance' of success. The emphasis was now on denying supplies to the enemy; on supporting, and thus saving, the Ukraine and its wheatlands and the other southern provinces.

When the Anglo-French conference opened, Milner stated that he and Cecil had been sent by the War Cabinet to discuss with the French government the provision of help for the various 'provincial governments' in Russia that 'showed signs' of opposing the Bolsheviks. The War Cabinet felt that the position was 'very critical' in Russia, said Cecil. But they must not simply antagonise the Bolsheviks without establishing effective resistance to Germany in southern Russia. He would like to know the French view of the 'real strength' of the parties there, and indeed of the 'various elements' throughout Russia. The crucial area was the Ukraine, which provided the bulk of Russia's food supplies. If all hope of Russian military support had to be definitely abandoned, 'the question of supplies became all important'. Under the armistice terms, these supplies could be shipped from Odessa to Constanza, on the Roumanian Black Sea coast, and thence up the Danube into Germany. If the Allies could make the Ukraine a barrier, they should clearly support it. But if they could not, they should secure friendly relations with the Bolsheviks and support them in their difficult negotiations with Germany, 'and in this way possibly prevent all Russian supplies from going to Germany'. All British reports from Jassy and Petrograd were unfavourable about the Ukraine, Cecil said. The British government felt under the 'strictest obligations of honour' to Roumania, which had fought magnificently, thanks largely to General Berthelot, in whom the British government, and it was believed the French government, had great confidence – but Roumania was now threatened with extinction. It would be dishonourable not to risk everything to save her, 'and, therefore, we must know whether the Ukraine could supply Roumania, and whether the reorganisation of the Ukraine was a real possibility'.[17]

Clemenceau replied that 'what had happened in Russia' was a phenomenon that defied prevision. He hoped the Ukraine could be organised, 'but we were really trusting to chance in deciding either for Petrograd or for the Ukraine'. He agreed that we must stand by Roumania. 'Honour came first.' No telegram reaching Paris had shown any 'uneasiness' about the Ukraine being able to supply Roumania. Possibly General Berthelot might be successful. General Barter, however, had all along opposed Berthelot's views. Cecil replied that Barter had now been recalled to Petrograd. Clemenceau concluded – on Berthelot's evidence – that there was a 'possibility' of resistance in the Ukraine, and it was vital to maintain a 'nucleus' of resistance for as long as possible.

On the other hand, the French Ambassador in Petrograd, M. Noulens, had had an interview with Trotsky about the French officers in the Ukraine and had asked him what he would do if the Germans did not accept his peace terms. 'Trotsky had replied that he would then make a revolutionary war, whatever that might mean.' This showed that Trotsky felt his position threatened. 'It was typical of such revolutionary Governments to start at the maximum of their power, and gradually dwindle away,' said Clemenceau. But in any case, the Russians did not want to fight.

As the Allies did not know the facts, Clemenceau said, he preferred to decide nothing. 'It was not right for us to risk everything on a gambler's last throw.' Allied officers must not get mixed up in civil war in Russia, but contact must be maintained with the Bolsheviks as long as possible. 'When supping with the devil we wanted, not merely a long spoon but an elastic spoon that could be stretched, but we must on no account interrupt the dinner.' On the whole, Clemenceau felt that Petrograd had 'less influence than it was thought; it was an artificial capital'. The Allies must give no ground for Bolshevik complaints about Allied action in the Ukraine, but they must support the Ukraine both to back up Roumania and to bar the road for supplies going to Germany. This was vital for the Allies. 'Huge German forces were about to attack us in the West, luckily for France not immediately.' Neither

France nor England were ready to meet such an attack. 'All his information went to show that it was really the last effort of the Germans.' Therefore, only one thing mattered, to shut off supplies for Germany by every possible means, and the most important source of supplies was from the Ukraine.

Cecil and Milner both agreed. Milner then explained that the French Ambassador in London had proposed a division of 'activity' in southern Russia: that France should look after Roumania and the Ukraine; that England should look after the rest of south-east Russia. The British government were ready to agree to this. 'At present, there was a good deal of confusion.'

But it was generally agreed, Milner went on, that the Allies should not at present take definite decisions: but as Clemenceau admitted, it was vital to keep the Ukraine shut off from Germany for the next three or four months. The Allies must, therefore support the Ukraine. 'But what if Trotsky were to say that by so doing we were fostering civil war, and that we must stop, or that he would join hands with Germany?' Clemenceau said he would deny that he was fostering civil war. The point was, Milner continued, 'whether we were prepared, in the ultimate resort, to quarrel with the Bolsheviks or not'. Clemenceau replied that he 'would lengthen the spoon to the uttermost limit, but that he would not let the Ukraine go'. Milner summed up the position by saying 'that if it came to that point, we would keep in with the Ukraine, and let the Bolsheviks join up with Germany, and with this', state the minutes, 'M. Clemenceau emphatically agreed'.[17]

The paper which Milner and Cecil had drawn up on their way to Paris was then read out. Cecil stressed that if these Anglo-French activities were to be effective, they must be supervised by two responsible men only; by General Berthelot in the Ukraine, and a British general in the Caucasus and Cossack districts. This was practical policy; there was no suggestion of spheres of interest, 'or subsequent political influence'. If it later seemed better to assign the Cossack regions to General Berthelot as well, the British would not oppose it. Clemenceau jumped on this and said that the Don Cossacks should be added to the Ukraine, ie, the French sphere. Cecil replied that the Allies should do what was best in practice. 'It was not a question of spheres of influence,' he emphasised. Information had reached London that a south-east union was being formed, together with the Caucasus states, based at Novocherkask in the Don country. This whole sphere should be under the British general. Clemenceau suggested that French and British officials could settle this matter on the spot. Cecil agreed; Berthelot would anyhow be fully occupied with the Ukraine alone. Clemenceau also agreed, but Foch 'insisted' that the Don Cossacks should be included with the Ukraine because Kaledin and Alexeiev, and Rostov and Novocherkask, were all in the Ukraine. (In fact, whether the British liked it or not, it *was* a question of British and French zones of interest in southern Russia.)

Cecil agreed that geographically these two towns were in the Ukraine, 'but it seemed for the moment better to keep up the South-Eastern Federation'. This, in fact, was the original French proposal, as put by the French Ambassador in London; but Foch stated categorically that Kornilov, Kaledin and Alexeiev, and their organisations, were at Novocherkask, 'and that the French must work there if they were to work properly in the Ukraine', for Shulgin, the present Cadet leader, was at Kiev, where the Ukrainian Rada sat, 'and the French were working with Shulgin'. (Here Foch was deceiving Milner and Cecil, probably unwittingly. Shulgin was not a Cadet at all. He was a landowner from south-west Russia, a staunch conservative, who had run a right-wing provincial paper in Kiev, and been elected to the Duma, where he joined the Progressive Bloc, which was roughly between the Cadets and the Octobrists. At the present moment, he was back in Kiev with certain Cadets.)

Cecil retorted that it would be a 'great error' for the Allies to associate too much with the Cadets. The Ukrainian Rada, which was strongly socialist, had placed the Russian General Scherbatchev in command of the whole Ukraine and the south Russian front and it would be very advisable for him to refrain from too much contact with 'reactionaries' such as Alexeiev and Kaledin. General Berthelot would do well to keep clear of such people. The British, working from the east, could keep in touch with them without incurring the same suspicion; the British position was 'much less compromising'. Politically, it was better to 'work' the Ukraine together with Roumania, rather than with the Don Cossacks.

The French Foreign Minister, M. Pichon, said that the Ukrainian Rada were pressing very hard for full French recognition. He proposed to be as sympathetic as possible, but not to recognise them officially. Cecil agreed; there should be unofficial relations, as at Petrograd. Pichon, however, suggested being more sympathetic to the Rada than to the Bolsheviks. Cecil agreed, 'provided we did so secretly'.

Pichon then raised the question of Finland. Unless the Allies went further, 'there was a risk that Finland would be on the German side'. The Finnish Senate was 'by no means gratified' with the British and French reply to their request for recognition of Finnish independence. Finland had a proper government, 'and Trotsky himself had more or less recognised its independence'. Cecil replied that if the Allies recognised Finland, they might then be driven to recognise Lithuania and

Courland (Latvia), 'which was what the Germans wished, for Lithuania and Courland would then by a plebiscite join Germany'. The best thing was to give Finland food, which Sweden should provide, and the British government would make it up to Sweden.

Pichon referred to the paper drawn up by Milner and Cecil and stressed that official relations with the Bolsheviks 'must be avoided at all costs'. Cecil agreed. 'Trotsky was evidently uneasy,' Pichon went on. The Allied attitude of reserve had been successful, 'and must not be abandoned'. Relations must continue to be semi-official and indirect. 'Our Embassies must be kept out of the matter.' Cecil more than agreed, 'because it was clear that Trotsky intensely desires our recognition, as he realises that he has cut himself off from the Western Powers.' This was an additional reason for the temporary withdrawal of Buchanan, 'without, of course, any rupture of relations'.

Cecil underlined the difficulty of obtaining roubles to finance southern Russia. It might be possible to use the Jews in Odessa and Kiev, via 'friendly' Jews in Western Europe, such as the Zionists. Milner advocated a clear boundary between the French and British 'efforts' in southern Russia. It was agreed to discuss this point that afternoon, after it had been discussed by Foch and the DMO.[17]

Later, when the meeting was resumed, Foch read out a draft convention between the French and British governments on the French and British 'spheres of activity' in south Russia, which he and the DMO had drawn up.

British zone: the Cossack areas, the Caucasus states.
French zone: Bessarabia, the Ukraine, the Crimea.

France, Foch emphasised, would operate north of the Black Sea against Germany and Austria, England south-east of the Black Sea against Turkey. But as the French had already agreed to advance 100 million francs to General Alexeiev at Novocherkask, who was forming an army to fight on against the Germans, ie, reopening the Eastern Front, and inter-Allied control was being organised, it was also agreed that the French would continue to supervise operations on the Don, until new arrangements were made with the British. All expenses would be pooled and shared equally between England and France.

The British and French ministers approved this convention, subject to the approval of their governments. Clemenceau said he had just learned that Trotsky was allowing the foreign missions in Russia to draw only small sums from Russian banks. But this, it was stressed, would not apply to banks in Odessa and Kiev. When Cecil asked how the French intended to finance southern Russia, Clemenceau said they were going to begin by trying to buy one million roubles. It was agreed that Berthelot would pass it on to Alexeiev via the Kiev and Odessa branches of the Crédit Lyonnais.[17]

The same day, the Supreme War Council at Versailles answered the War Cabinet's enquiry about whether the forces in southern Russia could resist a 'Bolshevik Army under German control'. If the Bolsheviks could act freely the Germans could obtain wheat from Odessa and oil from Batoum. If Allied military control of southern Russia were lost, the Black Sea ports of Odessa, Novorossisk and Batum must be retained as naval bases. Since the Black Sea remained closed to Allied warships, all groups in southern Russia who would fight on 'must be supported by all the means in our power', either along the Siberian railway from Vladivostok; or – as a result of successful military operations against Turkey – via Tiflis, in Georgia; or through the Dardanelles. The Supreme War Council, in fact, only gave an oblique reply to the War Cabinet, which offered a forlorn hope of resistance, and which, under the Anglo-French convention had, it seems, to be attempted by England.[18]

On December 26, Lord Robert Cecil submitted the Anglo-French convention to the War Cabinet, who approved it, and decided that General Knox should also be withdrawn with Buchanan, but that all personnel of the British missions now in Russia should proceed to southern Russia. This Anglo-French convention was much more than an *ad hoc* wartime arrangement. It was reconfirmed in London exactly a year later, just after the German armistice; tacitly, though unofficially, acknowledged at that time by the Americans; and claimed, indeed vociferously claimed, by the French as an 'international' agreement, until they were physically kicked out of their zone in March 1919. All the evidence suggests that this Anglo-French convention was to be the beginning of the division of the whole Russian Empire into Allied spheres of interest, as had previously happened in China; and subsequent events indeed showed that the victory of 'our friends' (*ie*, the anti-Bolshevik forces) in the Russian civil war would undoubtedly have resulted in a fragmentation of the Russian state.[18]

At first, Anglo-French efforts in their respective zones were totally unsuccessful. Indeed, the efforts of the French to 'befriend' the Ukraine were farcical. Even before December 23, Allied officers and agents (they were mainly French – Major Fitzwilliams was the British agent) had begun to descend on Kiev from both Russian GHQ at Mogilev, and from Roumania, and gave the Ukrainian Rada sizeable amounts of money, which Professor Kennan estimates at about 50 million roubles – and for which the Ukrainians were very grateful. 'Never was a political subsidy more disastrously wasted,' writes Kennan. As soon as it was paid over, the Ukrainians ran to the other side; and it was quickly evident that Austrian and German money, supported by a strong military presence in the background, was of paramount influence in Kiev. The allies had been mercilessly tricked. 'The plan failed, so it has to be called bad,' commented Fitzwilliams laconically. 'If it had succeeded, it would have been called good.'[19]

With the Ukraine lost, the Allies were back where they started. The British now could only make further, and indeed frantic, efforts to bolster up the Don Cossacks and volunteer army, which they now knew to be inherently weak and unstable. Further, as the French now claimed that they were in their zone, an Anglo-French row seemed to be in the offing as well, judging by the words used by Foch and Clemenceau to Cecil and Milner in Paris on December 23.

On December 31, Cecil informed the War Cabinet that a special 'Russia Committee' had been formed at the Foreign Office, which was responsible for all executive action in the British zone in southern Russia; he was the chairman, and both the War Office and the Treasury were represented.[20] In view of the power that the Russia committee wielded in the next few months, and the hash that it made of the vital question of finance for the Cossacks and others in southern Russia, it is of interest to note the personalities involved. The War Office was represented by the DMI (Major-General Macdonogh), the Treasury by Mr Dudley Ward, a Fellow of St John's College, Cambridge, and a former Assistant Editor of *The Economist*; from 1913 to 1914 he had been engaged in 'research works in Germany'. This had probably well equipped him to deal with wartime duties at the Treasury, which he had joined in 1914.

The Foreign Office was represented by Sir Ronald Graham, an Assistant Under-Secretary of State, who had been First Secretary at the British Embassy in St Petersburg in 1904, or by Sir George Clerk, a senior official at the Foreign Office, who – like Cecil – was hawkish on Russian affairs. But the Foreign Office had their own financial adviser on the Russia committee. This was Lieutenant-Colonel the Hon. Sidney Cornwallis Peel, a Fellow of Trinity College, Oxford, and – since 1912 – a member of the financial board of Oxford University. He was also vice-president of the Moroccan State Bank. This apparently qualified him to deal with the enormous intricacies of the Russian banks and their relationship with the English banks. Colonel Peel was almost certainly brought on to the Russia committee by Clerk (both had been at Eton and New College, Oxford) to ensure that any Treasury objections could be blocked. Peel (who in fact knew little about banking) engaged Samuel Guinness as his assistant. Guinness, then aged twenty-nine, had been at Winchester and Balliol, and had then undergone 'banking education in the United States and Germany'. He had become a temporary clerk in the Foreign Office and in 1916 had passed the Civil Service examination in International Law. But even Peel and Guinness combined were unable to cope with the problems arising from Colonel Keyes' proposals for financing Jaroszynski to obtain control of all the Russian banks (for England), or of founding a Cossack bank in southern Russia. In mid-1919, by which time various cross-payments and promissory notes had found their way back, out of the Russian maelstrom, to London for settlement, Peel was flummoxed. The Treasury, which then had to take over, were disconcerted by the muddle and confusion which they discovered. Determined to find a scapegoat, they settled on Guinness, since Colonel Peel was too well connected; (in 1919, his elder brother, Viscount Peel, had become Under Secretary of State for War, under Churchill). In the Foreign Office list (1920), Guinness's entry reads: 'Resigned August 1919, but continues in an honorary capacity to advise on financial matters.' The Treasury, in fact, had persuaded the Foreign Office to dismiss Guinness and make him sort out the affair of the Russian banks in his own time.

Despite this setback, Guinness had a distinguished banking career. After joining his family's merchant bankers as a partner, he became senior partner and in 1963 chairman; he also held many other banking directorships in the City of London.

The secretary to the Russia committee was Colonel F. H. Kisch, a very able General Staff officer, who specialised in Russian affairs.

# 7

## *The Bank Schemes*

As the peace talks proper between the Germans and the Russians got under way at Brest-Litovsk, the official German attitude to the Bolsheviks rapidly changed. Just as the talks opened, the Foreign Ministry in Berlin had received a succinct outline of the real Bolshevik position from Nasse, the German Military Attaché in Berne, and powerful spymaster, who was then in Berlin. There was a strong movement within the Bolshevik government, he warned, working to prevent the peace talks from coming to an end too quickly. 'One important reason for this is the wish not to antagonise the Entente too far; the other is the still existing hope that a revolution will break out in Germany, which would put the whole peace question on a different, and, for the Bolsheviks, far more advantageous basis.[1]

'The wish to maintain fairly good relations with the Entente has grown stronger lately for several reasons; its great influence, especially among the Russian bourgeoisie, and partly also among the right-wing Social-Revolutionaries [*ie*, right SR] is directed, in the last analysis, towards the frustration of the separate peace, and perhaps still more towards the destruction of German-Russian trade. It must be continually pointed out to the Russians that in this respect, also, the Entente is pursuing selfish ends; only Germany – because of her geographical position – is capable of assisting Russia to restore her economy quickly and effectively.' This was undoubtedly correct. 'The second factor which makes for procrastination is the hope of an early revolution in Germany. How far the Bolshevik leaders in fact believe in this is difficult to tell . . .

'Radek told my confidential agent that Germany was pressing for peace for two reasons: Germany wanted to launch a great offensive in the West in February 1918 and to have her rear free once and for all; but the main reason was that the water was already up to her neck. This became clear not only from the fact that the Central Powers negotiated so willingly with the revolutionary Bolshevik Government, but also from the manner in which they joined the negotiations. Members of the Foreign Ministry arrived at Brest-Litovsk in large numbers; from this the Bolsheviks could draw valuable conclusions. The Austrians in particular were so charming, so polite, and so anxious to oblige that they obviously made their German friends apprehensive. Behind every Austrian a Prussian planted himself, to make sure that their Allies did not go too far in their offers and promises . . .'[1] A copy of this shrewd report went to the German Under-Secretary of State, and to the German delegation at Brest-Litovsk – where the peace talks soon broke down. On December 27th, the Bolsheviks broke off the talks when told by the Germans that Poland and the Baltic states would become separate states under the peace treaty. Two days later, however, German military and naval officers arrived in Petrograd to discuss technical points in connection with the armistice; thus a link was maintained between the two sides.

But Nasse was now proved right. The Bolsheviks did believe that an early revolution was possible in Germany, and the Germans were now made to realise that they had been supporting and financing their own potential executioners. 'The latest publications of the Petersburg Telegraph Agency make it necessary to have serious words with Vorovski,' wired the Under-Secretary of State to Counsellor Riezler in Stockholm on January 4. 'They contain appeals to our nation, which include revolutionary matter, and calls to our soldiers to disobey orders and lay down their arms. This we must regard as improper and intolerable interference in our internal affairs. At the same time, libels are being published about us. We are portrayed as slave-drivers and oppressors of the workers. It is claimed that we put the workers' leaders into German concentration camps . . . It is surely impossible, in the long run, for a government which is engaged in peace negotiations with us, to use this kind of language about us,' he pointed out. 'Instead of securing peace for Russia . . . their procrastination of the peace settlement is simply playing into the hands of the Entente . . .'[1] A copy of this wire also went to Brest-Litovsk.

Meanwhile, Dr Helphand, now back in the German fold, was attacking the Bolshevik leadership in the new paper, aimed specifically at the local soldiers' and workers' councils, which he had launched on his return to Stockholm in early January. He especially attacked the Bolshevik dictatorship; this was quite undemocratic, he wrote, and Russia was simply not ready for the dictatorship of the proletariat. The whole Bolshevik programme amply demonstrated their 'terrible, boundless ignorance and lack of perception'. In fact, Bolshevik achievements to date were 'an insult to the splendid history of European revolutions', while the present soviets reminded him more of a 'Jewish cabal than of a modern democracy'. The Bolshevik leaders only stayed in power through the protection of their Red Army hirelings, 'like the multi-millionaires of America'. Like the Germans, Helphand was not enchanted with these revolutionaries whom he had nourished.[2]

In fact, the Germans still intended to stick to the Bolsheviks, and would not now even give undercover support to the SR. On January 9, the German Under-Secretary of State in Berlin wired Kühlmann at Brest-Litovsk that the German Minister in Copengagen had intercepted a letter from an SR member, who was close to the SR leader Chernov, to a friend in Copenhagen. 'This letter said that the Bolsheviks were now isolated, both morally and politically. The whole economic system and the Russian state were completely disorganised. The Bolsheviks would no more be able to maintain their power if they concluded peace, than if they failed to do so.' The SR were now convinced that social reforms in Russia could not be imposed by violence, and they would 'openly oppose the Bolsheviks, as soon as they were morally and physically capable of doing so', wrote the SR member. The conclusion of a peace, to which they were now moving, could only give one aim to all Russian democrats, 'namely mobilisation', he wrote, 'for Russia could not exist without the Baltic provinces . . .' If the German people really wanted to show a brotherly attitude to the Russian people, they would have to abandon all ideas of self-interest, and conclude an honest peace. 'Otherwise Russia would be forced to remobilise, and in thirty years there would be another war.' The German Minister stated that if the Foreign Ministry shared these views, the writer would be prepared to try to bring their mutual aims to fruition. 'In his opinion, the Bolsheviks would fall at the first shock, and he would not require large funds to bring this about.'[3] But the German Minister warned that since the rise of the left SR, Chernov had lost much of his influence. He therefore suggested telling the writer of the intercepted letter that the Germans could not take up relations with other Russian parties, since they were negotiating with the Bolsheviks.

'I agree,' replied Kühlmann from Brest-Litovsk.

But by early January, the Germans were nonetheless sure that the Bolsheviks were now really the allies of their opponents.

The breakdown in the peace negotiations led the War Cabinet to give serious consideration to a statement of their war aims (a subject broached at the Paris conference in early December, but taken no further) so as to try and influence the Bolsheviks in their favour. But the Cabinet realised that they were very ignorant of what was really happening in Petrograd, and of what Bolshevik intentions now really were.

[178]

On January 2, the War Cabinet took note of a despatch in that day's *Daily News*, from Arthur Ransome, its Petrograd correspondent, 'who is himself in full sympathy with the Bolshevik movement', announcing the threatened breakdown of the Bolshevik peace negotiations with the Central Powers. 'It was suggested,' state the Cabinet minutes, 'that M. Trotsky was, perhaps, finding himself face to face with an impossible situation involving a general peace at the expense of Russia, and that possibly Mr Arthur Ransome's despatch was a signal that M. Trotsky would like to get into touch with the Allies with a view to extricating himself from his difficulties'. Another theory was that Trotsky was trying to arrange a conference of the socialist parties of the different countries so as to extend the scope of his fanatical attacks on the existing order of civilisation. Considerable difference of opinion was expressed about Trotsky's motives, but it was generally agreed that it would be desirable to obtain more information.[4]

The War Cabinet instructed the Foreign Office to wire to Buchanan, asking him to get in touch with Arthur Ransome in order, if possible, to discover the precise meaning of his *Daily News* article, 'and what M. Trotsky was aiming at'.

Next day, Lord Robert Cecil warned the War Cabinet that although a hitch had occurred in the peace negotiations, the news from Russia 'was not encouraging'. General Knox had wired on the 1st 'that M. Trotsky and his friends had so ruined the Russian Army that if he does break off negotiations, the enemy will advance a few kilometres and capture his guns'. Buchanan had also wired that the Bolsheviks wished to know what American help they might expect, if they had to fight on. The Prime Minister asked the DMO whether he would prefer the Russians to fight on, at the price of losing their guns, as Cecil had suggested, or a separate peace. The DMO said he would prefer the former, as, though there was little hope for the north Russian front, the Austrians would be kept engaged in the south.[5]

Walter Long, the Colonial Secretary, suggested that it might be worth the War Cabinet's while to see a certain Mr Lattimore, an Englishman just back from Petrograd, where his brother, who was a bookseller, still lived. Lattimore could put the Prime Minister in touch with Trotsky. Cecil and General Smuts interviewed Mr Lattimore, who was waiting in the next room; but as he had left Petrograd a month before, no information of any value was obtained from him, 'beyond an expression of Mr Lattimore's personal opinion that M. Trotsky was an honest idealist'. This minor episode makes it clear that the War Cabinet realised that they gravely lacked up to date information about the Bolsheviks, and what was really happening in Petrograd.

The War Cabinet then considered the draft speech which the Prime

Minister was to make, containing a British declaration of war aims, in answer to a German statement of December 25 about their peace negotiations with the Bolsheviks.[5]

On the 4th, the War Cabinet continued their discussion of the speech, in particular a passage in which the Prime Minister proposed (as agreed by the Cabinet the day before) to inform the Bolsheviks that if they had not started unilateral negotiations with the enemy, 'we should have stood by the Russian democracy, as we intended to stand by the French democracy'. The Prime Minister argued that it was necessary to warn the Bolsheviks that we no longer considered ourselves bound to fight on in the interests of Russia, so that there should be no future misunderstanding; he also wished to give a similar hint to the enemy.

But it was stressed that this would be 'somewhat discouraging' to our friends in Russia, who did still wish to defend the Allies' interests, one of which was to prevent the Baltic states falling into German hands, 'since if this occurred the Baltic would become more than ever a German lake. For many years past, one of the greatest dangers to peace had been the desire of Russia to reach open water. If the Baltic were entirely under German control, the Black Sea exits practically subject to Turkish control, and Vladivostok very possibly in the hands of the Japanese. Russia would have no outlet except in the Arctic Ocean,' state the Cabinet minutes. 'It was impossible to imagine that this vast amorphous nation, when it recovered from its present prostration, would be content with these conditions, and Russian lack of access to the ocean might prove a constant source of future wars.' In fact, such a settlement was hardly consistent with a just and durable peace. The Prime Minister undertook to modify his speech accordingly.[6]

On January 5, Lloyd George delivered a major speech on war aims to a special trades union conference. He had to take into account the German terms to the Bolsheviks, with their alleged offer of independence to the Russian border states, especially to the Baltic states and Poland; General Smuts' secret negotiations with Austrian emissaries in Switzerland; a recent Labour Party manifesto on war aims, which had favourably impressed many people outside the Labour Party; the Conservative elder statesman Lord Lansdowne's recent letter, urging a compromise peace; and, above all, that Russia was withdrawing from the war. After consultation with all shades of political opinion, from Asquith to the Labour leaders, Lloyd George now came out in support of the French demand for Alsace-Lorraine, but denied that England wished to destroy Germany or Austria-Hungary, or even wished to deprive Turkey of Constantinople. He said nothing about the Baltic and other Russian border states, except that Poland must be independent. The three indispensable conditions for peace were the restoration of the sanctity of treaties, the right of self-determination, and the creation of some international organisation to prevent future wars.[7]

Three days later, President Wilson proclaimed his Fourteen Points before the Unites States Congress, in which he laid down principles for a liberal peace settlement, showed how European territorial problems could be settled by self-determination, and proposed a 'general association of nations' to preserve peace in the future. On Russia, he was more precise and added: 'The treatment accorded Russia by her sister nations in the months to come will be the acid test of their good will, of their comprehension of her needs as distinguished from their own interests, and of their intelligent and unselfish sympathy.'

The Bolsheviks treated President Wilson's speech with derision, and totally ignored Lloyd George's – though Trotsky stated, on the day the Prime Minister spoke, that Lloyd George doubtless hoped that the Germans would succeed in imposing a drastic peace on the Bolsheviks, so that German demands in the west would be minimised. In this surmise, Trotsky was, of course, perfectly correct; and it was only the War Cabinet which had prevented Lloyd George giving expression to this hope.

By depriving Russia of Poland and by renouncing Constantinople, it was thought that Lloyd George had renounced all the Allied secret treaties and was now in accord with President Wilson on general peace terms. This was not so. The other secret treaties, which did not concern Russia, remained in force – and Lloyd George certainly did not mean what he said about self-determination. Hankey records that he had pointed out to Lord Robert Cecil on the 4th what real self-determination would mean for the British Empire, and the two men had hastily watered down the Prime Minister's draft.[7]

By now, the British political agent to the Bolshevik government had been selected. On January 7, as Buchanan left Petrograd for London, 'saying that his mind had ceased to function properly, and that he was a completely broken man' (according to a report[8] by the Danish Ambassador in Petrograd, which was somehow intercepted by the German Minister in Copenhagen), Cecil, temporarily in charge of the Foreign Office while Balfour took a brief holiday, informed the War Cabinet that Robert Bruce Lockhart, the former British Consul in Moscow, would be leaving England for Petrograd at the end of the week. Meanwhile, instructions had been given that someone outside the British Embassy (of which Counsellor Lindley was now in charge) should get in touch with Trotsky. But, added Cecil (who felt that the Foreign Office was being by-passed, and that the whole arrangement would encourage the Bolsheviks), the Bolshevik representative in

London, Maxim Litvinov, was creating difficulties by demanding the funds and documents of the Russian Embassy, and the funds would probably be spent in spreading Bolshevik propaganda in England. Cecil was strongly opposed to allowing Litvinov to have them, but added that no fault could be found with him on personal grounds.

The Prime Minister, who by now probably realised that his speech on war aims had had no effect on the Bolsheviks, and who approved the despatch of Bruce Lockhart, reminded Cecil that there was a press report that Trotsky was quarrelling with the Germans, and that the SR party, which were the only alternative to the Bolsheviks, 'were quite as likely, if not more likely, to give in to German demands as was M. Trotsky'.[9]

On the 9th, Trotsky resumed the peace talks at Brest-Litovsk, determined to delay matters until a German revolution took place, but to seek Allied help in forming a Red Army if war had to be resumed. That day, the War Cabinet considered Lindley's latest telegram from Petrograd, urging that the British government should maintain contact with all *de facto* local Russian authorities. But the Cabinet decided that it 'would be better for the present not to commit ourselves so far', and to continue our present policy of maintaining contact with the Bolshevik government only through Bruce Lockhart. The despatch of a British political agent to the Bolshevik government did not, in fact, entail *de facto* recognition. British policy towards the Bolsheviks had not changed.[10]

Now that the Ukraine had literally sold out to the Central Powers, the British had no choice but to return to the support of the Don Cossacks and volunteer army in south Russia, whom they knew to be inherently weak and unstable, to try and prevent the Germans over-running the iron mines and wheatlands of south Russia. By the terms of the recent Anglo-French convention, it was agreed that the French would give financial support to General Alexeiev and his volunteer army, whom – it was half agreed – were in the French zone in south Russia, although the Cossack areas had definitely been assigned to the British, and Alexeiev was a guest, however temporary and unwelcome, of the Don Cossacks. An Anglo-French row thus seemed to be in the offing. But for most of December, little news reached London of what was happening in this crucial area of south Russia. The War Cabinet knew as little of 'our friends' in the south as they did of the Bolsheviks in the north.

Towards the end of December, however, the Anglo-French mission reached Novocherkask from Roumania and, as agreed in Paris on December 23, promised General Alexeiev 100 million francs for the volunteer army from French sources. At the same time, Boris Savinkov, former War Minister in the provisional government, arrived from Petrograd. He induced the Russian generals to form a political council (to lower their counter-revolutionary image), and to state that they were fighting for the constituent assembly.

On January 2, the War Cabinet noted that there was little news from French sources about the situation in south Russia, in fact, 'there was not that interchange of information between the French and British Governments which was so essential'. It was decided that the War Office should arrange for a 'regular interchange' of information with the French on the military situation 'in the respective British and French spheres in Russia'. The DMO then told the Cabinet that the Russian General Bicherakhov had gone to Kermanshah, in Persia, to rally loyal Russian troops there, 'and was confident that his efforts would be crowned with success'. The DMO said that he was arranging to feed these troops, and to send out to Mesopotamia, at the general's request, Russian officers in England and France.[11]

The War Cabinet also had to reconsider the position of the Roumanian army, which they had agreed on December 10 was so 'helpless' that Roumania should be allowed to make a separate peace. On January 7, Cecil informed the Cabinet that some of the Roumanian ministers were anxious to make a separate peace, but that the King of Roumania would dismiss them if we wished. Clemenceau, he said, was in favour of the King doing so. Cecil gathered that the CIGS did not foresee an Austro-German advance against the Roumanian army, at any rate for two or three months. He now had little faith in the Ukraine resisting such an advance; and only the fifteen 'good' Roumanian divisions could stop the Germans advancing into the Ukraine and capturing the supplies there. If we left it to the Roumanian government, they would inevitably make a separate peace. Only pressure from England and France would keep them in the war.[12]

Lord Milner pointed out that if Roumania stayed in the field, it would tie up some Austro-German divisions which would otherwise be available elsewhere. It was doubtful if it would suit German policy to overrun Roumania by force, as it seemed inevitable that Roumania, sooner or later, would form part of the Central Powers. He agreed that the Ukraine was now indeed a feeble reed to lean on, but there was an outside chance of 'something' materialising in the Ukraine, if Roumania held on; but if Roumania made peace, there could be no hope of 'rallying' the Ukraine. This was sheer wishful thinking. But the Prime Minister said that if Roumania stayed in the field, the Austrians would have an excuse for resisting German demands for the transfer of Austrian troops elsewhere. The War Cabinet decided that Cecil should inform the French government that we should do all in our power to keep Roumania in the war, and that she should be jointly informed of this. Only Sir Edward Carson dissented; Roumania, he said, should now be allowed to make a separate peace. But it was, in fact, now clear that both Roumania and the Ukraine, the left flank of the 'South-East Union' based on the Don, were a joint liability, not an asset, to the Allied cause and Allied hopes in southern Russia.[12]

On January 14, the War Cabinet were informed that a wire, sent on the 12th, had been received from Odessa, indicating a general 'deterioration' in the situation in southern Russia, and that Bolshevism was gaining ground in the Ukraine. Next day, Sir George Clerk informed the Russia committee (now in charge of all executive action in southern Russia) that their chairman, Lord Robert Cecil, wished them to consider what to do about the large quantity of military material and stores in Russia, which would probably fall into German hands unless some action could be taken. 'It had been suggested that it might perhaps be desirable to send Sir J. Norton-Griffiths to Russia on another mission of destruction.'[13]

This colourful character, an engineer and demolition expert who had worked in South Africa and Australia, was an extreme right-wing Tory MP known as 'Empire Jack' (whose grandson is the former Liberal Party leader, Mr Jeremy Thorpe). In mid-1917, Norton-Griffiths had organised the demolition of that crucial German vantage point on the Western Front, the Messines ridge. Later that year, as the Germans occupied more and more of Roumania, he had been sent out to fire the crops and oil wells; and succeeded to such an extent that he became known as 'The Angel of Destruction', and was liberally decorated.

The suggestion that Norton-Griffiths should now be sent out to devastate Russia was vetoed by the DMI. There would be the 'greatest difficulty' in destroying military material held by Bolshevik troops, he stated firmly, and General Poole would certainly be the best man to destroy the stores. It was decided to wire Poole in this sense.

Clerk then said that Mr Balfour wished the Russia committee to consider a report that General Alexeiev was short of funds. It was decided that the DMI should wire to General Foch enquiring whether the French 'had succeeded in actually placing ready money in the hands of the Cossack leaders'. The DMI mentioned that he had been told informally by the – highly unreliable – Count Horodysky that he thought he could raise $1\frac{1}{2}$ million roubles in Kiev 'at any moment'. Clerk promised to enquire further into the matter; he had been told that 'if we were prepared to pay a discount of 10%, we could raise all the roubles we required'. Dudley Ward, of the Treasury, suggested wiring to Lindley to ask 'what means he possessed of raising roubles'. To this the Russia committee agreed.[13]

Dudley Ward said that, with reference to a suggestion at the War Cabinet's meeting on the 11th that Russian banknotes should be forged, Messrs Waterlow, the banknote engravers, had told him that this would take at least three months. He intended to verify whether the French Mint 'had already printed and issued Ukraine paper money', as reported, and also proposed to enquire 'whether a distinctive note issue (distinct from a reproduction of current Russian notes) would be acceptable in the Caucasus'. Exactly what Dudley Ward intended by this is not clear; nevertheless the Russia Committee approved his proposal.[13]

The problems of keeping Allied and Russian supplies from the Germans by destruction or other means; of retaining or acquiring a place in the Russian 'sun' for British trade after the war; and thirdly of supplying 'our friends' in Russia with sufficient ready cash (a project to which General Poole himself was wholly opposed) – these were now the tasks of Poole's mission.

On December 29, Major Banting (Poole's Chief of Staff) was writing another letter to Colonel Byrne in London, outlining events in Petrograd (but this letter took many weeks to reach London). 'The comic-opera still continues here,' he wrote, 'the latest event is the arrival of a number of German officers – Naval & Military – to discuss the details of technical points in connection with the Armistice. They have brought a retinue of O.R.s [other ranks] to look after & presumably protect them. Some of them were put up in the Officers' quarters @ one of the Barracks, but they strongly objected to the near proximity of the Tovarish Soldiers & Red Guards & consequently rooms @ the Bristol Hotel were cleared for them. Railway transport is becoming much worse & the chief tactics of both sides, in the numerous civil wars which are going on, are to pull up whole lengths of railway track. Altho' prices are rising rapidly here, Petrograd somehow is not yet starving – food troubles are reported to be eminent [sic] in the near future, due to the wreckage of the railways.' Banting was off to Moscow that evening to discuss future British trade policy in Russia with some of the British firms here. Most thought that much could be done in the future, but the Germans would now have a free hand. 'I suppose many [in London] have laughed @ the idea of sending a Financial Business Expert out, as suggested in one of our recent cables, owing to the disturbed state of the country. It is really just the time now to start in & study the whole question so as to be ready to act when order is restored.' Banting enquired whether the present system of commercial attachés and consulates would be used to recover British trade after peace was declared. 'Out here @ any rate, an entirely new and powerful organisation is required at once, so as not to lose any opportunities of cutting out the Germans – the latter hold most of the Trump Cards. A new organisation will require about six months to get the hang of the show. Another point which appears to be of importance here is the Siberian trade. This is further away from Germany & the possibilities of development are enormous.'[14]

Major Banting's main point was taken up by the War Cabinet on January 1. The CIGS said he understood that the Germans in Petrograd now had a direct line between Petrograd and Berlin, via which they could transmit cypher messages. This was correct. Sir Arthur Steel-Maitland, joint Parliamentary Under-Secretary both to the Foreign Office and to the Board of Trade and head of the Department of Overseas Trade, drew the War Cabinet's attention to General Poole's wire (no. P.764) of December 26 to Colonel Byrne, stating that his supply mission could do much to stop supplies reaching the Germans, and that the British Embassy were being kept advised: 'Cable at once what stores are known to be needed most in Germany.' Poole suggested that he should concentrate on rubber, metals, cotton, fats, oil and chemical products. Each Ally should provide 10 million roubles to buy up these stores. 'I consider that British Government should at once send out an influential financial representative to consider the present [? position] and after peace [? organise] commercial intelligence branch in Russia. After a few months' time it will be too late to act. Americans are becoming more active and German influence is increasing rapidly,' warned Poole. 'Representative must be a real expert.' Local British businessmen could supply all the details about the possibilities, but it would take some weeks to decide on the policy to recommend to the British government. 'Do not allow the impression to get about that all commercial interest in Russia is at a standstill, as that is quite inaccurate. If properly managed, Russia will welcome British capital, etc.' The present organisation, involving the Commercial Attaché and the Consulate, was totally inadequate and quite out of date.

Steel-Maitland said there was no need to send an 'influential financial representative'. What Poole seemed to want was someone who could diagnose the present situation in Russia, and recommend to the British government the steps it should take to prevent the Germans getting hold of Russian businesses and supplies. The War Cabinet approved Poole's recommendation and left the selection of the individual to the Foreign Office and Steel-Maitland.[15]

But no action was taken to select a financial adviser for General Poole. On January 5, however, Colonel Byrne noted in his diary: 'Saw Sir

Arthur Steel-Maitland and expressed the opinion that the present is not the best time to despatch a Financial Expert to Russia, but that if General Poole was still anxious that one should be sent, his opinion should be given every consideration.' (Why Byrne felt that this was not the moment is not clear, as Poole and his mission had consistently pressed for the despatch of such an expert; but many of Poole's letters and despatches had still not reached London.) 'After consultation with Sir A. Steel-Maitland,' Byrne goes on, 'sent a wire to General Poole about the engagement of Professor Ipatiev [a Russian chemical expert].' In fact, it appears to have been agreed between Byrne and Steel-Maitland – and without their informing the Foreign Office or the Russia committee – that different experts should be attached to Poole's mission to prevent the different Russian commodities and supplies from falling into German hands; chemicals were highly important – so were metals. 'Saw Lt. Lessing and explained the present situation,' Byrne added the same day. This brief diary entry is explained by a letter to Byrne from Brigadier Finlayson, Poole's former Chief of Staff, from Perth, where he was on leave. 'I hear from Lessing that he is for Russia shortly at the General's request. I hope he'll be useful there & will enjoy it. I'm glad I don't deal in metals.'[16]

But in Petrograd, Poole's mission, which had still received no reply to its repeated requests for the despatch of a financial expert, now had to develop their own plans. On January 6, Major Banting wrote a long report for Colonel Byrne, enclosing various papers on British commercial interests in Russia, both current and after the war. 'It appears to us at this end,' he wrote, 'that Russia has been placed outside the picture as far as Gt. Britain is at the moment concerned, but it should be clearly understood that Germany can, if she really makes a serious effort, get out of Russia supplies next summer which would seriously reflect on the results of our sea blockade. On all sides German agents are appearing with a view to buying up existing stocks, for many of which Germany is prepared to offer goods in exchange, which is what Russia wants, especially the peasant class, who will give up their supplies of foodstuffs only in exchange for cheap clothing, boots, etc.; but not for money.'[16]

The Allied committee which had been started to prevent supplies going to Germany (known as *Tovaro Obmien*, or the Trade Barter Company) was now functioning, 'but can do no practical good until some funds are available – we have asked for ten million roubles as a start, and USA and French Missions have each asked for similar amounts.' There was, of course, some risk that the goods they bought could be requisitioned by the Bolsheviks and then handed over to

Germany for goods Russia wanted, 'but this is being very carefully watched and steps can be taken to prevent it in most cases. A further cable has been sent today again urging a sanction of roubles for this job.'

The Trade Barter Company could provide valuable data for the larger scheme outlined in Banting's paper, headed 'Proposals for British Commercial Situation in Russia', which were 'more or less on the same lines as outlined in the recommendations which we now find have been put forward by the British Embassy . . . The latter have included in their scheme proposals for immediate financial aid to certain parties in Russia, etc . . .'

Banting's paper stressed that in the present chaotic state of Russia, some British organisation should be started on the spot to stop Germany dominating Russia's economy. 'At the present moment, German commercial and banking agents are rapidly returning to Russia,' and though a separate peace had not yet been signed, and might not be for some time, it was 'universally agreed' that Russia would no longer fight on against Germany. 'If the present peace negotiations between Germany and Russia break down, Germany may possibly occupy Petrograd with a military force and Moscow also, but she cannot do more than occupy a comparatively small portion of Russia by military force. It is more probable, however, that Germany will adopt peaceful penetration into Russia,' wrote Banting; and in the interest of British trade relations, 'it is essential to start a definite scheme to counteract the same'.[16]

The first difficulty was the low rate of exchange of the Russian rouble and the German mark compared to the British pound sterling. 'This gives Germany an immediate advantage and emphasises the great importance of obtaining a controlling influence by Gt. Britain on the Russian financial market, *ie*, on the Russian banks,' wrote Banting. 'It must be clearly understood that in Russia all Banks are in reality Financial Groups acting as Company Promoters, etc; and ordinary banking business as understood in Gt. Britain is a very secondary item: consequently, the Russian Banks have a very powerful influence and control on all industrial enterprises in Russia. It is therefore necessary for Gt. Britain to obtain at once a controlling influence on the Banks, and this can be done as follows . . .' Some £15 million (about 400 million roubles, for the rate was rising) should be distributed on short-term deposits at eight or ten of the leading Russian banks, and if one of them was found to be obviously working for German and against British interests, 'then the deposit could be withdrawn, which would place the Bank in a difficult position – in most cases the Bank would prefer to meet the British demands rather than produce the money,' argued Banting.

These financial measures must be handled by a committee, which should have the full support of the British government, sitting in

Petrograd or Moscow, and consisting of a first-class British banking expert, a first-class British businessman, with long experience of Russian banking and business methods, and a local Russian representative. The first could readily be found in London. The second, to be chosen in consultation with the British Trading Corporation (a semi-governmental body), must be a man who understood the 'peculiarities' of Russian methods, 'and can advise the British banking expert, and criticise the local Russian representative. A precedent for this proposal,' added Banting, 'is found in the formation of the "British & Chinese Corporation" after the Boxer Risings in China under the official recognition of the British Government. In this case, Messrs Jardine Matheson & Co. took an active part in providing the knowledge of local conditions.'

This proposal, taken in conjunction with the Anglo-French convention of December 23 to parcel out Russia into Allied spheres of interest, demonstrates British official thinking about Russia, both in London and in Petrograd; the Bolshevik revolution was just another Boxer rising, after the suppression of which England would move in to clear matters up for herself – and the comparison with Jardine Matheson, the great opium dealers in the Far East, amply demonstrates the manner in which this clearing up would be done.

This committee sitting in Russia, Banting wrote, would be primarily responsible to the British government for the 'control and appropriation' in Russia of the huge sums owed to England as war debts, 'and to obtain as an offset against them investments in Railways, Mines, Forests and concessions generally – as it is most improbable that Russia can possibly be able to find the cash to pay the interest on the loans made for many years to come.'[16]

At present, the British government had no trade policy in Russia, and the Commercial Attaché and Consulate would be incapable of carrying out a policy as described. The men chosen must be first-class men, fully conversant with Russian business methods; otherwise the whole scheme was doomed to failure. 'Further, it is necessary to avoid active relations with the unscrupulous Russian commercial men, who have no doubt made much money, but who are not the type to be associated with a big British Government concern. Such men as Mr Benenson of the Russo-English Bank should be avoided.'

This was the main proposal of Poole's mission for protecting and expanding British trade in Russia. 'It is entirely and absolutely essential to have a first-class financial and commercial expert out here to co-ordinate the proposals of the various parties, as at present several proposals are sent home, all more or less alike,' stated Banting in his covering letter. 'As we see the various schemes, a total advance of about

£40,000,000 would be sufficient to cover all immediate needs of setting up a really sound campaign against Germany and her political and commercial aims in Russia and against the Allies generally.' (It is unclear how exactly the remaining £25 million was to be spent.)

Banting added a postscript – 'These notes have been very roughly draughted [sic] out @ a day's notice. General [Poole] is sending the official copies through by the next bag, but he is most anxious that you [ie, Colonel Byrne] are fully posted, as the Ambassador & Genl. Knox, etc. are just starting home – Admiral Stanley [the Chief Naval Attaché] will call & see you on his return. He is A.1 & fully in agreement with General [Poole].'[16]

Meanwhile, Colonel Byrne had succeeded in attaching one of his young officers, Captain Hicks, who was just back from Russia, to Bruce Lockhart as his assistant. On January 10, however, Byrne saw Mitchell Thompson (of the Restriction of Enemy Supplies Department at the Foreign Office), who said that he now had to treat Russia as a neutral, and as the Milner Committee had much information about supplies in Russia, it should be transferred to the Foreign Office. As the despatch of supplies to Russia had become a propaganda question, Byrne noted in his diary, and was closely connected with the prevention of important supplies falling into German hands, Byrne agreed, subject to Lord Milner's approval; but if any part of the Russia Supply Committee (as the Milner Committee was known) were handed over, the Foreign Office must assume full responsibility and act as agent for General Poole in London. Later that day, Milner told Byrne that he would agree to any proposal that Lord Robert Cecil might make on these lines – provided Byrne became a member of any committee that took the place of the Russia Supply Committee; this, of course, meant the Russia Committee, which the Foreign Office had packed with its own men.[16]

'Hicks left for Russia. I gave him a letter for Poole,' noted Colonel Byrne on the 11th. 'Bag in from Russia bringing letters up to December 14th.' There was now over three weeks' delay in the mail from Petrograd. In his letter to Poole, hastily written that day, Byrne stated: 'It has just been sprung on me that Lockhart is going out tonight, so I can only send a short note. I am sending Hicks back with Lockhart . . . Lessing goes out in the next steamer going in the ordinary way. I tried to get him out with Lockhart, but difficulties were in the way which I could not overcome. I am telling him everything that has gone on here, so that he can post you when he arrives. I think this is safer than trusting to putting anything on paper at present . . .'[16]

On the 15th, 'Lessing left for Petrograd,' notes Colonel Byrne in his diary. 'I talked very fully to him regarding Poole's decision [possibly that no more war supplies should be sent out to Russia] and I asked him to tell Poole to do all he could to stop half-baked schemes being suggested, and to see that any proposals made from Petrograd were practicable.'[16]

Lessing's despatch from London crossed a further batch of letters from Poole and his officers in Petrograd to Colonel Byrne, which give a good impression of local Russian affairs in mid-January. On the 14th, Captain Garstin stated: 'I haven't written for some time, but since the big change in November, things have altered very slightly. The Bolsheviks have consolidated their position, & all other parties, in P'grad, have faded away. I've jotted down one or two notes on things that might interest you.

'*Attitude to British*. Bad. We're considered quitters and weak-kneed. That is because the English out here, chiefly the business men, have chucked up the sponge & bolted, while Germans have been trying hard to get into what the English have left. Other Englishmen, not only civilians, have lost their tempers, cursed Russia, & departed. An Englishman in a temper is a comical sight, & the sight has been not uncommon. While the attitude of the Brit. Government in recognising no one, helping no one, wishing to help no one, is only making us unpopular with everyone. The silly perpetual attacks on the Bolsheviks in the English Press – Lenin as a German agent, etc., etc., mislead people at home, & infuriate the B[olshevik]s here. It's too childish. The French are worse, but the Yanks are playing more astutely. Anyhow, we are giving the impression of capitulation to Germany, which is terribly bad for our prestige, & our lack of any policy beyond a display of sulks, is not adding to the dignity of our position.

'*The Constituent Assembly* is a very doubtful factor. It has the blessing of the Allies, who presuppose its patriotism. There is no reason to expect anything from it except hot air, or to rely on what will probably be the most amorphous parliament on earth to do anything responsible & imperial. It will probably begin by making a weak peace to satisfy the electorate.

'*The Bolsheviks*, being led by Jews mostly, are the only party with a definite plan & method. Trotsky is as much against the German Imperialism as he is against ours, or what he imagines ours to be. He certainly represents the strongest anti-German party in Russia. In a land clamouring for peace, they have not yet made a dishonourable one. Being internationalists, they are not patriots, but then no one is, whatever they are.

'*The New States* are likely to upset the apple cart in the future unless the Allies come in & help them to Federate. They've got to be helped

from the outside. If we don't do it, there'll be endless troubles, &
annexations, etc. We ought to recognise them all, even the Bolsheviks;
help 'em all & federate them in the last act. Otherwise we're leaving
every possible inducement to Germany to run the show.

'We've got the chance of a lifetime in this country now. That's why
I spit blood at our capitulation. Merely bad temper, & weakness, & no
imagination. And our attitude on the fence is not even dignified.

'This letter is not only my own honest opinion, but also that of much
better people than myself. A rough digest.'[16]

Between January 16 and 18, Major Banting was again writing to
Colonel Byrne: 'This show is getting more & more wonderful, much to
the consternation of all diplomats. Troitsky [sic] & Lenin have novel
ideas about diplomacy & don't care a damn about diplomatic law and
past precedents. The Roumanian Minister & his staff were put in Peter
& Paul the other day at Troitsky's orders, presumably because the
Bolshevik commissars are not too popular in Roumania, but they were
released the next day after a united protest from all Ambassadors
(Allied & neutral) had been put up to Lenin. Another incident was an
attack and loot on the cellars of the Italian Embassy. I believe this
was really done by hooligans without the knowledge of Smolny
(Bolshevik Hd. Qtrs).

'The streets here are in an awful state. With an exceptional snowfall
and no one doing any work to clear it away, the surface is now full of
large holes. It is like going over a switch back railway when in a sleigh.
It is quite impossible at present for the cars, & anyhow there is a great
shortage of petrol . . . The food problem is getting more & more acute
here & what will happen in four or six weeks it is impossible to imagine.
Through sheer disorganisation by the Bolshevik regime, the railways
must sooner or later completely break down. Almost all the old management have now been cleared out . . .[16]

'There are all sorts of wild rumours that disorders will occur when the
Constituent Assembly meets tomorrow. Personally, it appears to us that
the Bolshevik will come out on top as there seems to be no one to take
their place. Some of the soldiers are reported to be against the Bolshevik, but I can't see them putting up a fight. They may "parlez"
but not much more.

'About the scheme for preventing goods in Russia being sent to
Germany. From the bag which is just in and cable T.751 it appears
that the Authorities at home are beginning to jib at the finance question.
If anything is to be done, prompt action is essential and it wd. appear
that the whole scheme may be upset & come under the "too-late"
policy. The Bolsheviks have taken complete control of the Banks, but
there are ways & means of negotiating business transactions over here –

an official statement is being prepared here to be forwarded home . . . One of the great difficulties, outside the financial one, at the present time in this scheme is the elimination of trade friction between the French & Americans & the British business people, as this scheme will have some influence on the after-the-war policy of the Allies over here. The French have a large amount of money invested in metallurgical & coal enterprises over here, but in general trade they are apparently far behind the British & the Americans before the war were out of the picture.' (Banting argued strongly that the whole scheme would break down if General Poole left, as he had considerable influence with the French and Americans, and nothing would be achieved if matters were left to the British Embassy. It was thus essential to send out the financial expert for whom they had pressed.)

'Petrograd may in a very short time be famine-stricken with dramatic results, but on the other hand it may scramble through. The present chaos does not appear to warrant the refusal of a really good man to come out here at once to avoid a possibility of the fatal "too late" policy in commercial matters now & after general peace is signed.

'The Press at Home is no doubt giving far too optimistic an idea of the general state of Russia to the public. It is possible that no one in England can realise that Troitsky is not tied by, & does not believe in, any precedents in European diplomacy & that Ambassadors may be arrested, etc . . . Troitsky is a crazy Internationalist Socialist of the extreme left & is out to smash the Upper Class here. He does not realise or care whether he smashes up Russia @ the same time, which he is certainly doing. He will use German or any other money to attain his end. Therefore until a strong business man arrives here, it seems fatal for the General to leave. It may be all rot staying on here, but I can't see the use of deserting a sinking ship until the last minute, as there is always a remote chance she may struggle into harbour.'[16]

At the same time, General Poole himself wrote to Colonel Byrne: 'I'm sending you by this mail a report of sorts on the work of this outfit. It's a sign of closing down when one begins to write what one has done, & mighty little it seems when it comes to setting down the cold facts on paper!

'Things are hopeless at the present time & I'm convinced they will get much worse before they begin to mend. The whole country is slowly but very surely toppling over & there will be a mighty crash. It will result, as far as I can see, in the annihilation of the *burgui* class – probably a good thing. They are rotten to the core and the country will heal quicker when they have been exterminated.

'But the great point to bear in mind is that it *will* heal, and that is what we have to look forward to. You will see at the end of my report I put forward suggestions for us to get a foothold for our Trade after the War. To do this means money. Now is of course a hopeless time to expect the Govt. to put up any money on such unstable guarantees. But we should surely make all our preparations beforehand, so as to be quite ready when the time comes. Therefore will you see Sir A. Steel-Maitland and discuss with him the desirability of sending out here *at once* a really live man who understands finance & business and who can advise the Govt. as to what line they should take? I am convinced he should be sent at once. If we haver, we shall be too late. Do it now. For the same reason I think we should get Prof. Ipatieff,* the Chemistry Expert. You will know the possibilities of the country, and you know also how the Britain [*sic*] can influence these half-baked Slavs – so you know the vast future for our Trade if only we act with some vigour.

'If you don't push this along at home, then nobody else will – and in five years' time we shall mildly wonder why it is that Germany has managed to collar the whole of Russia.

'You will no doubt hear of many wild-cat schemes put forward to help us in Russia. Each one of them involves much finance. I have looked into many – such as financing Alexeieff, financing Ukraine, etc. etc. In every case I can see exactly where the Russian comes in – he makes his "packet". In no case can I see where we come in except for the pleasure of paying!

'My scheme may prove equally "wild cat" – but anyhow we get a solid *quid pro quo*.

'Of all the schemes I have heard, the one I like best is to boost up the Northern Federation – with Archangel as centre. There we could easily consolidate the Govt. – one Man of War in the harbour would do that. We could reap a rich harvest in timber & railway concessions and control the two Northern Ports.

'I hope you will get some interest taken by the Authorities – it's all so pitiful now with this unending stream of little, little men who waste all their energies straining at gnats. Find us one big man and send him along.

'A little fighting yesterday. The Bolsheviks are still on top. The Constituent Assembly will develop into a talking machine & have no power.

'All well here. Happy New Year.'[16]

In London, the Treasury now evidently feared that the Bolsheviks would probably announce the cancellation of all British loans to Russia – the whole Russian debt of some £600 million. On the 15th, therefore,

---

* It appears that Colonel Byrne's wire, approving the appointment of Professor Ipatiev, had been mislaid.

the Chancellor of the Exchequer informed the War Cabinet that he intended to take over Russian private loans and Treasury bills. In 1915, he explained, as the Treasury had refused to make an advance to bolster up the Russian exchange rate, they had suggested that the Bank of England should provide the money, and this had been done by British firms taking up short-term bills worth £7·5 million. 'It was now contended, and undoubtedly with truth, that this money was provided not in the ordinary way of business, but in order to meet the wishes of the Government,' stated the Chancellor, 'and that therefore the Government should bear the liability.' Although the Chancellor denied any legal liability, he did not think the government should bear the whole loss and proposed to make the best arrangements he could with firms that had accepted these bills, 'subject to the avoidance of any appearance of treating them meanly'. The Bank of England had also issued £10 million of Russian Treasury bills, on behalf of the Russian government, and in the prospectus it was stated that the issue was made with the British government's approval. The Chancellor intended to make similar arrangements over these bills also. This the War Cabinet approved.[17]

The Home Secretary, Sir George Cave, then raised the question of Bolshevik propaganda in England. Should Litvinov's correspondence be censored? And should he not be warned that if he continued to spread propaganda, he might be expelled? Secondly, should any British newspaper publishing further Bolshevik propaganda be seized or prosecuted? Or did the British government prefer to rely on counter-propaganda? The Home Secretary added that present Bolshevik propaganda was a breach of the Defence of the Realm Act, and if it was spread in enemy or Allied countries, it would at once be stopped. In the past, he had deported men from this country for less objectionable propaganda. (At this time, Litvinov was mainly urging the British workers to help the Russian workers to make peace.) Litvinov had been invited to address a Trade Union meeting at Nottingham on the 23rd, and the Home Secretary felt that this Bolshevik agitation would have a bad effect on the British people in general. He drew the War Cabinet's attention to some of the front-page headlines in the Labour papers; the *Herald* printed a headline in large type – 'A People's Peace – Now or Never.'

Balfour pointed out that if Litvinov was deported it would be impossible to maintain 'our existing relations' with the Bolsheviks in Petrograd, where the situation was 'extremely critical', owing to the trouble which had arisen between the Diplomatic Corps and the Bolshevik government over the arrest of the Roumanian Minister. (On January 13, as Major Banting had related, the Roumanian envoy,

Diamandi, had been arrested in Petrograd to mark Bolshevik disapproval of Roumanian action against Bolshevik agitators in Roumania, and the mutinous Russian soldiers there whom the agitators had disaffected, all of which was naturally having a harmful effect on Roumanian troops stationed nearby. Diamandi's arrest had made all the other Allied ambassadors fear for their immunity.) Balfour stated that he had just had a wire from Petrograd that the whole Allied Diplomatic Corps had made a 'most solemn protest' against Diamandi's arrest, and they might all now have to leave.[17]

It was suggested that perhaps Litvinov's diplomatic privileges might be curtailed, though it seemed doubtful whether this 'enemy' propaganda was really doing much real harm amongst the British people as a whole. The Minister of Pensions (a Labour MP) did not think that the suppression of the Labour papers would have a bad effect, though instances were quoted of newspapers having been stopped under the Defence of the Realm Act, because they had published propaganda – in one case simply by stopping the supply of newsprint.

Balfour suggested that before any decision was taken about Litvinov, he himself should consult the Allies about what action they would take in similar circumstances, and also ask Lindley in Petrograd what effect Litvinov's deportation would have on the Bolshevik government. The War Cabinet approved Balfour's suggestion, and decided that the matter should be brought before them again at an early date.[17]

The question of Bolshevik propaganda in England, and the position of Litvinov, was again considered on the 22nd. The Home Secretary drew attention to a leaflet, printed for the British socialist party, for circulation to the Labour Party at their conference at Nottingham on the 23rd, which was a clear breach of the regulations, and had been seized by the police; a prosecution was being considered. The socialist paper *The Call*, which contained the gist of the leaflet, had also been seized. Litvinov's presence, stated the Home Secretary, was clearly being exploited in pacifist interests; and the British government must decide how he was to be treated. Cecil stated that, in his view, one of two courses should be adopted: complete freedom of speech, or drastic all-round repression. He believed free speech to be the wiser policy. 'To suppress small newspapers only gave them and their teachings a tremendous advertisement.' Litvinov should be dealt with in the light of general British policy towards the Bolsheviks. 'To drive him out of the country would be tantamount to a declaration of war against the Bolsheviks.' But he could be repatriated, like any other ambassador, as being *persona non grata*. Cecil had discussed the matter with Buchanan (now back in London), who rather thought a decision should be postponed as long as possible.[18]

The Minister of Labour agreed with the action taken by the Home Secretary. There was no doubt that the British socialist party's propaganda, backed in this case by the Independent Labour Party, was tending to undermine the British people's morale; and the house-to-house distribution of leaflets was a 'most damaging' method of propaganda. But he stressed the need, not for repression, but for a counter-offensive, especially in the smaller provincial papers. The War Cabinet approved the action taken by the Home Secretary, who should also seize the 'offending' printing presses, if possible. It was agreed that the local newspapers should be supplied with suitable material, as suggested by the Minister of Labour; but no action 'for the moment' should be taken against Litvinov.[18]

By now, however, there were wild and irrational fantasies and fears about Litvinov – even in Cabinet circles. His efforts to undermine the discipline of Russian Jews serving in the British army by the circulation of revolutionary pamphlets from a small propaganda bureau in the East End of London had led to a real fear that Litvinov was somehow going to raise a Red Army in the East End from amongst the Russian Jews living there who had not been conscripted.

On the 23rd, as the Labour conference opened at Nottingham, Balfour told the War Cabinet that under a convention between the British and late Russian governments, the ambassadors in both countries had been given power, without appeal, to grant exemptions from military service. Litvinov, as representative of the Bolshevik government, 'would undoubtedly exempt all the East End Jews from military service, if he could,' stated Balfour. 'This would create an intolerable position in the East End, where these Russian Jews were making large sums of money by supplanting British shopkeepers who had been called up for military service.'[19]

The DMO stated that there were about 25,000 Russians of military age in England, of whom only about 4,000 had so far been called up. 'From the counter-espionage point of view, it was most desirable that these aliens should either be got into the army, interned, or deported to Russia,' he stated firmly. As most of them were Jews, he had seen Dr Weizmann, president of the English Zionist Federation, who thought it important that the Jewish regiment, to which they were usually sent, should be despatched to Palestine as soon as possible. The regiment, now at Plymouth, had been told to prepare for service overseas and were waiting for ships. 'He [the DMO] feared that a majority of the remaining East End Jews cared very little for Zionism and were only anxious to make profits.' Under the convention, they could either choose to serve in the British army, or return to Russia. But there were no ships available to take them back to Russia, 'and this fact was known to a good many of the aliens'. Lord Derby added that there had been some trouble in the regiment at Plymouth, but their commander had spoken to them and they now all wanted to go to Palestine to fight. Derby trusted that the War Cabinet would stand firm, and continue to enforce the Military Service Acts in regard to these Russian Jews. 'Rather than allow them to remain in the East End, he thought that, failing their being got into the [British] army, the most practical suggestion would be to send them to a concentration camp at Aberdeen or Hull, to await transport to Russia.'

The War Cabinet agreed that the Military Service Acts should continue to be applied to Russian subjects in England, and if it was impossible to get them all into the British army, 'they should be sent to camps, as suggested by Lord Derby, and be made to understand that their return would not be permitted'.[19]

On the 17th, the Chancellor of the Exchequer announced that the British government would take over all private loans to Russia at 82% of their value, as signs had appeared that the Bolsheviks might be about to cancel the Russian debt to England. (The Bolsheviks had already taken a decision to this effect, though in fact no announcement was to be made for some while.) Balfour produced two wires from Lindley about the position of the Diplomatic Corps in Petrograd at that day's War Cabinet. Since it was possible that the British Embassy staff might be arrested, Lindley had destroyed a number of cyphers and documents, and, 'in the event of the Bolsheviks pushing matters to an extreme', was preparing to destroy the rest.[20]

George Barnes (Minister without Portfolio, and former leader of the Labour Party) stated that when he had mentioned the name of Trotsky at his meetings in Scotland during the past week, 'it had been received with cheers'. Since then, he understood that Arthur Henderson (the Labour Party secretary, and former Cabinet minister) had sent a message to the Bolsheviks. All this, and much else, 'led him to believe that a public statement of our policy towards the Bolsheviks ought to be made'. Balfour replied that, 'from a purely Foreign Office point of view', there would be great advantages in severing all relations with the Bolsheviks, who in making a separate peace, had broken the Treaty of London with the Allies, 'and were openly trying to raise revolutions in all countries'. But we still had 'great interests' in northern Russia and a number of British subjects there, whose position had to be considered. Relations of a 'practical kind' thus had to take place through agents. 'He [Balfour] was quite clear that we could not give full recognition to the Bolsheviks until they could show that they were representative of the Russian people.' By this, Balfour now seems to have been

[198]

implying that *de facto* recognition had been granted to the Bolsheviks. Lord Robert Cecil took careful note of Balfour's remark.[20]

That day, Sir George Clerk informed the Russia committee that it was highly important that the War Cabinet should be given the 'most complete and reliable' information obtainable on whether Germany was likely to be able to get food supplies from Russia before next harvest. The DMI stated what the position was in the Ukraine. The big landlords had sold the 1917 grain harvest and these stocks had no doubt been consumed by now. The small landowners were still holding on to the 1917 harvest and much of that of the previous year. It was decided to consider the matter further at their next meeeting, when the DMI hoped to have more information. Meanwhile, Dudley Ward would discover what information the Wheat Commission had.[21]

But at the Russia committee's meeting next day the question of a financial adviser to Lindley (not General Poole) was discussed, in spite of the apparent agreement between Steel-Maitland and Colonel Byrne that this was not the moment to send out such an adviser. 'Bag in from Russia with General Knox,' notes Colonel Byrne in his diary on the 18th. Knox, in fact, had arrived with Major Banting's paper of January 6, urging a massive injection of British capital into the Russian banks in order to obtain control of them for England. Byrne would appear to have passed Banting's paper immediately to the Russia committee, who were now told by Sir George Clerk that Steel-Maitland had 'strongly recommended' a Mr Herbert Guedalla as financial adviser to Lindley, and it was decided that Clerk should make further enquiries about him. Guedalla was a chartered accountant, who had founded his own finance house, the Imperial and Foreign Corporation, which promoted companies and share issues in the City. He had various Russian connections and directorships, and knew the Russian banker Benenson, who in turn knew Jaroszynski.[22]

A few days later (the 23rd), Colonel Byrne, whose Russia supply committee was about to be taken over by the Russia committee, sent two wires to General Poole. In the first (T.765), he officially approved the formation of the Trade Barter Company in Petrograd (known as *Tovaro Obmien*), to prevent supplies falling into German hands. Its objectives would be:

1. To ensure the safety of Allied supplies at Archangel.
2. To prevent the transport of all supplies to the enemy, and the production of any supplies likely to benefit him.
3. To secure all flax and platinum, etc. in Russia for ourselves.

'As regards objective no. 2,' added Byrne, 'no doubt you will be able to exploit the Russian talent for obstruction.' Poole was authorised to expend up to 10 million roubles on this project.[22] (*Tovaro Obmien* was in fact run by an Allied committee, with the French and Americans providing 10 million roubles each. It concentrated in particular on buying up sunflower-seed oil in the Kuban, glycerine at Petrograd and Kursk, and textiles, flax and hemp, and various metals, and mainly operated through the Russian co-operative societies. A man called Arthur Marshall (of the British Engineering Company of Russia and Siberia) actually ran *Tovaro Obmien* for General Poole, together with d'Arcy, the French Commercial Attaché, and an American called Stevens, of the National City Bank.)

Colonel Byrne's second wire to Poole (T.766) concerned the possible recovery from Russia of the guns and what was left of the ammunition supplied by England. 'Would there be any chance of the Russians disposing of any of their own material to us?' he asked.

This was the final action that Colonel Byrne took on the dissolution of the Milner Committee, or Russia supply Committee.[22]

On January 18, as Trotsky again broke off the peace talks at Brest-Litovsk on being told by the Germans that they would negotiate direct with the Ukrainian Rada (now more or less under German control), the Bolsheviks forcibly dissolved the first and only meeting of the Constituent Assembly (in which they only held 175 seats out of 707 – the SR had an overwhelming majority of 410 seats). This was a grand climacteric in British relations with the Bolsheviks, and led to action being taken.

By now, the DMI had heard from General Foch confirming that the French had been unable to provide General Alexeiev with any ready cash for the volunteer army, as agreed in Paris on December 23. As a result, Colonel Keyes had suddenly received orders from London to despatch 15 million roubles from Petrograd – at once and by any means – to the Don Cossacks and volunteer army at Novocherkask. Currency was by now very short in Petrograd. The British Embassy did not have this amount. Keyes decided that it would have to be provided by Jaroszynski.[23]

It is not clear whether Poole and Banting, when reporting to Colonel Byrne, had ever known that Lindley and Keyes in the British Embassy had all this time been actually carrying out their recommendations, with Foreign Office support, for purchasing the Russian banks, even though the banks had been nationalised some weeks before. For back in December, the Bolsheviks had been rightly alarmed at the contact between the Russian bankers and the Allied ambassadors, who they feared might give massive support to the Russian banks, which by late December were very short of cash, and thus enable them openly to finance their opponents. On December 27, therefore (as the decision in principle was taken to cancel the Russian foreign debt), Red Guards, many of them illiterate, had been sent to occupy the Petrograd and Moscow banks, which were declared to be nationalised. The bank clerks, however, came out on strike, and as the Bolsheviks could not replace them, the banks remained closed until late in January.

But for several weeks now, furious dealing in bank shares had been taking place under cover, as a result of Lindley's promise in early December that the British Embassy would guarantee the 6 million roubles in sterling necessary for Jaroszynski, on behalf of the British government, to buy out the Russian directors of the Russian Bank for Foreign Trade, who wished to leave Russia urgently to escape arrest. On January 4, Hugh Leech, now recovered from tonsilitis, had given Davidov, chairman of the Russian Bank for Foreign Trade, a promissory note on Leech's own account at the London City and Midland Bank in London for £151,500 (ie, 5 million roubles at 33), and Isidore Kon, Jaroszynski's financial agent, a similar note for £30,300 (1 million roubles). Both had then left rapidly for Stockholm, after the shares in the Russian Bank for Foreign Trade had been handed over to Jaroszynski, who transferred 6 million roubles to Leech's account at the Commercial and Industrial Bank in Petrograd. Thus Jaroszynski, acting as agent for the British government, now officially controlled the grain trade on the Volga.

(It was this minor deal with Kon that subsequently shed a little public light on these complicated transactions, for Kon was never paid, and later sued Leech. But when the case was heard in London in November 1920, both sides, and their eminent counsel, had good reason to say as little as possible – and the report of the case, taken on its own, is incomprehensible. In fact, Jaroszynski owed Kon this 1 million roubles, via Leech, for commission on the – subsequently cancelled – initial 50 million rouble loan from Benenson, and not for shares at all, as Kon falsely told Leech at the time.)

On January 11, Lindley finally informed the Foreign Office (not knowing that Leech had already signed the two promissory notes) that the directors of the Russian Bank for Foreign Trade wished to leave Russia at once to escape arrest, but would not go unless large funds were available for them abroad. He suggested that a banking group (in fact Jaroszynski), who wished to buy their controlling packet of shares, but had no foreign currency, should deposit 6 million roubles in Petrograd against the sterling equivalent for the bank directors in a London bank. 'Right for Embassy to put two people on board,' he added.[23]

The Foreign Office replied to Lindley on the 16th that they approved his proposal of the 11th – provided, it was emphasised to Lindley, that he in fact obtained 6 million roubles in cash, and the right to nominate two directors to the board of the bank. The Foreign Office, in fact, were approving British acquisition – and control – of the Russian Bank for Foreign Trade.

On the 17th, therefore, Keyes wired to London, again recommending the sterling equivalent of a 200 million rouble loan to Jaroszynski, to enable him to buy up all the five major Russian banks, and then set up a Cossack bank in south Russia, which could issue banknotes, and thus provide the Don Cossacks and volunteer army with 15 million roubles, as ordered from London. But once again, Keyes did not mention Jaroszynski by name – he simply referred to 'a financier'.[23]

Next day (the 18th), Hugh Leech at last told Lindley that he had already given the two promissory notes to the two Russian bankers, who had already left Russia; but Leech apparently said nothing about the transfer of the actual purchase money, *ie*, the 6 million roubles. Lindley simply asked him who the British Embassy should appoint as directors of the Russian Bank for Foreign Trade. 'Jaroszynski and me,' replied Leech (according to Lindley). On the 20th, therefore, Lindley (unaware that the 6 million roubles were now in Leech's account with the Commercial and Industrial Bank in Petrograd) replied to the Foreign Office wire of the 16th that as there were no rouble notes available, they should either be provided from London against security given by the London City and Midland Bank, or by another bank in Petrograd (in fact, by the Russian and English Bank, whose original temporary loan had enabled the crucial packet of shares in the Russian Bank for Foreign Trade to be transferred in the first place). This misunderstanding between Lindley and Leech demonstrates the hectic atmosphere now prevailing in Petrograd.[23]

When the Russia Committee met in London on the 21st, Lindley's wire of the day before had apparently not arrived. It was first agreed that Sir George Clerk should interview Mr Herbert Guedalla, the prospective financial adviser to Lindley, next day; but the interview should be non-committal, pending the completion of private enquiries by Colonel Peel (the Foreign Office's financial adviser on the Russia committee). The chairman, Lord Robert Cecil, then brought before the committee Colonel Keyes's wire of the 17th, containing his proposals for financing the Don Cossacks. 'Colonel Peel was in favour of adopting the scheme,' state the minutes, 'while admitting that the proposed financial procedure was decidedly irregular. Mr Ward (of the Treasury) sounded a note of caution. Sir G. Clerk emphasised two points:

a. With the Germans already at Petrograd, we must take action at once if we were to do so at all.
b. It was possible that at any moment we might be left without any British representative at Petrograd.'

The Russia committee agreed to Cecil's proposal that he should place the matter before the Cabinet, 'pointing out that the scheme, while offering great advantages, was of the nature of a gamble'. Thus the Foreign Office members, backed by their own financial adviser, had over-ridden the Treasury's initial objections.[24]

With the Bolshevik dissolution of the constituent assembly now known in London, the War Cabinet that took place later on the 21st, attended by Sir George Buchanan and General Knox, just back from Petrograd, was obviously to be of crucial importance. Some definite action would be taken – even though the Cabinet that day lost one of its more active members on the Russian question – Sir Edward Carson, who ostensibly resigned over disagreement with Lloyd George on the Irish question. ('I am not surprised,' records Hankey. 'He will not be missed.' Carson had not been a success in the Cabinet, and was not replaced.)[25]

Balfour first informed the War Cabinet that, in view of recent events in Petrograd, the Cabinet must 'very seriously' consider their relations with the Bolshevik government. We were the only Allied nation to have received a Bolshevik envoy, and in fact the only one to whom one had been sent. But the Bolsheviks would not mind quarrelling with us. 'It was a question, therefore, whether the Bolsheviks would commit some act which would provoke a rupture.' Balfour personally felt that we should postpone a rupture as long as possible, as the Bolsheviks clearly provided the Germans with more difficulties than the Social-Revolutionaries would. In fact, the Bolsheviks were more likely to postpone a separate peace between Russia and Germany, and stop the Germans getting supplies out of Russia, than any other party in Russia. They appeared determined, however, to spread what he described as 'passionate propaganda' both in this country, and also in Germany, where they believed conditions were very bad, and that internal trouble was 'inevitable' in the near future. There were two current views about Trotsky: one that he was in German pay, 'and was playing the German game'; the other, which seemed more probable, that he was a 'genuine fanatic' bent on spreading the doctrines of revolution throughout the world, 'but particularly in the two countries which he regarded as Imperialistic, viz, England and Germany'. This was a sound statement.[25]

Buchanan remarked that he had always been opposed to an open breach with the Bolsheviks. But it was clear that, sooner or later, we should have to choose between a rupture and complete mutual agreement over everything. He would prefer a rupture rather than allow large-scale Bolshevik propaganda in this country. He thought the Germans would clearly like to see a rupture between us and the Bolsheviks, and would like our envoys at Petrograd withdrawn so as to give them a clear field. 'Any step towards recognition by us would be exploited by the Bolsheviks in their own interests,' he warned. The SR had 'no backbone', and he agreed with Balfour that they would be 'less of a nuisance' to the Germans. Two things modified his view of avoiding a rupture with the Bolsheviks. First, the Bolshevik dispersal of the constituent assembly; secondly, the possibility of Japanese and American military support for the anti-Bolshevik forces in south Russia (a somewhat slim hope at this stage).

General Knox, when asked about the military situation, said that the very idea of a volunteer army in Russia was 'impossible'. At least 70% of the Russian troops on the northern and western fronts had disappeared since the revolution. When asked about the Germans obtaining food and supplies from south Russia, he said that 'even assuming a separate peace' it would be fully six months before the Germans could obtain anything important from south Russia. But after six months, they could get nearly all they needed, 'which would in effect break down the blockade'. But, as little corn had been sown in south Russia, there would be very little surplus corn for export unless the Germans could seize the land before April. 'The district of real importance was the Donetz coal basin, and whoever had effective possession of this, was in a position to hold up the transport and resources of practically the whole of Russia,' he emphasised. (And the Don Cossacks and the volunteer army were the nearest force.) A number of Russian officers had spoken to him in Petrograd about joining General Kaledin. 'As long, however, as we appeared to be giving any form of recognition or support to the Bolsheviks, it was not likely that they would take this step,' he warned. 'Our dealings with the Bolsheviks undoubtedly decreased the effectiveness of the moral and material support we were giving to the Cossacks,' Knox declared. The DMI said that it appeared that all the Russian armies on all fronts 'were rapidly melting away'.

Lord Robert Cecil stated that there had been 'considerable difficulties' in getting financial support to the Cossacks and 'other friendly persons' in south-east Russia. He drew attention to two wires received from Colonel Keyes (one sent in early December, the other on January 17), in which he suggested that if we could advance £5,000,000 (*ie*, 200 million roubles) to an 'un-named capitalist' (*ie*, Jaroszynski), it would be possible for us to get control of five banks that had branches in the 'friendly territory', which would enable us not only to finance the Cossacks, 'but also to obtain control of important industrial resources in south Russia'.

But Bonar Law (Chancellor of the Exchequer) 'felt some difficulty' in making such an advance to an unknown person, even on Colonel

Keyes' recommendation. At this, General Knox remarked that the 'unknown capitalist was probably Mr Poliakov'. The Cabinet minutes here state that it was 'subsequently ascertained' (from whom it is not clear – perhaps from William Sutherland, the Prime Minister's press secretary, who knew Lessing, who was a friend of Poliakov) that Poliakov was a Jewish banker from Rostov-on-Don, who was known to General Poole. This confusion of identity occasioned by Knox's chance remark was to prove disastrous.[25]

The War Cabinet approved the proposal. On the 22nd, Balfour was authorised to notify Keyes of this, via Lindley, in answer to his wire of the 17th. 'The Government are so anxious to give immediate financial assistance to our friends,' stated the reply, 'that if the advance can be utilised immediately to assist them, and on the understanding that the unnamed financier is P—— [*sic*], the Government will sanction the proposal. You see therefore that we are prepared to take this course entirely on your advice.'[26]

In Petrograd there was an acute shortage of rouble notes and when Hugh Leech assured Lindley that Jaroszynski had actually transferred the purchase money for the Russian Bank for Foreign Trade to Leech's account at the Commercial and Industrial Bank in Petrograd, Lindley had wired the Foreign Office again on January 22 that it would now be possible to transfer these 6 million roubles to southern Russia. The Foreign Office replied that they could be credited to the London City and Midland Bank against a promissory note – which, of course, Hugh Leech had long since given. Leech, in fact, was several jumps ahead of both Lindley and the Foreign Office. (On receipt of this later wire, Leech's partner, Firebrace, cancelled the temporary deal with the Russian banker Benenson, which had been designed to force Lindley's hand in the first place.)[27]

But as Colonel Keyes had only managed to raise 10 million roubles from secret funds, out of the 15 million which he had been ordered from London to send forthwith to the Don Cossacks, Keyes and Lindley asked Leech if his 6 million roubles really were in notes; if so, 5 million were to be sent to southern Russia at once. Leech went to see Jaroszynski, who had by now also acquired control of the International Bank (which in turn controlled the southern Russian grain trade), by purchasing the controlling packet of shares owned by the Russian bankers Wischnegradski and Chaikevitch, chairman and managing director respectively; and though Jaroszynski had failed to acquire the Volga-Kama Bank, which had extensive interests in the upper Volga region, he was still after the Siberian Bank, which controlled the Siberian grain trade, but could not induce Denisov, the managing director, to sell.[27]

But when approval was unexpectedly received from London – on about January 24 – for a British loan of 200 million roubles for the purchase of the five major Russian banks and the setting up of a Cossack bank in southern Russia, 'if the financier involved is Poliakov', both Keyes and Lindley were bewildered; neither could understand why Poliakov should be chosen. Teddy Lessing, who had been instructed on leaving England to tell Poole to stop 'half-baked' schemes, now, it seems, warned his friend Poliakov.

Poliakov, Poole and Keyes then got down to business with Jaroszynski, who was also baffled, for the British Embassy had already 'impressed upon Mr Jaroszynski and myself', Leech wrote later, 'that this project [ie, of sending money to southern Russia] was to be concealed with the greatest care from Mr Poliakov'. Both men disliked each other intensely. Jaroszynski regarded Poliakov's political views 'with the utmost suspicion', and Poliakov considered Jaroszynski to be a Russian financier 'of the bounder type'. (Keyes, in his secret service wires to London, which were later grudgingly handed over to the Foreign Office when law suits were pending, had given Jaroszynski the codename 'live wire'.) When Jaroszynski now produced his draft agreement for a British loan to himself of 200 million roubles for three years at $3\frac{1}{2}\%$, Poliakov turned it down; the most that he would recommend the British government to lend Jaroszynski, he told Poole and Keyes, was £500,000 – ie, one-tenth. Jaroszynski was furious. Poole and Keyes, who had strict instructions that the destination of this money was not to be revealed, were unwilling to say anything, thinking that Poliakov must have some special information (which he had not); and with the Cheka on the prowl outside, the two British officers had to keep silent as the two Russian financiers endlessly argued at cross-purposes.[27] Poole and Keyes finally had to force Jaroszynski to accept the smaller sum, and to raise the interest to $5\frac{1}{4}\%$, upon which Poliakov also insisted. Jaroszynski at last agreed that the smaller sum would now probably suffice, if the Volga-Kama bank was dropped from the scheme, and 'unless German action forced up the price of the Siberian bank', for with the British help he had already received, he now had an absolute majority in the Commercial and Industrial Bank, the Russian bank for Foreign Trade, and practical control of the International Bank. Keyes then asked Jaroszynski what security he would offer for this loan. He replied curtly that if he were also advanced what he needed to acquire control of the Siberian Bank, and to launch the Cossack bank in southern Russia (which amount he put at 30 million roubles), he would offer shares in industrial holdings worth 35 million roubles. These were 40,000 shares in the Russkaya Neft Company, 12,000 shares in the Ter Akopov Company and 30,000 shares in the Achinsk–Minusinsk Railway.

The first two were second-rate oil companies and the third was a branch line leading to some Siberian gold-quartz mines, and it was not clear whether these shares were free from mortgage, or even worth half 35 million roubles. (Indeed, Sir William Clark, of the Department of Overseas Trade, who brought a British Economic Mission out to Russia in July, mainly to investigate the muddle that had resulted from these bank deals, later remarked that Jaroszynski 'absolutely refused' to offer the actual bank shares themselves as security. 'He could hardly agree,' explained Clark, 'as the shares were all mortgaged in carrying on his "pyramiding" operations.')[27]

This security, however, was accepted by Poole and Keyes and the meeting then broke up. Hugh Leech, meanwhile, was investigating the best method of sending the 15 million roubles to Kornilov and Alexeiev. It was vital to find a reliable person both to carry the bank draft and to give a reasonable account of its use. An oil company seemed the best bet, he thought, and he first tried the Shell group; but finally he decided to use the Premier Oil and Pipeline Company, for which he himself had worked and for which he still held a power of attorney. This would give suitable cover, he thought, as the late Russian government owed the company large sums of money and the bearer could say that it was going to be used to buy up oil companies. So when Jaroszynski, on Keyes' instructions, gave Leech a draft for 15 million roubles, Leech made it payable to George Perkins, the general manager of the Premier Oil and Pipeline Company, at the Commercial and Industrial Bank in Ekaterinodar, and the draft was sent down to Perkins, who was then at Kiev. At the same time, Leech sent Perkins a secret message telling him to give the money to Kornilov, via General de Candolle, the British military envoy sent from Roumania, while Jaroszynski sent orders for the Kiev branch to put the Ekaterinodar branch in funds.[27]

The Don Cossacks, on whose behalf all this energy was being expended, having already refused to fight, now mutinied. On January 23, some Cossack delegates meeting north of Rostov formed a Military Revolutionary Committee, then turned on their *Ataman* Kaledin, who again had to appeal to Kornilov, whose small volunteer army of about 4,000 troops, now based at Rostov, suffered heavily. By late January, his small force had been driven out of all the nearby towns, save Rostov itself.[28]

Jaroszynski, meanwhile, was having no success in his attempt to buy the Siberian Bank, and hence to control the Siberian grain trade. Denisov, the main shareholder, mistrusted him; he had a shrewd idea that Jaroszynski would not be able to pay and consequently was not anxious to enter into any contract. Since the two men who had originally induced Buchanan to back the whole project were no longer around (Pokrovsky, the chairman of the Siberian Bank, and former Foreign Minister, was now in prison for failing to hand the Russian Red Cross funds over to the Bolsheviks, while Krivoshein, the former Minister of Agriculture, had simply disappeared), Keyes therefore asked Poliakov, who was anyhow a junior manager and director of the Siberian Bank, to arrange somehow for Jaroszynski to acquire control, as the Germans were known to be after this bank.[29]

All this had to be done very secretly. 'Judging by purely external signs, the power of the Bolsheviks seems to have secured itself to some extent during the last few days,' reported Count Mirbach, head of a German economic mission then in Petrograd, to the German Chancellor and Foreign Secretary, Kühlmann, on the 24th. 'Whether or how long this positive trend will last remains to be seen. Since political life here moves entirely in convulsive spasms, one must always be prepared to reckon with very brief stages. For the moment, however, the big planned coups of the Smolny government have been successful...'[30]

In London on the 24th, the War Cabinet continued their discussion of the 21st on the whole Russian question. Balfour recapitulated his previous appeals to the British government not to break off relations with the Bolsheviks, adding that he had wired to Lindley that he 'left it to his discretion as to when he and his staff should leave Petrograd should an emergency arise'. Lord Robert Cecil, who took a much harder line, saw that he had a ready ally in General Knox, and stated that while he 'fully concurred' in the present British policy, he thought the question should be more fully considered, in view of the 'strong representations' by General Knox that maintaining 'even informal relations' with the Bolsheviks tended to discourage 'friendly elements' in south Russia.[31]

The War Cabinet then adjourned until 6 p.m., when Allied intervention in Siberia was for the first time seriously and exhaustively considered. For while the British in the western theatre were much involved in erecting a barrier to German penetration into Russia, and especially into south Russia, all they could do to assist 'our friends' was to provide financial support. When they turned to Siberia, more definite projects could be entertained for restoring the eastern front against Germany. For the Far East was the only military theatre available from which Allied military support could be provided for the Don Cossacks and volunteer army; and the War Cabinet now took the crucial decision, in principle, to work for such armed Allied intervention in Russia from the Far East.

After the Bolshevik revolution, the War Cabinet did not fully consider the position in Siberia until December 7, just after the return of the

British ministers from the Allied conference in Paris (when it was decided that Russia could not be allowed to make a separate peace). In the Far East, it was feared, the Bolsheviks might seize the Siberian railway and rearm the many German prisoners in Siberia, who would despatch the enormous stocks of Allied supplies at Vladivostok to Germany. These fears were largely irrational. But there was an Allied power nearby which could, and – under certain circumstances – would take action in the Far East, namely Japan – which had been strongly urged at the Allied conference on December 1 to 'do something'. All Russians, however, hated and feared the Japanese, whose ambitions were limited to the domination of Manchuria, so as to be able to withstand western competition after the war; and Japan's main western rival was America, without whose consent she did not intend to take any action on Russian territory.

On December 3, by which time both Lloyd George and Clemenceau had left the Allied conference, General Foch put forward proposals for seizing the Siberian railway – proposals which were an exercise in kite-flying, in the absence of his political masters. In view of the Russian collapse and the German military and economic advance into Russia, the Siberian railway must be seized to restore good communications between Vladivostok and Moscow, argued Foch, and to reinforce the 'still healthy' elements in Russia (the Roumanians, Cossacks, Czecho-slovaks and Ukrainians, to be organised by General Berthelot's military mission) with American or Japanese troops. Foch in effect asked the Allied conference to approve the seizure of the Siberian railway from Vladivostok to Moscow by Japanese or American troops, who would pave the way for further troops from America or Japan to make a 'direct military intervention' into Russia from the Far East.[32]

Since writing his note, stated Foch, news had come of the Bolsheviks' seizure of Vladivostok. 'The German grip now extended from Petrograd to Vladivostok, and was threatening the interests of the United States and Japan in the extreme Orient,' he added. Even if the news of the Bolsheviks' seizure of Vladivostok was not true today (and it was not), it would be in a week or a month. 'We must put our hand on Vladivistok and on the whole line to Moscow at once.' Balfour suggested that a full-scale naval assault on Vladivostok would be a very formid-able operation. But Foch brushed this aside; the question of principle should be settled first by America and Japan. Balfour retorted that Foch's proposal 'was in essence an attack on Russia'. Foch replied that Allied intervention could take place 'without hostility to Russia'. America had vast stocks of war supplies at Vladivostok, destined for Russia and Roumania, 'and they might well claim to land troops to guard those stocks and to escort them to their destinations free from interference. This was not a declaration of war, but a means of ensuring supplies in times of trouble and unrest.'³²

Colonel House, a member of the United States delegation at the conference, said that such a plan had already been considered in Washington. 'The idea was a police force, not for the protection of the stores, but to keep the railways open in order to ensure food for the people of Russia.' The Japanese Ambassador warned that these good Allied intentions would be misinterpreted as an attack on Russia, while a police force would be too small to do any good. Colonel House agreed. All that America could do was to make an offer to Russia to run the railways in order to feed Russia. When Balfour asked to whom the offer was to be made, House suggested 'that we should proceed quietly under the present system', and let the American Railway Commission continue its work without raising any questions, until stopped by the Russians. Foch accepted House's suggestion, but urged that precautions be taken to anticipate Bolshevik disturbances, 'so that we might be able to keep Roumania and the loyal provinces supplied'. Balfour then proposed that the American Railway Commission should continue its work, and that both Colonel House and the Japanese Ambassador should consult their governments about landing a police force, if necessary. This was generally accepted, though no resolution on the subject was made.

Foch, having made his point, passed it to the CIGS in London, so that he could bring the necessary pressure on the War Cabinet.

On December 7, the CIGS duly proposed to the War Cabinet that Japan and perhaps America should be asked to send a force to police Vladivostok to protect the Allied stores, and later, if necessary, to obtain control of the Siberian railway, 'and open up communication with south Russia'. This was a new proposal, aimed at bringing some Allied support to the Don Cossacks, who were completely cut off. But it also was quite impractical – the Don Cossacks were more than 5,000 miles from Vladivostok. The War Cabinet considered whether the seizure of Vladivostok by Japanese or American forces 'might not do more harm than good, by strengthening Russian opposition to the Allies even among the most friendly sections of the population, and might even jeopardise the lives of the British Ambassador and other British subjects in Russia.' Similar fears had been expressed in Russia lest the recent démarche by General Barter at Russian GHQ, threatening dire Allied action if Russia made a separate peace, 'should imply an intention to let loose the Japanese against Russia. There was a real danger that Russia might not only make peace with Germany, but also might be provoked by us into fighting with the Germans against us'. On the other hand, an 'ambiguous and uncertain' policy towards the Bolshevik government was also fraught with 'serious disadvantages'. The War Cabinet simply decided that Balfour should wire to Washington and Tokyo (in conformity with the recent Allied decision in Paris to make enquiries about the protection of the Siberian railway) to ask if the conditions were now thought favourable by either America or Japan 'for the despatch of a police force to Vladivostok'.[32]

In reply, Lord Reading, the British Ambassador in Washington, stated that there had been no contact between America and Japan on the matter and that the American government had not yet reached any decision. The Japanese Ambassador, however, had told him some time ago that if German control of Russia seemed probable, Japan would mobilise and take the necessary counter-action.[33]

On December 12, however, the *Times* correspondent in Washington reported that Japanese troops had arrived at Vladivostok. But the Foreign Office were informed that the American government had been assured, through the Japanese Ambassador in Petrograd, that there was no 'landing in force'. Such an operation, the State Department pointed out, would be distinctly unfortunate if undertaken by Japan alone. The presence of even a few American officers in uniform, to co-operate with the Japanese, would have a far better effect and remove the impression of unilateral Japanese intervention. But, Robert Lansing, the Secretary of State, admitted in a further wire, if Japan had so acted to prevent Vladivostok and the Allied war supplies from falling into Bolshevik hands, he could not object.

In fact, no Japanese troops had been landed. But the need for some kind of intervention was reinforced by further news from Vladivostok, despatched in a wire from Buchanan in Petrograd on the 6th, though this did not reach the Foreign Office until the 14th. This reported strikes and general unrest, ships delayed, and serious dislocation of business, against which the Allied consuls had protested to the provisional government authorities, which were still in nominal control, though Bolshevik influence was now very strong. This protest was effectively supported by the arrival of the American admiral in his flagship, which had a salutary and restraining influence. His presence, it was felt, would also avoid the suggestion of unilateral Japanese intervention, which might follow the arrival of a Japanese warship, and he was invited to prolong his stay by a few days.[33]

On December 15, the British Ambassador in Tokyo reported the Japanese response to the War Cabinet's enquiry of the 7th about the despatch of a police force to Vladivostok. The Japanese Foreign Minister stated that Japan could not undertake to guard the Siberian railway from Vladivostok to Moscow, but would be willing to discuss a more modest operation up to Harbin, in central Manchuria, or even to Karymskaya, the junction of the Amur and the Chinese Eastern railways, in Russia itself. Participation by American troops would be unpopular in Japan and cause misunderstanding, the Foreign Minister said, but he would welcome British recommendations on how to prevent Bolshevik control of the entire Siberian railway. A Japanese warship was standing by to protect Allied life and property at Vladivostok, should the need arise.

On the 17th Balfour raised the matter with the CIGS, who replied on the 20th that Japanese and American troops should be used not only to guard the Allied stores, but ultimately to secure control of the whole Siberian railway. On the 21st, therefore, Balfour wired to Washington that he believed that, under certain circumstances, Japan would guard a portion of the railway from Vladivostok; he hoped that in that event the American government would co-operate and so avoid the political disadvantage of unilateral Japanese action. Secretary Lansing informed the British Ambassador that he knew that Japan had a force ready to protect her large colony in Vladivostok, if it were attacked, and he was afraid that such a landing might cause a violent outburst of feeling against the Allies and thus strengthen the Bolsheviks. In a further wire, it was stated that the American government disliked the idea of unilateral Japanese action as much as joint intervention by Japan and America.

On the 26th, the Japanese Ambassador in London had a discussion with Lord Robert Cecil, who inferred that Japan would, sooner or later, probably land a force at Vladivostok. Cecil urged consultation and co-operation with the American government, and then wired to Washington that if Japan should propose joint action with the American government, he hoped that it would not be hastily refused. The Japanese Ambassador in Washington, however, assured Secretary Lansing that no landing of Japanese troops was being contemplated. It might have a disastrous effect on Russian opinion which, in Lansing's view, would be still more hostile in the event of joint action by Japan and America. Colonel House concurred; if Japan intervened alone, there would certainly be pressure from a section of American opinion for America to participate – action to which, on both political and military grounds, the American government was strongly opposed.[33]

But the Japanese Ambassador in Washington was right. On the 27th, the Japanese government secretly decided against intervention. This was made clear in a memorandum from the Russian Embassy in London to the Foreign Office, reporting a discussion between the Russian Ambassador in Tokyo and the Japanese Foreign Minister, who declared that, save for some act of violence by the Bolsheviks against Japan, his country would not intervene; even if the Bolsheviks seized Vladivostok and the Siberian railway, Japan would not act except at the express desire of the Allies. And even then, if the occupation of Vladivostok became inevitable, Japan would give a solemn declaration that it was only temporary and was in no sense an act of conquest, but only undertaken to assist the local Russian authorities. Thus by the end of 1917, British efforts to secure small- or large-scale intervention in Siberia by Japan or America had had little success.[33]

But on January 1, when there was a further War Cabinet discussion about the Allied stores at Vladivostok, reports were circulating in London that the Bolsheviks were murdering and ravishing the population of Irkutsk, the large Siberian city near Lake Baikal, that the bodies of slaughtered children littered the streets, and that the French Consul and two French officers had also perished. (These reports were quite untrue, and may well have been deliberately spread by French or other Allied agents to urge on Japan.) When the War Cabinet discussed the Allied stores, 'which, unless safeguarded, might very probably fall into the hands of the enemy and be used against us' (so state the Cabinet minutes), Lord Robert Cecil stated that there were only two alternatives; either to leave the stores alone, or to encourage the Japanese to send a 'really strong force'. It would be of no value just to send a small British force.[34]

The CIGS agreed. 'It was undoubtedly of great importance to prevent the valuable war material at Vladivostok from falling into German hands.' (Of course, there was in fact no chance of this.) He recalled the War Cabinet decision of December 7, when Balfour was requested to make enquiries in Washington and Tokyo: 'but the United States government had refused to take action in the matter'. The CIGS felt that a force should now be sent, 'and that it must necessarily be Japanese or American, or both; for choice, it should not be solely Japanese, as in this case the Russians as a whole, not merely the Bolsheviks, would be opposed to this step. In order to show the Russians that the measures were purely protective, and had no sinister motives behind them, he thought it would be best to send a few Chinese and British troops to show the flag.' We could send two infantry companies from Hong Kong.

The War Cabinet felt that it was 'of the first importance' that some action should be taken immediately, and that the plan open to least objection was to allow the Japanese to occupy Vladivostok. 'This, of course, raised a very large question of policy, involving the possible exploitation of eastern Siberia by the Japanese, and probable resentment by the Russians.' These dangers, however, might be mitigated if all the Allies, or at least the Americans, British, and Chinese, participated. After some discussion, the War Cabinet decided that the cruiser *Suffolk* should be sent from Hong Kong to Vladivostok at once, and that the two infantry companies there should stand by; that Lord Robert

Cecil should inform the Japanese Ambassador that we were proposing joint action at Vladivostok, to protect the Allied stores, and should also wire to Colonel House, for the information of President Wilson, to explain the policy we now proposed, 'laying stress on the danger of the stores falling into the hands of the Germans', and asking for American co-operation.[34]

The Japanese, after giving assurances in late December that they would not intervene, or indeed take any action save at the express desire of the Allies, were incensed that the British were now taking unilateral action and despatching a warship. The Japanese Foreign Minister told the British Ambassador in Tokyo that he reproached the British government with lack of candour in passing on their proposals for safeguarding the Siberian railway and Vladivostok against German control. He was 'painfully affected' to learn that the British government disapproved of Japan acting alone, if intervention became necessary, and were inviting American co-operation. This would be very unpopular in Japan, even though relations with America were now much better than they had been in the past. He hoped the British government would trust Japan to fulfil this duty, especially as enemy action in eastern Russia and on the Siberian seaboard was of peculiar and intimate concern to Japan, who had her forces ready and could despatch them to the right places at very short notice. To emphasise his point, two Japanese warships were at once sent to Vladivostok.[35]

The Foreign Office (which was of course unaware that Japan had secretly decided against intervention on December 27) found this a 'surprising message'. The British Ambassador in Tokyo was instructed to reply that Lord Robert Cecil had explained in two interviews with the Japanese Ambassador in London why Allied intervention was preferable to unilateral action by Japan, and had been thanked for his frank statement by the Ambassador, who however could make no statement about Japanese policy; indeed, on December 26, he had said that he did not think the Japanese government had reached any decision on intervention. (This was correct. The decision was made on the 27th.) Since receiving the Japanese Foreign Minister's message about British reticence, the British Ambassador in Tokyo was informed, Lord Robert Cecil had passed it on to the Japanese Ambassador, who appeared much surprised, for he believed he had made the British position quite clear to the Japanese government. (He may well have done so; but the British had now changed their position.)[35]

The French now entered the lists. On January 7, they proposed nothing less than a joint Allied punitive expedition, which should march across Manchuria and exact due retribution for the alleged murder of the

French Consul at Irkutsk – cutting the Siberian railway *en route* to prevent the westward shipment of any Allied stores. Since it had been known in London for some days that the French Consul was in fact alive and well, this démarche was rendered null and void in London, though it continued to reverberate round the other Allied capitals for over two weeks.[35] But the British were now determined on some action. On the 7th, during a further short discussion by the War Cabinet, Lord Robert Cecil insisted that some British troops must accompany Japanese troops to Vladivostok, since 'the British Government desired to obtain the control of the Siberian railway, and if the Japanese went alone to Vladivostok, it would make this operation much more difficult'. (This was hardly consistent with the remark of the CIGS on the 1st that the despatch of British troops would assure the Russians that there were 'no sinister motives' behind a Japanese incursion into Siberia; but it underlines the fact that Lord Robert Cecil, and not anyone at the War Office, was the real hawk on Russian policy in the War Cabinet.)[36]

More alarmist reports – similar to the Irkutsk rumours – now reached London from the Far East. On the 8th, a wire arrived from Tokyo, urging that Japanese troops should occupy Vladivostok at once, since the Bolsheviks might send German submarines (apparently to be dismantled in the Baltic) down the Siberian railway in pieces and have them reassembled by German agents at Vladivostok, whence they could do much harm to Allied shipping. Though this caused concern at the Foreign Office, the Admiralty were unimpressed. 'It does not appear at all probable that any submarines will be sent by rail in sections to Vladivostok,' minuted the Naval Staff underneath this report. But it was considered important enough to be circulated to the War Cabinet. (It will be seen in the next chapter from what source this report probably originated.) On the 12th, the first Japanese warship reached Vladivostok and two days later was followed by the cruiser *Suffolk*.[37]

As direct action in Siberia was held up, the British government decided to support the local Cossacks on the railways. So did Japan. Thus when a Cossack *Ataman* called Semenov announced that he would seize the crucial junction of the Chinese Eastern railway with the main Siberian line, England and Japan separately decided to back him and urged the other Cossacks on the northern Amur line to join him.

But relations between England and Japan remained strained. On the 11th, the Japanese Ambassador in London informed the Foreign Office of a telegram he had received from the Japanese Foreign Minister, detailing the complaints he had made to the British Ambassador on being informed of the War Cabinet's decision of the 1st to despatch a cruiser to Vladivostok, and to invite American co-operation with the Japanese to protect the Allied stores. The Foreign Minister emphasised that Russia would take umbrage just as much at the despatch of an international force as at the despatch of a Japanese force; and in view of the strong national feeling on the matter in Japan, he could not support a request for the despatch of an American force to Siberia. A further telegram from the British Ambassador in Tokyo, recapitulating the same grievances and arguments, was received in London on the 14th.[38]

On the 17th, the British Ambassador wired again, indicating his preference for Japanese, as opposed to Allied intervention, since he believed that the Japanese would take independent action anyhow, if they thought it desirable. Lord Milner, on the 20th, wrote to Balfour, suggesting that the Allies should invite Japan to take military action in Siberia, when necessary, thus showing our appreciation of Japanese national feeling, our confidence in Japan, and further committing Japan to the war, and against Germany and German influence.[38]

At 6 p.m. on January 24, the War Cabinet again considered the question of Japanese intervention in Siberia. Balfour stated that in addition to the difficulty of securing Japanese military co-operation, there was the further difficulty that Japan might be satisfied with limited occupation of eastern Siberia and be unwilling to undertake our main objective, 'namely, the opening up of communications with South-Eastern Russia by securing control of the whole of the Siberian railway from Vladivostok to the Cossack country'. (This was a gigantic undertaking, verging indeed on the absurd, involving over 5,000 miles of railway.) He added that Lindley had just wired from Petrograd that the Danish Minister felt that the Germans had begun to doubt the value of a separate peace, owing to the 'appalling' conditions in Russia.[39]

There followed a recital of more rumours about Russia from third parties. Lord Robert Cecil said his latest information was that it was doubtful if Germany could get substantial supplies out of Russia, even if there was a separate peace. The manager of the Dreyfus Grain Company had told the Foreign Office that there were practically no cattle left, even in the Ukraine, owing to recent large-scale slaughtering. The Prime Minister urged the Foreign Office to obtain the views of a Mr Richards, of the Westinghouse Company, who was just back from Russia. Lord Hardinge, Permanent Under-Secretary at the Foreign Office, said that the French Ambassador had told him there was practically no corn left in southern Russia either, except in Odessa. The DMO agreed; as far as he could discover, there was very little corn left in the Ukraine and the Ukrainians were trying to get corn from the Kuban. Lord Milner said he had been told that the richest areas of Russia were Stavropol, the Kuban, and the Terek, north of the Caucasus; and between them and the rest of Russia to the north were the Don Cossacks, who should be able to stop supplies from this area reaching any other part of Russia. All this was reasonably accurate.

The War Cabinet then discussed the probable attitude of 'friendly elements' in Russia towards the Japanese. General Knox stated that when talking to Russian officers, he found no deep-seated hostility to the Japanese. They compared Japanese behaviour during the Russo-Japanese war very favourably with the Germans' barbarity. The DMO added that recent telegrams from Tiflis confirmed that Japanese intervention would not be unpopular, while a wire from Jassy showed that the Roumanians were anxious for it. (But these were both border states, who, though meant to form part of the 'South East Union', in fact disliked Russia and Russian centralism.)[39]

Lord Milner pointed out that the only possible supply line which offered any prospect of bringing prompt support to south Russia was the Siberian railway. 'In order to secure this railway it was well worth while playing upon Japanese sentiment, which might be flattered at being asked to do something for the Allies. The Japanese were a proud people, and the best policy would be to trust them openly.' The DMO agreed with Knox that little Japanese military support would be needed to obtain control of the Siberian railway, as all Siberia depended upon it, and a 'disciplined force' holding the important stations and vulnerable points, such as the bridge over the Yenisei river and the tunnels near Lake Baikal, could dominate Siberia. The Russian army was too powerless to put up serious resistance; even the Roumanian divisions could do a good deal, if they would only leave their own country. Milner added that Maklakov, the Cadet leader, now in Paris, agreed with this view. (But it was more than 5,000 miles from Vladivostok to southern Russia, and there were many vulnerable points; indeed, the enormous length of the line would require a huge 'disciplined' force. This argument also pre-supposed that the Siberian railway was working properly. In fact, it was in a lamentable state. It also assumed that the whole of the population along the railway would support the advancing force, or at any rate not oppose it.)

When asked what communications there were between the Siberian railway and the Don Cossack country, the DMO said that a branch line left the main railway at Chelyabinsk and ran some 400 miles south-west to Samara, on the Volga, 'which was on the edge of the Cossack country.' (In fact, it is nearer 600 miles from Chelyabinsk to Samara, and another 600 miles from Samara to Novocherkask, the Don Cossack capital – and south from Samara there was no line at all. There were, of course, some Cossacks east of the Volga, but their contacts with the Don Cossacks were very limited. In short, there was no direct link between the Siberian railway and the Don Cossacks.)[39]

These military arguments – of sheer desperation – were countered by the Foreign Office. Lord Robert Cecil stated firmly that he 'wished the Cabinet to realise that the proposal now made would probably result in the domination of the Japanese over the whole of Siberia, and would have far-reaching results upon the world's history, as it would make the Japanese a prodigious power in Asia, including the virtual domination of China'. Balfour doubted whether the Japanese could, in the long run, dominate so large a country as Siberia, 'inhabited by a considerable progressive Slav population'. Siberia contained some 9 to 10 million 'of the best Slavs in the world'. General Knox retorted that there was little national feeling in Siberia and the Don Cossacks would welcome military support, however small; they seemed afraid of the local Bolsheviks, 'but the Russian army was in such a state of cowardice and disorganisation that a small disciplined force could do almost anything'. (The alluring vision of the 'disciplined force' was to prove a constant temptation to arm-chair strategists. It was brought forward repeatedly, and when the Czechs appeared, it was justified.) Lord Curzon, the former Viceroy of India, said that Japan might well be content to occupy Vladivostok and dominate eastern Siberia, 'and would be unwilling to entertain the major proposition'. The Cabinet should bear in mind the point raised by the Indian government, when Japanese co-operation in Mesopotamia was being considered. 'This point was, in effect, that Japanese co-operation would enormously enhance the prestige of Asiatics as against Europeans, and would consequently react upon the attitude of Indians towards the British.'

Lord Robert Cecil emphasised that the great difficulty would be to secure American consent. The American Ambassador had told Balfour and himself that the American government hoped that Japan would not occupy Vladivostok. Balfour agreed that this was undoubtedly the American view, 'but recent events in Petrograd and the behaviour of the Bolsheviks might go far to cause the American government to change its view. The introduction of the Japanese would probably involve war with the Bolshevik Government,' he warned, 'and this we must be prepared to face.'[39]

At this, the Prime Minister launched into a general disquisition on Bolshevism. It was a growing menace to all civilised nations. 'Bolshevik doctrines were beginning to spread even in this country; they had undoubtedly spread in Austria; and indications in the Dutch newspapers showed that there was ground for believing that they were at work in Germany. M. Trotsky's view was that his pamphlets were more formidable than German guns. Any attempt of the Germans to interfere in Russia would be like an attempt to burgle a plague-house.' The Prime Minister clearly inferred that we should not interfere in Russia either – and war would mean interference. But our Allies, the French, he thought, 'would be only too ready to agree to Japanese intervention anywhere'.

But the Cabinet felt that while the Japanese government would favourably consider any Allied suggestion, they were unlikely to act on their own initiative, 'beyond an attempt on Vladivostok'. The DMO agreed; he had seen the Japanese Military Attaché, who thought the Japanese would favourably consider any proposals made by us, 'and that the Japanese only wished to know clearly what we wanted them to do'.

The War Cabinet thereupon decided that British policy should be 'to do all in their power' to open up communications between Vladivostok and south-east Russia along the Siberian railway, and that the Japanese should be urged to undertake military control of it from Vladivostok to Chelyabinsk. It was also decided that telegrams should be sent to Washington and Paris, explaining why the War Cabinet had reached this decision, 'and urging the American and French Governments to support their policy'.[39]

This far-reaching decision to launch the Japanese across the whole Eurasian continent, and practically into Europe proper by the back-door, was wrong on all counts – and emphasises how desperately it was felt in London that everything and anything must be done to reopen the Eastern Front against Germany and prevent her seizing Russian supplies. First, the Don Cossacks and the volunteer army were an inherently weak force; they were some 600 miles away from Samara, the nearest railway station on the Siberian railway – there was in fact no link between Novocherkask and Samara, and little indication that the Cossacks could seize Samara. Secondly, Japan had clearly stated that she would not occupy the entire Siberian railway – it was militarily absurd for any power even to consider undertaking 'military control' of more than 5,000 miles of railway in a foreign country. Thirdly, Japan insisted on carrying out her more modest schemes of conquest in Manchuria alone, without American co-operation, but with American consent. But America had made it abundantly clear that she disliked the idea of unilateral Japanese action as much as joint action by Japan and America; and as this only concerned Vladivostok and a small portion of the railway to the east, it was hardly likely that America would approve of Japanese 'military control' of the Siberian railway up to the Urals.

However misguided – and, in the event, academic – the War Cabinet's decision, it undoubtedly made easier the later, more practical, decisions its members were to take on Siberia. In principle, at least, they had crossed a Rubicon.

# 8

## Debate in the War Cabinet

SINCE January 18, the peace talks between the Germans and the Bolsheviks had been in abeyance. But in late January, after long deliberation, the Bolsheviks finally rejected the idea of a 'holy war' against the Germans, and accepted Trotsky's policy of 'no war – no peace'; and on January 30, Trotsky returned to Brest-Litovsk. Weak as the Bolsheviks' military position was in central Russia, they were now much stronger in the south. Dr Helphand advised the Foreign Ministry in Berlin that German relations with the Bolsheviks must now be handled 'with the greatest care', the German Under Secretary of State warned the German Eastern Command. 'He believes that the Bolsheviks' ideas will spread still further in Russia and that the [Ukrainian] Rada will not last much longer. He said that nobody would be able to drive out the Bolsheviks, now that they had occupied the Donetz basin and Kharkov, the centre of the industrial Ukraine, except with the help of German troops.' This was now true. Helphand here agreed with General Knox that whoever held the Donetz basin could put a stranglehold on practically all Russian resources and transport. Now that 'our friends' in south Russia had failed to keep the Bolsheviks out of the Donetz, it was more essential than ever for the British to come to some practical arrangement with the Bolshevik government.[1]

Early in February, Bruce Lockhart arrived in Petrograd to try to prevent the Bolsheviks from making a separate peace and to induce Trotsky to withhold all Russian supplies from the Germans, apparently promising British recognition in return. Mysterious documents which began to appear in Petrograd, apparently showing the Bolsheviks as paid German agents, nullified his efforts.

On February 2, Colonel Raymond Robins, of the American Red Cross, the unofficial American agent to the Bolshevik government (in fact, Lockhart's American counterpart), showed Edgar Sisson, the chief American propaganda agent in Russia, an English version of these documents, alleging Bolshevik complicity with the Germans from the early war period up to mid-1917; they had arrived clandestinely, he said. On the 4th, Russian versions of the documents were left at the Allied embassies and an English version at Sisson's office, and a Russian journalist called Eugène Semenov came to the American Embassy and showed the Ambassador a copy of a document, allegedly taken from the Bolshevik files, purporting to show that the Bolsheviks were even now taking both orders and money from the Germans. The next day, the American Ambassador sent for Sisson, who consulted Commander E. T. Boyce, head of British intelligence in Russia, who said that for the last three weeks he had received daily from a group of Russian officers copies of wires passing between the Bolsheviks in Petrograd and Brest-Litovsk and between the German economic mission in Petrograd and Berlin. This Russian 'wire group' knew and trusted Semenov, Boyce told Sisson; Semenov was dependable. Sisson therefore took all the various copies of the documents which Semenov produced and pressed him to obtain the originals.[2]

The provenance of these documents, which were to have a very considerable influence in Allied countries – and on some Allied governments – now seems definitely established by Professor Kennan. From the outbreak of war, a certain Anton Ossendowski, born in Poland, who had had a varied career, became a paid propagandist for certain Russian business interests who wished to eliminate German commercial influence in Russia; and he wrote numerous articles for the Suvorin newspapers, which had been violently anti-German long before the war, claiming that there was still an enormous network of German commercial intrigue going on in Russia.[3] But as his backers were also anxious to discredit their rivals, he was also able to indulge in profitable blackmail. By the time of the March revolution, he had become an editor of Suvorin's evening newspaper.

After the 'July days', he and Eugène Semenov, another editor on the same paper, were employed by Russian Military Intelligence to gather material proving that the Bolsheviks had received money from the Germans. (Their researches led to the exposure of Dr Helphand as the main German intermediary and financier of the Bolshevik movement.) When the Bolshevik revolution brought these activities, and sources of income, to an end, Ossendowski gave a letter to Semenov, who was well known to the Allied embassies, in which he asked the Allied ambassadors to give him 50,000 roubles to enable him to purchase, from 'official neutral sources abroad', a list of the firms working for German intelligence in Russia and in Allied and neutral countries, and a list of

[221]

the German spies in Russia. (This, of course, would have enabled him to exert some very profitable 'squeeze' on the firms and persons in question.) The Allied ambassadors, not surprisingly, declined this offer.[3]

Semenov then went down to the Don, probably with material alleging Bolshevik complicity with the Germans from the early war period up to mid-1917, which was published in full in the local press in December and January. Semenov had meanwhile returned to Petrograd to try to help obtain an Allied loan for the volunteer army.

Though the Russian officers' 'wire group' definitely produced some genuine material, and though the Bolshevik movement had definitely received, and still was receiving, substantial German financial support, all these present documents – alleging that the Bolshevik leaders were even now *personally* taking German money and carrying out German orders – were forgeries, though Ossendowski and his Polish and other assistants had woven in bits of accurate detail to give them colour. Captain George Hill, a British SIS agent then in Russia, infers that these documents (which later became known as the 'Sisson documents') were in circulation somewhat earlier than February and had first been bought at a 'very high figure' by another Secret Service, presumably the British. But after they were pronounced forgeries, they were put on the underground market again, he states, and bought by Sisson 'at a price which repaid the other Secret Service organisation in full'. Commander Boyce would thus have had good reason to cheer Sisson on.[4]

Initially, the documents were believed in nearly all the Allied countries and had a considerable effect on British policy; reports about them had already reached London by late January and were believed by those who found it convenient to accept them as genuine. They were also believed in Washington and had an even greater effect on American policy. Indeed, in September 1918, they were published in America with the backing of the American government, though the American Ambassador in London warned that by then the British considered them to be forgeries. In 1919, an official German publication, with a foreword by the German Prime Minister, stated that they were fraudulent. But in 1921, a German minister wrote of the same set of documents which had been published in Switzerland in 1919, 'The documents in this pamphlet were partly forged.' It was not until 1956 that Professor Kennan established their true provenance.[4]

On February 7, the War Cabinet considered a wire from Petrograd suggesting that they should give greater authority to Bruce Lockhart, 'and thereby pave the way for a fuller understanding with the Bolshevik Government'. There followed a decisive discussion on recognition of the

Bolsheviks, a step advocated by the Prime Minister, by Balfour, and by all British officials in Petrograd, but opposed by Lord Robert Cecil, who was supported by the War Office, and in particular by General Knox. Balfour stated that he thought Lockhart might be given fuller credentials, 'without our being committed to full recognition of the Bolshevik Government'. Lockhart was now in the same position as the British Consul at Helsinki, who dealt directly in political matters with the *de facto* Finnish government, and Picton Bagge, the former British Consul General at Odessa, now at Kiev, who dealt direct with the *de facto* Ukrainian government. Lockhart should therefore have direct dealings with the *de facto* Petrograd government.

'It was not possible for us to recognise the Bolsheviks as the governors of the whole of Russia,' stated Balfour, 'as the whole of Russia did not acknowledge their authority; besides which, such recognition would be clearly incompatible with the modified degree of recognition and support which we had been, or were, giving to the Ukraine and the Don Cossacks. By taking the step suggested, we did not either support or condemn Bolshevism as such, but merely facilitated dealings with the *de facto* Government in Petrograd.' At any moment, some incident, either in Russia or England, might break the 'very fragile thread' which maintained relations between the British and Bolshevik governments. 'We clearly could not go the full length of accrediting an Ambassador in Petrograd, and his [Balfour's] proposal would put our *de facto* relations with all the *de facto* Governments in Russia on an equality.' But it would be illusory to suppose that, by granting this new authority to Lockhart, we could induce the Bolshevik government to stop the spread of Bolshevik propaganda in England; for the whole position of Lenin and Trotsky would be undermined if such an undertaking were published in Russia, since the whole essence of the Bolshevik creed was that the belligerent nations should at once make peace, so that a general class war could begin instead. The question of the boundaries of Bolshevik authority in Russia would also prove a stumbling-block to any practical arrangement which Lockhart might be able to make in Petrograd. Finland alone had a clearly defined boundary; the Ukraine and the Cossack country had none.[5]

But Lord Robert Cecil doubted whether it was judicious that anything should be done to please or encourage a government which was behaving in such a manner. 'Such action might discourage what remained of the anti-Bolshevik elements, such as the Poles and Cossacks, and might prove helpful in the spread of Bolshevik propaganda in this country, as also in France and Italy.' The danger of the spread of Bolshevik propaganda in Italy was serious. 'Further, it looked as if M. Trotsky, at any rate, had taken German money, and that there was little chance of M. Trotsky being either willing or able to hold out against a separate peace.' Cecil added that, as he read the telegram, it seemed that Lockhart wanted fuller powers than those outlined by Balfour.

The Prime Minister retorted that it was no concern of the British government what socialist experiment or what form of government the Bolsheviks were trying to establish in Russia. He proceeded to read from a book called *The Elements of International Law* by the American authority George B. Davis, 'in which it appeared clear that recognition of one Government by another depended entirely upon *de facto* conditions'. In regard to Lockhart's demand, it should be borne in mind that the Bolsheviks were a 'formidable menace' to both Austria and Germany. The Austrian Empire was 'seriously embarrassed' by the spread of Bolshevism; while the 'dominant factor' in German politics today was the Brest-Litovsk situation. 'He [Lloyd George] had no fear that Bolshevism was a formidable menace to the internal peace of this country.' The recent by-election in Lancashire showed that 'even in an industrial constituency' the vast majority of the nation were opposed to revolution and wanted to bring the national war to a successful close. 'He therefore thought that the grant of fuller authority to Mr Lockhart might prove a useful opportunity for getting certain conditions agreed to by the Bolshevik Government in regard to their non-interference in the internal politics of Allied countries. He was also most anxious that the War Cabinet should not refuse the advice tendered to them by the British representatives in Russia, and he instanced several cases in the past where he thought errors had been made in refusing to accept such advice. The opinion he had formed of Mr Lockhart was such as to cause him to hesitate before rejecting any advice he offered.'[5]

But Lord Curzon agreed with Cecil. He had spoken to Buchanan the day before about Lockhart's proposal, and Buchanan thought 'that any further recognition of M. Trotsky would help Germany'. It would also help to spread Bolshevik propaganda in England. Lord Hardinge, the Permanent Under Secretary of State at the Foreign Office, stressed that 'full recognition of the Bolsheviks was not suggested'. Full recognition would involve direct dealings between Lindley and Trotsky, whereas the degree of recognition advocated by Lockhart would leave all dealings in the hands of an intermediary.

It was clear that the Cabinet were split down the middle on this issue. The Prime Minister was certain that further recognition of the Bolsheviks would affect matters in one way, his opponents were as certain that it would affect them in exactly the opposite direction. It was also clear that Lloyd George did not wholly agree with Balfour, and that Lord Robert Cecil was influenced by the 'Sisson documents', whose existence in Petrograd was now just coming to the attention of people in London, who believed them to be genuine. The Cabinet asked Balfour to prepare a draft reply to Lockhart's telegram for their consideration.

The Cabinet next had to consider a telegram to Lenin from Arthur Henderson (the Labour Party secretary and former Cabinet Minister, who had been out to Russia during negotiations for the abortive Stockholm Conference in 1917). The telegram, which had been held up by the censor (probably the one referred to by Barnes in the Cabinet on January 17) stated: 'British Labour Movement invites your party [to] send delegates [to] Inter-Allied Conference, London, Wednesday February 20th. British [Labour] movement secured general agreement on War Aims propose this document form agenda.' It was hoped that the presence of Bolshevik delegates would induce all Allied socialists to attend this meeting, which would be a preliminary to a meeting of the full International.

The Cabinet considered this message, but the minutes merely state that they decided 'not to prohibit the despatch of this telegram'. Bolshevik delegates were thus invited to London.

The War Cabinet then discussed wires from the British Military Attaché and the British Minister at Jassy, in Roumania, dated February 5 and January 30, about the possibility of a separate Roumanian peace. Balfour read out a wire from the Roumanian Prime Minister (which was received during the meeting), stating that the German General von Mackensen had issued an ultimatum that unless Roumania made peace forthwith, the armistice would be ended, and military action begun. The DMI stated that this ultimatum was a bluff. As long as the fifteen good Roumanian divisions could be supplied from Bessarabia (the province between Roumania and the Ukraine), the only danger was an advance from the Bukovina, to the north, where there were only ten poor Austrian divisions, and no German troops at all. Balfour added that the French took the 'strongest possible view' that the Roumanians should be discouraged from making a separate peace. If, however, they insisted upon doing so, Balfour thought it should be made quite clear that the Allies would be released from their undertaking given to Roumania when she entered the war, namely that the Allies would guarantee to supply her. The War Cabinet asked the Foreign Office to wire to Jassy, urging Roumania not to make a separate peace.[5]

On February 8, the War Cabinet considered Balfour's draft reply to Bruce Lockhart, with amendments suggested by Lord Robert Cecil and Philip Kerr, the Prime Minister's private secretary. There ensued 'a very lively discussion', records Thomas Jones, the assistant secretary to the Cabinet. The issue was indeed crucial; if some sort of recognition were given to the Bolshevik government, Bolshevik delegates could presumably come to the Labour conference in London on February 20. 'The PM seemed very much alive, almost as fresh and fit as though he had enjoyed a long holiday,' records Jones. 'The talk was swift and animated throughout.' This, however, is not reflected in the Cabinet minutes, which appear to exclude several statements by various ministers, which are to be found in Thomas Jones's draft notes of the meeting.[6]

Balfour ('more precise and vigorous than usual', comments Jones) began the discussion. Before the War Cabinet considered the draft reply to Bruce Lockhart, he stated, they should first consider three connected questions which had arisen since he had written his draft. First, he had received a formal protest that morning from Litvinov against the further enlistment of Russian subjects into the British army, which was accompanied by a threat to publish the correspondence about the matter. On January 23, the War Cabinet had instructed Lord Derby to consider the question (in fact, to arrange for the despatch of the Russian Jews in the East End to concentration camps, prior to their return to Russia, if they could not be got into the British army), but so far Derby had done nothing. Balfour feared an awkward incident; there could be no further delay in replying to Litvinov. Secondly, Balfour himself, Lord Robert Cecil and the DMO had the previous evening met Count Horodysky, who had implored them not to recognise the Bolsheviks, since, he claimed, there were now three Polish armies comprising more than 60,000 well-armed, well-fed and well-paid men, who had captured Krilenko, the Bolshevik C.-in-C., and his head-quarters' staff at Mogilev, and were about to march on Smolensk. (As usual, Horodysky's news was untrue.) Thirdly, Balfour went on, a wire had arrived that morning from the Bolsheviks, complaining that they were being prevented from removing stores from Vladivostok. There was also a wire from Lockhart, sent on the 6th, urging that visas be granted to Petrov and Chicherin to allow them to visit England, 'and regarding the recognition to be given to the Bolshevik Government'. In his closing paragraph, 'Mr Lockhart pleaded most earnestly that immediate consideration should be given to the policy which he advocated.'[6]

The Prime Minister ('who is half a Bolshevik himself', comments Hankey) re-emphasised what he had said the previous day about the 'inadvisability of refusing to accept the advice given by the man on the spot, viz Mr Lockhart'.

According to Thomas Jones, there was then this short exchange, not in the minutes.

*Lord Robert Cecil:* My view is that we have taken too much the view of the man on the spot. It was a mistake not to back Kornilov [*ie*, in September 1917].

*Prime Minister:* Both may be true. It may be that, to use a golfing term, we ought to have followed the stroke right through.

*Lord Robert Cecil:* I believe there was a moment when a strong telegram to Kerensky, 'You must co-operate with Kornilov', might have saved the situation.

*Prime Minister:* The soldiers might have refused. Here you have got emphatic advice.

*Balfour:* On what spot is Lockhart? Can he speak for all Russia? He says nothing about the Poles . . . Lockhart dogmatises about the effect the Bolsheviks are producing in Germany.

*Prime Minister:* My view is that Russia is our most powerful ally now in Germany, and especially in Austria . . . We want the Bolsheviks to make themselves a greater nuisance to the Germans than to us.

The Prime Minister, according to the Cabinet minutes, went on that he did not doubt Lockhart's belief that the Bolsheviks had a strong influence in Germany and Austria, and approved the general principles laid down by Balfour in his draft, 'that the internal politics of that part of Russia where the Bolsheviks were the *de facto* Government was no concern of ours'. He gathered, however, that the Polish armies referred to were fighting the Bolsheviks, not the Germans or Austrians. 'This was no concern of ours, and they could only be regarded as our friends if they diverted their armies against the Germans or Austrians, or, as was suggested, to the assistance of our Roumanian Allies.' By according limited recognition to the Bolshevik government, as suggested by Lockhart, we could influence them to treat the Roumanians better.

Lloyd George compared the present Russian situation with the Greek situation in 1916, when we had recognised King Constantine as the *de facto* ruler in one part of Greece and Venizelos in another part. Although King Constantine had been guilty of unfriendly acts towards ourselves and our Allies, this recognition had enabled us to give substantial help to the Venizelists, who remained under his rule.

It was argued that by according partial recognition to the Bolshevik government, we should be discouraging our friends in Russia. But the Ukrainians, whom we had regarded as our friends, had failed us.

(Jones here quotes the Prime Minister as saying: 'I don't see that we are doing more for Trotsky than for the Ukrainians – they are our worst enemies. Kaledin is funking – Alexeiev is fighting. We must not be too sure that the Poles are our friends. They are not fighting Germans. The Poles are fighting the Bolsheviks.')

The Prime Minister, according to the Cabinet minutes, then went on: 'The only people in Russia who could definitely be regarded as our friends were those who were willing to fight, not against the Bolsheviks, but against the Austrians and Germans.'[6]

Lord Robert Cecil stated that he disagreed with the Prime Minister. There had been a 'series of mistakes' over Russian policy during the past year. 'We had always tried to worship the rising sun, instead of standing firmly in support of those elements in Russia who were friendly to British aims and to the cause of the Allies.' It would be a 'fatal mistake' to do anything to dishearten the Armenians, the Poles or the Roumanians, and we should gain nothing by trying to conciliate our enemies. 'He [Cecil] thought it a great mistake to go hat in hand to the Bolsheviks at the time when the Bolsheviks were making war upon our Allies the Roumanians.' The Prime Minister agreed that the draft reply to Lockhart must include definite instructions about Roumania.

The Cabinet then considered a draft wire from the CIGS to General Foch, urging that all Polish troops, together with the two Czech divisions in the Ukraine, should be brought up on the Roumanian right flank, to prevent any German attempt to turn the Roumanian army by an advance north of the River Pruth, the eastern border of Roumania.

After further discussion (which 'got rather hot at one time', records Hankey, 'as they were getting to fundamentals, the rights of property owners, etc., when I hastily intervened, and brought them back to business'), the War Cabinet decided that Balfour's draft reply to Lockhart should be amended to include Philip Kerr's suggestions and the final passages of Lord Robert Cecil's proposals; it could then be despatched. This effectively nullified Lockhart's request, and the battle for recognition was now over. It was also agreed that the draft wire from the CIGS to Foch could be despatched.[6]

So ended this 'very amusing meeting', writes Hankey. 'You see, the moment we get to fundamentals, we are "Poles" apart,' said Lloyd George, 'laughing in his merry way, having thoroughly enjoyed himself . . .'

On February 10, as Trotsky suddenly announced his policy of 'no war, no peace', which again disrupted the peace talks at Brest-Litovsk, the Bolshevik government in Petrograd announced the repudiation of the entire Russian foreign debt. The Bolsheviks thus defied both the Germans and the Allies at one stroke. The Allied embassies in Petrograd made an immediate and joint reply refusing to recognise either the repudiation of the foreign debt, or the confiscation of Allied property in Russia, which would be reclaimed, they warned, at an 'opportune time'.[7]

At the War Cabinet on the 11th, permission was refused for Commissar Petrov to visit England from Petrograd. (He, it will be recalled, together with Chicherin, had only recently been detained in England for spreading defeatist propaganda amongst the Clyde shipworkers.) But as a visa had already been granted in Petrograd for Kamenev to come to England, and the French government had agreed to allow him to visit France under strict supervision, it was decided that Kamenev could visit England, provided he was kept under close observation. Their intention was undoubtedly to establish some sort of contact with the Bolshevik movement in London, even though the War Cabinet's refusal to recognise the Bolsheviks had presumably aborted Henderson's proposal for Bolshevik delegates to attend a Labour conference in London on February 20.[8]

That day (the 11th), the CIGS had a reply from General Foch in Paris, in answer to the War Cabinet's request of the 8th for Polish and Czech support for Roumania. There were, according to the French General Staff, three Polish divisions of some 40,000 men under formation in the Minsk–Mogilev area, and other contingents of unspecified strength were being assembled in the Ukraine. But they could not possibly be moved to the Roumanian front, as they had no horses and the railways were totally disorganised. (This hardly tallied with Count Horodysky's account of the 7th.) The Czech National Council in Paris, however, had given General Berthelot freedom of action in making such use as he thought best of the Czech contingents in the Ukraine, but he had been unable so far to move them to the Roumanian front 'owing to the difficulties raised by the Ukraine Government, which wished to keep this disciplined force, which has not been disorganised by Maximalism [ie, Bolshevism], in the Ukraine'. Foch could only leave it to Berthelot to make the best use he could of the Czech troops, in view of the chaotic conditions in south Russia.[9]

Foch's message was brought before the War Cabinet on the 11th. The DMI stated that General Ballard, the Military Attaché at Jassy, had on the 7th seen the Roumanian C.-in-C. who said that if he was concerned with the peace terms between Roumania and Germany, he would try to prevent guns and supplies being handed over to the enemy. It was in fact now clear that Roumania, the left flank of the 'South-East Union', was doomed. The DMI also reported that a wire from General de Candolle at Rostov stated that the situation there was 'becoming increasingly precarious, owing to the spread of Bolshevism, and that it was likely that General Alexeiev would be compelled to retire to Ekaterinodar [in the Kuban].'

On the Don, there had indeed been a disaster. As Kornilov thought that Bolshevik troops were advancing from the south on Rostov, the

[229]

last major Russian town on the lower Don still in anti-Bolshevik hands, he decided that his small volunteer army must leave, or it would be trapped. Kaledin begged him to remain. On the 11th, Kornilov urged Kaledin to collect all his supplies, and all the Cossacks who would fight, and withdraw with him. Kaledin refused, but was so dismayed at the general collapse that he retired to his room and shot himself. But no one in London or Petrograd was to know of this for some time.[10]

On January 25, Lord Robert Cecil had presided over another Russia committee meeting at which was considered a report on grain supplies in Russia, which appears to have indicated that there was practically no grain left in the Ukraine or southern Russia, except in Odessa. It was decided to send a wire to Odessa to discover how much there was there. Maynard Keynes told the committee that the Zionists in Russia were believed to have large sums of roubles in Petrograd, Rostov and elsewhere, and that these could possibly be taken on loan to avoid exchange-rate difficulties. This procedure was approved and Colonel Peel was instructed to deal with the matter. (But any idea that the Russian Zionists would give financial aid to what they would un-doubtedly consider to be neo-Tsarist armies was patently absurd.)[11]

Cecil then said that it was fairly evident that the Ukraine was about to make peace with Germany, and Roumania would probably do so also. The only course therefore was to try to persuade both countries to export as little of their remaining grain as possible to Germany. It had been suggested that we should induce them to sell surplus grain to the Cossacks; but the Ukraine wanted goods, not money, in return. Mitchell Thomson, of the Restriction of Enemy Supplies Department, said that apart from Odessa most of the grain still in the Ukraine was with small-holders, and to make real use of it, the Germans would have to provide payment in kind and actually shift it. Cecil asked if goods could be sent to the Ukraine from Archangel. Mitchell Thomson replied that although goods sent by rail from Archangel could avoid Petrograd and Moscow, they had to pass through Vologda, 'also a Bolshevik strong-hold'. It was decided to wire to General Poole and refer Cecil's enquiry to him; and also to wire to Picton Bagge, the British Consul at Kiev, to discover what goods would be most useful in the Ukraine for both barter and propaganda. It was further agreed to draft a wire for the DMI to send to General Foch, requesting him to instruct General Berthelot, in Roumania, to arrange for the Dreyfus Grain Company to buy up any grain available in the Ukraine for despatch to the Astrakhan, Orenberg and Ural Cossacks, east of the Volga, where there was also a great shortage of grain.[12]

On the 25th, Colonel Byrne wrote to General Poole to inform him that the Milner Committee (*ie*, the Russia Supply Committee) had been taken over by the Foreign Office. 'Knox, Stanley, and Co. have returned,' he went on, 'and they all have much the same information to give, namely that affairs are in a parlous state and that something must be done; but their recommendations as to what should be done are not easy to follow. It seems to me that you on the spot are in a better position to decide these matters than anybody else, and if I were in your place I should be inclined to act and report, rather than ask for instructions. This is, of course, the personal advice of myself and not the advice of the Secretary of the Milner Committee . . .'[12]

That same day, Poole replied to Byrne about the recovery of British guns and ammunition in Russia. 'The bulk of the British guns are in the possession of the Bolsheviks and [the] Ukraine,' Poole stated. 'It is necessary firstly to officially recognise each of these *de facto* . . . secondly to be prepared to offer a *quid pro quo*. Without recognition nothing can be done. I think that Buchanan will agree . . .' Without recognition, no Russian material could be acquired either, as Byrne had suggested. 'I am of opinion that nothing will be allowed to leave the country unless this policy is adopted. It is more likely to go to Germany.' This was indeed a strong argument.

On January 30, Byrne received another telegram from Poole, asking whether the financial adviser, for whom he had originally asked in his wire of December 26, was being sent out. For Poole now seems to have become partially aware of the banking transactions being engineered by Lindley and Keyes with Jaroszynski. 'I have received information that the London Banks are freely authorising the acceptance of roubles in exceedingly large amounts by Russian correspondents,' Poole went on, 'placing the equivalent sterling values at the disposal of Russian merchants'. Poole warned that this would either greatly increase the Russian debt to the Allies, or indirectly assist German economic intrigues. He suggested that all private financial transactions with Russia should be stopped in London, save for special cases approved by him 'and without any German taint'.[12]

On the 30th, Sir George Clerk informed the Russia committee that Herbert Guedalla had said that he could not accept the post of financial adviser to Lindley, if this meant that he would be acting in a subordinate and purely advisory capacity. (This, no doubt, was the result of the interview between Herbert Guedalla and Sir George Clerk, who wanted to keep financial control in the hands of the Russia committee – by which he meant Colonel Peel, the Foreign Office's own financial adviser, and not Dudley Ward, of the Treasury.) It was therefore decided that an approach should be made to someone in the Hudson's

Bay Company. But all this delay was only increasing the confusion between Petrograd and London.[13]

On February 1st, a member of Poole's staff wrote a further paper on British banking policy in Russia, which differed from Banting's paper of January 6, which had advocated British control of all the Russian banks. This new paper, although it argued against control of all the banks, took a much wider view. While British banking interests must be properly represented in Russia, 'in view of the huge stake in Russia now possessed by Great Britain', it argued, the Treasury should only back a scheme which combined all Russian interests, including banks, mining and finance houses, and British merchants in Russia. There should be a London group, called the 'British Bank of Russia', which should float two other groups:

1. The 'British Banking Corporation for Russia', which would conduct 'only orthodox banking business', and – like the Crédit Lyonnais, the National City Bank of New York, and the Netherlands Bank for Russian Trade – cater only for the business 'of their respective nationals, without undertaking any of the unorthodox transactions upon which the majority of the Russian banking institutions have in the past depended for the bulk of their profits'.[14]

2. Another group, some of whose capital might be allotted to 'approved Russian individuals', whose function should be to 'acquire control of and to operate and influence the operations of one or more of the existing Russian joint-stock banks and generally to undertake long-credit, industrial, loan, mortgage, investment, and financial transactions considered to be outside the scope of correct banking practice, but which are part and parcel of the system as it exists in Russia and to which serious attention is essential'. Now only a very few of the Russian banks were to come under direct British control.

Since previous German success in Russia had been largely due to their control of Russian transport, and since Russian banking and insurance were closely linked, this second group (in which the 'British Trade Corporation' should take the lead, though French and Russian interests might be invited to co-operate) should also control the transport and handling of goods by acquiring Russian concerns and placing them under British management, and should also persuade British insurance companies to form the 'British Insurance Company of Russia'.[14]

Handling of all these British financial interests in Russia would bring in an annual turnover of some £30 million. 'For a considerable number of years to come, it is certain that this sum will have to be capitalised by Russia and re-invested in the country by Great Britain.' Special banks would be needed in the Caucasus, where customs and habits were very different from those elsewhere, and in Turkestan and Siberia. But, the writer pointed out, 'The question of acquisition of entire or part control of existing Russian joint-stock banks is one that requires very close consideration before definite action is decided upon. The credit and standing of these banks has probably received a shock during the recent social upheavals from which they may never recover. It must be remembered that the bulk of deposits in Russian banks were utilised for what in London would be considered absolutely illegitimate and non-banking business. It is a grave question, therefore, if any of the Russian banks are today or will be in possession of realisable assets in excess of their liabilities. Acquisition by important British interests of any Russian bank however would at once have the effect of re-establishing the credit of such institution and of attracting depositors' money to the disadvantage of the other concerns not so favoured by such improvement in their status and credit. A danger therefore exists of British capital paying Russian (and perhaps German) holders of bank shares a price which is only justified by the fact that such a purchase is being made.'[14]

The formation of three distinct banking groups would ensure elasticity; if efforts were made to handle the whole matter by one group, or bank – like the 'National City Bank of New York' – transactions would have to be restricted to purely banking business. The writer finally outlined a complex scheme, whereby loans and mortgages could be interchanged on a short- and long-term basis. 'In this manner, practically an unlimited amount of banking capital could be made available by the London money market for Russia under conditions and under control at any rate equal to that offered in a similar manner by the German banks in the past . . .'

This was nothing less than a blueprint for a British takeover bid for the entire Russian economy – a giant extension of British economic imperialism, whereby a prostrated Russia could be reduced – or elevated – to the status of a British colony. But although the warning about the inherent danger in the purchase of the Russian banks was very timely, Jaroszynski's proposal, combining all these various propositions, was now going ahead with the help of a British loan. This long paper was, in fact, never sent to London. Perhaps the writer discovered on its completion that other members of Poole's mission were busily engaged in doing just what he was warning them against.[14]

Meanwhile, there was still no decision about a financial adviser for Lindley in Petrograd. On February 6, Colonel Peel had informed the Russia committee that the Hudson's Bay Company could not spare the person under consideration, so it was decided to ask Steel-Maitland to choose someone else.[15]

On the 8th, the Russia committee were told that Lindley had wired to say that Russia and Germany had now agreed to exchange 'certain commodities'. This was indeed serious. The DMI stressed that the information about the supply position in Russia was 'very conflicting'. He had just heard, from a recent arrival from Roumania, that in southern Russia 'white flour was plentiful and the fields were filled with cattle . . .' It was decided to reconsider the situation immediately.[15]

At the next meeting of the committee on the 9th, Captain Proctor (a member of Poole's mission, just back from Petrograd) strongly urged British retention of Archangel, which was the only port of entry into Russia. Lord Robert Cecil said he understood that Proctor believed that the Germans would seize Petrograd and Archangel, and asked how they would do this. Proctor replied that enemy prisoners had been concentrated near Petrograd; hundreds of German officers had been returned to Germany, but none of the men. 'There were today a very large number of prisoners actually in Petrograd, and some formations had been armed by Trotsky on the plea that such action was necessary in order to suppress the counter-revolutionary movement, which he alleged to be on foot in the city. The government offices in Petrograd were being filled with Jews imported into Russia, and if they were not Germans, they were certainly extremely anti-Ally. Lettish battalions had been concentrated at Petrograd and were being given specially favourable treatment. This was doubtless because the Letts were bi-lingual and would therefore be of great value to the Germans in their next move.' Cecil asked Proctor if his views were shared by other Englishmen at Petrograd. Proctor replied that 'this unfortunately had not been the case up to the time when he left Russia'. But he was con-vinced that Archangel and Petrograd could be seized in a single opera-tion. Trains had already run from Riga (which was now in German hands) to Petrograd. The 1½ million Austrian prisoners in Russia were anti-Bolshevik, he added.[16]

Cecil was right to question Proctor's views, which were not only not shared by his colleagues, but were largely nonsense. There was no evidence that Trotsky was at this stage arming German prisoners to suppress a counter-revolution, or importing pro-German Jews into Petrograd. Trotsky was, however, arming and giving specially favour-able treatment to the Letts. But in this he was buying the services of a Praetorian Guard to defend the Bolshevik leaders, since the Letts were violently anti-German, as they saw Latvia being occupied by the Germans. Nor was there any real evidence of whether the Austrian prisoners were especially pro- or anti-Bolshevik. But though Proctor's

[234]

views were false, and, on his own admission, not shared by his colleagues, Cecil's hawkish views were probably strengthened.

Further wires now arrived from Petrograd about recognition of the Bolsheviks and the rouble and supply position in Russia. 'I have been asked by Lockhart to cable you my views on the political situation as they tend to emphasise his own,' said General Poole in a wire which reached London on the 11th. 'Our proper policy as I have previously advised you, is to recognise at once the Bolshevik Government as the *de facto* Government of Petrograd, and [? every other national] force extending over the whole of Russia, more or less. I have always considered the French enthusiasm for Roumania, Ukraine and Don futile and hopeless and results have borne out my opinion. To hope for any military action from any section in Russia is useless and to finance them is in my judgement a waste. In my opinion the Bolshevik Government is not a German agent, it is, on the contrary, much more dangerous to German interests than the Russian army has been since the Revolution. We are only handicapping ourselves by not recognising the *de facto* Government. We could by recognising them gain material advantage, such as for instance blockading supplies [? for Germany] and getting supplies for ourselves. I consider the French are wrong in their ideas and should [? be urged to] change them.' But this wire came too late; already on the 8th the War Cabinet had decided against recognition.[17]

Two more wires from Poole reached London on the 11th. In a wire from him on the 8th, he reiterated his complaint of January 26 that he still did not yet know if a financial adviser was to be sent out, and again urged that most large-scale rouble transactions, via the London banks, should be stopped. 'I presume that it is fully appreciated in London that owing to actions of the Bolshevik regime, the rouble credits allocated against pounds sterling in London by the Russian Chancery of Credit may be and probably will be worthless,' he warned, 'Consequently I presume that British banks, etc. will now refuse until such time as the equivalent rouble credit in Russia can be realised to credit their clients with pounds sterling. These rouble credits may be made valid in the future when the ultimate settlement of Russian affairs is being made, and so may also British War Loans to Russia, but I think at present that they are not valid and no one can prophecy to what extent the Bolsheviks may reduce the chaos of banks and all finance in Russia.' There was thus a strong hint that the big bank deals arranged through Jaroszynski would also be invalid.

In another telegram received on the same day, Poole stated: 'I have discussed with Lockhart and Lindley the general situation out here and they agree with the following proposal – I consider that Germany will not be able to get much benefit in the way of supplies etc. from

Russia, at any rate before the spring, owing to the mad and destructive [? policy] of the Bolshevik regime.' The Trade Barter Company (*Tovaro Obmien*), run by Allied businessmen, was now in working order. 'Even if a separate peace is signed, there is no possible chance of any Russian military force being formed to operate against Germany and Austria,' he continued. If a financial adviser had been selected, Poole suggested that he should return to England to discuss matters with him first. Poole also asked that this wire (which supported General Knox's advice to the War Cabinet) should be shown to Lord Milner.[17]

As Lord Milner had handed matters over to the Russia Committee, this wire was read to them on the 12th and it was agreed that Poole should return to London.[18]

On the 13th, another British officer arrived in London from Petrograd and handed over to Colonel Byrne Captain Garstin's letter of January 14 (which stressed that the Bolsheviks were not German agents), and Poole's letter of January 19 – one of his many pleas for the despatch of a financial adviser. Byrne passed both letters on to Major Thornton, of the War Cabinet secretariat, adding that Garstin was 'employed with the propaganda people in Russia, and I have a good opinion of his abilities and power of judgement'.[19]

The same day, General Poole was writing another background letter to Colonel Byrne: 'The political situation is extraordinary. "No war & no peace" rather flummoxes us. I suppose the Huns will at once occupy Reval & the line of the lakes which was, I understand, the frontier they asked for. If they want to come here, there is not only nothing to stop them, but they would be welcomed by all the intellectuals. There are many reasons why they shouldn't come but two big ones why they should, *viz*:

1. The danger of Bolshevism to Germany.
2. The great financial stake the Germans have in this country which is endangered by the present B. Govt. tactics.

'You will have gathered from my recent cables to you that I am strongly of opinion that our policy at home is wrong & that we should do ourselves much better to recognise the B[olshevik]s as the *de facto* Govt. Indeed, I have written you about it before. I have always thought we were foolish to imagine that the S.E. federation & all the clap-trap nonsense that was talked of their possibilities was of the slightest use when it came to solid fact. As long as you will promise financial or moral support, you can find millions of Russians who will talk & promise anything. My own view is that Bolshevism is getting more hold every day & unless the civilised countries intervene it will stay for some considerable time in power. But in time saner counsels will prevail and we shall re-establish order & it will be a country of unlimited possibilities. If we are wise we shall now make all our preparations to be ready when that time comes. It is mainly with this idea that I have cabled you proposing to start the spadework with my organisation, as it is the only live British thing in Russia & I'm much afraid that unless we take it in hand nothing will be done except talk. But I also realise that it's no good building an edifice here unless one has a solid foundation at home & so if I am to take it on a first essential is a visit home to establish a satisfactory Russian section under Steel-Maitland's organisation & protection. By the time you get this they will have made up their minds if they want to use us & so in any case I ought to be on the way home. There is no doubt there are so many obvious mistakes in our present British organisations out here that a child couldn't help doing good if he tried to evolve some order. Of course, the chief one of all is the countless little shows who each work on their own – lack of co-ordination of effort. I think the latest effort of all is perhaps the limit, *viz* the cinemas for propaganda. At a considerable cost to the taxpayer – probably £40,000 – Bromhead [another British officer attached to Poole's mission] is hanging about outside with some two or three cinemas – mostly war propaganda! These would have been invaluable in June & July, when I was urging efforts to be made to get them, but somehow today the Russian public is not much interested in England's war efforts! The whole affair is more a tribute to our pertinacity than to our intelligence as a nation.[19]

'Life is not very pleasant nowadays. We personally have plenty of food but it is scarce in general. Wine is very scarce & hard to find. Highway robbery is very frequent even in frequented thoroughfares. Three nights ago du Castel [a French officer] was set upon & robbed at the corner of the Fontanka & Nevsky. I never go out at night without a revolver loose in my pocket & I never take my hand off it, so as to be ready to hurt someone if necessary, as I don't propose to let any Tovarisch rob me easily.

'The general situation at present is –

*Finland:* Pretty equal between Red & White Guards . . .
*Ukraine:* Bolsheviks have retaken Kiev . . . Allied influence there has not amounted to much.
*Don:* Bolshevism growing stronger. All the young Cossacks strongly tainted. Kaledin weak & has little power. Alexeiev practically told to clear out of the country . . . My secret service tells me not to count on his forces, who are mostly swashbucklers. The most that can be hoped from the Don, I think, is that they will be able to maintain internal order.
*Archangel:* Bolshevism growing in power . . .

[237]

*Moscow:* Bolshevism strong . . .
*Siberia:* A series of small republics with a strong tinge of Bolshevism &
anarchism. No probability of a central Govt. being formed in the near future.
*Caucasus:* International strife very acute. In N[orth] between the Cossacks
& tribesmen. In S[outh] between Tartars & Armenians . . .'[19]

All this was broadly true.

At noon on the 13th, with the battle for recognition of the Bolshevik
government now over, the War Cabinet considered Lord Derby's
report on what to do with the Russian Jews in the East End of London.
Balfour said that compulsory enlistment of Russian subjects into the
British army was 'impracticable', that Litvinov had made a protest
'practically denouncing the convention', and that news had come from
Russia 'that this convention was causing great irritation there and
damaging British interests'. In Russia, it was possible to exempt Englishmen from joining the Russian army, but there were no similar arrangements here, and if the cases in question were referred to Litvinov, 'he
would give exemption to every applicant'. To date, the question of
releasing Russian subjects already in the British army had not arisen,
but it might arise in the near future, and Balfour thought it would be
difficult to retain these men against their will, since Russia had made
peace and the men had been conscripted. But some of the men were
not necessarily Bolsheviks; they might be Ukrainians or Cossacks, in
which case Litvinov could hardly claim their release, since he did not
represent the Ukrainian or Cossack governments.[20]

The Home Secretary strongly urged that these Russians should not
be discharged from the British army and stressed that to stop recruiting
would leave a large number of Russians in the East End, 'where there
was bitter feeling against them, and where they would be a constant
source of trouble. He therefore recommended that, if practicable, these
Russians should be shipped to their own country.'

As no ships were available, it was suggested that these men be called
up forthwith, and if they refused to serve, they should be told that they
would be expelled from England at the end of the war. But in view of
the difficulties in passing the Aliens Act some years ago, it was felt that
it would be impossible to carry out such a threat. The War Cabinet
therefore agreed that 'if we had to break with the Bolsheviks, we should
break on grounds which would be supported by International Law, and
that to enforce the convention under existing circumstances, by which
we should be recruiting neutral subjects, would be indefensible'. It was
therefore decided to stop recruiting Russians for the moment, but not
to return those who had already joined the army, unless there was some
fresh development. The Home Secretary thus lost out, and the War

Office's project of putting Russian Jews in British concentration camps was abandoned.[20]

On February 15, Bruce Lockhart had his first interview with Trotsky, who asked for Allied military help and trade; if the Allies would stop supporting the Bolsheviks' opponents, he would co-operate by organising Bolshevik propaganda in Germany. He had documentary proof, he said, of Allied financial support for Alexeiev and Kaledin (news of whose suicide had still not reached Petrograd). Lockhart wired Balfour urging British compliance and co-operation. So did Lindley; if the British Embassy was to be of any use in Petrograd, 'or even to stay here at all', he warned Balfour on the 17th, they would have to abandon all support of the Don Cossack movement, 'which seems in any case to have completely collapsed'.[21]

On the 18th, the Germans began to advance on Petrograd. As the Russian soldiers fled, the Bolsheviks hastily accepted the German terms. But the Germans ignored this, and German troops drew nearer to Petrograd. Trotsky made an angry complaint to General Hoffmann (German commander on the Eastern Front), which was intercepted in London and read out to the War Cabinet on the 19th – by which time there was a new CIGS at the War Office. Sir Henry Wilson had replaced Robertson on the 16th; as a result, Derby had tried to resign, but Lloyd George would not let him go. Two simultaneous resignations at the War Office, with a major German attack on the Western Front pending, would be asking for trouble.[21]

On February 20, there arrived in London a wire from General Poole, whose disjointed phrasing probably reflects the desperation of the position in Petrograd – where Poole, it seems, had finally discovered all about the bank deals. 'Personal to Byrne from Poole. Please show following to Lord Milner – Upon our Government's policy in the near future does the success of our new venture, which apparently is approved of by the Foreign Office, largely depend. At present there is no doubt that the Bolshevik Government is most anti-German and there is a great chance now for us to strengthen British interests and ingratiate ourselves. Much would be done by the recognition of the *de facto* government, but the certain result will be an immediate expulsion from the country if we follow the policy of active support of certain other elements in Russia. That Trotsky will not stand it much longer I have on good authority. I certainly think that our policy should be to retain at all costs our position in this country.'[22]

Colonel Byrne passed this wire to Major Thornton, of the War Cabinet secretariat. But it was no good. That same day, Lord Robert

Cecil made British policy clear to the Russia committee, when they discussed what action to take about the Allied stores at Archangel. In mid-December, British naval personnel, accompanied by some of the local British community at Archangel, had been ordered to break through the ice and make for Murmansk, which was ice-free; this left the British stores at Archangel largely unattended. In mid-January, the British Consul recommended the despatch of a food-ship to Archangel, provided the stores and surplus products of the Archangel region were made available only to the Allies, and denied to both Bolsheviks and Germans; this would also enable the British to have first refusal of the commercial exploitation of this rich area after the war. But in late January, a Bolshevik commission arrived to take over Archangel and transport the stores by rail into the Russian interior. On February 10, the British Consul had reported that Archangel was now in Bolshevik hands, and soon the stores were on their way to Vologda.[23]

Cecil now stated that the Russia committee should work on the principle of denying to the Germans the stores most vital to them, rather than removing those stores most vital to us. The proposal for the despatch of a considerable force, including a landing detachment, to Archangel had been 'definitely rejected', but the despatch of a naval escort for the store-ships might still be considered. A Ministry of Shipping spokesman added that ships could easily get through to Archangel as early as April, owing to the very mild winter.[23]

Cecil then summarised the views of the Russia committee as follows: 'In view of the fact that it was the policy of H.M. Government not to recognise the Bolsheviks, no proposal for a transaction by agreement based on the recognition of the Bolsheviks could be entertained.' Further, since all the authorities agreed that any attempt to barter without such recognition would be useless, it was clearly impossible to try to secure the supplies by the exchange of commodities, without the use of force. The only solution, therefore, was the despatch of a store-ship to Archangel, accompanied by a warship, to deliver food to the inhabitants, 'and to *take* stores in exchange'.[23]

The Germans continued their advance towards Petrograd, but there was no response from London to Lockhart's request for British support for the Bolsheviks. On February 23, the Germans delivered much stiffer peace terms, with the stipulation that they would have to be accepted within forty-eight hours. On the 24th, as Trotsky furiously brandished copies of the forged 'Sisson documents' in Lockhart's face, Lenin insisted that the terms be accepted.

In spite of General Poole's warnings, the bank deals were now being finalised. On February 10, Lindley wired to the Foreign Office that agreement had been reached for a British loan of £500,000 to Jaroszynski (one tenth of what the War Cabinet had actually authorised) for three years at $5\frac{1}{4}\%$ to enable him to purchase control of most of the Russian banks for the British government. Two days later (the 12th), Jaroszynski asked Colonel Keyes to pay various sums of money (as shown below) into certain London banks for the various Russian bankers whose shares gave him complete control of the Russian Bank for Foreign Trade and the International Bank (which together controlled the entire grain trade on the Volga and in south Russia).[24]

*To the London County and Westminster Bank* (later the Westminster Bank).

£26,000 due to A. I. Wischnegradski (Chairman of the International Bank).
£26,000 due to E. G. Chaikevitch    (Managing Director        ”        ”   ).

*To the London City and Midland Bank* (now the Midland Bank).

£110,500 due to Davidov (Chairman of the Russian Bank for Foreign Trade)
and split between seven different Russians.

£162,500

Later in February, Jaroszynski again wrote to Colonel Keyes asking him to make a further payment of £40,472-15-4d to the London City and Midland Bank for a certain A. A. Lopukhin, whose name had been omitted by error from the list of seven Russians. (This was possibly the Russian Chief of Police, dismissed over the famous Azev affair, when that notorious 'agent provocateur' and Social Revolutionary had nearly succeeded, with the help of police funds, in assassinating the Tsar). Since the exchange rate was rising slightly from 33, it will be seen that the total payments made to the London City and Midland Bank approximate £151,515 (*ie*, 5 million roubles at 33), which was the amount due to Davidov, who had apparently made arrangements with the above eight Russians to provide him with ready money, probably in Stockholm.

There was confusion between Lindley and Keyes over these payments from the start. On February 13, Lindley wired the Foreign Office to say that £151,515 should be paid into Hugh Leech's account in London, as 5 million (out of the 6 million roubles) had been sent to southern Russia; he would wire about the disposal of the remaining 1 million roubles later. Keyes, however, did not for the moment agree to this. (Lindley never did wire about the remaining 1 million roubles, which became known both to baffled Treasury officials in London and to the British Embassy in Petrograd as the 'floating million'.)[24]

But Lindley was still one step behind Leech. Since neither the draft for 15 million roubles, nor Hugh Leech's letter, had ever reached the courier, George Perkins, at Kiev, owing to the fighting going on there, Leech had induced Jaroszynski to give him a second draft for 15 million roubles, which Leech this time gave to J. E. Coates, former cashier at the British Embassy, who was about to set out for southern Russia to join the banknote engravers and bank staff, who had already left Moscow for the Don to set up the Cossack bank. But on reaching Ekaterinodar, Coates found that General de Candolle had left, and the local banks had been nationalised. (When Coates eventually returned to Petrograd, he handed over this second draft to the British Consul, Woodhouse, at the urgent request of Poliakov, who was by then receiving angry telegrams from the Treasury in London.)[24]

When the news of Kaledin's suicide reached London is uncertain. They were very out of touch there with events in south Russia. But instructions now evidently went out that sterling commitments in Russia were to be generally reduced. It is also not clear when the news of Kaledin's suicide reached Petrograd. But Colonel Keyes, apparently with General Poole's backing, had already decided to proceed with the purchase of the Siberian bank, which controlled the grain trade in Siberia, as well as the gold and platinum trade, for the Germans were now making a determined effort to capture the Siberian Bank, and Jaroszynski was going to have to pay a much higher price than he expected.

Although the chairman was N. N. Pokrovsky, the former Tsarist Foreign Minister, this bank was effectively controlled by N. K. Denisov, an enterprising Don Cossack officer and engineer. It was the Siberian Bank (formerly closely connected with the Deutsche Bank) that had mainly been used by Helphand and the Germans to transfer money clandestinely (usually from the Disconto Gesellschaft in Berlin, via the Nya Bank in Stockholm) to Bolshevik agents in Petrograd, and it was because of its 'unprecedented prosperity' (was this due to Helphand's transactions?) that Denisov had bought control of it in 1916 from the then managing director, a Mr Tarnovsky, replacing him with a junior director, Nicolas Ass, while Denisov himself remained in the background. The Siberian Bank, whose 80,000 shares then stood at about 500 roubles each, continued to prosper, and after a 1-for-2 new issue, the 120,000 shares, following frantic speculation, stood late in 1917 at nearly 1,000 roubles each.

Jaroszynski was still set on buying up the Siberian Bank, but Denisov distrusted him. Colonel Keyes had therefore asked Poliakov (who was a junior director of the Siberian Bank himself) to work out some arrangement whereby Jaroszynski could acquire control. Poliakov had induced Denisov to sell his 36,000 shares, plus 8,000 over which he seems to have had control, making 44,000 in all, directly to Colonel Keyes himself – with an option to sell him a further 11,000, if he could deliver them, at 1,500 roubles per share. Jaroszynski was then to be allowed to take over these shares at cost price within three years.[24]

(From the full list of the Siberian Bank shares, which miraculously survives among Poliakov's papers, the figure of 36,000 shares appears to refer to 1,018 shares which were to be delivered with the contract, plus 34,992 which were lying mortgaged with the Russian Bank for Foreign Trade, the Azov-Don Bank, the Russo-Asiatic Bank, the International Bank, and the Union Bank of Moscow – making 36,010 shares in all. The figure of 8,000 shares appears to refer to 7,410 shares which were mortgaged with banks in Paris (the Banque Française de Banque et de Credit and the Paris branch of the International Bank); plus 323 which were mortgaged privately in Petrograd banks; and 248 shares, free of mortgage, held by the nominal managing director of the Siberian Bank, Nicholas Ass; making 7,981 in all. The figure of 11,000 shares appears to refer to 8,600 shares, which were held by the London branch of the Russo-Asiatic Bank, plus 1,052 lying at the British Treasury, and 1,322 which were held privately in Russia, free of mortgage; making 10,974 in all. These three totals, amounting to 54,965 shares, thus approximate to the above figure of 55,000.)[24]

This was a very good deal not only for Jaroszynski, but also for Denisov. Just before the Bolsheviks stopped all official dealings in bank shares, these shares had changed hands at about 500 roubles each, which was the most that had ever been advanced against them on mortgage by other banks, where the majority were anyhow held. But the Siberian Bank, in clandestine dealings, had suffered more than most from bad debts, etc., and the share prices on the black market had fallen. Denisov was therefore able to buy up further shares (apparently those held in London), which he could dispose of for 1,500 roubles at an enormous profit. (These negotiations did not remain entirely secret. On February 5, the American Ambassador in Petrograd had wired to Washington that the 'largest holder in well-known bank here [has] had bid for his holdings at highest market ever known, notwithstanding Soviet decree confiscating bank shares'. He assumed that this was from the Germans, but it probably refers to these British negotiations.)[24]

In mid-February, Colonel Keyes decided to act. Drawing upon secret funds, he purchased the Siberian Bank himself and made an immediate down payment to Denisov of the sterling equivalent of 15 million roubles, and gave Poliakov a power of attorney to act for him. 'We only forestalled the Germans by one day,' Keyes recalls, 'as the contract of a company formed in Norway had already been approved by the principal director, and was presented for signature in Christiania (Oslo) the day after the news was received that the shares had been sold in Petrograd.'

It is probable that this double operation was intended to provide Kornilov's volunteer army with some money, via the Siberian Bank, to keep it alive after the Don Cossack collapse (or the down payment may possibly have been the actual collateral for the second draft of 15 million roubles, which Leech gave to Coates before news of the death of Kaledin reached Petrograd) *and* to ensure British – and prevent German – control of the Siberian grain trade, when Japan, acting as the Allied mandatory power (as agreed by the War Cabinet on January 24), occupied Siberia and took control of the Siberian railway.

Colonel Keyes had no authority from either the War Cabinet or the Russia committee for this deal (the total cost of the 45,313 Siberian Bank shares held in Russia and France alone was £1,941,985). It was probably an SIS operation and obviously put through in a great hurry. Keyes agreed to pay Denisov £428,571 (*ie*, 15 million roubles at about 35) in London on March 1, and half the balance (£756,707) on January 28, 1919; and the rest (£87,067, *ie*, £756,707 – the other half of the balance – less £641,847, outstanding on the mortgaged shares, less £27,792 mortgage interest down to March 1, 1918), on July 30, 1919, and there were penalty clauses in the contract in case these sums were not paid on these dates.[24]

But even if Denisov delivered 55,000 of the existing 120,000 shares in the Siberian Bank (and the cost of the 9,652 shares held in London, on which Denisov had an option enabling him to sell them to Keyes, would amount to a further £413,657), the British government, and later Jaroszynski, were acquiring only 46% control, at a total cost of £2,355,642. Did Poliakov and Denisov conceal the 1-for-2 new share issue in 1917 from Colonel Keyes, giving him to understand that 55,000 shares – out of the previous total of 80,000 – gave him complete control? Were the new 40,000 shares non-voting shares? Hugh Leech (the usual intermediary in these bank deals) later claimed that he himself had nothing to do with the matter, and 'warned the Embassy that people would say that a commission had been taken'. Everything points to a great rush.

All these deals also involved Keyes in considerable personal danger. Ever since the Bolshevik revolution, in fact, the streets had been infested by bands of soldiers and sailors, and there were so many cases of robbery and murder every night that wise people never ventured out of their houses from dark till the morning. But it was 'impossible to meet anyone connected with financial matters except secretly by night,' recalls Keyes. 'Flats with entrances to two different streets were generally selected, the interviews always took place after 11 o'clock at night, and it was generally stipulated that I should wear a different fur coat and cap every time. There were anything up to 100 robberies with violence every night. Snow was not regularly cleared away, but was piled in great heaps at the sides of the streets, giving good cover to the armed gangs which infested the town. I was out for 22 nights out of the 28 in February, was attacked three times, twice with revolvers, and once with a bomb, saw three murders and several hold-ups, and got involved in two general mêlées.'[24]

In London, the Russia committee had no idea of the full scope of Keyes' bank deals; which might never have been put through if they had appointed a financial adviser to Lindley, as General Poole had constantly urged. On February 15, Dudley Ward, of the Treasury, submitted to the Russia committee a draft reply to Lindley's recent wire about Keyes' financial proposals, which stated that 'no advance of funds should be made to Yaroshinski [sic] until after Major Keyes [sic] had returned to England and explained the full bearing of his proposals'. (The wire in question may have been Lindley's wire of the 10th, confirming that the British loan of £500,000 had been put through, or a later one up to February 13; but it clearly made no mention of the Siberian Bank deal.) In reply to Dudley Ward, Lord Robert Cecil said that 'while agreeing that no further obligations should be entered into . . . we could not repudiate any action which had already been taken on the strength of the authority which had been given to Major Keyes, who, it appeared, had pledged himself to the extent of half a million pounds'. (In fact, Keyes had pledged the British government to a further £2·35 million.) In view of Cecil's remarks, which expressed the general feeling of the Russia committee, Dudley Ward agreed to refer the draft reply back to the Treasury. Cecil then read out General Poole's telegram (despatched from Petrograd on the 7th and received on the 11th), 'urging the desirability of recognising the Bolsheviks'. This drew no response from the committee.[25]

They were no better, in fact much worse, advised by the time of their next meeting on the 18th, when Dudley Ward brought before the committee Lindley's wire of February 7, regarding the transfer of the 5 million roubles, via Kiev, for General de Candolle to pass on to Kornilov at Rostov. For Dudley Ward urged that the proposal (which had long since gone through) should be vetoed, not only because of the difficulties involved in the transaction, but because General de Candolle had reported that the 'South-East Union' had 'ample credit at their disposal'. This was untrue – and what the 'South-East Union' desperately wanted was not credit but cash. But the Russia committee agreed with Dudley Ward, who undertook to draft the necessary reply to Lindley. The breakdown in communications between Lindley and Keyes in Petrograd and the Russia committee in London was complete – solely because of the Russia committee's refusal to despatch a financial adviser to Petrograd, as constantly urged by General Poole and others.[25]

The Russia committee now decided to terminate all further banking transactions of any kind via the British Embassy in Petrograd. On the 20th, Sir Ronald Graham (Assistant Under Secretary of State at the Foreign Office) stated that they had received many applications from people with property in Russia, and he read out a draft reply to the applicants: 'Owing to the restrictions of banking transactions which had been imposed by the Bolsheviks, the transfer of bank balances to the Embassy credit was no longer possible, and it was undesirable that telegrams suggesting such transfers should be despatched from England to banks in Russia. The British Embassy at Petrograd would accept deposits of notes, etc. for such custody as they could offer, but this could only be done at the depositor's risk.' In view of what the Foreign Office itself had been up to with Jaroszynski, while the Bolsheviks were restricting banking transactions, this was a hypocritical reply; but it was approved by the Russia committee.[25]

It is possible that Colonel Keyes, through his acquisition of the Siberian Bank, managed to deliver the desperately needed finance to Kornilov and Alexeiev on the Don. For by February 21, when the volunteer army pulled out of Rostov, Alexeiev had received 15 million roubles via the Rostov branch of the State Bank, so it is said; without which, as the historian David Footman has remarked, the 'formation of any appreciable force would have been impossible'. In view of subsequent British claims that they had 'called the Volunteer Army into the field', and of their previous complete failure to deliver a single rouble to the Don, it is obviously of crucial importance to discover *where* this 15 million roubles came from. All that can be said is that it was possibly delivered through the Siberian Bank.[26]

The few remaining Don Cossacks would not come with the volunteer army as they pulled out of Rostov. Alexeiev urged that their little force be disbanded and that small groups should reassemble later in the Caucasus. Kornilov urged that they go to the Kuban. Others wanted a withdrawal into the steppe. Kornilov finally prevailed, and the volunteer army set out across the frozen steppe on the 'ice campaign' towards the Kuban Cossack capital of Ekaterinodar. Alexeiev and Denikin, both of them ill, were carried out on carts, their only money in a wooden box beside them. Kornilov refused a horse and marched on foot. Just before they left, Alexeiev wrote to a friend, 'We are moving out into the steppe. We can return only by God's mercy. But we must light a torch so that there will be one gleam of light in the darkness enveloping Russia.'[26]

On the 24th, as the Germans drew ever nearer to Petrograd, Poole and Keyes drew up two letters of agreement with Jaroszynski, one covering Keyes's purchase of the Siberian Bank, the other the British loan of £500,000 to Jaroszynski for him to purchase control of the other Russian banks; both these letters were antedated to October 28, 1917 (*ie*, not only before the Bolsheviks nationalised the Russian banks, but before they had even seized power), and gave the British government the right, *inter alia*, to nominate two directors to the board of each bank; in fact, to control them. The two letters were taken to Lindley, who, after some slight alterations, approved them. They were then signed by both parties. Their intention was clear: if the Germans were defeated and the Bolsheviks suppressed, the British government, through their agent Jaroszynski, would control the entire Russian and Siberian grain trade – and thus most of the Russian economy.[27]

The Bolsheviks now retaliated. On February 25, a short wire reached London from General Poole stating that the Bolsheviks were now forcing the remaining Russian bank directors to sign over the balances and other valuables held by them in banks in England, France and America. On the 20th, the Azov-Don Bank had been ordered to hand 1,200,000 American dollars over to Commissar Saalkind and others, who were about to go on missions abroad; but the bank had managed to delay matters. 'There is a great danger of the boards of the Russian banks being compelled to pay such valuta deposited abroad,' warned Poole. 'It is obvious that the valuta is required for the spreading abroad of Bolshevik propaganda.'[28]

This and similar wires disturbed the Home Secretary, who was evidently indignant at the War Cabinet's decision of February 11 to allow Bolshevik emissaries to visit London, where anti-Bolshevik feeling was now rising. Recent speeches by the Bolshevik envoy, Maxim Litvinov, had, he said, shown a quieter tone since the warning given to him after his proclamation in the *Woolwich Pioneer*, the Home Secretary informed the War Cabinet on February 25, but his activities must be stopped. It appeared that Litvinov's real name was David Finkelstein, and that he had later adopted various aliases, among them Gustav Graf Buchman, Harrison, and only more recently Litvinov. It might be possible to obtain evidence 'connecting him with the robbery at a bank at Tiflis some years ago. This robbery was organised from Berlin,' said the Home Secretary. [The facts of the matter were that on June 12, 1907, Stalin had held up the Tiflis Treasury and got away with a large sum of money. As it consisted of banknotes of high denomination, it was smuggled out of the country, and Lenin had ordered a Bolshevik party member called Maxim Wallach, who lived in Paris, to dispose of the proceeds there. He failed to do so and was arrested by the French police. In 1908, after spending several years in France, he had to come to London, where he called himself Maxim Harrison, and had worked for various publishing houses and had become the Bolshevik party representative in London under the name of Litvinov. During the war, he had worked for the purchasing commission of the Russian delegation in London. The idea that Stalin had robbed the Tiflis Treasury in 1907 on German orders was absurd, and shows that anti-German sentiments were rising in London as well.] Litvinov's most recent activities, the Home Secretary reminded the War Cabinet, had included attempts to undermine the discipline of Russian Jews in the British army, the formation of a Bolshevik propaganda bureau in the East End, and the enlistment of Red Guards in London.[29]

Action against Litvinov, however, was imperilled by the arrival in Aberdeen, (on the 23rd), and subsequently in London, of three Bolsheviks from Moscow, namely Kamenev, a member of the Central Committee en route for France as Bolshevik representative in Paris, Saalkind, who was on his way to Switzerland, and a diplomatic courier. It was possible that they were going to break their journey to attend the Labour conference suggested by Henderson in his wire to Lenin of February 7, but made abortive by the War Cabinet's refusal to grant recognition to the Bolshevik government. Kamenev, it was now stated, was found to have on him a cheque for £5,000 drawn on an English bank, which had been seized and deposited at Scotland Yard. The three agents had brought a good deal of baggage, some of it personal, some under diplomatic seal. It was proposed to search their personal baggage and to endeavour to get Litvinov to open the sealed bags in the presence of someone from the Home Office.[29]

The previous afternoon, the Home Secretary went on, the police had raided the Communist club in Soho, 'and found a meeting of Russian revolutionaries taking place'. One of the three new arrivals was present, but it was not felt proper to arrest him with the thirty-seven other revolutionaries who had been detained. A watch was being kept on the three envoys, 'and it was proposed that M. Saalkind, who had a passport for Switzerland, should be hastened on his way thither'. Some papers, including the club's register, had been seized. The register showed that Litvinov was a member of the club, under the name of

'Harrison', which was subsequently changed in the register to Litvinov. Kamenev, it was understood, had intended to proceed to France, but now proposed to stay in England.

The DMI said that the War Office were 'considerably perturbed' by the attempts of Bolshevik agents to undermine discipline in the British army and he trusted that action would be taken to stop this sort of thing. 'He understood that M. Litvinov was accused not only of being connected with the bank robbery at Tiflis, but also of forgery. A telegram had been sent to Tiflis with a view to obtaining further information . . .'

The War Cabinet decided that the Bolshevik envoys should be watched, and could be deported if sufficient evidence against them came to light; but no action was to be taken against Litvinov without the War Cabinet's authority.

The question of the withdrawal of the British Embassy in Petrograd was then discussed. Buchanan stated that the time had now come for our envoys to leave Russia. Lord Robert Cecil thought there was 'serious risk' of our envoys in Petrograd falling into the hands of the Germans, 'who might very soon be in a position to send a body of troops to Petrograd'. We could no longer leave it to the Englishmen on the spot to decide whether to leave their posts; they should be instructed to withdraw as soon as possible. The DMI said that we would still be able to obtain information from Intelligence officers and secret agents, who would remain on in Petrograd. It was pointed out that it would be impossible to despatch cypher telegrams if the British Embassy were withdrawn, but Balfour said that the whole point of our envoys remaining in Petrograd was that it gave us some chance of influencing Bolshevik policy in our favour; the German terms accepted by the Bolsheviks made this no longer possible. It was therefore decided that Lindley and his staff should return to England as soon as possible.

Hankey was angry at this 'thoroughly stupid' decision, made in Lloyd George's absence; and that afternoon, personally intervened at the Foreign Office and Home Office. As a result, it was agreed that someone with a proper cypher should remain in Petrograd.[29]

# 9

## Brest-Litovsk — The Allied Failure

On February 25, the War Cabinet took a further major decision on Siberian policy, exactly a month after they had decided that they should 'do all in their power' to open up communications between Vladivostok and south-east Russia along the Siberian railway to bring support to the Don Cossacks and the volunteer army, and that the Japanese should be urged to undertake military control of it from Vladivostok to Chelyabinsk; also, that America and France should be urged to support this policy.

On January 26, Balfour had accordingly wired to Washington, Paris and Rome that Japan should be invited to act as Allied mandatory to protect the Siberian railway, which was the only effective means of bringing support to 'our friends' in south Russia, and countering German influence; this proposal, of course, excluded any suggestion of future Japanese control or annexation of Russian territory. On the 30th, the French Ambassador in London informed the Foreign Office that the French government approved the proposal, and this news was passed to Sir William Wiseman, the chief British intelligence agent in America and an intimate friend of Colonel House, who was President Wilson's close adviser. The British proposal had, unfortunately, reached Washington at a moment when relations between America and Japan were cool. On the 25th, the British Ambassador in Tokyo had wired that his American colleague had been instructed to inform the Japanese Foreign Minister that the American government rejected the French proposal (of January 7) for the despatch of a joint Allied punitive expedition to Irkutsk to avenge the murder of the French Consul (who was, in fact, alive and well), and indeed deprecated any foreign intervention in Siberia, which was likely to be distasteful, dangerous, and perhaps disastrous to Russia; it was also considered in Washington that the despatch of one, not two, Japanese warships to Vladivostok would have been sufficient. This message was coolly received in Tokyo.[1]

Meanwhile, the War Office admitted that they did not have sufficient information to work out a detailed scheme for control of the Siberian railway. They suggested that the Japanese be asked whether such a scheme would be feasible, and whether they would put it into operation; the War Office felt that as there would be no organised military opposition, the Japanese army should be able to control the entire railway. This admission of military ignorance was passed on to Paris by the Foreign Office on January 31.

A message then arrived from Wiseman in New York saying that the President promised to give careful consideration to Balfour's proposal for Japan to act as Allied mandatory after he had consulted General Tasker Bliss (the American military representative to the Supreme War Council in Paris) on what military advantages could be expected from this move; but Wiseman's impression was that the President would decline to agree on the grounds that (a) Japan would decline the offer, and (b) that intervention would cause strong anti-Ally and pro-German sentiment to spring up in Russia. Balfour replied, via Wiseman, to Colonel House on February 2 that he agreed that caution was necessary in dealing with a difficult and ever-changing situation. Meanwhile, the attempt by the Cossack *Ataman* Semenov to seize the junction of the Chinese Eastern and the main Siberian railway (for which he was to receive arms and money from both England and Japan) was said to be progressing favourably. Balfour thus suggested that the Allied invitation to Japan to secure the entire Siberian railway should now be deferred until there was more definite news of Semenov's progress.

On the 6th, the British Ambassador in Rome wired that the Italian Foreign Minister would prefer Allied intervention in Siberia, rather than sole Japanese action, as proposed by Balfour, which would reduce European prestige in Asia; he also doubted whether Japan would go any further west than would suit her own particular interests. This message was also passed on to New York. On the 8th, however, Balfour again wired to Colonel House, via Wiseman, that the latest news of Semenov's expedition was not quite so satisfactory. It now appeared that even if Semenov were successful, his operations would be limited to a small part of the railway, and the Japanese were sending agents to report on the Siberian position, no doubt with a view to taking immediate action if Vladivostok was threatened. Balfour consequently urged the American government to give further consideration to his proposal that Japan should act as Allied mandatory.[1]

Balfour's wire to House was more timely than he realised. On the same day, the 8th, the Japanese Foreign Minister told the British and American ambassadors in Tokyo that the time had come for Allied agreement on action to prevent the spread of German influence in Siberia. Control of the railways up to the junction of the Chinese Eastern with the main Siberian railway would keep German influence out of the Far East, he said, inferring this to be the limit of Japanese action. He hinted that Japan might move only with Allied, and not American approval, for America, which was not a party to the London Pact of 1914, could not be expected to take the same attitude as England and France to a separate Russian peace. On the 12th, however, Balfour told the French Ambassador in London that it was impossible for the Allies to press for Japanese intervention without American consent. On the 13th, the American government made its position clear. The Secretary of State, Robert Lansing, instructed his ambassadors to inform the British, French, Japanese and Chinese governments that America could not approve of Japanese action in Siberia. Russia, he added, would not welcome foreign intervention, which was at present inopportune, but if it later became unavoidable, there should be joint Allied action, not intervention by one mandatory power. To emphasise this situation, the American cruiser *Brooklyn* was sent to Vladivostok.[2]

On the 14th, Balfour brought the matter of Japanese intervention in Siberia before the War Cabinet for the first time since January 24 and promised to circulate a fresh paper. Two days later, the French Ambassador sent him a memorandum recapitulating the dangers of the Siberian situation at some length; only Japanese action could avert them. The French government suggested a Japanese advance to the Urals, and a simultaneous Japanese guarantee not to seize any Russian territory. On the same day, the 16th, the British Ambassador in Rome reported that the Italian Foreign Minister had modified his original views of Balfour's proposal of January 26 and would not now oppose an invitation to Japan to act as Allied mandatory in eastern Russia, on the assumption that this would enjoy American consent.[3]

On February 20 (by which time the Don Cossacks had collapsed, their *Ataman* Kaledin had shot himself, the Germans had renewed their advance into Russia, and the British government had purchased the Siberian Bank), the War Cabinet again considered the Siberian situation, but as it was changing from day to day, it was difficult to take a decision. Balfour outlined the present position. 'It was no longer a question of bringing help to the Cossacks by means of Japanese intervention, as it was now clear that the Cossacks no longer existed as an efficient fighting force. There were two principal theories upon the subject of Japanese action: one was the French, which saw in Japan the only means of countering German influence in Russia; the other was the American, which, apart from jealousy and suspicion of Japanese enterprises, considered the Japs [*sic*] as the worst possible agents of the Allies in Russia.' It was agreed to raise the matter again at an early date, when the Prime Minister could attend the Cabinet.[4]

When the Bolsheviks finally accepted the German peace terms, Japan seemed ready to strike. On the 23rd, the British Ambassador in Tokyo wired to say that his French colleague had proposed to the Japanese Foreign Minister that France and Japan should co-operate to prevent Russian food and supplies from falling into German hands by buying up stocks in Russia, by diverting rolling-stock from west to east, and by stopping the entry of food and supplies from Japan into Siberia. The Japanese Foreign Minister replied that this was impracticable without control of the Siberian railway, and he deplored the withholding of Allied consent to Japanese intervention. He again suggested that if England and France agreed, Japan could go ahead without American consent, and could certainly proceed as far as Irkutsk, perhaps even further. For the third time, he hinted that Japan might possibly break from the Entente so as to be free to intervene in Siberia and thus secure what she wanted in the Far East, and might then come to terms with Germany on the basis of a common hostility to Bolshevism.[5]

This was the background to a further lengthy discussion about Siberian intervention by the War Cabinet (in the absence of the Prime Minister) on February 25. Balfour stated that two days before, he had seen the Japanese Ambassador, who said that Japan wished to seize the Siberian railway junction in the Far East 'at once' to safeguard Vladivostok. Balfour had asked him if Japan would in fact seize the entire Siberian railway up to the Urals, to deny the railway and Siberian produce to the Germans. The Japanese Ambassador took the point, but said he had received no instructions. Balfour then asked if Japan would act as Allied mandatory, and gathered that the Japanese government fully understood that they would go into Siberia simply as a move against Germany and would disavow any intention of annexing Russian territory; but he also gathered that the Japanese were 'vehemently opposed' to any small Allied contingents being attached to the Japanese force, as this would make Japanese public opinion suspicious, 'owing to the impression that was generally felt in Japan that, earlier in the war, the British had tried to curtail Japanese activities'. This had deeply injured Japanese *amour-propre* and made it most difficult to persuade the Japanese to agree to co-operate with the Allies, save for Russians like Semenov. 'This being the case,' said Balfour to the Cabinet, 'we should have a difficult task in persuading President Wilson to agree to our policy.'[6]

[253]

France favoured Japanese intervention only on the 'distinct under-standing' that Japan would take control of the entire Siberian railway. Lord Robert Cecil thought we should ask the Japanese government to consider seizing the Siberian railway as far as Chelyabinsk, the junction east of the Urals; this, he gathered from talking to Englishmen and Russians who knew Siberia, would not produce a bad effect on public opinion in Siberia. Buchanan agreed; the Russian attitude to the Japanese had undergone a 'considerable change' in the last few months, but it should be clearly pointed out to the Russians that the Japanese were only being brought in 'to save Asiatic Russia from being dominated entirely by Germany'.

Lord Milner felt that Russia would very soon have a German-con-trolled government at Petrograd, 'either under the Bolsheviks or a pro-German Czar'. There was little point in having small Allied con-tingents attached to the Japanese force. 'The great thing, in his view, was to remove the suspicion regarding our attitude which existed in the minds of the Japanese. We had steadily snubbed the Japanese and treated them as a convenience, and, looking to the future, he thought it was most essential that we should take such action as would remove this sense of grievance.' The DMI agreed; as far as he could gather from Japanese officers in England, 'if we trusted the Japanese we should get a great deal more out of them than we had hitherto'. Walter Long, the Colonial Secretary, did not think that the Dominion governments would object to Japanese intervention; but if the British Ambassador in Washington were informed that the British government approved of it, he should be asked to consult the Canadian envoy in Washington about it.

Subject to the Prime Minister's approval, the War Cabinet requested Balfour to inform the British Ambassador in Washington that the British government 'viewed with favour the idea of Japanese inter-vention in Siberia up to Chelyabinsk', and give the reasons which had led to this decision, namely the denial of the Siberian railway and Siberian grain and produce to the Germans, and to ask the British Ambassador to obtain American agreement to this policy. Balfour was also asked to wire this decision to the British Ambassador in Tokyo, 'leaving it to his discretion to make such preliminary and tentative approaches to the Japanese to act, as he might think fit'.[6]

Hankey thought this also a 'thoroughly stupid' decision, 'which, in my opinion,' he records, 'will do no good, and may result in the starting of the "Yellow Peril".' But as it was a matter of high policy, he took no action except to see that Lloyd George was informed. 'The PM rang me up later and expressed himself very dissatisfied with the Cabinet's decisions,' he writes.[6]

[254]

On the 26th, however, Balfour informed the War Cabinet that the Prime Minister had approved his draft telegram to Washington and a copy had been sent to Tokyo; but Balfour would not approach the Japanese Ambassador in London until the American view had been obtained. Thus, exactly a month after the first British proposal of January 24, that Japan should seize more than 5,000 miles of the Siberian railway, the War Cabinet, in full knowledge of strong American objections (in face of which Japan would not move), were again making exactly the same proposal to America; by this time, however (and unknown to the Cabinet), Colonel Keyes, through his purchase of the Siberian Bank, had acquired what was imagined to be legal control of the entire Siberian grain trade and most of the Siberian economy.

The Germans refused to stop their advance into Russia until the peace treaty was actually signed, and the Bolshevik delegates were delayed by the disrupted railways on their return to Brest-Litovsk. The Allied embassies in Petrograd concluded that the Germans might well seize the Russian capital and decided to leave. On February 26, the DMI told the War Cabinet that the German advance was being made by very small forces. 'In telegrams received at the end of the previous week,' he added, 'it was stated that M. Trotsky had talked of the possibility of guerrilla warfare taking place.'

The War Cabinet then had to give further attention to southern Russia, especially to the Caucasus, with its large stocks of grain in the Kuban and the Terek, now that the Don Cossacks and the volunteer army to the north had collapsed. The old Russian Caucasus army had entirely disintegrated. 'The Russian troops were completely demoralised, and bands of armed Armenians were committing all sorts of excesses,' stated the DMI. He asked what policy was to be adopted south of the Caucasus in Persia (where the British had a vital interest in protecting the Persian oilfields) in view of the fact that General Dunsterville, who had been sent from Baghdad with a British mission and some armoured cars to train local Georgian and Armenian troops to prevent Turkish forces crossing the Caucasus range, had been unable to get through. The CIGS suggested that Dunsterville should try to raise levies at Kermanshah, in central Persia, midway between the Caspian and the Persian Gulf, and that as soon as the snow melted, General Marshall should support him with cavalry and armoured cars to be sent up from Kasr-i-Shirin (north-east of what are now the Iraqui oilfields, on the Baghdad–Kermanshah road). 'It was most important to secure the safety of the roads leading from Mesopotamia through Kermanshah to Teheran and to the Caspian Sea,' said the DMI. The matter had been discussed the previous day by the Persian committee.

and the War Office had been asked to report on the military situation. [7]

The Cabinet were told that the Persian committee had also wired to the British Minister at Teheran to ask for his opinion on the War Office proposals. Hitherto, we had been giving substantial financial support to democratic elements in Persia in an attempt to conciliate them, and had been prepared to withdraw our troops and make other concessions, in return for a *quid pro quo*. The British Minister, however, had urged military occupation of north-west Persia to repel Tartars, Bolsheviks and Persian extremists. The Persian committee was against this and had suggested alternatives, which so far, had come to nothing. The War Office were pressing for military action, 'but, as this would be tantamount to declaring war on Persia, it was necessary that the matter should be examined from every side'. The DMI said the matter was one of considerable urgency, 'as disorder was spreading from the Caspian along the road to Kasr-i-Shirin'. The War Cabinet referred the matter back to the Persian committee, which was to meet as soon as a reply came from the British Minister in Teheran. There the matter was left. [7]

On the 28th, the Prime Minister drew the War Cabinet's attention to the 'very conflicting information from Russia'. He took up the DMI's remark of the 26th, and 'asked whether the possibilities of a formidable guerrilla warfare [in Russia] had not been under-rated. History in Spain and elsewhere had shown that large numbers of troops could be occupied by these means, particularly in forest country.' The DMO admitted that in Russia guerrilla warfare 'might still be very trouble-some' to the enemy. But nothing was in fact done to support Bolshevik forces against the Germans. [8]

Balfour then stated that he had given instructions that Kamenev and his colleagues, who had recently arrived from Russia, 'should be treated with every consideration, and that he had stopped their being sent straight to France, as had been suggested, and he had since heard that the French Government would not receive them'. Kamenev was being allowed to stay in England until arrangements could be made for his return to Russia; most of his baggage, Balfour added, had not been opened or examined by the police. Balfour, in fact, made it clear that he was opposed to the rabid anti-Bolshevism now gaining ground in England. [8]

The Russia committee was anxious about the bank deals engineered by Colonel Keyes in Petrograd. That day, Dudley Ward, of the Treasury, warned his colleagues that the 'whole question' of British financial policy towards Russia 'might be brought to a head at any moment by some overt act of hostility'. This anxiety was shared in

Petrograd. The same day, while Lockhart managed to obtain a Bolshevik exit visa for Colonel Keyes only by a subterfuge, Lindley and Keyes, in the fever of their departure, burnt the letters of agreement with Jaroszynski, who buried his own copies in the ground 'somewhere in Petrograd' (where, as far as history relates, they still are); but Keyes had duly signed the power of attorney for Poliakov the day before, and the major part of Keyes' agreement with Denisov has miraculously survived.[9]

That evening, Hugh Leech came to say farewell to Keyes, and 'brought him up a box of cigars just before he left for the train, and his last words to me', Leech later reported, 'were to the effect that I should do all I could to immediately render liquid the floating million . . . I told him that I would do what I could, but did not see much prospect of doing anything in their absence.' That night, the British Embassy hurriedly left the Russian capital. (When passing through Oslo, Keyes met Denisov, who handed over 1,018 Siberian bank shares, which Keyes deposited at the British Legation. Denisov then asked Keyes to alter his payment to $1\frac{1}{2}$ million francs to be credited to him at the Société Française de Banque et de Crédit, with the balance paid to the London City and Midland Bank. This alarmed the French, who at once sent a representative to London 'to try and get on even terms with us'; but Keyes, on arrival, was instructed to give him no information about the Siberian Bank.)[9]

On February 26, Balfour had informed the British Ambassador in Washington of the War Cabinet's decision of the 25th, namely that the British government approved of Japanese intervention in Siberia up to Chelyabinsk in the Urals, so as to deny both the Siberian railway and Siberian produce to the Germans; the background to this decision was given and American approval was requested. On the 27th, Balfour privately informed Colonel House, via Wiseman, that the Japanese government was preparing Japanese public opinion for action in Siberia and that it would thereafter be more difficult to control Japanese policy in Siberia, if she entered the area independently and not as Allied mandatory. On the same day, the French Ambassador in Washington informed Secretary Lansing that the Japanese Foreign Minister had told the French Ambassador in Tokyo that he was 'ready to pledge his country to act so far as the Ural mountains'. This latter, indeed crucial, message must be viewed with scepticism. The French were ready to adopt all and any methods to promote Japanese intervention in Siberia, including the propagation of downright untruths; the recent incident of the 'murder' of the French Consul in Irkutsk was to be the first of a series. The Japanese Foreign Minister, who was himself much more interventionist than his colleagues in the Japanese government, certainly knew this and played on it. So it is doubtful whether the Japanese Foreign Minister really pledged Japan to advance to the Urals, and even if he did, it is unlikely that he meant it.[10]

These various wires and notes (together with news of the imminent conclusion of peace between the Germans and the Bolsheviks) had a powerful effect on Secretary Lansing, who now swung right round, and induced both President Wilson and his adviser House to agree to the British proposal that Japan should act in Siberia as Allied mandatory. On March 1, the President himself drafted a note to the Japanese government in this sense, which was shown that same day both to the British chargé d'affaires and the French Ambassador. The British Embassy at once wired this important message to the Foreign Office. On March 2, Wiseman wired from New York confirming that the President approved the British proposal, and if England, France and Italy invited Japan to act as Allied mandatory, he would send a separate, but similar, invitation to Japan.[10]

From Petrograd, Bruce Lockhart was imploring Balfour not to let Japan loose in Russia. On March 1, he had his first interview with Lenin, who stated that he was willing to accept Allied military support in the event of further German aggression. On the 2nd, he saw Trotsky, who was very disturbed at reports that Japan would probably occupy Vladivostok; this, Trotsky emphasised, would throw the whole Russian nation into the arms of Germany and make any further resistance to the Germans useless. That day, therefore, Lockhart wired to Balfour, strongly urging that the Bolsheviks be given Allied support and that Japan should be restrained; Russia would chiefly blame England, he warned, if Japan descended on Siberia. On the 3rd, the peace treaty between the German and Bolshevik governments was signed at Brest-Litovsk. That day, the Russian journalist, Eugène Semenov, told the American propaganda agent, Edgar Sisson (who was still assiduously collecting copies of the forged documents) that his group in Petrograd had carried out a successful raid on the Bolshevik offices, and he presented Sisson with originals of alleged documents from the Germans. No originals of alleged Bolshevik documents to the Germans were produced, only photographic copies. Sisson bought the whole lot – and at once left Russia with his 'scoop'. General Poole had also left, via Finland. 'He is now waiting at Helsingfors for Swedish boat to take him to Stockholm,' stated Major Macalpine, who was left in charge of the British Supply Mission, in a wire which reached London on the 4th. Poole and Major Banting should reach Stockholm about March 9.[11]

In northern Russia, Archangel was frozen throughout the long Russian winter and the only port of entry for British ships was Murmansk, which the Gulf Stream keeps ice-free. In January, a Bolshevik commission had arrived at Archangel to take over the town and the mass of Allied stores there. The British government had confirmed that they had no intention of withdrawing British naval forces from Murmansk; the British presence would remain in northern Russia. But throughout February, there were continual fears that the Germans would seize the port and surrounding area, either through Finland, or by advancing up the railway from Petrograd, after they had taken the Russian capital. On February 12, just after the former Russian Naval Commander of Murmansk had been assassinated, Admiral Kemp, the British Naval Commander, and the British Consul had a secret meeting with two Russian officers, who were trusted by the local soviet, and it was decided to set up a local authority to co-operate with British naval forces to defend the Murmansk area. On the 16th, the town soviet, the local Russian Fleet soviet, and the Railway Workers' Union, formed a joint body (hereafter referred to as the Murmansk soviet). When the Germans resumed their advance into Russia late in February, Admiral Kemp wired to the Admiralty that a British expeditionary force of at least 6,000 men was needed to prevent the Germans seizing Murmansk; the local Russians would only resist the Germans if the British were clearly seen to be the stronger. As there were no troops available, Kemp's request was turned down. But it was decided to send a British cruiser to Murmansk, and to ask for a French and an American cruiser to be sent as well. When this request was made to Paris and Washington, the French at once agreed. On March 1, the CIGS told the War Cabinet that there was also a project afoot for the despatch of a small British demolition party of twenty men to both Murmansk and Archangel, and he was asked to discuss the matter with the Admiralty.[12]

At Murmansk, however, there was now great anxiety about a German attack, which was thought imminent. On March 1, the head of the Murmansk soviet therefore wired to Petrograd to ask what help the local defence force could accept from the 'friendly powers'. Trotsky, wrongly informed that the peace talks had again been broken off and that the German advance had resumed, sent back an immediate reply (later to become notorious as a key document in Stalin's denunciation of Trotsky as an Allied agent) that they must accept 'any and all assistance' from the Allies to resist the Germans. On the 2nd, therefore, members of the Murmansk soviet reached an agreement – by word of mouth – with Admiral Kemp, the British Consul, and a French officer, to set up a military council of three people to defend the Murmansk region – one to be appointed by the Murmansk soviet and one each by the British and French, who agreed not to interfere in local affairs, but to supply food and arms and material for the local Russian troops.[12]

On March 4, the War Cabinet considered the position in both Siberia and northern Russia. Balfour, referring to the British proposal of February 25, stated that the American government 'had agreed to Japanese intervention in Siberia', subject to their usual proviso that they would not subscribe to a joint Allied declaration, but would later issue their own 'supporting the Allied policy'. Balfour added that he had drafted a telegram to Tokyo, stating that America had consented, 'and that the next move was with Japan'. He had also drafted his idea of the sort of declaration that the Allies should make. The telegram, he hoped, would be sent that afternoon.[13]

The First Sea Lord then read out to the War Cabinet a telegram from Admiral Kemp at Murmansk, 'which stated that the local soviet had received a telegram from M. Trotsky, saying that [as] peace negotiations had apparently broken off and that measures were being taken to defend Petrograd to the last drop of blood, it was the duty of the [Murmansk] soviet to do everything they could do to defend the Murman line, and ordering them to co-operate with Allied Missions in everything'. (This is an accurate paraphrase of Trotsky's actual wire.) The First Sea Lord went on to report Kemp's agreement with the Murmansk soviet and the decision to send British and French cruisers to the port, but no troop reinforcements. He then read out the draft instructions which he proposed to send to Admiral Kemp, which emphasised that the Admiral 'was not to undertake operations against the Bolsheviks except in a case of extreme urgency'.

The War Cabinet decided that the Admiralty should inform Admiral Kemp 'that we cannot send land forces; that naval reinforcements are coming; and that he should be authorised to land the troops, if, in his judgement, any useful assistance could be given by them to any Russian forces against the Germans'. There can be no doubt whatever that the War Cabinet's decision to authorise the landing of British troops in northern Russia was influenced by the American decision to approve Japanese intervention in Siberia.[13]

That afternoon, Balfour wired to both the British Ambassador in Tokyo and to Bruce Lockhart in Petrograd. In his wire (no. 198) to Tokyo, he stated that America now approved of Japanese intervention in principle. If, therefore, the Japanese Foreign Minister would issue a declaration that the Allies, by intervention in Siberia, only wished to help Russia to preserve intact the Russian provinces, to see Russia both politically and economically strong and independent, and to prevent Germany destroying Russia, seizing Russian provinces, dictating Russian policy and exploiting Russian commerce, then the British Ambassador was to negotiate with his French and Italian colleagues (after consultation with their governments) a joint Allied invitation to Japan to act as Allied mandatory to protect the Siberian railway as far as Chelyabinsk, or at any rate to Omsk, so as to prevent a German seizure of Siberian grain and produce.[14]

In his wire to Petrograd, Balfour warned Bruce Lockhart that Japanese intervention in Siberia was imminent. The British government, he stated, in answer to Lockhart's reproaches at the lack of Allied military support for the Bolsheviks, would gladly help them resist the Germans; and he detailed the recent agreement between British officers and the Murmansk soviet. But the Bolshevik regime had achieved nothing; it had abandoned Allied military stores, and had failed to make the Russians fight or the Germans retire. But the Japanese intention to thwart German penetration to the Pacific coast coincided with British interests in preventing the Germans from seizing the Allied stores at Vladivostok and the Siberian harvests, which could supplement the Ukraine's meagre grain supplies. To avoid these dangers, Japan would certainly move, said Balfour, and it was better that she should do so, even from the Russian point of view, as Allied mandatory, rather than alone. The sense of Balfour's telegrams to Tokyo and Petrograd was conveyed to Wiseman in New York, for transmission to Colonel House.[14]

But the Prime Minister had not abandoned the Bolsheviks. 'I am anxious to get a paper on the possibilities of Russia from the point of view of guerrilla warfare,' he minuted to the CIGS on March 5. 'The Russian Army as an organised force has completely broken up. It is not impossible, however, that organised bands may be formed which would give the Germans infinite trouble and absorb large masses of troops in protecting lines of communication.' This drew no response from the War Office.[15]

On the 5th, the War Cabinet considered Bruce Lockhart's recent wire, 'in which he had urged a suspension of the proposed intervention of Japan in Siberia', and Balfour's reply of the 4th, in which he had explained British policy. This reply was approved, 'subject to the suggestion that it might have been added that if the Bolsheviks proposed to put up a fight against the Germans, they might enlist the Japanese as allies'. Balfour undertook to consider whether a further telegram in this sense should be despatched. The War Cabinet also approved Balfour's telegram no. 198 to Tokyo, 'in which he initiated the invitation to the Japanese to take action'.[16]

In Petrograd, Bruce Lockhart that day had a further lengthy discussion with Trotsky, after which he sent Balfour another appeal for British support for the Bolsheviks. A special congress of soviets would meet in Moscow on the 12th to consider ratification of the Brest-Litovsk peace treaty. If some Allied support was by then on offer, the Bolsheviks would either declare a sort of jihad against Germany, or force Germany to declare war against Russia. But if Japan were given *carte blanche* by the Allies to enter Siberia, or if England, as was rumoured, was at once to occupy northern Russia, the Bolsheviks would be driven into German arms. So said Trotsky, according to Lockhart, who urged Balfour to try to secure a Bolshevik invitation for England and America to co-operate in the defence of Archangel and Vladivostok. But Japanese intervention must be stopped. If Lockhart could assure Lenin that we would support him in fighting Germany, Lockhart was sure that war would be declared. 'This is our last chance,' he warned.[17]

On March 6, Admiral Kemp landed a force of 130 Royal Marines at Murmansk, as authorised by the War Cabinet's decision of the 4th. The same day, Balfour replied to Lockhart, in accordance with the War Cabinet's observations of the 5th. If Japan intervened, stated the Foreign Secretary, she would come in as an ally of Russia. If, therefore, Trotsky wanted British support against the Germans, why did he not also try to obtain Japanese support?[17]

But Japanese intervention was no longer imminent. President Wilson's approving note to the Japanese government of March 1, which had that day been privately shown to the British and French ambassadors in Washington, had not been sent. On the 4th, Wiseman had wired from New York to say that Colonel House, though anxious to assist the Allies, still felt that Japanese intervention was fraught with danger, even in the opinion of conservative American statesmen. Such action would be misrepresented by the Germans as an invasion of Russia; it would be said that we were using a Yellow race to destroy a White race. This might have a disastrous effect on American opinion, leading to friction between the American and Japanese people and creating a formidable anti-war party in America, with consequent diminution of the present almost unanimous support of the war administration. The President would send his promised note to the Japanese government, reported Wiseman, associating himself with the Allies, but hoped that means could be found to prevent German propaganda from bearing fruit. Colonel House, in fact, had drawn the President back from the abyss of intervention.[18]

On the 5th, both Wiseman and the British Ambassador in Washington informed Balfour of President Wilson's new note to the Japanese government, which was quite different from the draft of March 1; though the present danger in Russia was admitted, and it was agreed that Japan rather than any other Allied power should intervene if necessary, it was felt that even if Japanese intentions – in which the President expressed the same faith as before – were announced in a declaration to the Russian people, they were certain to be misconstrued and discredited by German propaganda, with disastrous effects in Russia. The President now appeared to believe that nothing but harm could come of Japanese intervention. But the presidential lapse of March 1 had undoubtedly precipitated the War Cabinet's decision of March 4, which had resulted in the landing of British troops at Murmansk on March 6.[18]

Balfour did not give up hope. On the 6th, he wired back to Wiseman that the unconditional surrender of the Bolsheviks to Germany at Brest-Litovsk made immediate action in Siberia imperative, and it was preferable that Japan should act as Allied mandatory, rather than alone. The Bolsheviks said that they still intended to organise resistance to German aggression, in spite of their peace treaty. We had suggested, through Bruce Lockhart, that they should invite help from Japan and Roumania, but to allay suspicion, both in England and America, it was to be made abundantly clear that this action was suggested in the sole interest of the Russian people. The same day, Balfour saw the Japanese Ambassador in London, and showed him his telegram (no. 198) of March 4 to Tokyo, instructing the British Ambassador to negotiate a joint Allied invitation to Japan to act as Allied mandatory in Siberia.[18]

But, in fact, Lockhart had unwittingly been misinforming Balfour of the Bolshevik government's willingness to resume hostilities against the Germans. In their talks and half-promises to the young British agent, Lenin and Trotsky were mainly concerned in preventing Japanese intervention, which they knew depended just as much on England, the leader of the Western Alliance, as on American consent; and Lockhart was the only Allied political agent in Petrograd with direct access to the head of his government, and his advisers. Colonel Raymond Robins, the American unofficial agent, had no such access to President Wilson or his advisers. Nor were Lenin and Trotsky as open with Lockhart as he imagined. He evidently knew nothing of the secret Bolshevik party congress, which met in Petrograd between March 6 and 8, to decide whether to recommend ratification of the peace treaty to the congress of soviets, due to meet in Moscow on the 12th. On the 7th, Lenin opposed any renewal of the war and demanded immediate ratification, to gain a little time before the inevitable Japanese invasion, and the continued German penetration of Russia, only temporarily delayed by the peace treaty. With the Bolshevik party congress supporting Lenin, ratification in Moscow was inevitable. But Lockhart knew none of this.[19]

In Tokyo, the Japanese Foreign Minister, the most enthusiastic interventionist in the Japanese government, saw that, with America still opposed, he could not carry his colleagues. On the 7th, therefore, he told the British Ambassador that it would be difficult for Japan to act as Allied mandatory, if she could not count on American help with finance and steel, etc. It might be wise, therefore, to pause in the hope of obtaining President Wilson's support later on. We should not thereby disappoint Japan, which had been pleased that the demand for Allied participation had been dropped.[20]

On the 9th, however, Balfour wired back to Tokyo, requesting the British Ambassador to proceed at once with the instructions contained in his telegram no. 198 of March 4, ie, to obtain a satisfactory declaration from the Japanese Foreign Minister, and then negotiate for a joint Allied invitation to Japan to act as Allied mandatory; the only modification in the previous instructions was that the Ambassador was to report on his conversation with the Japanese Foreign Minister before negotiating with his Allied colleagues.[20]

On March 11, the War Cabinet again considered the position in both northern Russia and Siberia. Balfour asked what action the Admiralty had taken about the proposal to despatch a demolition party to northern Russia. The protection of the Allied stores at Archangel and Murmansk had a 'big bearing' on Allied policy generally. The Deputy First Sea Lord replied that, if necessary, an armed icebreaker, flying the White Ensign, would be despatched to Archangel, and British and French cruisers were on their way to Murmansk. The Secretary of State for War read out a letter from the French Military Attaché, urging the despatch of ships to bring away the most urgently needed Allied stores at Archangel; these, he intimated, were French stores, and should be brought away first. (As Archangel was ice-bound, this was impossible, of course.) As the matter was to be considered by the Allied Naval Council, the War Cabinet left the subject.[21]

Balfour then explained the present position regarding Japanese intervention in Siberia. 'America had first acquiesced in the proposed enterprise, but had since reverted to her misgivings.' As a result of this change of attitude, the British Ambassador in Tokyo had not acted on the instructions contained in Balfour's wire no. 198 of March 4, and the Japanese government had therefore not yet been officially approached about intervention in Siberia as Allied mandatory. On the 9th, Balfour had wired again to Tokyo, authorising the British Ambassador to proceed at once on the previous instructions in wire no. 198, the only modification being that he was to report to the Foreign Office on his talks with the Japanese Foreign Minister before negotiating, with his French and Italian colleagues, a joint Allied invitation.

In the discussion that now followed, the opinion was expressed that Japan was unlikely to act 'in view of the lukewarmness of the American attitude', and that the Japanese government's state of mind could be inferred from the British Ambassador's wire from Tokyo of the 7th. 'It seemed that the situation was materially altered. Not only had Japanese eagerness abated in consequence of American reluctance, but most of the advice received from Russia dissuaded us from encouraging or countenancing a Japanese invasion of Siberia, as certain to drive Russia into league with Germany. As against this view,' state the Cabinet minutes, 'it was urged that Russia, even if animated with hatred of Germany, was quite unable, without foreign assistance, to make any sort of resistance to the Germans. General Knox and Captain Proctor [a member of Poole's mission in Petrograd, from where he had just returned] were instanced as among those who considered the situation lost unless Japan acted, and acted soon. There was little prospect of any hardening of the Russians if left to themselves; and to wait for an invitation from them to Japan would be to wait for an uncertainty and, in any case, to wait too long.'[21]

But the War Cabinet's attention was drawn 'to a two-fold risk of the policy of Japanese intervention in Siberia:

a. Russian hatred of Germany, a foundation it might be possible to build on, would be transferred to us, for letting loose Asia on a temporarily prostrate Russia.

b. There was a possibility of a rift on a matter of cardinal policy between ourselves and the United States of America, to secure which was one of the aims of German policy.

Japan, in any case, would not go far west, as she had ceased to feel confident that her Allies were on the winning side. We should not prevail on her to go far enough to engage in serious armed conflict with the Germans. All we needed for our immediate purpose was protection of the stores at Vladivostok. This could be done without the invasion of Siberia up to the Urals and running the risk of incurring all the odium and reaping none of the benefit.'

But Balfour emphasised 'that it was [too] early to assume that America would not go with us, and that Japan would refuse to go west.' He urged that the result of our démarche at Tokyo should be awaited. If the present American view, as expressed in the British Ambassador's wire from Washington of March 5, had already been made known to Japan, as inferred from Wiseman's telegram of the 6th (which was in fact true), we should first obtain the considered opinion of the Japanese government, with the alternatives clearly before it.[21]

So the War Cabinet decided to await the result of the British

Ambassador's talks with the Japanese Foreign Minister. This report was, in fact, despatched from Tokyo that same day. The Japanese Foreign Minister wanted certain further information before any Japanese declaration could be made, stated the British Ambassador. First, were British and American views so divergent on Japanese intervention that, in the words of the American acting Secretary of State, Japan 'would have to choose between the United States of America and the Allies', or words to that effect? Secondly, if a long expedition was obligatory, and America declined to provide money or metals, where was Japan to find them? The British Ambassador enclosed in his report the formal invitation to Japan to act as Allied mandatory, which had been negotiated by the Allied ambassadors in Tokyo. It is uncertain when this reached London, but it amply justified the War Cabinet's fears. On the 12th, the War Cabinet's attention was drawn to a further telegram from Wiseman, 'which indicated that hope should not be abandoned of another change in American policy on the subject of Japanese intervention in Siberia'. Next day, however, the Deputy Chief of the Naval Staff advised the War Cabinet of the receipt of a telegram from the British Naval Attaché, who was still at Petrograd, warning that any Japanese action might drive the Russians into German arms. 'The Naval Attaché was repeatedly being questioned as to how far we were working in accordance with the Japanese, and requested information.'[22]

But the arguments put forward towards the end of the War Cabinet's meeting on the 11th seem to have been accepted; Japan was still a doubtful quantity and would not go nearly far enough into Siberia to defeat German designs. The most that could be hoped for was Japanese protection of the stores at Vladivostok. The Bolsheviks did not want the Japanese under any conditions. On the 14th, Lockhart wired to Balfour that he had sounded Trotsky about obtaining Japanese support, as instructed by the Foreign Secretary on the 6th, but the idea had been angrily scouted. Germany, stated Trotsky, had already offered him an alliance with Japan against England and America, but Russia preferred to fall fighting against both Germans and Japanese. Only Germany could benefit by Japanese intervention, said Trotsky; and he denounced British foreign policy as cowardly and ignorant.[22]

On March 11, Kühlmann, the German Secretary of State, during a short visit to Bucharest, gave his views on the Russian situation, in answer to the German Treasury's request for guidance on a few comments on foreign policy to be made in the Reichstag. 'The over-all situation is so uncertain,' Kühlmann wired, 'that I should advise against making any comments on foreign policy, if not absolutely necessary.' In view of the latest reports from Russia, and of the opposition to the ratification of the German treaties which existed there, 'I would especially recommend moderation in the evaluation of the positive results achieved at Brest. One could probably say that the Eastern sky was beginning to lighten, but it would perhaps be better not, as yet, to assume that the transition from war on two fronts to war on a single front is definitely assured.'[23]

Various matters, however, were being ratified or at least clarified, in London. On March 7, Colonel Peel had brought the question of Colonel Keyes' financial operations and bank deals before the Russia committee, whose general feeling was that 'any obligation' which Keyes had entered into on behalf of the British government 'should be carried out', in view of the 'definite authority' which had been given to Keyes. But certain payments should be postponed pending Lindley's return to England. It thus appeared that the Russia committee, under Lord Robert Cecil's chairmanship, now approved even the Siberian Bank deal.[24]

The War Cabinet appeared to approve as well. On the 12th, their attention was called to a message from President Wilson expressing sympathy with the Russian people, on the opening of the congress of soviets in Moscow. 'It was pointed out that this document did on behalf of the United States exactly what Mr Lockhart had urged the British Government to do,' state the Cabinet minutes. 'The American public, however, had not the same cause for resentment against Russia as the European Allies, who had made great investments in Russia, and who had been deserted in the midst of the struggle.' The first speaker may have been either the Prime Minister, or Balfour; the second was probably Lord Robert Cecil. This was the view on Russia of a divided Cabinet.[25]

On the 14th, Wiseman wired from New York that the President's message to the Russian people was intended to allay both American and Russian fears of intervention, and added that the President now had in mind the despatch of an American civil mission, attached to the Japanese force, to help to reorganise Russia. But if he did not receive a sympathetic reply from Russia, he was unlikely to proceed further with the idea. That afternoon, Balfour made a statement on British policy towards Russia in the House of Commons. Russia, he stated, could never reap the fruits of her revolution if dominated and penetrated by Germany; and the only way to escape this was to invite Allied intervention from the Far East. On the 17th, this statement was wired to Lockhart in Petrograd.[26]

But it was too late. The day before, Lenin had induced the congress of soviets in Moscow to ratify the peace treaty; and Russia withdrew from the war. British efforts to restore the Eastern Front with Russian troops had been unsuccessful. While exerting every effort to support a phantom Don Cossack and volunteer army in southern Russia, the War Cabinet had not only failed to encourage, but had doubly antagonised the *de facto* Bolshevik government, with its small force of Red Guards, in central Russia; which, by half believing their own false propaganda, they had now half convinced themselves was run by paid German agents. As a result the Germans were free to transfer all their troops, and all the Russian and Siberian grain, oil and minerals that they could seize, to the Western Front. The Allied position was desperate. The only hope now was to restore the Eastern Front with Allied troops – by Allied military intervention in Russia.

By the Treaty of Brest-Litovsk, the War Cabinet in London had at least broached the idea. On January 24, they had decided 'to do all in their power' to open up communications between Vladivostok and south-east Russia along the Siberian railway to bring support to the Don Cossacks and volunteer army; and to urge Japan to undertake military control of the railway from Vladivostok to Chelyabinsk. This idea was rejected by the American government on February 13. On the 25th, with the Don Cossacks and volunteer army out of the picture, and Russian withdrawal from the war imminent, the War Cabinet now decided that they 'viewed with favour' the idea of Japanese intervention in Siberia up to Chelyabinsk, so as to deny to the Germans both the Siberian railway, and Siberian grain and produce (which the British claimed to have bought through the Russian bank deals). It was suggested that Japan act as Allied mandatory. In early March, as President Wilson gave tentative, verbal approval to the British proposal, the Murmansk soviet, with Trotsky's approval, agreed with British officers to co-operate in defending the Murmansk area from German incursion. The War Cabinet, on hearing of this approval in both Washington and Petrograd, thereupon agreed to small-scale British intervention in north Russia – and 130 Royal Marines landed at Murmansk on March 6.

But as President Wilson drew back from involvement in Siberia, Bruce Lockhart raised the idea of obtaining a Bolshevik invitation for England and America to help defend both Archangel and Vladivostok, a project designed to offset the danger of Japanese intervention. At this point came the Brest-Litovsk Treaty, which took Russia out of the war. The War Cabinet now anyhow had doubts about Japan, which was still regarded as a doubtful quantity, and which obviously would not go far enough into Siberia to defeat German designs. Japan, in fact, could only be trusted to guard the Vladivostok stores. In Washington, President Wilson was considering the despatch of an American civil commission, to be attached to any Japanese force that intervened – provided that the Bolsheviks agreed. Thus by mid-March, the idea of Allied intervention was already coming to depend on a Bolshevik invitation, and to be limited to guarding Russia's northern and far-eastern ports, Murmansk and Vladivostok, against German attack.

But although the British were already ashore at Murmansk with Bolshevik approval, they were not considered – whatever General Poole might like to foresee, or Lenin and Trotsky might like to say – to be after Russian territory in north Russia. Everyone knew that Japan, although she would not move without American consent, was after Russian territory in the Far East. This was the nub of the problem of Siberian intervention.

Would the Americans come to think the price worth paying?

# Sources

CHAPTER I

1. Commander Oliver Locker-Lampson's report to the Admiralty, dated March 19th, 1917 (now in the Locker-Lampson Papers).

2. Alexander Kerensky, *Russia and History's Turning Point*, London, 1966, pp. 108–110; M. Philips Price, *My Reminiscences of the Russian Revolution*, London, 1921, pp. 89–90, 130–2, 134–40.

3. Z. A. B. Zeman and W. B. Scharlau, *The Merchant of Revolution: The Life of Alexander Israel Helphand*, London, 1965, pp. 5–205.

4. Z. A. B. Zeman, *Germany and the Revolution in Russia, 1915–1918*, London, 1958, pp. vii–xi (hereafter referred to as 'Zeman').

5. Professor George Katkov, *Russia 1917*, London, 1967, pp. 63, 74, 76–7, 83, 97–8.


CHAPTER 2

1. This description of the British Embassy in St Petersburg is taken from I. E. Grabar and V. N. Lazarev, *Istoriya Russkogo Iskusstva*, Moscow, 1961, Tome 6, p. 205; G. H. Hamilton, *The Art and Architecture of Russia*, Penguin, 1954, pp. 163–202; Harold Nicolson, *Sir Arthur Nicolson, First Lord Carnock*, London, 1930, pp. 203–5; Meriel Buchanan, *Diplomacy and Foreign Courts*, London, 1928, pp. 133–49; and *Recollections of Imperial Russia*, London, 1923, p. 11 *et seq*; R. H. Bruce Lockhart, *Memoirs of a British Agent*, London, 1932, pp. 117–18.

2. Thomas Jones, *Whitehall Diary*, London, 1969, pp. 40, 66–7, 220, 243; Stephen Roskill, *Hankey, Man of Secrets* volume 1, 1877–1918, London, 1970, pp. 329, 360, 402, 434–5, 490; Duff Cooper, *Old Men Forget*, London, 1953, p. 93; Louis Fischer, *Men and Politics*, London, 1941, p. 503; *Lloyd George*, a diary by Frances Stevenson, edited by A. J. P. Taylor, London, 1971, pp. 34, 136 (hereafter referred to as 'Lloyd George diary').

3. *Whitehall Diary*, pp. 127, 233; Hankey, pp. 229, 364; Lloyd George diary, p. 129; *Lord Riddell's Intimate Diary of the Peace Conference and After*, London, 1933, p. 87; Lady Violet Bonham Carter, *Winston Churchill as I Knew Him*, London, 1965, p. 277.

4. *Whitehall Diary*, pp. 239, 243, 253; Hankey, pp. 271–2; Lloyd George diary, p. 76; Riddell, pp. 387, 389, 410–12.

5. *Whitehall Diary*, pp. 14, 65.

6. Lloyd George diary, p. 148.

7. *Whitehall Diary*, p. 52; Hankey, pp. 494, 497; Frances Lloyd George, *The Years That are Past*, London, 1967, p. 154.

8. Hankey, pp. 212, 325, 355, 384; Lloyd George diary, pp. 126–7.

9. Hankey, p. 559; Bonham Carter, p. 193.

10. *Whitehall Diary*, pp. 148, 254; Lloyd George diary, p. 134; Riddell, p. 25; Lord David Cecil, *The Cecils of Hatfield House*, London, 1973, pp. 294, 304–6.

11. *Whitehall Diary*, pp. 41, 43.

12. Roy Jenkins, *Asquith*, London, 1964, p. 383; Major-General Sir C. E. Callwell, *Field-Marshal Sir Henry Wilson: His Life and Diaries*, Volume 2, London, 1927, pp. 71, 82–3; Hankey, p. 444; Frances Lloyd George, p. 154.

13. This account of the Allied Mission to Russia is taken from Callwell, vol. 1, pp. 301–28; and the *National Review*, vol. 115, July to December 1940.

14. Sir George Buchanan, *My Mission to Russia and other Diplomatic Memories*, London, 1923, diary entry for February 18; Major-General Sir Alfred Knox, *With the Russian Army, 1914–1917*, London, 1921, diary entries for March 8 and 10.

15. Katkov, pp. 262–82.

16. Knox, March 12, 13 and 15.

17. Buchanan, April 9, 10 and 16.

18. Zeman and Scharlau, pp. 206–34.

19. Katkov, pp. 105–15.

20. Buchanan, May 21.

21. Robert D. Warth, *The Allies and the Russian Revolution*, Duke University, 1954, pp. 66–89.

22. Kerensky, pp. 286, 359–62.

23. King George V's letter is in the Locker-Lampson papers.

24. Warth, pp. 113–15; Kerensky, p. 290.

25. This account is taken from Commander Locker-Lampson's report to the Admiralty, August 16, 1917. General Kornilov's letter and the First Lord's message are in the Locker-Lampson papers.

26. Zeman and Scharlau, pp. 206–34; Katkov, pp. 105–15.

27. *Whitehall Diary*, pp. 28, 59; Hankey, p. 398; Frances Lloyd George, pp. 109–10; Riddell, pp. 113–14.

28. Hankey, p. 409.

29. Lloyd George diary, pp. 115, 225; Riddell, pp. 113, 116, 303, 381.

30. War Cabinet 200a; W.O. 33/924.

31. Warth, p. 119; General Basil Gurko, *War and Revolution in Russia, 1914–17*, New York, 1919, pp. 164–5; W. H. Chamberlin, *The Russian Revolution*, vol. 1, London, 1935, pp. 192–222.

32. War Cabinet 204.

33. Commander Oliver Locker-Lampson's report, August 16, 1917.

34. War Cabinet 205.

35. War Cabinet 208; Chamberlin, vol. 1, pp. 192–222.

36. W.O. 33/924.

37. War Cabinet 213.

38. Lloyd George diary, p. 284; Warth, pp. 66–89.

39. War Cabinet 215.

40. Cabinet Paper G.T. 1705.

41. Cabinet Paper G.T. 1751.

42. Chamberlin, vol. 1, pp. 192–222; W.O. 33/924.

43. Commander Oliver Locker-Lampson's report, August 16, 1917.

44. Private information from one of Locker-Lampson's former officers.

45. War Cabinet 217.

46. Chamberlin, vol. 1, pp. 192–222.

47. W.O. 33/924.
48. Zeman, no. 68.
49. Zeman and Scharlau, pp. 206–34; Zeman, no. 69.
50. Kerensky, p. 325.
51. Cabinet Paper G.T. 1793; War Cabinet 221; W.O. 33/924.
52. Cabinet Paper G.T. 1828.
53. Cabinet Paper G.T. 1829.
54. Cabinet Paper G.T. 1844.
55. Chamberlin, vol. 1, pp. 192–222.
56. Kerensky, pp. 363–9.
57. W.O. 33/924.
58. War Cabinet 223; W.O. 33/924.

CHAPTER 3

1. Cabinet paper G.T. 1886.
2. Cabinet paper G.T. 1865.
3. Cabinet paper G.T. 1885.
4. Cabinet paper G.T. 1911; Chamberlin, vol. 1, pp. 192–222; Kerensky, p. 372.
5. W.O. 33/924.
6. Cabinet paper G.T. 1896.
7. W.O. 33/924.
8. Cabinet paper G.T. 1938; Buchanan, September 3.
9. Cabinet paper G.T. 1930.
10. War Cabinet 226; Cabinet paper G.T. 1936; Chamberlin, vol. 1, pp. 192–222.
11. W.O. 33/924; Cabinet papers G.T. 1943 and 1954; Chamberlin, vol. 1, pp. 192–222.
12. Cabinet paper G.T. 1966; Chamberlin, vol. pp. 192–222.
13. W.O. 33/924.
14. Buchanan, September 5.
15. Cabinet papers G.T. 1991 and 1993.
16. War Cabinet 229.
17. Chamberlin, vol. 1, pp. 192–222; Buchanan, September 8.
18. W.O. 33/924; Chamberlin, vol. 1, 192–222.
19. Cabinet papers G.T. 2011 and 2006.
20. War Cabinet 230.
21. Cabinet paper G.T. 2021.
22. Cabinet paper G.T. 2027.
23. Kerensky, pp. 341–56; 359–92.
24. Krasny Arkhiv, no. 24 (*Foreign Diplomats on the Revolution of 1917*).
25. Private information from Locker-Lampson's former officer.
26. W.O. 33/924.
27. War Cabinet 231.
28. Kerensky, pp. 354–5; 398; 400–2.
29. Cabinet paper G.T. 2048.
30. Cabinet paper G.T. 2044.
31. War Cabinet 233.
32. This letter is in Cab. 27/189.
33. W.O. 106/1036.
34. Cabinet paper G.T. 2071.
35. War Cabinet 234 and 235.

36. Cabinet paper G.T. 2077.
37. W.O. 33/924.
38. War Cabinet 238 and 240.
39. Zeman, no. 71; Katkov, pp. 105–15.
40. War Cabinet 243; Kerensky, pp. 354–5; 398; 400–2.
41. Buchanan, pp. 187–9, 192–200; Kerensky, pp. 387–8.
42. War Cabinet 247b and 248.
43. This letter is in Cab. 27/189.
44. War Cabinet 255; Cabinet paper G.T. 2337; Katkov, pp. 39, 41, 141.
45. Buchanan, October 25; Cab. 27/189.
46. Lloyd George Papers. F60/2/36.
47. War Cabinet 262.
48. Knox, November 1; Cab. 27/189.
49. These letters are in Cab. 27/189.
50. War Cabinet 265.
51. Knox, November 6; Buchanan, November 5.
52. Knox, November 8; Buchanan, November 7 and 8.
53. This letter is in Cab. 27/189.
54. Chamberlin, vol. 1, pp. 192–222.


CHAPTER 4

1. These letters are in Cab. 27/189; Knox, November 8 and 12.
2. Colonel J. F. Neilson's report, November 19.
3. Knox, November 14; Buchanan, November 19, 20 and 21.
4. Zeman, nos. 73, 74, 77, 81, 82.
5. Zeman and Scharlau, pp. 235–43.
6. Zeman, nos. 72, 75, 78, 79, 80, 83; Katkov, p. 97.
7. Zeman and Scharlau, pp. 235–43; Zeman, nos. 72, 86, 89, 90, 91, 92.
8. Callwell, p. 19.
9. War Cabinet 274 and 275.
10. War Cabinet 279; Hankey, diary entry for November 27.
11. War Cabinet 280.
12. War Cabinet 281; David Footman, *Civil War in Russia*, London, 1961, p. 44.
13. This description of the Russian banking scene, and of its later development, is taken from W.O. 0149/7335; from wires, reports and minutes in F.O. 371/3964, 3977, 3979, 3988, 3994, 3995, 3996, 4021, 4022, 4023, 4024, 4029, 4038; from certain general sources (hereafter referred to as 'The Bank Schemes').
14. The Bank Schemes; Buchanan, November 25; Knox, pp. 726–7; Professor Richard H. Ullman, *Intervention and the War*, London, 1961, pp. 22–23, 43.
15. War Cabinet 282.
16. Buchanan, November 27, 28; Knox, November 28; Ullman, p. 23; Cab. 27/189.
17. War Cabinet 285.
18. War Cabinet 286.
19. War Cabinet 288.


CHAPTER 5

1. These minutes are in Cab. 28/3.
2. The Bank Schemes; Ullman, p. 44.

3. The Bank Schemes.
4. These letters are in Cab. 27/189.
5. The Bank Schemes; Keyes papers (India Office): Mss Eur F. 131/22.
6. Knox, December 3; Buchanan, December 3 and 4.
7. Cab. 28/3.
8. War Cabinet 289; Cabinet Paper G.T. 3705 in Cab. 24/43.
9. War Cabinet 290.
10. Ullman, pp. 25–28; 45–48.
11. The Bank Schemes.
12. These letters are in Cab. 27/189.


CHAPTER 6

1. Zeman, nos. 93, 94, 95, 98.
2. Zeman, nos. 99, 100, 101, 102, 107; Zeman and Scharlau, p. 243–51.
3. Zeman, nos. 104, 106, 108, 109, 110, 111; Zeman and Scharlau, p. 243–51.
4. Buchanan, December 6, 7, 8.
5. Footman, p. 35–50; Ullman, p. 49, 52.
6. This report and these letters are in Cab. 27/189.
7. Footman, p. 47–9.
8. War Cabinet 294.
9. War Cabinet 295.
10. This report is in Cab. 27/189.
11. War Cabinet 298 and 299.
12. War Cabinet 302.
13. War Cabinet 303; Hankey, December 23.
14. Colonel Byrne's diary is in Cab. 27/189.
15. War Cabinet 304.
16. Cab. 27/189.
17. This paper and these minutes are in Cab. 28/3.
18. War Cabinet 306; Ullman, p. 56.
19. Professor George F. Kennan, *Russia Leaves the War*, London, 1956, p. 184; Edgar Sisson, *One Hundred Red Days*, Yale University, 1931, p. 269.
20. War Cabinet 308.


CHAPTER 7

1. Zeman, nos. 112, 113.
2. Zeman and Scharlau, p. 243–51.
3. Zeman, no. 114.
4. War Cabinet 311.
5. War Cabinet 312.
6. War Cabinet 314.
7. Ullman, p. 65; Kennan, p. 261; Hankey, January 4.
8. Zeman, no. 115.
9. War Cabinet 316.
10. War Cabinet 319.
11. War Cabinet 311.
12. War Cabinet 316.
13. War Cabinet 321; F.O. 95/802.

14. These letters are in Cab. 27/189.
15. War Cabinet 309.
16. Cab. 27/189.
17. War Cabinet 322.
18. War Cabinet 328.
19. War Cabinet 329.
20. War Cabinet 324; Philips Price, p. 209–11.
21. F.O. 95/802.
22. Cab. 27/189.
23. The Bank Schemes.
24. F.O. 95/802.
25. War Cabinet 327; Hankey, January 19.
26. War Cabinet 328.
27. The Bank Schemes; Keyes papers.
28. Footman, p. 55.
29. The Bank Schemes; Keyes papers.
30. Zeman, no. 116.
31. War Cabinet 330.
32. Cab. 28/3; War Cabinet 294.
33. Foreign Office summary of correspondence, etc. concerning Allied intervention in East Russia, dated June 21, 1918, covering the period December 7, 1917 to June 13, 1918; in file 'J.C.C.D. – Russia 1918' in the Davidson Papers in the Beaverbrook Library.
34. War Cabinet 309a.
35. Foreign Office summary.
36. War Cabinet 316.
37. Admiralty Files, China 1918.
38. Foreign Office summary.
39. War Cabinet 330a.

CHAPTER 8

1. Zeman, no. 117.
2. Sisson, pp. 291–5, 357.
3. Professor George F. Kennan, *The Journal of Modern History*, June 1956.
4. Captain George Hill, *Go Spy the Land*, London, 1932, pp. 200–4; Zeman, p. x.
5. War Cabinet 340.
6. War Cabinet 341; *Whitehall Diary*, pp. 48–52; Hankey, February 8.
7. Ullman, p. 70.
8. War Cabinet 342.
9. Cabinet Paper G.T. 3602.
10. Footman, pp. 56–7.
11. F.O. 95/802.
12. Cab. 27/189.
13. F.O. 95/802.
14. Cab. 27/189.
15. F.O. 95/802.
16. W.O. 106/1560.
17. Cab. 27/189.
18. F.O. 95/802.
19. Cab. 27/189.

20. War Cabinet 345.
21. Ullman, pp. 72–4; War Cabinet 349.
22. Cab. 27/189.
23. F.O. 95/802; Ullman, pp. 111–13.
24. The Bank Schemes; Ullman, p. 70; *Papers relating to the Foreign Relations of the United States: Russia 1918*, Washington, 1931–2, pp. 368–9 (hereafter referred to as 'Russia 1918'); Keyes papers.
25. F.O. 95/802.
26. Footman, pp. 52, 57–61.
27. The Bank Schemes.
28. Cab. 27/189.
29. War Cabinet 353; Hankey, February 25.

CHAPTER 9

1. Foreign Office summary.
2. Ullman, pp. 95–105; Foreign Office summary.
3. War Cabinet 346; Foreign Office summary.
4. War Cabinet 350.
5. Foreign Office summary.
6. War Cabinet 353; Hankey, February 25.
7. War Cabinet 354.
8. War Cabinet 356.
9. F.O. 95/802; Lockhart, p. 54; The Bank Schemes; Keyes papers.
10. Foreign Office summary; Ullman, pp. 105–8.
11. Ullman, pp. 120–21; Sisson, pp. 358–66; Cab. 27/189.
12. Ullman, pp. 109–17; War Cabinet 357.
13. War Cabinet 358.
14. Foreign Office summary.
15. Lloyd George Papers, F47/7/18.
16. War Cabinet 359.
17. Ullman, pp. 122–3.
18. Foreign Office summary.
19. Ullman, pp. 123–4.
20. Foreign Office summary.
21. War Cabinet 363.
22. Foreign Office summary; War Cabinet 364 and 365.
23. Zeman, no. 119.
24. F.O. 95/802.
25. War Cabinet 364.
26. Foreign Office summary.

# Index

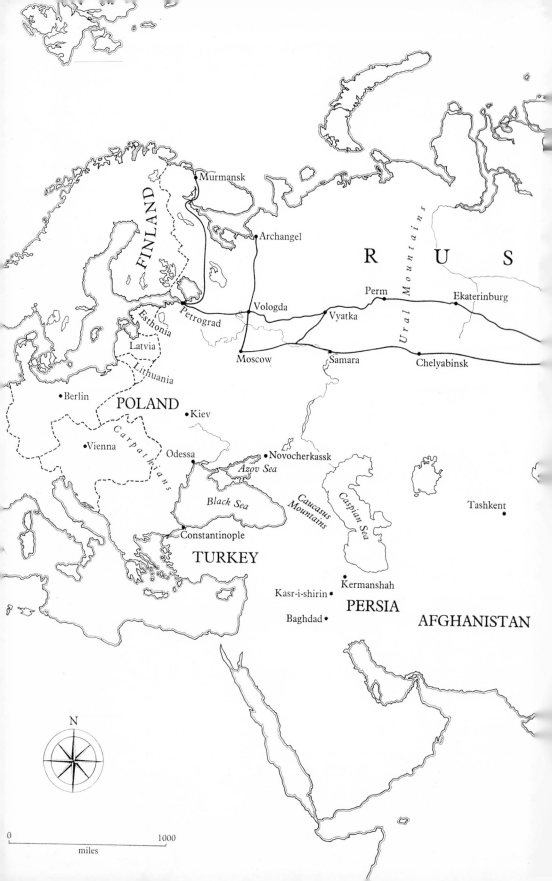